Eva Ries
Precarious Flânerie and the Ethics of the Self in Contemporary Anglophone Fiction

Buchreihe der Anglia/ ANGLIA Book Series

Edited by
Andrew James Johnston, Ursula Lenker, Martin Middeke, Gabriele Rippl, Daniel Stein

Advisory Board
Laurel Brinton, Philip Durkin, Olga Fischer, Susan Irvine, Christopher A. Jones, Terttu Nevalainen, Ad Putter, James Simpson, Emily Thornbury, Derek Attridge, Elisabeth Bronfen, Ursula K. Heise, Verena Lobsien, Liliane Louvel, Christopher Morash, Susana Onega, Martin Puchner, Peter Schneck

Volume 76

Eva Ries

Precarious Flânerie and the Ethics of the Self in Contemporary Anglophone Fiction

—

DE GRUYTER

ISBN 978-3-11-153092-5
e-ISBN (PDF) 978-3-11-076749-0
e-ISBN (EPUB) 978-3-11-076752-0
ISSN 0340-5435

Library of Congress Control Number: 2022932905

Bibliographic information published by the Deutsche Nationalbibliothek
The Deutsche Nationalbibliothek lists this publication in the Deutsche Nationalbibliografie; detailed bibliographic data are available on the internet at http://dnb.dnb.de.

© 2024 Walter de Gruyter GmbH, Berlin/Boston
This volume is text- and page-identical with the hardback published in 2022.

www.degruyter.com

Acknowledgments

I would like to express my sincerest gratitude to a number of people who contributed in one way or the other to this book. First and foremost, I am very grateful to Martin Middeke, who was not only the supervisor of my PhD project, but also introduced me to Butler's writings on precariousness. His continuous support and advice have greatly contributed to the genesis of this monograph and have helped to refine my argumentation.

I am also very much indebted to Günter Butzer who agreed to co-supervise my PhD and whose seminars first acquainted me with Foucault's late writings on the ethics of the self. Moreover, thanks are also due to Hubert Zapf, for agreeing to join the board of supervisors at short notice.

My gratitude also goes to Wolfgang Müller for many enlightening discussions on the subject of flânerie and particularly for his comments on early conceptualizations of my thesis.

I am very grateful to my colleagues Martin Riedelsheimer, Korbinian Stöckl, Christina Schönberger-Stepien, and Leila Vaziri for their input and many insightful conversations on the topic.

For preparing the manuscript, thanks are also due to Felix Boeger and, in particular, Victoria Müller, whose organizational talent and meticulous proofreading proved once more priceless.

Moreover, I would like to thank Teresa Herzgsell and Martin Riedelsheimer for reading part of my manuscript and their invaluable advice.

Writing one's thesis during a global pandemic is not an easy thing and it would have been multiple times as hard if it weren't for the support of a number of friends, all of whom deserve to be named here individually: Sina Abel, Annika Becker, Sophia Brocker, Verena Gawert, Korbinian Grabmeier, Marco Milling, Felix Nölte, Rebekka Reinholz, Elisabeth Rowley, Angela Ruf, Johanna Salger, Vanessa Schäfer, Teresa Thoma and, most of all, Iris Schmidt.

Thanks are also due to my parents, Petra Kranz-Watermann, for her support, financial and otherwise, and Hubert Ries, for supplying my ever-growing library with a steady influx of books since my early childhood, thus getting me interested in literature in the first place.

Contents

1   **The Return of the Flâneur** —— 1

2   **Flânerie and its Discontents** —— 13
2.1   The History of the Flâneur as a Literary Trope —— 14
2.2   Walter Benjamin's Continuum of Strolling —— 32
2.3   Flânerie and/as Performance —— 44
2.4   Flânerie and Other Media: A Brief History of Flânerie and Intermediality —— 51
2.5   Excursus: Flânerie *sans la lettre:* The Flâneur in the Anglophone Literary Tradition —— 54
2.6   Synopsis: The Aesthetics of the Flânerie Text —— 66

3   **Michel Foucault's Ethics of the Self** —— 69
3.1   The Aesthetics of Existence —— 72
3.2   The Techniques of the Self —— 75
3.2.1   Writing the Self —— 75
3.2.2   Reflexivity and Truth-Speaking —— 79
3.3   The Subject of Experience —— 83

4   **Judith Butler's Precarious Subjects** —— 88
4.1   Discourse and Materialization —— 88
4.2   Sovereign Melancholia and Resistance as "Promiscuous Obedience" —— 90
4.3   Precarious Subjects —— 94

5   **Synopsis: Ethical Subjects and the Flânerie Text** —— 105

6   **The End of Flânerie? The Sovereign Subject and Precarious City Life in Ian McEwan's *Saturday*** —— 111
6.1   A Flâneur without Flânerie: Henry Perowne as Benjaminian 'Man of the Crowd' —— 111
6.2   Technologies of Domination in *Saturday*: The Flâneur as Sovereign Subject —— 116
6.3   Precarious City Life: Ambiguous Transformations —— 120
6.4   Precarious Interpretations: Strolling through the Memory Space of Literature —— 126

7	**Flânerie as Technique of the Self —— 132**
7.1	Precarious Flânerie in Siri Hustvedt's *The Blindfold* —— 132
7.1.1	Streetwalking the Metropolis: The Female Gaze and the City —— 134
7.1.2	Flânerie as Resistance in *The Blindfold* —— 139
7.1.3	The Logic of "War and Struggle": Discourse, Power and *parrēsia* in *The Blindfold* —— 150
7.2	Precarious Truth-Speaking in Teju Cole's *Open City* —— 166
7.2.1	Traveler, Migrant and Nomad: The Triple Dilemma of the Postcolonial Flâneur —— 167
7.2.2	Representation and Knowledge-Formation in *Open City* —— 172
7.2.3	Flânerie as Technique of the Self in *Open City* —— 176
7.2.4	Truthfulness and *parrēsia* in *Open City* —— 184
7.2.5	Parrēsiastic Aesthetics of Existence: Truthfulness and Critique in *Open City* —— 195

8	**City Matters: Affect and Media in Precarious Performances of Subjectivity —— 203**
8.1	Performing the City: Precarious Ethical Subjects in Dionne Brand's *What We All Long For* —— 203
8.1.1	The City as Fluid Materiality: Affects, Matter and Textuality in *What We All Long For* —— 206
8.1.2	(Un-)Grievable Lives: Global and Local Structures of Power in *What We All Long For* —— 210
8.1.3	Metropolitan Aesthetics of Existence: Encounters with the Precarious City —— 224
8.1.4	City of Longing and Belonging: Affect and Identity in *What We All Long For* —— 236
8.2	Turning Film into Scripture: Intermedial Encounters in Robin Robertson's *The Long Take* —— 242
8.2.1	The Ultimate Flânerie Text: Formal Peculiarities and the Aesthetics of Transgression in *The Long Take* —— 243
8.2.2	"A Way to Lose More Slowly": Flânerie as a Technique of the Self in *The Long Take* —— 250
8.2.3	History Repeating Itself? Precariousness and Circular Performances of Sovereignty in *The Long Take* —— 255
8.2.4	The Aestheticization of City Life: Film Noir and the Tradition of Flânerie in *The Long Take* —— 262

9	**Conclusion —— 270**

Works Cited —— 278

Index —— 296

1 The Return of the Flâneur

> Imagine standing by a window at night, on the sixth or seventeenth or forty-third floor of a building. The city reveals itself as a set of cells, a hundred thousand windows, some darkened and some flooded with green or white or golden light. Inside, strangers swim to and fro, attending to the business of their private hours. You can see them, but you can't reach them, and so this commonplace urban phenomenon, available in any city of the world on any night, conveys to even the most social a tremor of loneliness, its uneasy combination of separation and exposure.
>
> [...] Cities can be lonely places, and in admitting this we see that loneliness doesn't necessarily require physical solitude, but rather an absence or paucity of connection, closeness, kinship: an inability, for one reason or another, to find as much intimacy as desired. [...] Hardly any wonder, then, that it can reach its apotheosis in a crowd. (Laing 2016: 3–4)

As Olivia Laing remarks at the beginning of her 2016 collection of essays entitled *The Lonely City: Adventures in the Art of Being Alone*, cities are home to a paradoxical feeling: a lack of connection or closeness, commonly associated with loneliness, despite the physical proximity of others. What is more, it is an increase of physical proximity that might lead to this feeling's "apotheosis in a crowd." In her book, Laing recounts her experience of a particularly lonely time in New York City and argues for the possibility of treating feelings of isolation by means of art as a form of mediated communication. During her stay in New York, she often embarks on aimless strolls through the city and although *The Lonely City* is not primarily an account of New York itself, the rambling structure of her essays, which all center on individual stories of loneliness, imitates the motion of aimlessly strolling from thought to thought. New York then only forms the material backdrop to the symbolic city through which Laing moves and which she at the same time produces in her text – that is, the eponymous 'lonely city' inhabited by those for whom "[l]oneliness is collective; it is a city" (Laing 2016: 281). Her artistic project then aims at "creat[ing] intimacy" and "healing wounds", thus establishing a community of the vulnerable that resists the "gentrification [of] emotions" in late capitalism (Laing 2016: 280). In order to do so, Laing engages in what is commonly known as the practice of flânerie both on a metaphorical and a material level.

In this, her approach is decidedly different from more prototypical cases of flânerie. Roughly 150 years earlier, Charles Baudelaire, the godfather of the urban practice of flânerie, understood the paradoxical situation of the individual in the modern metropolis as a privilege rather than a burden. For him, "multitude [and] solitude" are "identical terms" which are "interchangeable by the active and fertile poet" (Baudelaire 1970: 20). This poet frequently takes up the role of the "solitary stroller" who thanks to his imagination "enters as he likes into each man's personality" (Baudelaire 1970: 20). The ability to be "alone in a bustling crowd" (Baudelaire 197: 20) is then a prerequisite for the imaginative kind of communion that Baudelaire suggests and turns the strolling observer into "a prince enjoying his incognito wherever he goes" (Baudelaire 1972: 400).

Laing herself refers to this Baudelairian art of projection – what Walter Benjamin calls "filling the hollow space created in him [the flâneur] by such isolation" (2006: 58) – and points out that any such practice would be utterly unattractive to her since she "found the idea abhorrent, in fact, a dandyish disinclination to engage with the *reality* of other people" (2016: 222–223; my emphasis). Thus, she distinguishes between a dialogical representation of the city that embraces the difference of individual vulnerabilities and a totalizing gaze onto the city that subsumes the inhabitants under the sovereign interpretation of the flâneur. Where Laing establishes vulnerability as a value that resists tendencies of homogenization, Baudelaire emphasizes the analogy with sovereignty and superiority. Although both authors address a somewhat similar basic constellation – that is, the paradoxical tension between distance and proximity in the metropolis – their attitudes towards this constellation are diametrically opposed to each other: where Baudelaire deliberately seeks the anonymity and alienation of the metropolis in order to achieve a sense of superiority *qua* imagination, Laing tries to escape it by means of engaging with a community of isolated and vulnerable others whose discourse mingles with her own.

Laing's text, however, ties in with a tendency that has become particularly prevalent in contemporary flânerie texts which increasingly focus on aspects of sociality and relationality in the city and which establish relationality as a value instead of a problem. The continuum that opens up between the two versions of flânerie mentioned above is then intrinsically linked to the fact that the flâneur's experience is, despite an internal distance from the crowd, an essentially social one. Indeed, from its very beginnings, the literary trope of the flâneur has been used to reflect on the status of the subject and its relation to a fast-transforming environment produced by others. Contrary to other pedestrian figures like the stroller or the wanderer, the flâneur is inseparably tied to manmade processes of acceleration, industrialization, and mechanization. The natural habitat of the flâneur is then actually non-natural; it is built, maintained, and constantly transformed by humans and thus juxtaposes the isolated practice of the individual flâneur with a complex web of social relations that becomes manifest in the various constituents of the city, such as crowds, buildings, and the diverse sphere of city streets. Social interaction takes place on a direct material level when the flâneur is jostled by the city crowds on their way through the city or on the mediated level of signification when buildings, signposts, and advertising turn into a text that can be deciphered by the flâneur. Yet, as the contrast between Laing and Baudelaire implies, the attitude of many flânerie texts towards the flâneur's relation with his environment has decisively changed in recent years and it is precisely this shift towards an emphasis on and positive evaluation of the relationality and post-sovereign status of subjects in contemporary flânerie texts that I focus on in this book.

However, examining flânerie in contemporary literature raises a few problems. The main problem is that the flâneur is dead. Or rather, the flâneur has been proclaimed dead in several contexts for the last hundred years, most notably in the work of Walter Benjamin who famously interpreted the flâneur as being symptomatic of the subject's integration into and subjection to capitalism. For Benjamin, "the department store is the last promenade for the flâneur" (Benjamin 2006: 85) and, following this assumption, the 'death' of the flâneur becomes linked to several factors all of which are rooted in processes of industrialization and commodification, as I will discuss in relation to Edgar Allan Poe's short story "The Man of the Crowd" (1840), which Benjamin considered a prime example of the end of flânerie.

First of all, this end is linked to processes of acceleration that turn the leisurely practice of strolling into a compulsive necessity for movement that Benjamin translates into the image of the flâneur's intoxication by the streets:

> An intoxication comes over the man who walks long and aimlessly through the streets. With each step, the walk takes on greater momentum; ever weaker grow the temptations of shops, of bistros, of smiling women, ever more irresistible the magnetism of the next street-corner, of a distant mass of foliage, of a street name. Then comes hunger. Our man wants nothing to do with the myriad possibilities offered to sate his appetite. Like an ascetic animal, he flits through unknown districts – until, utterly exhausted, he stumbles into his room, which receives him coldly and wears a strange air. (Benjamin 2002: 417)

Similarly, Poe's narrator, who is symptomatic of the 'end of flânerie' according to Benjamin, is magnetically attracted to the fast-moving crowd and thus drawn out onto the street for the sake of examining one of its constituents, the eponymous 'man of the crowd', until he grows "wearied unto death" (Poe 1965: 145).

Second, the 'death of the flâneur' is tied to processes of commodification so that Poe's narrator strolling through a market while following the 'man of the crowd' becomes, for Benjamin, "the figuration of his [the flâneur's] end" (Benjamin 1972: 54). This is further emphasized by the overall analogy between the flâneur and the commodity, which Benjamin draws repeatedly in his writings on the flâneur. Third, as the connection with Poe's story also implies, this death is interwoven with a loss of intellectual control since the 'man of the crowd', an *uncanny* double of the crowd itself as well as of the unnamed narrator, "*lässt sich nicht lesen*" (Poe 1965: 145; original emphasis) – the phrase is also translated at the beginning of the story, yet refers to an actual book there instead of to the 'man of the crowd': "it does not permit itself to be read" (Poe 1965: 134) – despite all the efforts made by the narrator, who follows the man for twenty-four hours through the British capital, yet cannot arrive at any conclusion as to how to classify him.

While Poe's story serves as a condensed illustration of the processes that contribute to the death of the flâneur, Benjamin also mentions historical developments that led to the disappearance of the flâneur as a socio-historical phenomenon. The flâneur's decline is, according to Benjamin, closely related to the transformation of his actual historical urban environment and therefore aligns with the process of 'Haussmannization', a project of profound renewal and reorganization of the city of Paris championed by Baron Haussmann towards the middle of the nineteenth century. Haussmann's plans were predominantly aimed at impeding any further attempts at revolution by facilitating the military's access to the city through the creation of broad avenues, and at adapting the city to the demands of capitalism and industrialization. Thus, what unites all of the abovementioned characteristics is a linkage between the death of the flâneur and the negotiation of dynamics of resistance and subjection, accompanied by a decline in flânerie's potential for resistance and by a certain loss of the flâneur's autonomy.[1]

Despite Benjamin's prophecies of doom, the flâneur is in fact *not* dead, and it is especially the '(un-)dead' status of the flâneur that has proven particularly fruitful within theoretical and literary re-workings of the practice of flânerie. Most notably, Zygmunt Bauman re-interpreted the flâneur as one of the prime modes of postmodernist experience in terms of an uncritical affirmation and acceptance of the decentering of the self based on the utter lack of consequences of the flâneur's actions. Flânerie is, according to Bauman, the "ultimate play" (2015: 142) that becomes manifest in the connection between consumption and the production of an identity based on this consumption. The unqualified affirmation of this "degenerate utopia" (Bauman 2015: 151) then turns the flâneur from cultural critic into an uncritical fellow traveler. Although Bauman thus essentially reinterprets the flâneur and now reads him as the prime representative of the crowd instead of its counter-image, the flâneur, paradoxically, lives on *because* of his death.

---

[1] Nevertheless, it was also Benjamin himself who pronounced the 'return of the flâneur' in German literature at the beginning of the twentieth century and so posed a conundrum for all later scholars focusing on flânerie by simply resurrecting the flâneur in a mostly different context – that is, Benjamin does not offer any explanation for the sudden resurrection of the flâneur despite the persistence of the circumstances that led to his downfall.

Discourse on the flâneur's afterlife then quite necessarily bears traces of Benjamin's theses on the death of the flâneur in its connection with two phenomena central to human experience in the twentieth and twenty-first centuries, namely consumerism and acceleration. The dynamics associated with consumerism and their relation to the death of the flâneur can be linked to Benjamin's reflections on the decline of the Parisian Arcades – a diverse space associated with shopping, but also with more dubious kinds of consumption like prostitution or gambling – and the ensuing rise of the (not so diverse) department store and the shopping mall – associated with shopping and consumption of a more 'family-friendly' kind. In this, the transition from Arcade to shopping mall is marked by the introduction of various means of surveillance – such as security services or cameras – that keep the unruly outside of such normative areas (see Featherstone 1998: 914). Whereas the Parisian Arcades could then still serve as a breeding ground for revolutionary ideas (see Köhn 1989: 43), the shopping mall and its consumers are firmly embedded in a framework of societal normativity and could be understood as another kind of 'Haussmannization' that takes precautions against the rebellious potential of the city.[2]

Acceleration, in turn, might contribute to the 'death of the flâneur' in a variety of ways. First of all, it has frequently been argued that the increase of traffic inhibits flânerie and relegates the flâneur to areas in which he can still stroll around so that "[f]lâneurs like tigers, or preindustrial tribes are cordoned off on reservations, preserved within the artificially created environments of pedestrian streets, parks and underground passageways" (Buck-Morss 1989: 344). Any kind of resistant potential is therefore tamed and deprived of its possible societal impact since the flâneur no longer has full access to the actual space of the city.

Moreover, acceleration in general has been said to destabilize the flâneur as reading subject since it minimizes time for reflection and therefore contributes further to the gradual loss of the flâneur's critical potential (see Fuest 2008: 167). As the example of "The Man of the Crowd" implies, acceleration and a decline in hermeneutic capabilities might ultimately result in what could be called the psychopathological flipside of flânerie (see Porombka 1999: 292–296). According to Stephan Porombka, this kind of flânerie compensates for the subject's exhaustion vis-à-vis the demands of the experience of modernity, yet might ultimately result in a violent outcome (1999: 303–308) and aligns with what Dietmar Voss calls "frustrated delusions of grandeur and power" (2001: 47; my trans.). Thus, if the leisurely practice of flânerie is reduced to the bare necessity for

---

[2] On the close relation between cities and resistance in general see Ehland and Fischer (2018a and 2018b).

movement because the flâneur has to keep up with a constant increase in acceleration, the interplay between perception, reflection, and movement characteristic of prototypical models of flânerie is reduced and the flânerie itself becomes manic.

Harald Neumeyer, by contrast, suggests a different – preliminary – end of flânerie in Germany and France due to the historical circumstances of World War II. Here, movement is not necessarily accelerated, but stylized when the flâneur becomes a soldier and strolling is turned into marching so that a different 'man of the crowd' is construed. After World War II, it is then not only the subject who has lost its ability to 'make sense', but the cities themselves, now likewise deprived of their identity and dissolved into meaningless, empty surfaces that cannot offer anything of interest to the flâneur (see Ortheil 1986: 37).

Hence, all those meditations on a possible end of flânerie dwell on different modes of subjection to the demands of modern life, capitalism, or ideology, even if it is only the subjection to a compulsive affirmation of one's sovereignty, as the psychopathological variations of flânerie imply. The return of the flâneur would then have to entail the resurrection of his potential for resistance or at least a partial autonomy and, in fact, as studies of contemporary literary flânerie show, the flâneur as a literary trope has indeed not lost his potential for practices of resistance (see, for example, Gomolla 2009; Keidel 2006; Riedl 2017), although this resistance might occur in a more varied and complex way. What is more, flânerie as a practice of resistance has in fact been revived by activists and theorists alike. Thus, Guy Debord and the situationists promoted the practice of *dérive*, a kind of aimless drifting, as part of their program of 'psychogeography' which aimed at "the study of the precise laws and specific effects of the geographical environment" (Debord 2006: 8). Since then, psychogeography has become a burgeoning field especially on the British literary scene, with representatives such as Iain Sinclair, Will Self, and Peter Ackroyd. On a theoretical level, it ties in with Michel De Certeau's conceptualization of strolling through the city as a performative speech act that interprets – and therefore possibly defers – the scopic regime of the city (see De Certeau 1988). The performative potential of walking has in turn been rediscovered by performance artists from all over the world who incorporate practices of flânerie in their art works (see e.g. Fischer 2011; Mock 2009). Contemporary flânerie, therefore, has to be located within a contested field of subjection and resistance, with every potential 'death of the flâneur' already inviting his next revival, and vice versa.[3]

---

[3] This also remains true for the flâneur's most recent reincarnation, the so-called 'cyberflâneur'. While some scholars praise the potential of a virtual flâneur who strolls through the 'streets' of

Drawing on the social preconditions of flânerie mentioned at the start of the chapter, the flâneur might be said to constantly oscillate between being part of the city crowd and being different from it with respect to external appearance as well as internal experience. While earlier examples of flânerie often indulge in a dialectics of distance and proximity with regard to the crowd, I will show that more recent examples of flânerie literature move beyond these dialectical dynamics and create complex webs of relations of sameness and difference that build on a variety of paradoxical features which the trope of the flâneur accumulated in the course of the centuries, yet which it also partly contained from its very beginning. Moreover, those flânerie texts take a belated 'ethical turn' by engaging with those webs of relations. In the same way that Olivia Laing establishes vulnerability as a shared human quality in order to resist the sameness of various kinds of 'gentrification', a considerable number of contemporary flânerie texts use the paradoxical constellation of flânerie in order to establish ethical norms while at the same time affirming the value of difference by disrupting societal norms of sameness. In those texts, literature acquires a two-fold function: on the one hand, it defers the common norm of sovereign subjectivity according to which subjects exist independently outside of social relations and establishes a sense of a shared condition of precariousness *sensu* Judith Butler as a new norm; on the other hand, it transfers Michel Foucault's reflections on a new form of non-normative ethical subjectivity to the material (albeit fictional) reality of cities in the twentieth and twenty-first centuries. Here, an ethical strand emerges which, in my opinion, can best be analyzed by using Foucault's as well as Butler's concepts of ethical subjectivity as an interpretative lens, with a specific focus on what Foucault calls 'techniques of the self' and on Butler's concept of precariousness as an ontological 'fiction', where the Foucauldian techniques of the self directly contribute to the development of a post-sovereign subjectivity. Both approaches frequently coalesce in Butler's conception of performance as a practice of resistance, which occurs on several levels in the texts I analyze. My argument then ties in with recent developments in research

---

the data city (see e.g. Featherstone 1998) others already claim the "Death of the Cyberflâneur" (Morozov 2012) due to the 'Haussmannization' of the internet by means of social media and, of course, capitalism. Therefore, Christiane Schneider's conclusion regarding the death of the flâneur certainly has a point: "The flâneur will not have a long life to live. Whoever issues his birth certificate, adds the death notice immediately. But it is precisely those conjurations and swan songs recited with verve until today that ensure the survival of the flâneur" (1996: 152; my trans.) – "Dem Flaneur ist kein langes Leben beschieden. Wer immer seine Geburtsurkunde ausstellt, liefert die Todesanzeige gerne gleich mit. Aber gerade in diesen bis heute mit Verve vorgetragenen Beschwörungen und Abgesängen scheint sein Überleben gesichert."

on Anglophone city texts, as well as city texts in general, which often conceptualize strolling through the city in terms of Michel De Certeau's "Walking in the City" as performance (see Weymann-Teschke 2018: 44–74; Löffler 2017: 36–41; Riedl 2017: 106; Nigg 2017: 40–53).[4] My study's additional focus on the *ethical* implications of such performances, however, suggests reading the practice of flânerie as one of the central paradigms for the negotiation of ethical subjectivity in contemporary literature. What is more, I claim that literature can be considered the ideal realm for reflecting on the models put forward by Foucault and Butler since fiction itself already implies the particularity of any model discussed due to its explicit separation from factual reality.

Foucault's and Butler's theoretical approaches are particularly apt for the analysis of contemporary flânerie texts for several reasons that inevitably have to take into account the thesis of the 'end of flânerie': due to quite a number of affinities between Benjamin, "the patron saint of cultural studies" (Solnit 2001: 198), and Foucault, a link can be established between the philosopher proclaiming the end of flânerie and the theoretician pronouncing the death of the subject. Benjamin and Foucault share a focus on materiality's entanglement with discourses of power and consequently both access the death of the subject (in Benjamin's case, the flâneur) through the prism of the individual's subjection to discourses of power, although Foucault's approach offers a much broader con-

---

[4] Nevertheless, I do not focus on walking in general, but on the practice of flânerie in particular because it is in the trope of the flâneur that several aspects of walking in the city become particularly marked and therefore allow for a more detailed analysis of those very features. While flânerie texts certainly showcase the material experience of the city – a characteristic they share with most city texts that include representations of walking in the city – their focus on a particularly aimless kind of walking heightens the overall transformative potential of the city and adds to the possibility of resistance (on the city's potential for transformation see Pietrzak-Franger, Pleßke and Voigts 2018). Thus, flânerie could be understood as a kind of walking whose potential for resistance is particularly marked (on the subversive potential of walking in general see, for example, Fischer [2011: 103] or Blair 2019). At the same time, the tradition of flânerie is closely linked with the profession of the writer – of fictional as well as factual texts – and therefore entails a kind of systematic representation often related to hegemonic discourses of power. Especially the gaze of the flâneur – which is usually the prerequisite for the representation of the city in text – bears an analogy with appropriation and projection so that flânerie – paradoxically – not only emphasizes walking's potential for resistance, but just as much its connection to practices of appropriation and dominance (for a brief summary of the ambivalent character of walking with regard to power, see e.g. Nigg [2017: 67–68]). In my opinion, flânerie texts therefore lend themselves even more readily to analyses of subjectivity after the so-called 'death of the subject' because they include a heightened focus on discourses of domination and resistance, which in themselves are increasingly foregrounded by contemporary city literature (see Rosenthal 2009: 236; 2017: 78).

ceptualization of subjectivity. While Benjamin does not offer any explanation for the return of the flâneur and leaves open the question of whether the brief return of the flâneur in Franz Hessel's as well as his own writings is a mere relic of past times or whether it constitutes an actualized version of the other versions of the flâneur, Foucault 'resurrects' the subject in a new form in his studies on sexuality. I therefore suggest reconceptualizing the return of the flâneur in terms of Foucault's resurrection of the subject since the conditions of the death of the subject and the death of the flâneur are – to a certain extent – similar, or rather because the death of the flâneur can be integrated into Foucault's overall thesis on the death of the subject.[5] More importantly, it is the notion of flânerie as *techne*, brought forward in Benjamin's autobiographical writings, that allows for establishing a connection between flânerie and Foucauldian technologies of the self. While this reconceptualization of flânerie in terms of an ethics of the self already opens up a pathway to examining the recent ethical turn in Anglophone flânerie texts, it is ultimately only the "normative aspiration" (2004a: 219) in Butler's ethical writings that accounts for the common normative streak regarding post-sovereign subjectivity that can be identified in contemporary Anglophone city texts.

The five case studies I am conducting then access the analysis of post-sovereign subjectivity from a variety of perspectives that combine into a broad overview of those forms of subjectivity in terms of differing markers of identity with regard to race, class, and gender, and that, furthermore, respond to the Foucauldian framework's emphasis on difference and particularity. First of all, the five texts I am examining are by authors with very different racial backgrounds

---

[5] This is also suggested by Keith Tester who points out that "Benjamin's comments on the rationalization of Paris are not very far removed from what would now be called a Foucauldian analysis of discipline" (2015: 19–20) and Sigrid Weigel whose analysis of the genealogy of the analogy between city and woman also includes reflections on the connection between Benjamin and Foucault as well as the implication that flânerie can be understood in terms of Foucauldian subject formation (1990: 184–187 and 212–215). Moreover, Foucault himself mentions his proximity to the writings of the Frankfurt School in an interview with Duccio Trombadori (1991: 116–119). While this can certainly be seen as proof of an affinity between Foucault's and Benjamin's thought, it has to be noted that 1) an identification of Benjamin's work with the Frankfurt School is, at least, open to debate (Schmidt 1994), 2) Foucault does not refer to Benjamin, but rather to Horkheimer, Adorno, and Marcuse in this context, and 3) that he explicitly points out that the Frankfurt School's conception of the subject deviates from his own (Foucault 1991: 120–124). This last aspect, however, is particularly interesting in the context of my study since it fits the assumption that the 'death of the flâneur' as a sovereign subject can be counteracted by means of the development of a post-sovereign subjectivity that draws on Foucauldian techniques of the self.

and regional affiliations, ranging from the New York-based white writer Siri Hustvedt to the also New York-based Nigerian-American writer Teju Cole, to Toronto-based Caribbean-Canadian author Dionne Brand, to London-based Scottish author Robin Robertson and London-based British novelist Ian McEwan. Second, they differ with regard to gender with Hustvedt and Brand potentially representing a 'female' perspective and Cole, Robertson, and McEwan representing a 'male' perspective. The texts' protagonists, in turn, either align with or add to this variety of perspectives: Hustvedt's and Cole's protagonists are explicitly framed as *alter egos* of their authors; the different backgrounds of *What We All Long For*'s five main characters juxtapose Africadian, Asian-Canadian, Caribbean-Canadian, Italo-Caribbean-Canadian perspectives with the perspective of a Vietnamese refugee; Robertson's protagonist comes from rural Canada; and McEwan's Henry Perowne also aligns with his author's national and ethnic background. Class differences are just as pronounced, with some characters experiencing utter poverty (Dionne Brand's character Quy) while others find themselves in a particularly precarious financial situation (Robertson's Walker or Hustvedt's Iris Vegan) and yet others could be associated with an extremely well-off upper-middle class (McEwan's Henry Perowne).

This selection of texts aims at taking into account a large variety of voices from the 'center' as well as from the 'margins' in order to represent an array of modes of subjectivity that is as vast as possible and that engages with the analysis of practices of resistance and dynamics of power from a multitude of vantage points. Moreover, this approach also retains a focus on the power dynamics that are intrinsic to Great Britain's colonial history. Nevertheless, precisely because this study aims at tracing flânerie as a practice of resistance from a variety of angles, there are former colonies that, due to restrictions of space, had to be left out, most notably the Indian subcontinent, even though Anglophone Indian literature features quite a number of interesting flânerie texts as well, such as Amit Chaudhuri's *A New World* (2000) and *Odysseus Abroad* (2015), Suketu Mehta's *Maximum City: Bombay Lost and Found* (2004), or Aravind Adiga's *The White Tiger* (2008). A most useful examination of flânerie in Anglophone Indian literature can be found in Sandten (2012; 2020), however.

Precarious Flânerie and the Ethics of the Self in Contemporary Anglophone Fiction[6] can be situated within a burgeoning field of new-found interest in the trope of the flâneur, particularly in German-language publications, for reasons

---

[6] The term 'precarious flânerie' has also been used by Natalia Lettenewitsch in her article on "Prekäre Flanerie: Filmische Streif- und Beutezüge durch Berlin". However, Lettenewitsch's use of the term mostly focuses on the aspect of financial precarity and does not carry the ethical implications I intend to transmit.

discussed below. Quite a number of publications have appeared in recent years on the return of the flâneur in contemporary literature, starting with Matthias Keidel's *Die Wiederkehr der Flaneure: Literarische Flanerie und flanierendes Denken zwischen Wahrnehmung und Reflexion* in 2006 which scrutinizes the paradigm of 'strolling thought' in German literature from the 1970s to the 1990s. Stephanie Gomolla has analyzed the trope of the flâneur in French literature from the 1950s onwards in *Distanz und Nähe: Der Flaneur in der französischen Literatur zwischen Moderne und Postmoderne* (2009) and Eva Riedl examines the flâneur in the works of the German author W.G. Sebald in her monograph entitled *Raumbegehren: Zum Flaneur bei W.G. Sebald und Walter Benjamin* (2017). Jan Rhein addresses the question from a comparative vantage point and compares instances of flânerie in the works of Jacques Réda, Stephan Wackwitz, Orhan Pamuk and Cees Nooteboom in *Flaneure in der Gegenwartsliteratur: Réda, Wackwitz, Pamuk, Nooteboom* (2015). Moreover, several works focus on the connection between interculturality and flânerie, such as Rolf Goebel's *Benjamin Heute: Großstadtdiskurs, Postkolonialität und Flanerie zwischen den Kulturen* (2001), Jannica Budde's *Interkulturelle Stadtnomadinnen: Inszenierungen weiblicher Flanerie- und Migrationserfahrung in der deutsch-türkischen und türkischen Gegenwartsliteratur am Beispiel von Aysel Özakin, Emine Sevgi Özdamar und Aslı Erdoğan* (2017), or Jule Thiemann, who analyzes the nexus between flânerie and migration in *(Post-)Migrantische Flanerie: Transareale Kartierung in Berlin-Romanen der Jahrtausendwende* (2019). Nevertheless, there has so far been no monograph on flânerie in contemporary Anglophone literature, although the trope is frequently alluded to in individual articles or chapters within monographs on city literature.[7] This is partly due to the fact that the topic of flânerie in itself is somewhat underresearched in English as well as American studies since the flâneur is a phenomenon mostly associated with French and German literature. However, as Isabel Vila-Cabanes's study on the flâneur in nineteenth-century British literature, entitled *The Flâneur in Nineteenth-Century British Literary Culture: "The Worlds of London Unknown"* (2018), proves, practices of flânerie are in fact as present in British literature as they are in other national literatures.[8]

In chapter two, I delineate the theoretical framework of the book. I begin by offering a brief overview of the history of the flâneur as a literary trope in French and German literature before moving on to my take on a three-fold conceptual-

---

[7] See e.g. Artt (2018), Dinter (2019), Faisst (2018), Hartwiger (2016), Munt (1995), Rosenthal (2009; 2011; 2016; 2017), Sandten (2012; 2020), Vermeulen (2013; 2015), Williams (1997).
[8] For an overview of publications containing individual chapters on British flânerie – as opposed to Vila-Cabanes's monograph which focuses on British flânerie exclusively – see chapter 2.5.

ization of flânerie that draws on some of Benjamin's main theses on flânerie. I then summarize the central theses on flânerie as performance and their connection to the work of Michel De Certeau; recapitulate the history of flânerie from the point of view of intermediality; and discuss the appearance of the trope of the flâneur in Anglophone literature. The theory chapter on flânerie concludes with a heuristic model of what I would call the 'flânerie text' that builds on characteristics recurring throughout the previous sections.

Chapters three and four focus on the conceptualization of Foucault's and Butler's theories of ethical subjectivity with a specific emphasis on the Foucauldian 'techniques of the self' and Butler's theses on precariousness as *conditio humana*, while chapter five offers a synopsis of the theoretical underpinnings of my study along with a more detailed account of my overall thesis. The various case studies in the remaining chapters then build different strands of my argument. The analysis of Ian McEwan's *Saturday* focuses on technologies of domination as a counterpoint to the more positively evaluated technologies of the self and thus marks the possible borders of the concept of ethical subjectivity. Hustvedt's and Cole's novels, in which the relation between their respective protagonists and their authors is one of 'repetition with a difference', form prototypical examples of a Foucauldian 'aesthetics of existence', with the texts themselves reflecting the processes of (trans-)formation in the two protagonists. Finally, since this study also aims at analyzing different factors that might contribute to modes of subjection as well as resistance in individual characters' techniques of the self, such as the circulation of affect or different kinds of media and intermediality, I examine the texts written by Brand and Robertson, which explore those themes in detail.

As these five analyses show, contemporary Anglophone flânerie texts negotiate variants of post-sovereign subjectivity while at the same time affirming the shared human condition of vulnerability and relationality, thus deferring the norm of sovereign subjectivity.

2 Flânerie and its Discontents

"Definitions are at best difficult and, at worst, a contradiction of what the flâneur means. In himself, the flâneur is, in fact, a very obscure thing" (Tester 2015: 7), states Keith Tester in the introduction to his compilation on flânerie. He thus sums up an overall problem faced by research on flânerie (Neumeyer 1999: 17), namely that flânerie itself is difficult to define due to the heterogeneous history of the flâneur as a socio-historical phenomenon, and even more so as a literary trope. When looking at manifestations of flânerie in contemporary city texts, the situation becomes even more complex, not only due to the transformations that the trope has undergone since the appearance of the first flânerie texts,[9] but also due to the cultural significance of the appropriation of the phenomenon by Benjamin in his historical-materialist analysis of the nineteenth century. While Benjamin's writings on the flâneur can thus hardly be ignored as a primary point of reference for contemporary flânerie texts, it is impossible to say what, precisely, constitutes a flâneur for Benjamin due to the often contradictory observations that he makes on flânerie throughout his works.[10] In the following I will argue that the phenomenon of the flâneur both in its literary and socio-historical manifestations has become increasingly ambivalently semanticized in the course of the centuries, and that this has turned it into a particularly paradoxical concept. Beyond a minimal definition of flânerie, according to which the term refers to the act of strolling aimlessly through the space of the city, the flâneur comprises a number of rather contradictory characteristics that complicate any kind of fixed definition. While some aspects of this paradoxical constellation can be considered to be engrained in the phenomenon of flânerie from its very beginning, the vision of the flâneur as an ambivalent figure has been further emphasized by Benjamin's functionalization of it, which explicitly places it in an overall framework of subjection and resistance and thus paves the way for the reconceptualization of walking as a practice of resistance within spatial theory in the second half of the twentieth century.

---

9 For an overview of different functionalizations of the practice of flânerie in French and German literature over a considerable time span see e.g. Keidel (2006: 12–46).
10 For an extensive discussion of the impossibility of using Benjamin for definitions of flânerie see Neumeyer (1999: 14–17 and 380–387); Vila-Cabanes (2016: 5–15).

https://doi.org/10.1515/9783110767490-003

2.1 The History of the Flâneur as a Literary Trope

A first difficulty in establishing any fixed definition of flânerie is the fact that flânerie is from a contemporary point of view only accessible as an essentially textually mediated phenomenon.[11] Since the flâneur as a socio-historical phenomenon has long since disappeared from the streets of everyday metropolises, the actual practice of flânerie can only be traced in textual sources, a high percentage of which consists of fictional or at least semi-literary forms of writing that cannot be claimed to constitute examples of factual speech. The so-called 'physiologies', essays and sketches from which descriptions of the flâneur can be drawn, only portrayed aestheticized stereotypes or an exaggerated version of anything that a real-life flâneur might have been. Although flânerie was a particularly prominent socio-historical phenomenon in Paris in the nineteenth century, it is still rather what has been *written* – in the form of sketches or brief essays – about those extraliterary flâneurs as types that serves as a basis for the flâneur as a trope in literature (see also Solnit 2001: 200). Thus, most monographs on the topic introduce their definitions of flânerie by referring to the flâneur as a socio-historical phenomenon coming into existence roughly at the beginning of the nineteenth century[12] and then base their actual definitions on literary and semi-literary descriptions of flânerie, following the assumption that artists and writers claimed the phenomenon of flânerie for themselves and functionalized it as their mode of experiencing reality,[13] whereas others doubt that the type ever existed in an extraliterary reality.[14] In any case, defini-

---

[11] See also Müller (2013: 206) as well as Shields (2015: 62), who point out that flânerie as a phenomenon is predominantly mediated through literary texts.
[12] See Vila-Cabanes (2016: 17), Köhn (1989: 27–34), Rhein (2015: 12–13), Keidel (2006: 13–15).
[13] Gomolla (2009: 10), Köhn (1989: 27–35), Severin (1988: 7–12), and Keidel (2006: 12–15) proceed in a similar way.
[14] Cf. for example Schneider (1996: 152; my trans.): "The figure of the flâneur, of whose actual empirical existence no one has ever been certain, has always been an object and a trigger for the intellectual projection of desires and might have only been invented to reflect on the phenomenon of the metropolis and its perception." – "Die Figur des Flaneurs, von der keiner so recht weiß, ob sie empirisch jemals existiert hat, war schon immer Gegenstand und Auslöser intellektueller Wunschprojektionen und wurde vielleicht überhaupt erst erfunden, um über das Phänomen der großen Stadt und ihrer Wahrnehmung nachzudenken." Similarly, Rebecca Solnit states in her monograph *Wanderlust* (2001: 200): "The only problem with the flâneur is that he did not exist, except as a type, an ideal, and a character in literature."

tions of flânerie are thus already based on a plethora of reference texts, none of which can be assumed to have produced a prototypical flâneur.[15]

Likewise, the origin of the flâneur is blurred both on an etymological and a phenomenological level. Whereas it is quite clear that the term 'flâneur' derives from the verb 'flâner' (*TLFi* s.v. *flâneur, euse*, adj. subst.), hypotheses on the etymology of 'flâner' differ. Several sources point out that 'flâner' derives from the Old Norse 'flana', which can be translated as "'run close to look at something, stare, make eyes'" (Aasen, qtd. in Brynhildsvoll 2020: 52) or "to run giddily here and there" (Solnit 2001: 198)[16] – and is thus almost diametrically opposed to the slow movement that the verb 'flâner' suggests – but it has also been pointed out that the term 'flâneur' might have derived from an Irish term for 'libertine' (Solnit 2001: 198; Wilson 1992: 93).[17] Apart from these etymological complications, the flâneur as a socio-historical phenomenon is preceded by his occurrence as a structural paradigm in cases of flânerie *avant la lettre* such as, most notably, Louis-Sébastien Mercier's *Tableau de Paris*, published in 1781 (Köhn 1989: 17–25), long before the term 'flâneur' was explicitly mentioned for the first time in a literary text, the anonymous *Le Flâneur au salon ou Mr. Bon-Homme: Examen joyeux des tableaux, mêlé de Vaudevilles* (1806), which suggests that by the turn of the century the flâneur was already established as a socio-historical phenomenon (Vila-Cabanes 2016: 24). The *Tableau de Paris* is particularly noteworthy because Mercier's social criticism projects a type of flânerie that is very different from the disinterested, leisurely strolls of M. Bonhomme and there-

---

[15] Common examples frequently mentioned in research on flânerie are Louis Huart's *Physiologie du Flaneur*, Louis-Sébastien Mercier's *Tableau de Paris*, Charles Baudelaire's *Paris Spleen*, Franz Hessel's *Walking in Berlin*. See also Rob Shields (2015: 62): "The notion of *flânerie* is essentially a literary gloss: it is uneasily tied to any sociological reality."

[16] Knut Brynhildsvoll refers to Ivar Aasen's dictionary for his translation whereas Solnit's translation mostly coincides with the information provided by the *Trésor de la langue française* (*TLFi* s.v. *flâner* v.).

[17] Although references to the thesis that 'flâner' derived from 'flana' predominate, the connection to 'libertine' is just as interesting since it has also been noted that early flâneurs adopted their style from British gentlemen in the course of a French "anglomania" which was caused by the strong influence that Britain exerted on France in economic terms. As Robert L. Herbert points out, "[t]he British were the principal foreign investors in French commerce and industry and were the most influential foreigners in Paris in the 1830s and the 1840s. They financed, built and staffed, most of the French railways, they were major suppliers of agricultural and industrial equipment, they were the source of new ideas about animal breeding, and they were the originators of the terms, and often the conventions, of early modern sports, above all, horse-racing, rowing, sailing and running ('le footing')" (Herbert 1988: 34).

fore raises the question as to which text might be considered to be more 'prototypical' with regard to a definition of flânerie.

This diversity in anything that might be called a flâneur intensifies even further if seen from a diachronic perspective, due to the production of ever more versions of flânerie over time. Thus, while even the most minimalistic definitions of flânerie usually refer to it as a practice of aimless wandering within the space of the city,[18] the abovementioned M. Bonhomme, in fact, does not wander the city without an aim (Vila-Cabanes 2016: 26). And whereas many early descriptions put an emphasis on the idleness of the flâneur (Vila-Cabanes 2016: 23–33), Baudelaire refers to the flâneur as someone whose basic aim is to "merge with the crowd" (1972: 399) and who is explicitly contrasted with any kind of 'lazy' behavior:

> The man who loves to lose himself in a crowd enjoys feverish delights that the egoist locked up in himself as in a box, and the *slothful* man like a mollusk in his shell, will be eternally deprived of. (Baudelaire 1970: 20; my emphasis)

Many definitions of flânerie put an emphasis on the act of observation that accompanies the practice of walking,[19] but this aspect is of secondary importance in the dandyesque flâneurs' performance of flânerie. As Barbey d'Aurevilly remarks, this kind of flânerie was to be considered as "an attitude of protest against the vulgarized, materialistic civilization of the bourgeois century" (D'Aurevilly, qtd. in Herbert 1988: 34). Therefore, the dandyesque flâneur's aim resides predominantly in his desire to be seen, whereas especially latter-day flâneurs depend on their anonymity in the crowd in order to be able to observe the goings-on of the city (Keidel 2006: 15). The differing stages in the development of the practice of flânerie thus add ever new characteristics to the trope, more often than not partly obliterating essential characteristics of older versions of the flâneur in new functionalizations of the trope.

Consequently, existing definitions of flânerie differ a lot in the emphases they put on various characteristics of the flâneur. Isabel Vila-Cabanes, for example, defines the flâneur as

> a person – in the nineteenth century usually male – who goes for a stroll around the city with no particular purpose or destination. Often in an idle mood, the explorer of the modern metropolis saunters around the streets, observing and describing the urban environment and reflecting on it. The existence of the flâneur is paradoxical, since he is in the crowd but is not really a part of it. He is detached from the masses and acts as a spectator

---

18 Cf. Neumeyer (1999: 17) or Müller (2013: 214).
19 Cf. for example, Keidel (2006: 12) or Vila-Cabanes (2016: 15).

who experiences society in his own way. In the anonymity of the streets, the flaneur finds the best atmosphere to let his thoughts run free, for what he observes induces thought processes in him. (2016: 15)[20]

Matthias Keidel, by contrast, immediately links the flâneur to the production of texts:

> I understand the term 'flâneur' as referring to writers who roam through the metropolis and produce texts poised in the tension between descriptive perception and reflection on what has been seen. The manner in which the change between perception and reflection is motivated, determines the type of strolling thought at hand, which in turn directly or indirectly correlates with the strolling movement of the author – thus, the thought process is literally structured by the writer's feet. Those texts are then not motivated by any kind of philosophical systemic thought, but by immediate sense impressions, by the author-subject's reaction to the metropolis as context of perception and the incentives for thought it provides. (Keidel 2006: 12; my trans.)[21]

While both definitions do share certain characteristics such as the emphasis on a link between observation and reflection, they are quite obviously based on different stages of flânerie. Moreover, Vila-Cabanes seems to refer to the flâneur primarily as a literary motif, while Keidel draws an explicit connection between the author as an extraliterary entity and the practice of flânerie. And whereas Vila-Cabanes emphasizes the fact that the flâneur's wanderings through the city are aimless, Keidel includes this aspect at best implicitly by referring to the flâneur's activity of 'roaming' through the metropolis. What is more, Vila-Cabanes's flâneur is decidedly 'idle', whereas the profession of the writer in Keidel's definition suggests the opposite. Lastly, the presence of the crowd as a criterion is entirely missing from Keidel, yet features prominently in Vila-Cabanes's description.

The excerpts drawn from the history of flânerie texts that I referred to above might seem to comprise a rather eclectic selection of writings on flânerie, but they show what is problematic about any kind of fixed definition of flânerie.

---

20 Vila-Cabanes adds here another flânerie text to those that have already been mentioned, namely Auguste de Lacroix's essay "The Flâneur" (1841) which she uses as a basis for her definition of flânerie.
21 "Als Flaneure werden hierbei durch die Großstadt schweifende Literaten verstanden, die ihre Texte in den Spannungsbogen von beschreibender Wahrnehmung und Reflexion des Gesehenen stellen. Die Art und Weise, wie der Wechsel zwischen Wahrnehmung und Reflexion motiviert wird, ist bestimmend für verschiedene Arten flanierenden Denkens, das jeweils direkt oder indirekt mit einer Gehbewegung des Autors zusammenhängt – der Gedankengang wird also im wörtlichen Sinne von den Füßen strukturiert. Motivation dieser Texte ist kein philosophisch systematisches Denken, sondern der unmittelbare Sinneseindruck, die Reaktion des Autor-Subjekts auf den Wahrnehmungskontext der Großstadt und die damit verbundenen 'Denk-Anreize.'"

Not only can the flâneur be found in a variety of forms, which complicate or make it even impossible to come up with any fixed definition of flânerie, but the type also comprises contradictory attributes in itself. As the abovementioned quote by Keith Tester suggests, whenever the flâneur is tied to a specific definition in terms of content, the risk is that this definition creates an image of the flâneur that misses substantial aspects of the tradition of the trope. As a firmer basis for the selection of works in this book, I have therefore chosen Harald Neumeyer's minimal definition of flânerie according to which it is to be understood as an open paradigm of strolling aimlessly through the space of the city which can be functionalized in various ways (Neumeyer 1999: 17). Yet, since the texts I examine negotiate the flânerie trope by drawing on certain characteristics that have frequently appeared in the tradition, despite not being present in each and every extant example of flânerie, I present here a brief overview of those characteristics as well as the problems they might give rise to when attributed to flânerie.

Starting with Neumeyer's minimal definition, three aspects have to be discussed in detail: the action of strolling, the aimlessness of this strolling, and the space of the city. In relation to the first, it is worth clarifying that I use the term 'strolling' to translate the German word '*streifen*' which Neumeyer uses in his definition, since it captures the ambivalence of the term chosen by him.[22] According to the Oxford English Dictionary, the activity of 'strolling' can be defined as "to walk or ramble in a careless, haphazard, or leisurely fashion as inclination directs; often simply to take a walk" (*OED* s.v. *stroll* v.[2a]). While the term might thus suggest a "leisurely" and thus rather slow way of moving through the city, it does not restrict the manner of walking to this option and just like the German term *streifen* rather emphasizes the aimlessness of this movement. Whereas many definitions of flânerie also feature a reference to the slowness of flânerie (see e.g. Gomolla 2009: 32), the practice cannot be reduced to this aspect – especially in the context of contemporary flânerie texts – since such a characterization of flânerie overemphasizes one pole of a continuum within which the flâneur has to be positioned with regard to velocity. On the one hand, the flâneur might well be understood as a contrast to the fast-moving crowd in the city: he protests industrialized progress by, as Walter Benjamin points out in a much-quoted statement, taking turtles for a walk and adapting to the animals' pace

---

[22] 'Streifen': "ohne erkennbares Ziel, ohne eine bestimmte Richtung einzuhalten wandern, ziehen: irgendwo herumwandern, -ziehen" (Duden s.v. *streifen* v.[4a]). The emphasis in this definition is clearly on the aimless character of this kind of walking while the definition does not specify whether this movement might be considered slow or fast.

(Benjamin 2006: 84).[23] Accordingly, the *Trésor de la langue française* also defines the verb 'flâner' as "[a]vancer lentement et sans direction precise" (*TLFi* s.v. *flâner* v.^A), thus emphasizing the slowness of the movement as much as its aimlessness. This might be especially justified in the context of flânerie as a socio-historical phenomenon since the aspect of leisure – and thus the corresponding slow movement – is central to the socio-historical phenomenon of the Parisian flâneurs. On the other hand, the flâneur also stands for a dynamization of vision and thus for acceleration if contrasted with an otherwise static spectator. As Neumeyer points out, the phenomenon of the crowd demands an observer who is just as dynamic as the crowd itself and can adapt to its fast-moving changes (1999: 33). Moreover, it might sometimes be difficult to judge if a character in a literary text can be considered to walk slowly through the city, with the situation becoming even more complicated if a text features flânerie as an overall structural paradigm rather than taking the form of one or more characters. The flâneur, therefore, has to be located within a dialectics of acceleration and deceleration since he is participating in the overall acceleration of the industrialized city, but at the same time is contrasted with a crowd that is moving even faster, and becomes therefore emblematic of processes of deceleration.

While the term 'strolling' only refers to movement that is undertaken by foot, current research in flânerie has shown that other modes of movement, such as riding a bike or driving a car, might qualify as flânerie as well.[24] Thus, while 'traditional' flânerie still has to be considered as occurring on foot, other forms might be possible as long as they comply with the characteristic of aimlessness and as long as it is taken into account that those forms always already constitute a deviation from more prototypical forms and thus carry additional meaning.

The second aspect, the aimlessness of the movement of the flâneur, is likewise contested. With regard to this characteristic, Neumeyer specifies that 'aimlessness' should not be equated with a lack of intention, but can rather be combined with different intentions, thus serving differing functions. Only if the intention of the flâneur actually influences the direction of his movement

---

23 Solnit, however, laconically remarks that, although Benjamin's quote is frequently employed as proof of the flâneur's preference for slow movement, no one has so far presented actual historical evidence of a specific individual engaging in such behaviour (Solnit 2001: 200). Benjamin's anecdote might thus rather be considered of metaphorical value than as a historically accurate description.
24 See, for example, Pleßke (2014: 293) on the possibility of interpreting Henry Perowne, the protagonist of Ian McEwan's *Saturday*, as a flâneur. Another interesting case in point in this context is Don DeLillo's novel *Cosmopolis* (2003), in which the protagonist Eric Packer seems to 'stroll' aimlessly through the city in his car.

through the city does he stop being a flâneur (Neumeyer 1999: 52). Aimlessness is thus restricted to a situation in which the flâneur never has a concrete aim towards which he is directing his steps. This is not to say that Neumeyer excludes the possibility that the intention of the flâneur might influence his flânerie on the level of perception. He admits that different functionalizations of flânerie lead to different modes of perception and thus might produce varying results (Neumeyer 1999: 54). Yet, if the functionalization of the flâneur influences his overall perception, why should it not just as well influence the direction that his walks take? Thus, when faced with a decision on which way to take at a crossing, the flâneur's choice might – intentionally or unintentionally – be influenced by the overall function that his flânerie is supposed to have. It is therefore questionable whether the movement of the flâneur can unequivocally be judged to be aimless at all times. The aimlessness of the flâneur rather has to be considered a constantly endangered characteristic and a reflection on the freedom of the strolling subject itself. While the movement of the flâneur is thus predominantly aimless, those instances in which he seems to deviate from aimlessness form part of flânerie and could serve the negotiation of relationships of subjection and freedom.

Lastly, the space of the city as the natural 'habitat' of the flâneur, the third aspect of the definition, serves, first and foremost, to distinguish the flâneur from his predecessor (Jauß 1989: 190), the person who strolls through nature (Neumeyer 1999: 11; Groh 1987: 51; Gomolla 2009: 8). The transfer of the stroller who is located in nature to the space of the city causes a variety of modifications with regard to the movement as well as the perception of those who stroll. First of all, the path of the stroller in nature is not only predetermined, but also free from obstacles, whereas the flâneur might be able to choose from a variety of routes, but might also have to face a plethora of hindrances such as the crowd itself, construction work, or traffic. The movement of the solitary stroller is thus transformed from a linear practice into the disrupted and distracted zigzag-form of urban flânerie: while the city is the space that makes flânerie possible, it can make it impossible as well. Similarly, the objects of the stroller's observation have changed. The flâneur can no longer indulge in the tranquility and harmony of nature, but he observes the crowd in its ever-changing configurations and is confronted with the intruding stimuli of modern technology that the city offers. While the flâneur thus directs his gaze towards the city as an object, the city might redirect the flâneur's gaze towards ever new attractions, and this turns the flâneur from a subject into an object himself.[25]

---

[25] See for entire paragraph Neumeyer (1999: 12–13).

One central constituent of the environment that the city offers to the flâneur is the crowd. As Baudelaire points out, "[t]he crowd is his [the flâneur's] domain, just as the air is the bird's, and water that of the fish. His passion and his profession is to merge with the crowd" (Baudelaire 1972: 399). Yet, 'merging' in this context does not in fact refer to a complete incorporation into the crowd. Here, the relationship between flâneur and crowd could rather be described as a dialectical motion between merging with the crowd – that is, identification – and distancing himself internally from the crowd (Gomolla 2009: 31). Consequently, the attitude of the flâneur could, as Rüdiger Severin puts it, be described as "sympathetic indifference" (Severin 1988: 3; my trans.)[26] and thus as inherently paradoxical. The relationship between the flâneur and the crowd is thus also essentially ambivalent and can take up a variety of meanings in its individual manifestations. Indeed, the crowd itself is not necessarily essential to flânerie. As Benjamin's autobiographical writings *Berlin Childhood around 1900* (1938) or his collection of aphorisms, titled *One-Way Street* (1928), suggest, the flâneur might not need the crowd as his "natural domain", and might just as much focus on buildings, architecture, or the signs that the city itself offers him. While the encounter between flâneur and crowd has become a staple in many flânerie texts, this does not hold true for all of them. The crowd is a frequent, yet not essential characteristic of flânerie texts.

All of the abovementioned characteristics thus situate the flâneur within a tension between opposing poles of deceleration and acceleration, freedom and subjection, and facilitation and hindrance of flânerie. While those are the only qualities that can be attributed to all of the cases of flânerie that I analyze in this book, a couple of characteristics, like the encounter with the crowd, do occur frequently, but not always in the specific context of flânerie; these are of particular importance for my analyses since the texts I examine draw on them deliberately.

Firstly, flânerie is always accompanied by certain specific modes of perception, amongst which visual perception prevails. Benjamin, drawing on Georg Simmel, refers to the "marked preponderance of visual activity" (Simmel, qtd. in Benjamin 2006: 69) that determines the relationships between people in the city. The flâneur has thus frequently been characterized as an observer of life in the city, and hence as reliant on the city dweller's preferred mode of perception. At the same time, as has been mentioned at the beginning of this chapter, the flâneur might not just be the subject, but might become the object of observation as well. Especially in the case of the dandyesque flâneurs flaunting their

---

26 "[t]eilnehmende[] Teilnahmslosigkeit" (Severin 1988: 3).

supposed moral superiority, an emphasis is rather put on their being perceived by the public than vice versa. Fittingly, the tension between seeing and being seen in the history of the trope of the flâneur can thus further be specified in the flâneur's differentiation from two types that are often confused with him because they share some of his characteristics: the dandy and the *badaud*. While the dandy could be associated with the concept of 'being seen', the *badaud*, that is, the gawper, is the epitome of 'seeing' because his whole identity condenses into the pleasure of watching. In both cases, the border between these types and the flâneur is often not clear cut.

This holds especially true for those flâneurs who could be associated with the practices of the dandy (Gomolla 2009: 38–39; Keidel 2006: 14; Müller 2013: 206) as they demonstratively took their idleness to the streets. Consequently, the dandy has by some scholars been seen as a subtype of the flâneur,[27] whereas others classify him as the parent category to the flâneur (Gomolla 2009: 39).[28] Moreover, while many sources confirm a partial overlapping of the characteristics of the dandy and the flâneur (see Hohmann 2000: 130; Wuthenow 1978: 190; Herbert 1988: 34–35; Köhn 1989: 28–30; Keidel 2006: 14),[29] Müller (2013: 209) and Vila-Cabanes (2016: 44) distinguish between the flâneur and the dandy explicitly by reference to the dandy's emphasis on performance and visibility. Drawing on Margaret Rose's (2007) analysis of nineteenth-century 'physiological' writings, Müller points out that the flâneur's contemporaries in fact perceived him as a type distinct from the co-existing phenomenon of the dandy (2013: 210). Müller's and Vila-Cabanes's objections are important because they draw attention to the fact that the thesis of the transformation of the dandy into the flâneur is often too readily accepted. While I would not quite agree that the physiologies' explicit differentiation between the flâneur and the dandy suffices as proof that the flâneur and the dandy were perceived as two distinct phenomena by their contemporaries, since this argument is based on the problematic assumption that the physiologies can be read as factual accounts of

---

[27] Angela Hohmann refers to the dandy as "the first socio-historically proven manifestation of the flâneur" (2000: 130; my trans.).

[28] See for example Ralph-Rainer Wuthenow who refers to the flâneur as one "manifestation of the dandy" among others (1978: 190).

[29] See e.g. Herbert (1988: 34–35): "By the early 1860s, the Parisian *flâneur* had absorbed many of the leading characteristics of the dandy. The dandy was not necessarily a *flâneur*, but the *flâneur* was almost always a dandy. In his British top hat and formal clothes, however, the *flâneur* was not immediately distinguished from the mass of French upper-class men of the Second Empire."

contemporary socio-historical reality,[30] I also hold that assumptions regarding the dandy simply as a stage of development in the evolution of the flâneur are questionable (see also Zauner-Schneider 1995: 106). Moreover, descriptions that equate the flâneur with the dandy on the grounds of his "British top hat and formal clothes" (see fn. 28) have to be problematized since several sources confirm that British dandyism underwent profound changes when it was transferred to French society (see Moers 1960: 107–117; Rossbach 2002: 14). However, it might be this translation that introduces a blurring of the boundary between dandy and flâneur: while the so-called "bourgeois flâneur" (Ferguson 2015: 26; Vila-Cabanes 2016: 40–43) can indeed be associated with the outward appearance of the British dandy, as the descriptions of the flâneur in a variety of sources confirm (see e.g. Vila-Cabanes 2016: 30–31; Gomolla 2009: 36; De Lacroix 1840: 65 or Huart 1841: 49, 80, 57) – that is, with the rather discreet, refined style of Beau Brummel[31] – the French actualization of the British phenomenon might in fact be perceived as distinct from the bourgeois flâneur's purely external emulation of fashionable British attitudes.[32]

What is more, Köhn, for example, illustrates the thesis that the dandyesque flâneurs of the first half of the nineteenth century were mostly aristocrats who cultivated a specific style of life – or a certain aesthetics of existence – that aimed at distancing them by means of manners, clothing, gestus, and habitus from the bourgeoisie by drawing on the journalistic work of Honoré de Balzac (Köhn 1989: 28; see Balzac 2010: ch. 45). It has to be noted, however, that Balzac refers here to practices communicating 'elegance' when strolling along the boulevards, but distinguishes those practices quite explicitly from dandyism (see Balzac 2010: ch. 39), and furthermore, seems indeed to distinguish between flâneur and dandy (Balzac 2010: ch. 40). The fact that Balzac frequently refers back to Brummel when reflecting on what he terms 'elegant life' (see Balzac 2010: ch. 40 and 48) further attests to the distinction between British dandyism (embodied by Brummel) and its French actualization, and to the assumption that many arguments claiming the merging of the flâneur with the dandy resulted from a combination of practices of strolling with an adoption of the specific style of Brummel. Müller's critique, thus, certainly holds true in cases like Köhn (1989: 28–30), Keidel (2006: 14), and Riedl (2017: 84). While Köhn bases

---

30 See also Neumeyer, who points out that the description of 'ideal types' need not necessarily represent the reality of nineteenth-century Paris (1999: 89).
31 For a description of Brummel's type of style, see Rossbach (2002: 13).
32 See Moers (1960: 108): "In the new century the fascination was with manners, and dandy manners were the English export." Moers's account further suggests that dandyism was indeed a practice common beyond the realm of the aristocracy.

his account mostly on the aforementioned quotes from Balzac, Keidel and Riedl simply reproduce Köhn's argument without adding further proof. Neumeyer (1999: 81, 149, 154), however, proves the blurring of the line between dandy and flâneur in a variety of sources.

Crucially, Baudelaire also seems to oscillate between the role of the flâneur and the dandy and includes both types in his analysis of modernity in "The Painter of Modern Life" (Müller 2013: 211; Harvey 2003: 14). However, I do not quite agree with Müller's assumption that the concept of the flâneur is ultimately more important for Baudelaire, since his argument is built on a perceived balance between the I and the non-I in Baudelaire's writing (2013: 211). The poet, who refers to the flâneur as "a prince enjoying his incognito wherever he goes", and whom Neumeyer, for example, identifies as the "sovereign of the city" (1999: 135; my trans.) could just as well be interpreted as exploiting the dialectical relationship between I and non-I for the sake of self-stylization, thus further contributing to the blurring of the border between flâneur and dandy.

Particularly relevant for my analysis, then, is that the blurring of the border between flânerie and dandyism is usually linked to aiming at a performance of distinction. Just like the idle pose of the aristocratic boulevardiers, the bourgeois "flâneur's ostentatious inaction offers evidence of superior social status" (Ferguson 2015: 26). While the aristocratic idlers Balzac refers to in his journalistic writings aim at performing their superiority with regard to manners and education, the bourgeois flâneur flaunts his economic success, and hence his financial freedom. Adopting the style of the British dandy seems here all the more fitting in terms of a contemporary French 'anglomania' that was based on an association between 'Britishness' and economic success. Once again, the focus is placed on a performance of flânerie that aims at 'being seen' by others and at distinguishing oneself from a crowd that is deemed inferior to oneself. In both cases, the explicit performance of flânerie aims at the display of superior social status, although the bourgeois flâneurs already form part of flânerie as a mass phenomenon.

This is not to say that flânerie is always linked to dandyism. As Matthias Keidel, drawing on Köhn and Kracauer, suggests, the terms 'flâneur' and 'dandy' can no longer be used synonymously once journalists and writers start to adopt and adapt the practices of flânerie (2006: 14) because the purpose of their flânerie simply shifts.[33] Since flânerie had already become a mass phenom-

---

33 The practice of the flâneur was adopted by writers and journalists when the production and distribution of newspapers on a daily basis became possible due to technological progress and the inclusion of advertisements, which allowed distributors to lower prices and thus make the papers available to a wider audience (see Keidel 2006: 14; Neumeyer 1999: 89–91; Köhn 1989: 34; Kracauer 1994: 73).

enon towards the middle of the nineteenth century, the flânerie which had previously been used as a deliberate performance of idleness and thus to stand out from the crowd could now also be used to blend in with the crowd of bourgeois flâneurs in order to obtain information regarding social life in the city. While Baudelaire often fuses dandyism and flânerie in his writings, he also argues that the aim of the flâneur is to "merge with the crowd" and thus lets the performance of the dandy be entirely obliterated by the anonymity and invisibility of the flâneur, or rather relegates the activity of self-stylization to the act of writing and the artistic products that will result from it. Hence, the flâneur could be distinguished from the dandy through his focus on the act of observation which can be contrasted with the dandy's desire to be recognized within the city. Yet, since this does not hold true for some of the first flâneurs who actually coincide with the adaptation of the dandy to the streets of Paris, the border between the flâneur and the dandy is always already a contested one and the concept of performance might recur in later manifestations of flânerie in terms of a dialectics between 'seeing' and 'being seen'.

The *badaud*, by contrast, can be located at the other end of this spectrum. He dissolves into the activity of seeing and thus succumbs to the spectacle of the city. This characteristic becomes especially clear in his relationship to the crowd: while the gawper merges indistinguishably with the crowd and is overtaken by the phenomena of the city, the flâneur keeps his individuality (Gomolla 2009: 40; see also Shaya 2004: 50). Yet, as Neumeyer points out, this differentiation, which draws on Victor Fournel's distinction between *badaud* and flâneur in *L'Odyssee d'un flâneur ou Ce qu'on voit dans les rues de Paris* (1867), rather conflates the *badaud* with the passer-by and does not specify in what way the *badaud*'s manner of 'seeing' differs from that of the flâneur (Neumeyer 1999: 79). When Fournel describes the flâneur's specific manner of observation, he does so by resorting to the example of Poe's "The Man of the Crowd", in which the nameless narrator watches the passing crowd through the window of a coffeehouse before he decides to follow the unknown man he has seen in its midst (Fournel 1867: 269–271; Neumeyer 1999: 80). For Fournel, the important characteristic here is the distance between the flâneur and the crowd which turns the flâneur into a distant reader of the crowd (Fournel 1867: 269; Neumeyer 1999: 79), yet what he fails to specify is in what way this distance is linked to the motion of the flâneur (Neumeyer 1999: 80); evidently, his example for this manner of observation – Poe's nameless narrator – cannot be called a flâneur. Moreover, Fournel introduces an intermediate type between the flâneur and the *badaud*, called the 'badaud parfait', who seems to be a spectator like the flâneur, and he frequently mixes up the characteristics of the *badaud* and the flâneur, thus further complicating any strict distinction between flâneur and *badaud* (Neumeyer 1999: 80). It therefore remains largely unclear in what way the flâneur's mode of perception differs from that of the *badaud*. Similarly, M. Bonhomme, the first specimen of the literary trope of the flâneur, is described as a "very close first cousin" (*The Flaneur in the Salon* 2016: 103) of M. Muzard, a name that evokes the type of the *musard*, an equivalent of the *badaud*. This first flânerie text then still implies a close connection between the *badaud*'s fascination with the metropolitan spectacle and the flâneur's observation of city life.

Although he does not draw a distinction between the flâneur's and the *badaud*'s modes of perception, Fournel emphasizes that the flâneur "observes and reflects" (Fournel 1867: 270; my trans.) and thus may be said to create an inner distance towards his objects of observation (Gomolla 2009: 40; Vila-Cabanes 2016: 45–47). The border between *badaud* and flâneur might be blurred, given Fournel's confusion of their characteristics, but he introduces the activity of reflection as an important benchmark. The only problem with this characteristic of flânerie is that it is of no use when applied to the flânerie text: as soon as the perception of the flâneur is translated into text or as soon as the spectacle of the city has registered within the consciousness of a strolling character, reflection can be assumed to take place. While prototypical cases of flânerie can thus easily be recognized due to a high level of reflection, it is difficult to say where reflection stops within the confines of the literary text. Neumeyer's argument is especially important here because it marks the aspect that links the flâneur with the *badaud*, that is, their common mode of perception, which reveals the flâneur's underlying fascination with the spectacle of the metropolis.

Returning to the overall spectrum delineated by the dandy and the *badaud*, the flâneur can be located in between the two.[34] Predominant, albeit not exclusive characteristics can be found in the act of observation which distinguishes the flâneur from the dandy, and the act of reflection which distinguishes the flâneur from the *badaud*, although in both cases the borders remain blurred thus causing some of the characteristics of the dandy and the *badaud* to infiltrate examples of flânerie.

Linked to the paradigm of visual perception, or rather to the combination of visual perception with reflection, is the metaphor of the flâneur as a reader of the city (Gomolla 2009: 35; Neumeyer 1999: 83). This aspect can best be exemplified by a quote from Franz Hessel's *Walking in Berlin:*

> The flaneur reads the street, and human faces, displays, window dressings, café terraces, trains, cars, and trees become letters that yield the words, sentences, and pages of a

---

[34] See also Mazlish (2015: 49): "The passage to the *flâneur* and his modernity runs through the dandy on the one side and the masses, or, crowd, on the other."

book that is always new. To correctly play the flaneur, you cannot have anything too particular in mind. On the stretch of road between Wittenbergplatz and Halensee, there are now so many possibilities to run errands, eat, drink, to go to a theater, film, or cabaret, that it's easy to promenade without the risk of developing a set goal, leaving oneself to the unforeseen adventures of the eye. (Hessel 2017: 133)

For the flâneur, the whole city consists of signifiers.[35] From people to buildings and even to trees, everything carries meaning, thus creating "unknown adventures of the eye". This kind of reading also includes actual signs that might be found on posters, advertisements, or street signs, as the chapter "Enseignes et affiches" in Fournel's *L'Odyssee d'un flâneur ou Ce qu'on voit dans les rues de Paris* suggests.

This metaphor recurs in various functionalizations of the flâneur, such as the historiographer or the sociologist. For Benjamin and Kracauer, for example, the flâneur can decipher the signs of the past in the city. He walks back "into a vanished time" (Benjamin 2002: 416) and he ensures that "the past remains attached to the places where it was at home during its lifetime" (Kracauer 1980: 173; my trans.).[36] The flâneur as sociologist appears in texts ranging from the beginning of the nineteenth century to the present. While the early physiologies, with their analysis of social types representative of certain professions or even entire classes of the population, could already be considered to constitute attempts at sociology in their interpretation of the metropolitan crowd (see also Gomolla 2009: 38), it is the research conducted on the flâneur in the twentieth and twenty-first centuries that emphasizes this analogy (Frisby 2015: 81–110; Gilloch 1999: 109). As the above examples show, the act of reading might then also form part of the construction of the identity of the flâneur since he creates his own identity in relation to the identity of the crowd, which he has deciphered by means of his practice of flânerie (Neumeyer 1999: 59). At the same time, the flâneur's interpretation might be linked to processes of projection, dissemination, or deconstruction and need not necessarily adhere to truth as a value. Thus, the strolling lyrical I of Baudelaire's *Parisian Scenes (Tableaux parisiens)* interprets the people he encounters on the streets of Paris and invents stories about them without aiming at any kind of truthfulness (Neumeyer 1999: 59). The focus here lies entirely on the construction of the identity of the lyrical I as a "sovereign of the city" who creates his own city based on individual interpretations.

---

35 Neumeyer refers in this context to the city as a "reservoir of signifiers" (1999: 80; my trans.).
36 "das Vergangene an den Orten haften [bleibt], an denen es zu Lebzeiten hauste."

This process of identity construction ties in with another common characteristic of the flâneur: his resistance to mass phenomena such as acceleration or technological progress (see also Gomolla 2009: 31).[37] Thus, the flâneur's complex tension between distance and proximity to the crowd as well as attention and indifference could be linked to what Georg Simmel, for example, refers to as the "resistance of the individual to being levelled, swallowed up in the social-technological mechanism" (1971: 324). Moreover, as mentioned above, the flâneur has been described as distinct from the crowd due to his individuality. This individuality becomes manifest in a variety of attributes that juxtapose the flâneur with the crowd and present him in a state of opposition to the crowd. First of all, the aimlessness of his walks contrasts with the purposeful motion of the crowd that is subjected to timetables, schedules, and the rhythms of industrialized society (Hohmann 2000: 154; Gomolla 2009: 33). Thus, the flâneur's contemporaries at the beginning of the nineteenth century criticize him for his idleness and lack of productivity (Gomolla 2009: 33; Vila-Cabanes 2016: 23). The second attribute, his slowness, has even been deemed suspicious by Franz Hessel's fellow citizens, as he remarks that "I attract wary glances whenever I try to play the flaneur among the industrious; I believe they take me for a pickpocket" (Hessel 2017: 1). While slowness might not necessarily be one of the constitutive characteristics of the flâneur, whenever it occurs it traditionally functions as a marker of the resistance of the flâneur with regard to the general processes of acceleration that accompany rapidly progressing industrialization (Gomolla 2009: 32–34). The slowness of the flâneur is then closely related to the act of reflection that might follow the flâneur's perception of the city. The inner distance which Fournel postulated as the primary feature that distinguishes the flâneur from the *badaud*, and which forms the precondition for any act of reflection, is then best exemplified in the work of Charles Baudelaire who, as mentioned earlier, repeatedly describes flânerie in terms of a dialectics of merging with the crowd and keeping an inner distance from it (Baudelaire 1972: 399–400; Gomolla 2009: 31; Neumeyer 1999: 135). What is more, the entire relationship between flânerie and artistic production necessarily entails reflection. Nevertheless, while those three aspects – aimlessness, slowness, and reflection – are usually linked to flânerie as a performance of resistance, they might equally well be turned into modes of subjection or compulsion and thus cannot be said to be exclusively linked to resistance and the aspiration to freedom this

---

37 Likewise, Leonhard Fuest refers to flânerie as the "chiffre of a lost time" (2008: 169).

connection might imply.[38] They indicate, however, that resistance becomes manifest not only in the artistic production that the flâneur creates based on his strolls through the city, but also in the actual practice of strolling that deviates from the normative demands of an increasingly industrialized environment.

As Benjamin's observations on flânerie imply, it is especially the connection between artist and flâneur that has been linked to a negotiation of resistance and subjection in the history of the paradigm of flânerie. That of the artist is also still the profession most frequently associated with the activity of flânerie and thus further contributes to the constant deferral of the identity of the flâneur since it precipitates the incorporation of the basic practice of flânerie (that of aimlessly strolling through the space of the city) into a variety of different artistic programmes – most notably, Charles Baudelaire's reflections on modernity or Louis Aragon's surrealist agenda – as well as individual artistic works. Those functionalizations give rise to a few more ambivalences to be detected in the history of the literary trope of the flâneur. Thus, research on flânerie frequently refers to Louis-Sébastien Mercier's *Tableau de Paris* in the context of the flâneur *avant la lettre* (Vila-Cabanes 2016: 17–21; Vila-Cabanes 2015: 74) or as a paradigm for the entire genre of what could be called a flânerie text (Köhn 1989: 17). Mercier's text, which was published in 1781 and thus prior to the French Revolution, describes the city of Paris and its population in 1,049 short chapters, each focusing on a different aspect of Parisian daily life. The *Tableau de Paris* thus consists of a plethora of miniature pictures that combine into one large mosaic-like image of the city. Later examples of literary flânerie, like Baudelaire's *Parisian Scenes* (*Tableaux parisiens*), seem to draw on this practice of representing the totality of the city by means of a variety of miniature images, although the title of Baudelaire's collection of poems already indicates a shift in meaning by deferring the singular of the *Tableau* to the plurality and fragmentation of the *Tableaux*. Attempts at the totality of a bird's-eye view can thus be juxtaposed with the modern subject's experience of fragmentation and disorientation.[39] Moreover, Baudelaire's text differs from Mercier's project in a few other ways. While Mercier's *Tableau* is a decidedly political text with an often moralizing message (Köhn 1989: 19), Baudelaire refrains from putting the poems of the *Tableaux* into a political

---

38 As Eva Riedl (2017: 117) remarks, flânerie as a strategy of refusal could just as well be combined with the 'death of the flâneur' which then results in obsessive forms of walking whose extreme end could – as Stefan Porombka suggests – be found in running amok. Nevertheless, both Porombka and Riedl also link compulsive forms of flânerie to processes of assimilation.
39 Interestingly, this ambivalence recurs within the structure of both works since Mercier aims at the production of one large picture out of 1,049 miniatures and Baudelaire compensates for the experience of fragmentation by means of the creation of a 'sovereign' strolling subject.

context (Köhn 1989: 61). Mercier accordingly tends towards an authentic representation of historical reality as an ideal, whereas Baudelaire's depiction of the French capital flaunts its subjective character by projecting the lyrical I's imagined stories onto the people he encounters on the streets of Paris. The genre that Baudelaire uses also corresponds with the subjectivity of his approach, thus translating the city into a collection of poems, while Mercier's *Tableau* consists of small sketches that could best be described as a variant of the essay and its proximity to factual writing. The two artists open up a continuum between different kinds of literary flânerie, ranging from factual writing to entirely fictional accounts and from prose to poetry. Ambivalences with regard to the functionalization of the practice of flânerie thus recur on the level of form and genre, resulting in a reproduction of this generic hybridity within individual texts such as Baudelaire's *Paris Spleen* which does tend towards a more political depiction of Parisian city life (see Köhn 1989: 71–73). Concerning this new style of poetry, the prose poem, Baudelaire remarks the following:

> Which one of us, in his moments of ambition, has not dreamed of the miracle of a poetic prose, musical without rhythm and rhyme, supple enough and rugged enough to adapt itself to the lyrical impulses of the soul, the undulations of reverie, the jibes of conscience? It was, above all, out of my exploration of huge cities, out of the medley of their innumerable interrelations, that this haunting ideal was born. (Baudelaire 1970: ix–x)

The *Paris Spleen*, which according to Fritz Nies could be called "nothing less than a single great flânerie of the imagination" (Nies 1964: 264–265; my trans.), then constitute Baudelaire's attempt at reproducing this "haunting ideal" and thus represent the overall hybridity of flânerie on a structural level.

What is more, the hybridity between factual and fictional writing also implies the blurring of another border, namely that between the artist and the philosopher or between the artist and the journalist. A particularly prominent example of the dissolution of this border can be found in Walter Benjamin who not only uses flânerie in literary works like the *One-Way Street*, but also employs what could be called 'strolling thought' (Keidel 2006; Köhn 1989: 207) in his philosophical writings on *The Paris of the Second Empire* where he moreover engages with other examples of flânerie on the level of content (see Buck-Morss 1986: 99).

Ultimately, the blurring of several of those borders coalesces in the topos of the flâneur as a representative of the 'subject of modernity' or 'experience of modernity' which has most prominently been proposed by Walter Benjamin. Consequently, Neumeyer, who analyzes the varying functionalizations of flânerie within different conceptions of a socio-historical as well as aesthetic modernity, introduces his thesis by means of a summary of the many contradictions that can be found in Benjamin – and thus emphasizes the plurality of the trope as a representative of modernity – before he presents his detailed analysis of those functionalizations (see Neumeyer 1999: 14–25). As Neumeyer shows, the heterogeneity of the trope of the flâneur causes a corresponding heterogeneity in the conceptions of modernity that result from it since various artists functionalize the basic practice of flânerie in different ways and thus create different conceptions of modernity.[40]

Hence, the fundamentally paradoxical constellation of the flâneur looms large in the history of the trope.[41] This is not to say that the paradox itself is a characteristic that pertains to each and every variant of flânerie, but rather that, like the other characteristics, it features frequently and occurs again on the meta-level of an overall definition of the flâneur, so that definitions are in fact "difficult and at worst a contradiction of what the flâneur means". While it is impossible to take all the minute variations in the functionalization of the paradigm of flânerie into account, I nevertheless suggest that it is especially Benjamin's work on the flâneur that is an important point of reference due to its prominence in the history of the flâneur as cultural icon.[42] I would like to argue that the texts I analyze refer back to aspects of Benjamin's heterogeneous (and also incomplete) concept of flânerie and combine those in order to come up with their own complex observations. Benjamin's theses on flânerie thus do not lose their significance within writings on flânerie – as some research on flânerie suggests[43] – but become important for contemporary reconceptualizations pre-

---

[40] Eva Riedl (2017: 97), however, correctly points out that Neumeyer's method is somewhat tautological and one might ask whether the plurality of the flâneur does not rather derive from the plurality of modernity than the other way around – as Neumeyer's concept suggests.

[41] For a description of the flâneur as a predominantly paradoxical phenomenon see also Parsons (2000: 18–20) and Piggott (2012: 158).

[42] This very general observation is an assessment that most of today's scholarship on flânerie agrees on despite various internal contradictions in Benjamin's writings on the flâneur (see Neumeyer 1999: 14; Müller 2013: 216; Riedl 2017: 21; Vila-Cabanes 2016: 15; Rhein 2015: 10; Thiemann 2019: 65–66). The extent to which Benjamin's remarks are then integrated into individual analyses, however, varies. Thus, contrary to most contemporary research on flânerie which usually refers to Benjamin as one stage in the development of the flâneur, but refrains from using the problematic tensions in Benjamin's observations on the phenomenon of the flâneur in particular as backdrop for their analyses, I agree with Riedl (2017: 21), who explicitly points out that the paradoxical structure of Benjamin's attempts at a 'theory of flânerie' could be seen as an opportunity, rather than a problem.

[43] Neither is it true that especially Benjamin's theses on the analogy between flâneur and commodity have disappeared from contemporary flânerie texts, as Keidel (2006: 42–43) claims. Although there might be more examples to be found in English literature than in German texts, novels such as Christian Kracht's *Faserland* (1995) prove Keidel wrong. See also Biendarra (2002).

cisely because of the specific meaning that Benjamin adds to his flâneur's partly paradoxical basic structure, relocating him within the dynamics of sovereignty and subjection.

2.2 Walter Benjamin's Continuum of Strolling

By now, the observation that Benjamin's writings on the flâneur can by no means be configurated into one coherent concept, has become almost commonplace in scholarship on flânerie.[44] Thus, Benjamin's transition from the chapter on bohemia to the chapter on the flâneur in *The Paris of the Second Empire in Baudelaire* already opens up a couple of questions on which attributes actually pertain to the flâneur in Benjamin's writings. There, he explicitly addresses the flâneur's link to the profession of writing and then points out that the writer "goes to the marketplace as a flâneur – supposedly to look around, but in truth to find a buyer" (Benjamin 2006: 66). Unfortunately, the translation does not grasp the full meaning of the German original, in which Benjamin states that the flâneur goes to the marketplace "*wie er meint*, um ihn anzusehen, und in Wahrheit doch schon, um einen Käufer zu finden" (Benjamin 2013: 32; my emphasis). Thus, while the translation to a certain extent suggests that the flâneur deceives others when pretending to look around, the German original explicitly states that he deceives himself (*wie er meint:* 'as he believes'). What is even more important is the question of where exactly the practice of flânerie starts: can the writer also be a flâneur if he is outside the marketplace or is the practice of flânerie perhaps – as the quote seems to suggest – closely linked to the marketplace itself and can therefore only be practiced inside anything that might be considered a marketplace? In other words, is it the *pretence* of looking around the marketplace, while actually trying to find a buyer, that constitutes the writer as flâneur, or is it the mere act of 'looking around' that in fact constitutes the practice of flânerie? While it might seem logical to understand flânerie as a role that is taken up by the writer before entering the marketplace so that the practice of flânerie only consists of the act of looking around, it is precisely the gist of Benjamin's argument following his short introductory phrase that shows flânerie and capitalism to be inseparably linked (Schmider and Werner 2011: 573). The definition of the term 'flâneur' therefore seems to oscillate between the subjection of the

---

[44] See e.g. Neumeyer (1999: 14–24), Keidel (2006: 41–46), Vila-Cabanes (2016: 5–15), Gomolla (2009: 10), and see also Solnit (2001: 199).

flâneur to the market and his possible existence outside the marketplace.[45] The situation becomes even more complex given the various other imprecisions in Benjamin's comments on the flâneur. An example frequently referred to[46] is Benjamin's contradictory categorization of the eponymous 'man of the crowd' who is pursued by the narrator in Poe's short story: while Benjamin refers to this man as a flâneur in his chapter on the flâneur in *The Paris of the Second Empire in Baudelaire*,[47] he also assigns an unhurried habit to the flâneur in general within the very same chapter (Benjamin 2006: 84), although the harassed behaviour of the 'man of the crowd' does not comply with this description. Benjamin then fully contradicts himself when he claims in *On Some Motifs in Baudelaire*, the revised version of his chapter on the flâneur in *The Paris of the Second Empire in Baudelaire*, that the unknown man cannot be called a flâneur:

> Baudelaire was moved to equate the man of the crowd, whom Poe's narrator follows throughout the length and breadth of nocturnal London, with the flâneur. It is hard to accept this view. The man of the crowd is no flâneur. In him, composure has given way to manic behavior. (Benjamin 2006: 188)

In a very similar way, Benjamin bases many of his theses on the analogy between flâneur and commodity in his analysis of the life and poetry of Baudelaire and their socio-cultural context, while he denies Baudelaire the status of flâneur at the end of his essay (Neumeyer 1999: 16):

> If one tries to imagine this rhythm and investigate this mode of work, it turns out that Baudelaire's flâneur was not a self-portrait of the poet to the extent that this might be assumed. An important trait of the real-life Baudelaire – that is, of the man committed to his work – has been omitted from this portrayal: his absentmindedness. – In the flâneur, the joy of watching prevails over all. (Benjamin 2006: 98)

Therefore, it is difficult to come up with any kind of unified concept of flânerie based on Benjamin's writings. Nevertheless, it cannot be assumed that Benjamin's theses on flânerie had no historico-cultural impact. As Neumeyer, for example, correctly points out, most secondary literature on flânerie still includes extensive chapters on Benjamin's writings on the flâneur (1999: 14), even though they are at the same time dismissed as a theoretical framework.

---

45 See also Schmider and Werner (2011: 573), who point out that Benjamin's changing definition of flânerie derives from the transitory character of the type who, analogous to the in-between state of his hometown Paris, oscillates between two poles.
46 See Neumeyer (1999: 15); see Vila-Cabanes (2016: 12); see Müller (2013: 208).
47 See Benjamin (2006: 79): "This unknown man is the flâneur."

In the following, I will suggest three variations of the trope of the flâneur to be used as heuristic models for my analysis based on Benjamin's contradictory observations on the flâneur. I will argue that he depicts a continuum that is only defined *ex negativo* by other types that delimit its borders without themselves constituting cases of flânerie in *The Paris of the Second Empire in Baudelaire* and its revised version *On Some Motifs in Baudelaire*.[48] The flâneur himself thus becomes a boundary that is placed under scrutiny by Benjamin. Many attributes that Benjamin assigns to the trope can be linked to this continuum which at the same time sheds new light on the relationship between subjection and sovereignty in the strolling subject. As Michael Makropoulus points out in his article on "Benjamin's Theory of Massculture", Benjamin seldom offers definitions of the terms he uses, yet it is often possible to construct a 'coordinate system' based on his texts which makes it possible to assign certain attributes to these terms (Makropulous 2007: 277; my trans.). Following this assumption, I will connect several observations that Benjamin makes in his writings on Baudelaire to each of the two parts of the overall analogy that Benjamin draws between flâneur and commodity: the flâneur who enters the market in order to observe it on the one hand, and the flâneur who enters the market in order to find a buyer on the other hand. This division is of course not clearly demarcated in Benjamin's writings but marks the poles between which the flâneur moves back and forth without ever being determined by only one of them. The heuristic model that can be created based on this approach does not represent a complete conceptualization of the flâneur in Benjamin, but only serves to illuminate certain areas of tension that can be linked to Benjamin's basic thesis of the incorporation of the flâneur into the market.

Moreover, it helps to illustrate how in Benjamin's descriptions of flânerie the practice is in various ways linked to an illusory idea of sovereignty that only veils an actual subjection of the flâneur.[49] While the idea of a dialectics of sovereignty and subjection also occurs in concepts of flânerie before Benjamin, the argument that this sovereignty is always already an illusion is most poignantly described in his writings and can thus be seen as a forerunner of the specific constellation of sovereignty and subjection in the texts I analyze. Furthermore, and this is the third variation of the trope to be extracted from Benjamin's work, he mentions an additional form of flânerie as *techne* that involves a subject consciously giving up a status of sovereign subjectivity, which then allows for drawing a direct con-

---

48 Parts of this chapter have already been published in Ries (2020).
49 See also Voss (2001: 46), who claims that the flâneur becomes subjected to the societal conditions of modernity precisely because he imagines himself to be their subject.

nection between the flâneur and the theorizations of Foucault and Butler and for conceptualizing the complex dynamics of subjection and resistance in contemporary flânerie texts.

Benjamin's description of the flâneur as a transitional character is linked to his tripartite division between Berlin, Paris, and London in his chapter on the flâneur in *The Paris of the Second Empire in Baudelaire*. Those three metropolises are representative of different stages of industrialization as well as of the incorporation of the individual into the crowd:[50] while Berlin still makes it possible for the individual to get an overview of the market and to "look around" from an elevated as well as distanced position, the citizen of London always already forms part of the crowd and only enters the café as a consumer – according to Benjamin, although this is in no way an accurate description of the actions of the nameless narrator of Poe's "The Man of the Crowd", to which Benjamin refers in this passage (Benjamin 2006: 80) – in order to "leave it again, attracted by the magnet of the mass which constantly has him in its range" (Benjamin 2006: 80). The difference between the two lies in their "observation posts" (Benjamin 2006: 80). While Berlin's man of leisure, whom Benjamin uses as an example, observes the crowd from a window of his own house – Benjamin even compares this window to a loge in the theatre (Benjamin 2006: 80) and thus refers to the man of leisure in his topographical position 'above' the crowd – the London citizen only stays for a short while in the coffee house, from where he watches the crowd, and almost immediately returns to the street. Berlin's man of leisure then still seems to be in a sovereign state from which he observes the market, while the 'man of the crowd' cannot stay apart from the crowd and is therefore subjected to its constant attraction. In both cases, the characters described are attracted to the crowd and cannot look away from it, both are therefore subjected to this attraction.[51]

In his revised version of *The Paris of the Second Empire in Baudelaire*, titled *On Some Motifs in Baudelaire*, Benjamin adds a temporal dimension to his differentiation between the three cities, according to which London is the most industrialized, Berlin the most "provincial" (Benjamin 2006: 183) and Paris is in between the two other cities (Benjamin 2006: 188–189). Paris's transitional state then forms the basis for the character of the flâneur who is also in a state be-

---

50 See Benjamin (2006: 79–80 and 84–85); Schmider and Werner (2011: 572).
51 See also Benjamin (2006: 189), where he mentions that the man of leisure in E.T.A. Hoffmann's story that Benjamin uses as an example of depictions of the city crowd in Berlin "has lost the use of his legs", so that due to his sickness he cannot join the crowd on the street. The superiority displayed in the 'art of seeing' is thus also supposed to replace the state of subjection to his sickness.

tween those of the two other characters (Schmider and Werner 2011: 573). Benjamin describes this in the following way:

> In comparison, Baudelaire's Paris preserved some features that dated back to the old days. Arcades where the flâneur would not be exposed to the sight of carriages, which did not recognize pedestrians as rivals, were enjoying undiminished popularity. There was the pedestrian who would let himself be jostled by the crowd, but there was also the flâneur, who demanded elbow room and was unwilling to forgo the life of a gentleman of leisure. Let the many attend to their daily affairs; the man of leisure can indulge in the perambulations of the flâneur only if as such he is already out of place. He is as much out of place in an atmosphere of complete leisure as in the feverish turmoil of the city. (Benjamin 2006: 188)

Paris thus forms a space in between the stages of the two other cities and the flâneur is a transitional character who moves inside the crowd, but does not belong to it (Schmider and Werner 2011: 573). The arcades function here as a synecdoche for the transitional space of the city of Paris and are situated between the interior space of the man of leisure and the street of the London citizen; they are "the classical form of the *intérieur* [, in which] the street presents itself to the flâneur" (Benjamin 2006: 85). In analogy to the division between the three cities, Benjamin arranges their three human representatives: "London has its man of the crowd. His counterpart, as it were, is Nante, the boy who loiters on the street corner, a popular figure in Berlin before the March Revolution of 1848. The Parisian flâneur might be said to stand midway between them" (Benjamin 2006: 188–189).[52]

This tripartition also shows to some extent why there are so many contradictory attributes in Benjamin's descriptions of the flâneur. Since the character is only an intermediary state between 'man of the crowd' and immobile onlooker, he combines attributes pertaining to both extremes without being reducible to either one of them (Schmider and Werner 2011: 573). Thus, the Benjaminian flâ-

---

[52] Interestingly, Benjamin switches here from using E.T.A. Hoffmann's protagonist as representative of Berlin and replaces him with Nante, who does not observe the crowd from a window in an elevated position, but is already standing on the street and watches the crowd from his position at a street corner. Nevertheless, Benjamin adds that his way of observing the crowd can be compared to that of Hoffmann's man of leisure who observes the crowd from above so that the following characteristics might also hold true for Nante: "His attitude toward the crowd is, rather, one of superiority, inspired as it is by his observation post at the window of an apartment building. From this vantage point he scrutinizes the throng; it is market day, and all the passers-by feel in their element. His opera glasses enable him to pick out individual genre scenes. Employing the glasses is thoroughly in keeping with the inner disposition of their user. He confesses he would like to initiate his visitor in the 'principles of the art of seeing'" (Benjamin 2006: 189).

neur can be 'calm' and 'manic' at the same time, when he moves slowly, yet the crowd entices him to become a part of it. This is not yet the case for Berlin's man of leisure, whose slowness, which congeals into standing still, forms – as is the case with Berlin's Nante – the limit to one side of a Benjaminian description of flânerie. The driven, externally controlled and rushed movement of the 'man of the crowd' forms the other extreme of Benjamin's description. That Benjamin rejects the 'man of the crowd' as a flâneur in his revised version of *The Paris of the Second Empire in Baudelaire* makes sense if the 'man of the crowd' thus constitutes the limit case of an individual that has been completely incorporated into the crowd. Nevertheless, it remains unclear when precisely the Benjaminian flâneur turns into the 'man of the crowd' and several characteristics could be added to each of the poles of the continuum, such as deceleration vs. acceleration, reflection vs. fascination or resistance vs. assimilation, with the possibility of contradictory features occurring within a specific example of flânerie so that an assimilation to the crowd might still be articulated in the decelerated practice of strolling if the flâneur joins a crowd of window-shoppers, for example.

A resurfacing characteristic of Benjamin's different modes of flânerie is the illusory quality of the supposed sovereignty of the flâneur. What Benjamin sees as the beginnings of flânerie is already explicitly linked to a performance of sovereignty. The sentence leading up to the chapter on the flâneur in *The Paris of the Second Empire in Baudelaire* is followed by the observation that "[o]nce a writer had entered the marketplace, he looked around as if in a panorama. A special literary genre has captured the writer's first attempts to orient himself. This is the genre of panoramic literature" (Benjamin 2006: 66). What Benjamin calls "panoramic literature" refers to the physiologies, the sketches mentioned above that aimed at portraying the several types of people to be found in the city in an anecdotal as well as ironic manner (Vila-Cabanes 2016: 36). Benjamin now links this genre to the idea that people can be classified according to various types and can thus be instantly 'known', thus granting the observer a position of sovereignty:

> They [the physiologies] assured people that everyone could – unencumbered by any factual knowledge – make out the profession, character, background, and lifestyle of passers-by. The physiologies present this ability as a gift which a good fairy lays in the cradle of the big-city dweller. [...] Delvau, Baudelaire's friend and the most interesting among the minor masters of the feuilleton, claimed that he could divide the Parisian public according to its various strata as easily as a geologist distinguishes the layers in rocks. (Benjamin 2006: 70–71)

If the physiologies mark the beginning of flânerie for Benjamin, then the performance of sovereignty acted out in them is linked to the flâneur as a writer of physiologies. Yet, this sovereignty remains illusory since the physiologies

> were just the thing to brush [...] disquieting notions [about the potentially criminal nature of other citizens] aside as insignificant. They constituted, so to speak, the blinkers of the 'narrow-minded city animal' that Marx wrote about. (Benjamin 2006: 69)

The physiologies thus only served the aim of giving city-dwellers as optimistic an image of each other as possible, thereby excluding more authentic representations of the city. The sovereign gesture of an analysis of the crowd remains an illusion.

Benjamin then moves on to predominantly literary depictions of flânerie and again links them to a performance of sovereignty, although this performance is now based less on the idea of the deception of the reader – namely that the sovereign analysis of the crowd is only an illusion intended to gloss over the more sinister truths of individuals in the nineteenth-century crowd – than on the idea that the sovereignty of the flâneur is already put into question by the presence of crime in the city and now has to be reinstated by the flâneur-as-detective. Flânerie is therefore offered as a technique that can be used as a means for the detective to do his work, as Benjamin claims in the following statement: "In times of terror, when everyone is something of a conspirator, everybody will be in the position of having to play detective. Flânerie gives the individual the best prospects of doing so" (Benjamin 2006: 72). The flâneur-as-detective still performs sovereignty in the sense that he is the one able to find the criminal even within an anonymous crowd, yet "the detective story, regardless of its sober calculations, also participates in the phantasmagoria of Parisian life. It does not yet glorify the criminal, though it does glorify his adversaries and, above all, the hunting grounds where they pursue him" (Benjamin 2006: 72). The sovereignty of the detective is then the result of a glorification of the type, a point further emphasized when Benjamin links the detective story to his analysis of "The Man of the Crowd" which is, according to him, "something like an X-ray of a detective story" (Benjamin 2006: 79); that is, the story's focus on the 'unreadability' of the man of the crowd (and by extension the crowd itself) could be interpreted in terms of an uncanny inversion of the detective's presumed ability to read the clues of the criminal's presence in the crowd.

In his description of Poe's short story Benjamin already hints at the subjection of the flâneur in what he calls a department store – in fact, the unnamed narrator of Poe's story as well as the man he follows end up temporarily in a market, that is, a place that offers none of the vertical transformation of architecture suggested by Benjamin's terminology. According to Benjamin, the advent of the department store signifies the end of flânerie since it forms a decayed example of the *intérieur* that had once been the arcades, the flâneur's favourite haunt. In this way, Poe's short story already "prefigures [the] end" (Benjamin 2006: 85) of flânerie. The flâneur now "roam[s] through the labyrinth of commodities as he had once roamed through the labyrinth of the city" (Benjamin 2006: 85).

Following this analysis, Benjamin likens the flâneur himself to a commodity intoxicated by the crowd of buyers that surrounds him. The vocabulary used by Benjamin now emphasizes the subjection of the flâneur to the crowd. The flâneur has become addicted to this crowd, which forms the veil through which he perceives the city (Benjamin 2006: 90).

While Benjamin only hints here at the ways in which the flâneur becomes incorporated into capitalism, he specifies his theses on the subjection of the individual to the crowd in *On Some Motifs in Baudelaire*. This incorporation takes place in the realm of perception. As Benjamin explains in the chapter following his delineation of the tripartite division between Berlin, Paris and London, life in the city in modernity becomes predominantly characterized by the sensation of 'shock' (Benjamin 2006: 126). Moving through the city "involves the individual in a series of shocks and collisions" (Benjamin 2006: 191); in order to navigate through the city's spaces one has to pay attention to "traffic signals" (Benjamin 2006: 191) for orientation and thus "technology has subjected the human sensorium to a complex kind of training" (Benjamin 2006: 191). The sensation of 'shock' that the passer-by experiences in the crowd can then, according to Benjamin, be compared with the situation of the worker who becomes subjected to the workings of the machine (Benjamin 2006: 191). In a similar way that the passer-by learns to react to the demands of modernity's city life, the worker reacts to the demands of the machine. In this context, Benjamin quotes Marx, who claims that "It is a common characteristic of all capitalist production [...] that the worker does not make use of the working conditions. The working conditions make use of the worker; but it takes machinery to give this reversal a technologically concrete form" (Marx, qtd. in Benjamin 2006: 191). Similarly, the passer-by in the city of the nineteenth century becomes subjected to the workings of an industrialized city, that is, a city that is formed according to the demands of capitalism. Ultimately, with the industrialization of the city constantly progressing, flânerie becomes impossible since it has to adapt to those conditions and reduces the flâneur's perception to issues of navigation, which is why the flâneur is replaced by the 'man of the crowd' in Benjamin's continuum.

Yet, in *The Paris of the Second Empire in Baudelaire*, the 'man of the crowd' is still a flâneur and the description of his end in the department store is linked to the intoxication of the flâneur as commodity via the crowd.[53] In this analogy, the flâneur retains at best a temporal sovereignty by means of his subjection to the market, since "the concentration of customers which makes up the market, which in turn makes the commodity a commodity, enhances its attractiveness to the average buyer. [...] Some of the commodity's charms were based on the market, and each of these turned into a means of power" (Benjamin 2006: 86). The flâneur's sovereignty as a skilled observer of modern city life is now replaced by the commodity's "means of power" and is conditioned by the flâneur's subjection to the market, which highlights the limited range of his power. Thus, the illusory nature of the flâneur's sovereignty ties in with the continuum delineated above, with the impression of sovereignty becoming increasingly tenuous towards the pole marked by the 'man of the crowd'. In Benjamin's description of the earliest flâneurs – the authors of the physiologies – the supposed sovereignty of their analysis of the city crowds is still emphasized, even though they are also already subject to the demands of their customers. With an increase in circulation, this subjection becomes more and more discernible. What is more, the analogy suggests that the commodity's power does not lie in the sovereignty of the observer who gains a superior status due to his knowledge of the city, but derives from fashioning oneself and one's writings according to the demands of the market.

My analysis of contemporary flânerie texts is therefore based on the assumption that both poles between which the flâneur resides only contain an illusory notion of sovereignty. Especially the flâneur's incorporation into the crowd emphasizes the illusory character of this sovereignty although the strolling subject is not necessarily aware of the 'loss' – or more accurately the non-existence – of his sovereignty and therefore does not even react to it. Functionalizations of flânerie that emphasize the manic habit of a flâneur similar to the 'man of the crowd' might thus stress the subjection to a given system while functionalizations that emphasize the flâneur's idle and slowed-down behaviour – and the mode of observation that this entails – might accentuate the notion of sovereignty that his gaze aims to establish; in both cases, violence might be needed to claim their equally illusory sovereignty. The blurring of the border between the two sides which results from Benjamin's paradoxical combination of both variants of the flâneur already implies the connection between the necessity to constantly repeat the performance of this sovereignty and the subjection of the sub-

---

53 In fact, Benjamin describes his whole project as a "deciphering of flânerie as an intoxication produced by the structure of the commodity market" (Benjamin 1974: 1122; my trans.) – "Dechiffrierung der Flânerie als eines durch die Struktur des Warenmarktes erzeugten Rausches."

ject which needs to be repressed by means of this repeated performance. Those two functionalizations will serve as the frame of reference to analyze how contemporary flânerie texts emphasize the subject's entanglement with discourses of power. There is, however, a third aspect which surfaces in Benjamin's writings on the flâneur when Benjamin refers to flânerie as a kind of *techne*.

Despite his thesis regarding the end of the flâneur in the department store Benjamin claims "The Flaneur's Return" in his review of Franz Hessel's *Walking in Berlin* and describes his practice of flânerie in terms of "a walking remembrance" (Benjamin 2017: xiii).[54] Moreover, in the notes to his *Arcades Project*, Benjamin points out that the city can serve as a pathway into the past for the flâneur:

> The street conducts the flâneur into a vanished time. For him, every street is precipitous. It leads downward – if not to the mythical Mothers, then into a past that can be all the more spellbinding because it is not his own, not private. Nevertheless, it always remains the time of a childhood. (Benjamin 2002: 524)

As the quotation suggests, flânerie offers the opportunity to travel back in time through the medium of the flâneur's perception of the city. This past should not be the flâneur's own private past although it always remains "the time of a childhood".[55] It should then be possible for the flâneur to remember the past by means of (slowly) walking through and perceiving the city and thus Benjamin also uses flânerie in *A Berlin Chronicle* in order to recall what is repressed and what is past and to make it visible again.[56] But as Neumeyer points out, this re-discovery of the past remains limited to the world of myth that has been sedimented within the metropolis and moreover needs the statues and monuments that are present in the city for the flâneur to be able to see this world (1999: 371–372). Hence, similar to Benjamin's concept of flânerie in his writings on Baudelaire, the *Arcades Project*'s comments on flânerie further complicate any fixed conceptualizations of flânerie based on Benjamin's texts. What is more, Benja-

---

[54] Nevertheless, it has to be pointed out that Benjamin wrote the review on Hessel's book in 1929, before he came up with his theses on the 'death of the flâneur' in the 1930s. This, however, does not solve the overall problem when Benjamin states at the end of his review: "Here [in Berlin], and not in Paris, does one see how the flaneur may diverge from the philosophical walker and take on the traits of a were-wolf roaming restlessly in the social wilderness, as Poe has depicted for posterity in his *Man of the Crowd*" (2017: xviii–xix).
[55] Those remarks also contain traces of Benjamin's earlier comments on flânerie in his review of *Walking in Berlin*, according to which flânerie can indeed be used to re-discover one's childhood (see also Neumeyer 1999: 373).
[56] See Neumeyer (1999: 371): "Verdrängte wie Vergangene."

min's thesis on the flâneur as mnemotechnician hardly fits with his analogy between flâneur and commodity or even implies an entirely new functionalization of flânerie.[57]

However, his art of 'walking remembrance' is bound up with flânerie as a certain kind of *techne* that entails giving oneself up to the city (see Neumeyer 1999: 369). Here, getting lost in the city due to simple ignorance of the place itself would not qualify as flânerie:

> Not to find one's way in a city may well be uninteresting and banal. It requires ignorance – nothing more. But to lose oneself in a city – as one loses oneself in a forest – that calls for quite a different schooling. Then, signboards and street names, passers-by, roofs, kiosks, or bars must speak to the wanderer like a cracking twig under his feet in the forest, like the startling call of a bittern in the distance; like the sudden stillness of a clearing with a lily standing erect at its center. Paris taught me this art of straying; it fulfilled a dream that had shown its first traces in the labyrinths on the blotting pages of my school exercise books. (Benjamin 1978: 8–9)

The paragraph then ends with a reference to the "endless *flâneries*" (Benjamin 1978: 9) that Benjamin undertook in Paris, and moves on to Hessel, whom Benjamin also mentions as a teacher in the art of walking the city. Likewise, in his review of *Walking in Berlin*, he quotes Hessel's description of the flâneur's specific form of perception – "We only see what looks at us" (Hessel 1999: 318, qtd. and trans. in Benjamin 2017: xviii) – and comments that the philosophy of the flâneur has never been more aptly described than Hessel did with those words (Benjamin 2017: xviii). Hessel's quote fits very well, as Neumeyer points out, with the description of the "straying" that Paris has taught Benjamin, in which the status of the subject is assigned to supposed objects of observation like "signboards and street names, passers-by, roofs".

Strolling is here described in terms of a *techne*, which needs to be learned either from the city as teacher – as is the case with the city of Paris in the example mentioned above – or by means of the writings of a strolling predecessor – as is the case with Hessel's description of flânerie (Neumeyer 1999: 369 and 371). What remains unclear is how, precisely, the city might become a teacher to the peripatetic, particularly since the process of learning to stroll seems to be paradoxical, as the flâneur would have to have already learned the practice of flânerie in order to be able to perceive the elements of the city as speaking to him (Neumeyer 1999: 369). This incongruity in the actual description of the technique of flânerie seems to align with the indecisiveness in Benjamin's overall

---

[57] On the general incompatibility of the different concepts of flânerie in Benjamin's work, see Keidel (2006: 41).

definition of flânerie. The only defining characteristic of this technique of flânerie seems to be the giving up of the sovereignty of the flâneur who lets himself be seduced by objects as well as passers-by in the city. Yet, this conscious giving up of one's own sovereignty is essentially different from the state of subjection in which the flâneur as commodity finds himself: whereas the latter tries to perform his sovereignty by means of the instrumentalization of the objects of observation – that is, the different elements of the city – and is not aware of the state of subjection he is in, the former surrenders willingly to giving up his own sovereignty – this, at least, seems to be a constitutive characteristic, if not the entire aim of this technique of flânerie – and assigns the status of subjects to the objects by letting them speak to him and allowing them to subject him. The actual technique of flânerie remains unspecified in this and can be re-interpreted by succeeding flâneurs in ever new variations. The sole constitutive characteristic of this kind of flânerie is a partly conscious, yet in its actual manifestation largely unclear, giving up of one's sovereignty, which consists in a subjection to singular objects instead of a subjection to a general discourse of power that assigns a position of seeming sovereignty to the subject.

Therefore, I would like to propose a tripartite model of the flâneur in Benjamin as an additional frame of reference for my analysis. The first and second parts of this model are constituted by the two poles of the abovementioned continuum: the flâneur who has already been turned into a commodity and thus has been almost entirely transformed into a passer-by, and the flâneur as pseudo-sovereign counterpart to the crowd and the mechanisms it is subjected to. This continuum can be understood in terms of what Angelika Wellmann calls a "historico-aporetical continuous form" (1991: 153)[58] which, over time, leads to the flâneur's incorporation into the crowd and thus is representative of the modern subject's loss of sovereignty.[59] At the same time, the second pole – and second part of the model – potentially emphasizes the sovereignty of an individual who is opposed to the crowd and turns the crowd into an object of representation by means of his artistic production. The last part of this tripartite model is constituted by the concept of flânerie as *techne*, which does not prescribe any definition of flânerie as a technique apart from the giving up of one's sovereignty. Especially this last conception of flânerie could be linked to Neumeyer's minimal definition of strolling aimlessly through the city.

---

58 "historisch-aporetische Verlaufsform."
59 See also Wellmann (1991: 142; my trans.): "For, according to Benjamin, the ostentatiously demonstrated 'self-possession' has long been rendered invalid within the social reality of the nineteenth century." – "Denn nach Benjamins Auffassung ist in der Wirklichkeit des 19. Jahrhunderts der ostentativ zur Schau gestellte 'Selbst-Besitz' längst hinfällig geworden."

Still, although those conclusions can be drawn from Benjamin's writings on the flâneur, this is not to say that they offer any useful definition of flânerie itself. The flâneur in Benjamin is a signifier that Benjamin implicitly assigns to various signifieds ranging from the flâneur-as-journalist to the flâneur-as-writer as well as the flâneur-as-motif-in-literature; while Benjamin's definitions already assume an idea of the flâneur that seems to be given, the attributes that he assigns to the flâneur remain contradictory (see also Neumeyer 1999: 17). Yet, at the same time Benjamin's observations on flânerie can hardly be ignored when looking at contemporary flânerie texts, since they have had a lasting influence not only on the academic discussion of flânerie, but even more so on the primary literature of flânerie. There, the flâneur or the paradigm of flânerie might occur as a trope or structural principle which is always implicitly referencing former variations of itself. It is then especially the flâneur's complex entanglement with power and the negotiation of resistance to a normalizing power that resurface in post-Benjaminian manifestations of flânerie.

2.3 Flânerie and/as Performance

Benjamin and his historical-materialist functionalization of the flâneur paved the way for further appropriations of the trope in the wake of the spatial as well as the performative turn which emphasize walking as a material practice. The link between materialism and the flâneur can already be found in Benjamin's writings on the Parisian Arcades. As has been mentioned above, Benjamin sees the walker in the city as subjected to the technology that the city imposes and this subjection takes place in a material way by directly affecting the body and sensory perception. Moreover, some scholars have claimed that in Benjamin the flâneur's practices of recollecting the hidden past of the city can be understood as a matter of performance (Berg 2009: 223).[60]

---

[60] Benjamin is thus also an important predecessor of other historical-materialist approaches within spatial theory, the most prominent example of which is that of Henri Lefebvre (Parker 2015: 19). Like Benjamin, Lefebvre has his origins in Marxist thought, yet transferred his attention to the examination of the 'politics of space' (Parker 2015: 20). Lefebvre's "three-dimensional dialectics of space" – "dreidimensionale Dialektik des Raums" (Schmid 2005: 30; my trans.) – which assumes a productive interaction between three different kinds of spaces – mental space (*espace conçu*), physical or perceived space (*espace perçu*) and social or lived space (*espace vécu*) – then forms the basis for many other approaches in the overall context of the spatial turn (Nigg 2017: 55; Bachmann-Medick 2009: 291).

2.3 Flânerie and/as Performance — 45

Spatiality is important to the study of flânerie texts not only because of flânerie's tendency to result in the representation of the metropolitan space via the medium of the flânerie text, but also because the production of space is already intrinsically linked with movement. Thus, space has to be primarily understood through the prism of motion:

> Space and spatiality need to be experienced for their conceptualization in thought to become possible. That is, those movements which we exert with our bodies and as bodies in space only produce what we call space from a historical, cultural or individual perspective. This is also the vantage point from which our conceptualization of other bodies in space develops. (Böhme 2005: xv; my trans.)[61]

In this quote, Hartmut Böhme especially emphasizes the corporeal and material nature of this kind of motion. Movement is here understood as a bodily practice and delineated in terms of experience which only then enables practitioners to form an understanding of the space they traverse. Necessarily, the mode of movement that is the most fitting for a corporeal experience of space is found in walking itself, with some scholars even suggesting walking as a general model for literature and spatiality (Nigg 2017: 11; Bachmann-Medick 2009: 257).

In this context, Michel de Certeau's chapter on "Walking in the City" from his monograph on *The Practice of Everyday Life* has become a central point of reference within research on city literature and spatial practices.[62] De Certeau distinguishes here between two ways of assessing spatiality, the *carte* and the *parcours*. The *carte*, which can be likened to a panoramic, panoptic[63] view of the city, is explained by means of an image that might feel slightly uncanny for any post-9/11 audience:

> To be lifted to the summit of the World Trade Center is to be lifted out of the city's grasp. One's body is no longer clasped by the streets that turn and return it according to an anonymous law; nor is it possessed, whether as player or played, by the rumble of so many differences and by the nervousness of New York traffic. When one goes up there, he leaves behind the mass that carries off and mixes up in itself any identity of authors or spectators.

---

[61] "Raum und Räumlichkeit muss, um überhaupt gedacht werden zu können, erfahren werden. Dies bedeutet: die Bewegungen, die wir mit unserem Körper und als Körper im Raum vollziehen, erschließen erst das, was wir historisch, kulturell, individuell als Raum verstehen. Von daher erschließen wir auch, was Bewegung fremder Körper im Raum ist".
[62] See for example Nigg (2017: 41–53), Weymann-Teschke (2018: 44–51) and Rosenthal (2011: 49–72; 2017: 78).
[63] De Certeau directly refers to Foucault's concept of the panopticon in this context (1988: 92) as his whole study also aims at examining the "popular procedures [that] manipulate the mechanisms of discipline" as discussed by Foucault (1988: xiv).

> An Icarus flying above these waters, he can ignore the devices of Daedalus in mobile and endless labyrinths far below. His elevation transfigures him into a voyeur. It puts him at a distance. It transforms the bewitching world by which one was "possessed" into a text that lies before one's eyes. It allows one to read it, to be a solar Eye, looking down like a god. The exaltation of a scopic or gnostic drive. The fiction of knowledge is related to this lust to be a viewpoint and nothing more. (De Certeau 1988: 92)

The voyeur here is likened to a god whose sovereign perspective onto the city allows the city to become decipherable and the voyeur to no longer be subjected to the structure of the street and the rhythms of the traffic. While looking down on the city still relates to affective drives and lust, the voyeur lacks any corporeal presence and is reduced to being "a viewpoint and nothing more". The comparison with Icarus, moreover, implies delusion and a fall-to-come, although the voyeur might be able to ignore the "devices of Daedalus" at the moment. The knowledge that the voyeur might acquire from his reading then also remains a fiction since his image of the city is distorted due to the distance of his position. Thus, de Certeau describes at the beginning of the chapter how the city's "agitation is momentarily arrested by vision. A gigantic mass immobilized before the eyes" (1988: 91). The buildings, instead, become a "wave of verticals" (1988: 91), suggesting an illusionary dynamic in the actually static parts of the city while actual motion is brought to a standstill by vision.

By contrast, the *parcours* deprives its practitioners of the totalizing vision of the voyeur so that "[i]t is as though the practices organizing a bustling city were characterized by their blindness" (de Certeau 1988: 93).[64] Those who are "'down below'", the walkers or "*Wandersmänner* [...] follow the thicks and thins of an urban 'text' they write without being able to read it" (Certeau 1988: 93). The walkers are thus subject and object at the same time (Nigg 2017: 47) and perform – and thus necessarily defer – a text they are also subjected to. Their experience of the city takes a bodily form when "follow[ing] the thicks and thins" of the urban text. While the text of the city is readable from the incorporeal viewpoint of the voyeur, the text produced by the walkers defies representation due to its constant deferral:

> The networks of these moving, intersecting writings compose a manifold story that has neither author nor spectator, shaped out of fragments of trajectories and alterations of spaces: in relation to representation, it remains daily and indefinitely other. (De Certeau 1988: 93)

---

64 Interestingly, Riedl (2017: 331–339) refers in this context to the opposing modes of optic experience and haptic events in Benjamin's essay on "The Work of Art in the Age of Mechanical Reproduction" and links them in her analysis with de Certeau's differentiation between *carte* and *parcours*.

De Certeau goes on to describe those networks in terms of the literary, referring to "intertwining, unrecognized poems", a "poetic and mythic experience of space" and a "metaphorical city" which "slips into the clear text of the planned and readable city" (de Certeau 1988: 93). The practices of the *parcours* and the *carte* are therefore intertwined with each other, with the walker's spatial practice of everyday life resisting the domination of the panoptical *carte*. The *parcours* thus becomes a practice of resistance that is taken up by citizens in their everyday lives.[65] As has been mentioned above, those practices can be described in terms of performativity since, according to de Certeau, they can be likened to speech acts:

> The act of walking is to the urban system what the speech act is to language or to the statements uttered. At the most elementary level, it has a triple "enunciative" function: it is a process of *appropriation* of the topographical system on the part of the pedestrian (just as the speaker appropriates and takes on the language); it is a spatial acting-out of the place (just as the speech act is an acoustic acting out of language); and it implies *relations* among differentiated positions, that is, among pragmatic "contracts" in the form of movement (just as verbal enunciation is an "allocution," "posits another opposite" the speaker and puts contracts between interlocutors into action). (De Certeau 1988: 98; original emphasis)

Those speech acts recur in various ways in twentieth-century urban life, thus skateboarding (Borden 2000), or the parcours as a sport in which practitioners try to find alternative ways through the city such as jumping from one roof to another, can be understood as manifestations of de Certeau's *parcours* (Nigg 2017: 87). Yet, the practice also figures prominently in many artistic forms of interaction with the city such as situationist or interventionist techniques or performance art in general.[66]

Especially the situationist Guy Debord's concept of 'psychogeography', delineated for the first time in his "Introduction to a Critique of Urban Geography" in 1955, has gained new interest in English studies in recent years (see Berensmeyer and Löffler 2018; Coverley 2010; Löffler 2017; Richardson 2015) due to a rising number of contemporary British authors, such as Iain Sinclair, Will Self or Peter Ackroyd, explicitly identifying with the practice of psychogeography. According to Debord, psychogeography

---

[65] However, the actual political effects of this still mostly private practice have also been subject to debate since the resistance performed by means of resistant modes of walking often lacks any larger political agenda (see Ahearne 1995: 185).
[66] See e.g. Fischer's study on *Walking Artists* (2011) which analyzes various functionalizations of walking in contemporary performance art.

sets for itself the study of the precise laws and specific effects of the geographical environment, whether consciously organized or not, on the emotions and behaviour of the individuals. The charmingly vague adjective *psychogeographical* can be applied to the findings arrived at by this type of investigation, to their influence on human feelings, and more generally to any situation or conduct that seems to reflect the same spirit of discovery. (Debord 2006: 8; original emphasis)

The methods that the situationists suggest for this kind of study could be described in terms of a 'radical flânerie' (Nigg 2017: 84) which is characterized by techniques of *déambulation* (strolling around), *dérive* (drifting) and *détournement* (detour, misuse in the sense of a de- and re-contextualization). According to Debord, *déambulation*, for example, manifests itself as "a technique of rapid passage through varied ambiances" (Debord 1995: 64; my trans.) in order to create new spaces in the city and to de-normalize everyday life. The specific aim here is to construct, live and create unforeseeable situations and psychic topographies which allow for new contextualizations (Nigg 2017: 85; Fischer 2011: 117). The situation itself is an arranged and constructed moment (o.A. 1976) which can only be described as a new fleeting context, not as any kind of fixed space (Nigg 2017: 85).

Situationist performances could thus be understood as a new, updated form of flânerie (Nigg 2017: 84) that productively engages with the city as a lived space *sensu* Henri Lefebvre (see also Fischer 2011: 107) or as a variation of the *parcours* that reinterprets the urban system. As Debord's description already indicates, this new flânerie can also be deliberately accelerated and might thus pay tribute to the continuing acceleration of the twentieth-century city by adjusting the pace of resistant modes of movement so as to respond to a changed urban environment – the proximity to modes of subjection to acceleration then ties in with the flâneur's overall precarious balancing between resistance and subjection. While Nigg argues that the situationists' *dérive* cannot be considered an example of flânerie because it produces new spaces instead of simply representing a specific perspective onto the city (Nigg 2017: 85), I contest that this is actually the case since Nigg's definition of flânerie only covers its panoramic manifestations. As the history of flânerie delineated in chapter 2.1 indicates, flânerie can in fact be understood in terms of a performance practice that might actively contribute to the re-signification of spaces in the city. Not only is the dandyesque flâneur's showcasing of his superiority decidedly performative, but especially Benjamin's conception of flânerie as *techne* clearly deviates from any panoramic – and thus potentially sovereign – perspective onto the city by aiming to engage with the space of the city in a different, non-sovereign mode. As Nigg also mentions in her chapter on flânerie, the flâneur experiences the city in a direct, bodily way so that the texts he produces focus on "life as the city" (Köhn 1989: 217; my trans.; qtd. in Nigg 2017: 76). The materiality of this experience then has the potential to be translated into the form of the texts he creates which mirror the fragmented nature of perception in the city and thus undermine structures of power by defying linearity and attempts at totality. I therefore disagree with Nigg's thesis that flânerie always tends to be more focused on the production of knowledge and thus necessarily aligns with existing structures of power (cf. Nigg 2017: 77). Nevertheless, it is especially the flâneur as dandy who already represents the overall paradox in which flânerie is caught. While his practice aims at resistance to bourgeois society's focus on usefulness and production, it also refers back to former structures of power, namely that of France's absolutist monarchy. The fact that the flâneur is always already suspended between resistance and the affirmation of discourses of power and cannot be pinned down on one or the other side of this spectrum then becomes especially discernible in flânerie as performance.

One interesting counterexample to Nigg's thesis regarding the flâneur's association with power can be found in the poetry of William Blake, which has repeatedly been cited as a representative of early forms of psychogeography (Coverley 2010: 41–44; Löffler 2017: 1–3; Berensmeyer 2018: 167). Thus, Blake's poem "London" not only constitutes an exemplary case of flânerie, but could also be interpreted as a precursor to psychogeographical writings. Here, the lyrical I wanders the streets of London and focuses their perception onto a number of distressing sounds (a "cry" [Blake 1996: l. 9], a "sigh" [Blake 1996: l. 11], a "curse" [Blake 1996: l. 14]) which are then translated into powerful images by means of synaesthetic and catachrestic metaphors so that "the hapless soldier's sigh" (Blake 1996: l. 11) is turned into "blood [running] down Palace walls" (Blake 1996: l. 12). The image uncovers the power structures responsible for the suffering of the population of the city and by extension the whole country, the implication being that soldiers are sacrificed for the sake of imperialism and thus the blood is on the hands (or walls) of the Crown (or the Palace). The poem revels in sensory perception and the bodily experience of the city through the lyrical I, culminating in the image of the "mind-forged manacles" (Blake 1996: l. 8) impressed on the citizens of the British capital. Consequently, psychogeographic flânerie and thus a flânerie that actively produces new spaces instead of representing spaces according to existing systems of knowledge can already be found in literary texts long before the situationists came into existence.

Nevertheless, it has to be pointed out that flânerie cannot be reduced to psychogeography itself. While flânerie is a mode of walking that can be made to serve a variety of functionalizations, the function of psychogeographical modes of walking is fixed since psychogeography usually aims at the "study of the precise laws and the effects of the geographical environment".[67] Moreover, although psychogeography is mostly understood in terms of 'urban walking' (see Richardson 2015b: 5), there are theoretical (see Stein 1987; Stein and Niederland 1989) as well as literary approaches (see Papadimitriou 2013; Sinclair 2003) which focus on landscapes or suburban areas as the "geographical environment" under scrutiny. As I will show in my analysis, contemporary flânerie texts might include psychogeographic elements, but they also reach far beyond the limits of psychogeography by negotiating ethical questions on a level that transcends the much more local concerns of psychogeography.

Neither can flânerie simply be equated with de Certeau's concept of the *parcours*. While the *parcours* belongs to the practices of everyday life and thus also includes walks that necessarily do have an aim, flânerie is always aimless. Flânerie can thus be described in terms of the *parcours*, but not every spatial practice that can be described in terms of the *parcours* constitutes an example of flânerie. Moreover, any translation of the spatial practice of the *parcours* into text is necessarily problematic and runs the risk of turning the pedestrian's walk into a readable text. As can be seen in the passages quoted above, scripture can be located in between the concepts of the *carte* and the *parcours* so that the flânerie text could just as well constitute an intermediate stage between the practices of the *carte* and the *parcours*.

Overall, the bodily experience of the city linked to a poststructuralist conception of space is central to the nexus between flânerie and performance. This connection originates from the ambivalent nature of walking itself. On the one hand, walking produces in-between spaces, constantly crosses borders and entails motion and the fleeting character of situations. On the other hand, walking is a product and the embodiment of motion (Nigg 2017: 69), a physical form of action that takes place within the material environment of the city and that allows for multiple kinds of sensory perception (Weymann-Teschke 2017: 61; Boutin 2012: 131). The practice of flânerie is then a modified version of walking as a performative engagement with space. The aimlessness of flânerie might enhance the resistant qualities of walking, as can be seen in the practices of the situationists. Especially in an extremely rapidly accelerating social sphere tending towards abstraction and virtualization like the societies of the twentieth and twenty-first centuries, the material aspects of flânerie as bodily interaction with the space

---

[67] Although the re-contextualization of psychogeography in contemporary British fiction, in particular, certainly broadened the overall concept of psychogeography, even wide-ranging approaches like Richardson's still define it in terms of "a method of walking that responds to and critiques the terrain" (2015b: 4); that is, the focus lies primarily on matters of geography instead of an interaction with the human representatives of the city.

of the city become a medium of resistance by creating new spaces in the city and also reflect the ways in which the body might be subjected to the material and scopic structures of power present in the city. This reflection might be manifested in a direct bodily reaction, but also in the artistic product of the flâneur's walks – that is, the text that follows from flânerie. However, since flânerie texts often either implicitly or explicitly also include other media, scripture is not the only medium that serves the representation of the material practice of flânerie, although it might be the most prominent one. In the following, I will briefly delineate flânerie's entanglement with other media and the intermediality resulting from it in the flânerie text.

2.4 Flânerie and Other Media: A Brief History of Flânerie and Intermediality

Unfortunately, so far there has been no study that focuses exclusively on the connection between intermediality and flânerie.[68] This is all the more surprising given that flânerie has from its very beginnings dealt with intermediality[69] in its various forms. The practice of walking itself already harbors the potential to imbue the text with a material quality that reproduces the sense-impressions of the city and thus offers modes of perception that draw on the multi-sensory experience of theatrical performance and performance art. Among this variety of sense-impressions it is especially the sense of sight that is emphasized

---

[68] See also Müller (2013: 225) who points out that an examination of flânerie from the point of view of studies of intermediality is an important desideratum in research on flânerie. This is particularly interesting since the trope of the flâneur has in fact been examined by both literary studies scholars and art historians focusing on visual representations of flânerie, yet the specific entanglements between different media within flânerie literature have not been analyzed so far. Only Jörn Glasenapp, Georgiana Banita and Judith Ellenbürger's anthology *Die Lust zu gehen: Weibliche Flanerie in Literatur und Film* (2019), which traces intermedial connections between literature and film in cultural products featuring female flânerie, constitutes an exception.

[69] The term 'intermediality' here refers to examples of overt as well as covert intermediality, that is, cases in which texts directly include other media such as paintings or photographs as well as cases in which texts mirror the basic structure of another medium as is, for example, the case with the imitation of filmic techniques in narrative texts (see Rippl 2012: 320; see also Wolf 2001: 284 and 2005: 253–255). This definition also complies with Irina Rajewsky's differentiation between "media combination" and "intermedial references", with the former referring to "the combination of at least two medial forms of articulation" (2005: 52) and the latter representing media-products that emulate characteristics of another medium. In both cases, simply mentioning another medium or work of art does not suffice as an example of intermediality (Rippl 2012: 319–320).

through intermedial connections to visual representation. Thus, the 'tableau' forms a central metaphor in both Mercier's genre-paradigmatic *Tableau de Paris* and Baudelaire's *Parisian Scenes* (*Tableaux parisiens*), suggesting visual representation alongside corporeal materiality by means of its proximity to the medium of the *tableau vivant*. Moreover, Baudelaire describes flânerie itself by means of the example of Constantin Guys, "The Painter of Modern Life", thus deliberately blurring the line between the flâneur as a painter and the flâneur as a writer in his theoretical observations on flânerie. However, while those examples only account for cases of covert intermediality, the "preponderance of visual activity" in the practice of flânerie does also produce examples of overt intermediality, such as the physiologies, which often included pictures alongside their description of the different social types in the city (see, for example, De Lacroix 1840; Huart 2007).

Consequently, photography became a major addendum to the flâneur's repertoire, as attested by Fournel, who also refers to the flâneur as a "daguerréotype mobile" (Fournel 1867: 268), or more recently by Susan Sontag, who points out that "photography first comes into its own as an extension of the middle-class *flâneur*" (Sontag 1990: 55; Gomolla 2009: 64). While those examples might not constitute cases of intermediality, they demonstrate that flânerie was from its very beginnings connected with a variety of media, each of which emphasized different characteristics of flânerie. Whereas writing might focus on the aspect of reflection and thought, visual media like painting and photography foreground the aspect of observation. The advent of film at the end of the nineteenth century offered new opportunities for city dwellers since the movie camera combines the strolling motion with the reproduction of visual perception so that it can be considered to be "a technological double of the flâneur's presence" (Gleber 1999: 137).[70] As Petra Désiré Nolan shows, it is especially the so-called 'film noir' that adapts several characteristics of the flâneur for its protagonists, who often exist in a state of alienation from their fellow human beings and stroll or drive aimlessly through deserted streets (Nolan 2004: 113). While the camera itself can thus be likened to the flâneur's roving eye, the film also features the flâneur as protagonist.

Yet, the flâneur is not just the object or producer of artistic artefacts, but also their recipient. Thus, Siegfried Kracauer describes the moviegoer in terms of flânerie (Gomolla 2009: 70):

---

[70] For further research that focuses on the affinity between camera and flâneur see e.g. Kaiser (2007; 2008) and Kock (1994: 224; my trans.) who points out that "the pan or the tracking of the camera" correspond with "the intuition or the gaze of the flâneur". – "[D]er Schwenk oder die Fahrt der Kamera [entsprechen] der Intuition oder dem Blick des Flaneurs."

2.4 Flânerie and Other Media: A Brief History of Flânerie and Intermediality — 53

While the audience at the premiere craves the societal event and lets itself be seduced by "world-famous stars", the true enthusiast's passion is dedicated to the "Unofficial, the Unobserved". Driven by a "thirst for adventure", similar to that of the "roaming camera", he prefers to stroll "randomly through the cinemas" to "make discoveries at a distance from the road". For, like the "true collector", he encounters his "real happiness" in the "finds" he did not look for, but that he "captured on his expeditions" unexpectedly and "as if by chance". (Mülder-Bach 2004: 571; my trans.)[71]

Since the moviegoer can be likened to the strolling camera and since he is searching for contents that only chance can present to him, the similarity with the flâneur is obvious. This idea of the flâneur as a recipient of art recurs in relation to other media as well: Franz Hessel describes the flâneur as a reader of the city, and even very early descriptions of the flâneur like the anonymous sketch of M. Bonhomme depict characters strolling through art galleries and musing in front of paintings (Vila-Cabanes 2016: 27). Hence, since the history of flânerie is embedded in a variety of media, intersections between different media within one single flânerie text are likely to occur and can feature various kinds of intermediality: *The Blindfold* and *Open City* contain several examples of ekphrasis, *What We All Long For* features extensive descriptions of installations as well as photography, and *The Long Take* not only structurally mimics the medium of film, but also includes actual photographs in the running text. Those intermedial references are often accompanied by a reflection on the strolling protagonists' mode of perception and thus, following Benjamin, one of the means of their subjection. Through a defamiliarization of the media employed, especially in cases of covert intermediality, the structural principles of certain modes of reception can be emphasized and thus brought into focus, so that it is not only the flânerie text which becomes a means of reflection, but also other artistic products that might be included in it. Intermediality in general can thus add to the resistant and reflexive potential of the flânerie text.

Since this chapter has so far been concerned with the history of flânerie on an international scale, there still remains a caveat regarding the analysis of flâ-

---

[71] The quotation is from Inka Mülder-Bach's editorial note to the sixth volume of Kracauer's *Collected Works* and summarizes his description of the moviegoer, employing direct quotations from his description. – "Während das Premierenpublikum das gesellschaftliche Ereignis sucht und sich von 'weltberühmten Stars' verführen lässt, gilt die Leidenschaft des wahren Liebhabers dem 'Inoffiziellen, Unbeobachteten'. Getrieben von einem 'Abenteuerdrang', der dem der 'umherschweifenden Kamera' gleicht, schlendert er am liebsten 'aufs Geratwohl durch die Kinos' um 'abseits von der Heerstraße seine Entdeckungen zu machen'. Denn wie der 'wahre Sammler' findet er sein 'eigentliches Glück' in den 'Besitzstücken', die er nicht gesucht hat, sondern 'auf seinen Streifzügen' überraschend und 'wie durch Zufall erbeutet'".

nerie in contemporary Anglophone literature. Research on flânerie has mostly focused on French and German literature, raising the question of whether there is any such thing as an Anglophone history of flânerie. The question will be discussed in the following section.

2.5 Excursus: Flânerie *sans la lettre:* The Flâneur in the Anglophone Literary Tradition

The first thing worth noting in this context is the fact that the Anglophone tradition of flânerie is a largely neglected field of study, even though the occurrence of flânerie is by no means restricted to the French and German literary traditions. What is more, the versatility of the trope leads to a variety of in- and exclusions of literary examples within existing scholarship on flânerie that often entail divergent interpretations. To name but one example, Joseph Addison and Richard Steele's 'Mr Spectator', the eponymous protagonist and voice of *The Spectator*, has been identified as a precursor to a tradition of 'proper' – that is, nineteenth-century – flânerie that has mostly been discussed by Isabel Vila-Cabanes (2018: 45–46), whereas Dana Brand sees the publication as a whole as a "fully developed" (Brand 1991: 39) version of what he terms the 'Benjaminian flâneur'. The discrepancy with regard to classification is caused by 1) their different conceptualizations of flânerie and 2) the levels *in* the publication itself on which they locate flânerie – that is, for Brand, the practice of flânerie is suggested both by 'Mr Spectator' and the magazine itself, whereas Vila-Cabanes mostly focuses on the fictional character. However, the central problem that recurs with many examinations of an Anglophone tradition of flânerie lies in an issue of translation: the term 'flâneur' itself rarely appears even in British publications contemporaneous with the peak of the French tradition of flânerie[72] so that any identification of flânerie in Anglophone literature has to rely mostly on

---

[72] Vila-Cabanes suggests the following explanations for the relative absence of the term 'flâneur' in British publications of the nineteenth century: "It is difficult to establish why British society remained reluctant to incorporate the French term in their everyday vocabulary. Unlike in the early decades of the nineteenth century, when the Napoleonic wars took place and animosity towards French culture may have been a reason, the 1830s and 1840s bear witness to a growing connection between France and Britain, which is for instance illustrated in the collaborative productions of the periodical press. Although English language was rather kin to French words and the French urban figure was also known in British society, a reason which may have contributed to the reluctance of British authors to adopt the word *flâneur* later in the century may be an affirmation of cultural independence" (2018: 254).

the signified rather than the signifier and thus invites deferral of already blurry origins. To further complicate the issue, the rapid development of industrialization and the concomitant growth of London as a metropolis suggest that practices of flânerie that are closely tied to the rise of the metropolis itself might have occurred *avant la lettre* in the United Kingdom.

As Brand and Jonathan Conlin, for example, argue, the practice of flânerie has indeed been a recurrent trope in British literature throughout the eighteenth and nineteenth centuries with predecessors occurring as early as the sixteenth (see Brand 1991: 14) and the seventeenth centuries (see Brand 1991: 15–27 and Conlin 2014: 20). Regarding flânerie as a socio-historical phenomenon Vila-Cabanes points out that "[t]he practice of sauntering up and down the city streets and enjoying the urban landscape becomes a popular activity in Britain already in the late seventeenth and early eighteenth centuries" (2018: 121). As contemporary sources like the diaries of Samuel Pepys, Joseph Addison and Richard Steele's *Spectator*, or John Gay's poem *Trivia* imply, strolling was not restricted to the aristocracy, but, as in France, can be considered a rather bourgeois activity in Britain.

With regard to the appearance of flânerie in American and New English Literatures similar problems occur; that is, the term 'flâneur' is rarely used even though practices of flânerie appear frequently in city texts within those areas. Since research on flânerie is even scarcer in the fields of American and New English Literatures, quite a number of desiderata arise, such as individual studies on the development of the trope of flânerie in American literature of the twentieth and twenty-first centuries or the appearance of practices of flânerie in other Anglophone literatures across the centuries, as well as a book-long examination of any kind of 'postcolonial flânerie'.[73]

The bulk of research on flânerie in Anglophone literature is then still mostly restricted to British literature, even though here too there are few publications on the topic. To date, only Vila-Cabanes's monograph *The Flaneur in Nineteenth-Century British Literary Culture: "The World of London Unknown"* (2018) focuses exclusively on the study of British flânerie texts,[74] while Dana Brand's *The Spectator and the City in Nineteenth-Century American Literature* contains two chapters on the development of flânerie in the United Kingdom (Brand 1991: 14–63)

---

73 For an overview of research on postcolonial flânerie see section 7.2.1 below.
74 While very few studies focus exclusively on the tradition of British flânerie, there are quite a large number of short publications on the occurrence of the flâneur in individual works in the Anglophone tradition. See e.g. Briggs (2014), Carluccio (2020), Conlin (2014), Gregori (2005), Hollington (1981), Müller and Vila-Cabanes (2012), Murail (2016), Pogossian (2016), Roob (2018), Tseng (2006), and Vila-Cabanes (2014; 2020).

and then goes on to examine whether Brand's particular model of flânerie could be adapted to American literature of the nineteenth century.

Apart from those two studies, there are a number of monographs that include analyses of the trope of the flâneur – or strolling spectator – in specific works or the works of particular authors, such as John Rignall's *Realist Fiction and the Strolling Spectator* (1992) which features interpretations of the trope of the flâneur in the works of Sir Walter Scott, Charles Dickens's *Bleak House*, Henry James's *The Ambassadors*, and Ford Madox Ford's *The Good Soldier*, or Margaret Rose's *Flaneurs and Idlers* (2007), a comparative analysis of the flâneur in French and British physiologies of the 1840s, most notably Louis Huart's *Physiologie du Flâneur* and Albert Smith's *The Natural History of the Idler upon Town*. Additionally, Martina Lauster presents a comparative overview of the trope of the flâneur (among other modes of perception) in British, French, German, and Austrian journalism in the nineteenth century in *Sketches of the Nineteenth Century: European Journalism and its Physiologies, 1830–50* (2007) and Gillian Piggott traces the trajectory of the flâneur in the works of Charles Dickens in *Dickens and Benjamin: Moments of Revelation, Fragments of Modernity* (2012). In *American Flaneur: The Cosmic Physiognomy of Edgar Allan Poe* (2004), James V. Werner contributes to research on the tradition of the flâneur in American literature by reading the work of Edgar Allan Poe through the interpretative lens of flânerie. Moreover, Deborah Epstein Nord compares accounts of male and female flânerie in nineteenth-century British literature in *Walking the Victorian Streets: Women, Representation and the City* (1995) and Deborah L. Parsons discusses the works of writers such as Virginia Woolf, Jean Rhys, and Doris Lessing from the vantage point of the concept of the flâneuse in *Streetwalking the Metropolis: Women, the City and Modernity* (2003).[75]

Finally, there have been a number of compilations that include analyses of British versions of the flâneur, such as Klaus Benesch and François Specq's *Walking and the Aesthetics of Modernity: Pedestrian Mobility in Literature and the Arts* (2016), which features essays on flânerie in the works of Thomas De Quincey, Iain Sinclair, and Peter Ackroyd; Richard Wrigley's *The Flâneur Abroad: Historical and International Perspectives* (2014), which contains two articles on early British flânerie dating back to the seventeenth and eighteenth centuries; Alexandra Becquet and Claire Davison-Pégon's *Ford Madox Ford's Cosmopolis: Psychogeography*, Flânerie *and the Cultures of Paris* (2016) and the most recent publication, Oliver Bock and Isabel Vila-Cabanes's *Urban Walking: The Flâneur as an Icon of Metropolitan Culture in Literature and Film* (2020), which includes essays

---

75 For an overview of the history of the flâneuse see section 7.1.1 below.

2.5 Excursus: Flânerie *sans la lettre:* The Flâneur in the Anglophone — 57

on flânerie in selected works by Arthur Machen, Virginia Woolf, and Ian McEwan.

Research on flânerie in American literature is, as mentioned above, even less common. The only book-long study that focuses on the appearance of the trope of the flâneur in American literature is Brand's monograph on the strolling spectator in pre-Civil War American literature. Here, Brand convincingly shows that the flâneur, understood as a Baudelairian as well as Benjaminian embodiment of "the consciousness of modernity" (1991: 13), also appears in the writings of Poe, Hawthorne, and Whitman and that "[d]espite a strong native tradition of antiurbanism and despite the widespread [sic] perception of the inferiority of American cities as compared with those of Europe, many Americans [...] were fascinated by the cosmopolitan mode of being exemplified by the flâneur" (1991: 9). However, various manifestations of flânerie recur in American literature in the course of the twentieth century in works as disparate as John Dos Passos's *Manhattan Transfer* (1925), Nella Larson's *Quicksand* (1928), or Paul Auster's *City of Glass* (1985). While there are no individual studies tracing the history of the trope over this broader period, research on American as well as Canadian city literature in the twenty-first century frequently employs the trope of the flâneur as an additional interpretative lens in its analyses of the representation of the city (see, for example, Rosenthal 2011: 48; Weymann-Teschke 2018: 61–69).

With regard to flânerie in the New English Literatures, a plethora of articles on the occurrence of flânerie in the works of individual authors exist, but no individual studies on the trope. An examination of flânerie in Indian Anglophone literature can be found in two publications by Cecile Sandten (2012; 2020). Two interesting approaches towards flânerie from a global perspective can be found in Wrigley's compilation on *The Flâneur Abroad* (2014) and Kelly Comfort and Marylaura Papalas's *New Directions in Flânerie: Global Perspectives for the Twenty-First Century* (2021).

I will not attempt to give an overview of what might be called a history of Anglophone flânerie since this is not the object of my study and there is, in my opinion, not enough secondary material to effectively cover this vast field based on a definition as broad as the one mentioned above. While Vila-Cabanes has collected an impressive array of primary texts featuring instances of flânerie, I do not quite agree with her narrow definition of flânerie, which mostly excludes any kind of political motivation on the part of the flâneur (see Vila-Cabanes 2018: 19 and 2016: 19), and therefore would suggest expanding the notion of what could be called a British tradition of flânerie to include textual examples featuring flânerie as a practice of resistance.[76] I certainly agree with Vila-Cabanes's thesis that there is a tendency in British literature for flâneur writings to shift from more affirmative depictions of the city towards increasingly uncanny representations (Vila-Cabanes 2018: 255), but I would like to put additional emphasis on the existence of a socially critical flâneur within an Anglophone tradition of flânerie. Thus, I concur with Neumeyer's assumption that the aimless motion of the flâneur is not necessarily devoid of intentionality. What is more, there are actually quite a lot of flâneurs to be found in French as well as British literature who dabble in social criticism. Not only is Mercier's representation of the city in the *Tableau de Paris* subjected to his political agenda, but Romanticist depictions of London also often focus on the alienating and exploitative aspects of city life and commodity culture. A prominent example would be William Blake's poem "London", which has already been discussed in the chapter on flânerie as performance. In this short text, the lyrical I powerfully attacks institutions like the crown, the church, and marriage as well as the entire process of industrialization and capitalism and presents them as direct causes of the suffering of the London population.

In the following, I will discuss two issues that, in my opinion, need to be particularly highlighted in the history of the literary trope of the flâneur within a British tradition; these are, 1) the fact that the British flâneur occurred almost a century earlier than his French counterpart and is, due to the importance of trade in Great Britain, very explicitly linked to the market itself, and 2) that there is indeed a flânerie in the British literary tradition that aims at producing a socially critical gaze onto the city. In this, I will focus my discussion on one publication and one author that could be deemed central to an examination of British flânerie and that constitute the two cases most frequently referred to in this context: Addison and Steele's *Spectator* and the work of Charles Dickens.

Although the notion of one *single* Benjaminian concept of the flâneur is highly problematic – for the reasons explained above – Brand's thesis on the Spectator being "suited to become the poet of capitalism" (1991: 35) is particularly noteworthy. He convincingly shows that the flâneur partakes in the promotion of capitalism by creating benevolent representations of trade and the marketplace as well as the aesthetics of circulation (Brand 1991: 35–38). Especially essay no. 454, titled "Twenty-Four Hours in London", is highly reminiscent of "the paradoxical nature of the flâneur's relationship to the commercial culture

---

[76] Although the other publications offer interesting readings of individual works, they vary, at times significantly, in their definitions of flânerie and therefore do not quite allow for a unified account of the history of British or even Anglophone flânerie.

and spaces in which his mode of consciousness develops" (Brand 1991: 36). In this essay, which meta-reflexively mirrors the structure of the whole publication, Mr Spectator tries to cure his nightly insomnia by going to London in the early morning and spends the rest of his day aimlessly driving and strolling through the city in general and its marketplaces in particular. According to Brand, Mr Spectator's cure can be understood as also the cause of his insomnia since "the spectacle of urban commercial life is all-absorbing" and "a true appreciation of it demands and creates a restless consciousness in search of distraction, incapable of rest" (1991: 36). While the essay itself might not necessarily suggest this cause-and-effect relationship between urban commodity culture and the flâneur's restlessness, it nevertheless refers back to the flâneur's paradoxical relationship of subjection and attraction to the market, which is engrained in the magazine's condition of production. Thus, the *Spectator* needs to be sold to frequenters of the same social space that it portrays since it was mostly distributed to coffeehouses and clubs in the city. The fiction on which the whole publication relies is the fiction of the strolling spectator who encounters his material during his rambles through the city to which the product of Mr Spectator's flânerie is supposed to be sold. The title of the publication almost literally engenders Benjamin's analogy between flâneur and commodity. Mr Spectator, the flâneur, becomes *The Spectator*, the commodity.

The city that Mr Spectator walks is often represented through the metaphor of the marketplace (see e.g. Addison and Steele 1967: I, 212; III, 402, 405). Thus, during his rambles through the city in essay no. 454, his main focus lies on markets like Covent-Garden or the Royal Exchange (Addison and Steele 1967: III, 403, 404–405). In both cases, the depiction of the markets is charged with attraction by foregrounding the "agreeable young Women" (Addison and Steele 1967: III, 403) and "agreeable females" with "pretty hands" and "agreeable faces" (Addison and Steele 1967: III, 404) who could be encountered in those places shopping and selling the commodities displayed. This active promotion of capitalist culture by charging its central places with positive affect becomes especially manifest in essay no. 69, which focuses on the description of the Royal Exchange. With no understatement, Mr Spectator introduces his essay with the words "[t]here is no Place in Town which I so much love to frequent as the *Royal Exchange*" (Addison and Steele 1967: I, 212) and he concludes with general praise of the English merchant:

> For these Reasons there are not more useful Members in a Commonwealth than Merchants. They knit Mankind together in a mutual Intercourse of good Offices, distribute the Gifts of Nature, find Work for the Poor, add Wealth to the Rich, and Magnificence to the Great. Our *English* Merchant converts the Tin of his own Country into Gold, and exchanges his Wooll

[sic] for Rubies. The *Mahometans* are cloathed in our *British* Manufacture, and the Inhabitants of the Frozen Zone warmed with the Fleeces of our Sheep. (Addison and Steele 1967: I, 214)

The *laudatio* on those different constituents of capitalist trade finally culminates in this statement in the last sentences of the essay:

> Trade, without enlarging the *British* Territories, has given us a kind of additional Empire: It has multiplied the Number of the Rich, made our Landed Estates infinitely more Valuable than they were formerly, and added to them an Accession of other Estates as valuable as the Lands themselves. (Addison and Steele 1967: I, 214–215)

The Spectator then is, despite its various claims to objectivity (see e. g. Addison and Steele 1967: I, 1 and 5), very decidedly affirmative of capitalism and its various components. As Brand points out, this affirmation of capitalism also extends to *The Spectator*'s aesthetics which accepts the "value of novelty, change, and the flood of objects in and of themselves" (1991: 38). Brand derives this assumption from Mr Spectator's conclusion to essay no. 454 in which he recommends keeping one's "mind open to Gratification" and being "ready to receive it from any thing it meets with" (Addison and Steele 1967: III, 415), which Brand then links to the Benjaminian concept of *Erlebnis* – that is, "experience as consumption and collection" (1991: 37). *The Spectator* certainly engages in this kind of "'phantasmagoria of the idler'" (Benjamin, qtd. In Brand 1991: 37) by aimlessly delighting in various images of the city which in their totality present themselves to the reader as the spectacle of the metropolis. The genre of the periodical essay fits particularly well the ephemeral rhythms of the modern metropolis with its up-to-date topics and publication on a daily or weekly basis and thus mirrors the processes of constant circulation and consumption.[77] Whereas I disagree with Brand's assumption of a single concept of flânerie that could be extracted from Benjamin's writings, he is certainly right in emphasizing *The Spectator*'s affirmation of commodity culture and in relating it to Benjamin's writings on the flâneur. Nevertheless, I think the comparison could be taken even further given the socio-historical contexts of *The Spectator* and those parts of French history on which Benjamin focuses in his essay on "The Flâneur".

The publication of *The Spectator* largely aligns with the rise of the literary market. While literary production before the eighteenth century mostly depended on patronage by the court or individual aristocrats, new copyright legislation at

---

[77] For an overview of the generic characteristics of the periodical essay see DeMaria (2005: 527–540).

2.5 Excursus: Flânerie *sans la lettre:* The Flâneur in the Anglophone

the beginning of the eighteenth century allowed for independent literary production (Schwalm 2012: 39). Addison and Steele's success thus primarily depended on their products being bought by the crowd. Similarly, in Benjamin's wide-ranging discussion of the rise of the literary market in France, which precedes the chapter on the flâneur in his Baudelaire book (see Benjamin 2006: 46–66), he refers, for example, to the practice of 'hack-writing' which was also common in England in conjunction with the rise of the literary market (Schwalm 2012: 39). The parallel that can be drawn between *The Spectator* and Benjaminian remarks on the flâneur is therefore not limited only to the representation and affirmation of a consciousness adapted to commodity culture, but could also be extended to some of the socio-historical conditions that Benjamin explicitly names: it is not just the flâneur's consciousness that adapts to the aesthetics of consumption; his whole existence is now subjected to capitalism as well.

This is particularly interesting because *The Spectator*'s blatant promotion of capitalist culture stresses the parallel that Benjamin draws by explicitly linking the periodical essay's aesthetics of the ephemeral with commodity culture. That *The Spectator* can serve as a convincing example of the analogy between flâneur and commodity is also suggested by Benjamin's remark that flânerie was not possible in London at the beginning of the nineteenth century due to the already advanced progress of industrialization and capitalism at that time. If the flâneur originated in the United Kingdom one century prior to the French flâneur, then it comes as no surprise that nineteenth-century London cannot afford the same kind of flânerie as eighteenth-century London and that the French flâneur of the nineteenth century whom Benjamin describes would rather be analogous to Mr Spectator than to any of his successors in the nineteenth century.

Even if compared with French manifestations of the flâneur *avant la lettre* such as Mercier's *Tableau de Paris* (1781), British variants like *The Spectator* or Samuel Johnson's *The Rambler* (1750–1752) occurred much earlier. The comparison between *The Spectator* and the *Tableau de Paris*, moreover, points to another significant difference. Whereas *The Spectator* claims to be apolitical – although it has been widely acknowledged that the publication promoted Whiggish interests – and mostly focuses on topics which are not too openly political, like manners, morals, or the depiction of everyday life in the city (Vila-Cabanes 2018: 38), the *Tableau de Paris* directly criticizes existing political structures in pre-revolutionary France. The roots of British flânerie can thus be found not in political resistance, but rather in an affirmation of the system of capitalism linked to a focus on morality and normativity.

Nevertheless, social criticism does occur in British flânerie literature in the nineteenth century, particularly in the work of Charles Dickens. A case in point is Charles Dickens's *Sketches by Boz*, a collection of his early journalistic writings. While I agree with Vila-Cabanes that those short pieces often convey an unbiased representation of the city (Vila-Cabanes 2018: 114–115), I also maintain that Dickens's alter ego Boz is *not* "pre-eminently distanced from the urban spectacle" (Vila-Cabanes 2018: 115), but that he rather finds himself in an essentially paradoxical relationship with the city due to the "constant awareness of mortality" and the recurring "theme of individual social and economic decline" (Brand 1991: 56) that the *Sketches* display. That his social criticism might not just be considered a side note can already be seen in the very first essay in the collection, titled "The Streets – Morning". Here, Boz describes the routine of everyday life on the streets of London in the morning. Although a large part of this essay is actually taken up by a rather detached description of city life in the morning, the essay finally culminates in the following passages:

> The shops are now completely opened, and apprentices and shopmen are busily engaged in cleaning and decking the windows for the day. The bakers' shops in town are filled with servants and children waiting for the drawing of the first batch of rolls – an operation which was performed a full hour ago in the suburbs: for the early clerk population of Somers and Camden Towns, Islington, and Pentonville, are fast pouring into the city, or directing their steps towards Chancery Lane and the Inns of Court. Middle-aged men, whose salaries have by no means increased in the same proportion as their families, plod steadily along, apparently with no object in view but the counting house; knowing by sight almost everybody they meet or overtake, for they have seen them every morning (Sundays excepted) during the last twenty years, but speaking to no one. If they do happen to overtake a personal acquaintance, they just exchange a hurried salutation and keep walking on, either by his side or in front of him, as his rate of walking may chance to be. As to stopping to shake hands or to take the friend's arm, they seem to think that as it is not included in their salary, they have no right to do it. Small office lads in large hats, who are made men before they are boys, hurry along in pairs, with their first coat carefully brushed, and the white trousers of last Sunday plentifully besmeared with dust and ink. It evidently requires a considerable mental struggle to avoid investing part of the day's dinner money in the purchase of the stale tarts so temptingly exposed in dusty tins at the pastry cooks' doors: but a consciousness of their own importance and the receipt of seven shillings a week, with the prospect of an early rise to eight, comes to their aid, and they accordingly put their hats a little more on one side, and look under the bonnets of all the milliners' and stay makers' apprentices they meet – poor girls! – the hardest worked, the worst paid, and too often, the worst used class of the community. (Dickens 1994: 53–54)

The image that Dickens creates here is noteworthy due to its appeal to totality. The groups of people represented in this passage account for a large part of the London population and even suggest a certain circularity. While it starts off with the description of the "[m]iddle-aged men, whose salaries have by no means increased in the same proportion as their families" and thus directly criticizes the economic situation in which this part of the population finds itself, it then moves on to the "[s]mall office lads [...], who are made men before they are boys" and keep themselves from buying stale pastry through attempts at flirtation with "the milliners' and stay makers' apprentices [...] the hardest worked, worst paid, and too often, the worst used class of the community", thus suggesting that those small office lads will in time turn into middle-aged men caring for families they cannot really support on their salary.

While the office boys' future might still be open at this time, the description of the middle-aged men already bodes ill for their prospects. Moreover, the passage openly addresses the commodification of the population: every group is seen through the lens of money and acts on its basis – to the point that the middle-aged men seem to refrain from interaction because they are not paid for it – and none of the different groups seems to earn enough.

This culmination of the panoramic description of London's streets in the morning is paralleled by a scene in the corresponding essay "The Streets – Night". Before concluding his description of the streets by night with the depiction of a gentlemen's club, Boz focuses on an impoverished ballad singer who tries to raise some money by singing on the streets:

> There was another, but it has ceased. That wretched woman with the infant in her arms, round whose meagre form the remnant of her own scanty shawl is carefully wrapped, has been attempting to sing some popular ballad, in the hope of wringing a few pence from the compassionate passer-by. A brutal laugh at her weak voice is all she has gained. The tears fall thick and fast down her own pale face; the child is cold and hungry, and its low half stifled wailing adds to the misery of its wretched mother, as she moans aloud, and sinks despairingly down on a cold damp doorstep.
>
> Singing! How few of those who pass such a miserable creature as this, think of the anguish of heart, the sinking of soul and spirit, which the very effort of singing produces. Bitter mockery! Disease, neglect, and starvation, faintly articulating the words of the joyous ditty, that has enlivened your hours of feasting and merriment, God knows how often!
>
> It is no subject of jeering. The weak tremulous voice tells a fearful tale of want and famishing; and the feeble singer of this roaring song may turn away, only to die of cold and hunger. (Dickens 1994: 58–59)

Boz clearly empathizes with the woman, appealing to his readers to recognize the "anguish of heart" which the "very effort of singing" might produce in her. What is more, this passage is juxtaposed with the description of the party at the club which also features performances of songs. However, Boz's description of the participants of the party is by no means as sympathetic as his account of the ballad singer:

> The 'professional gentlemen' are in the very height of their glory, and bestow condescending nods, or even a word or two of recognition, on the better-known frequenters of the room, in the most bland and patronising manner possible. (Dickens 1994: 59)

The inclusion of this scene actually departs from the overall topic of the essay – a description of London's streets by night – and can thus only be understood as an addendum to the depiction of the ballad singer which serves as a critique of the inequality represented by the juxtaposition of these two scenes. Thus, the description of the streets by night, like that of the streets in the morning, culminates in social criticism.

Yet, both endings might also imply an alternative interpretation of Boz's apparently purposeless flânerie through the city. As the structure of both essays suggests, the representation of the city is just a pretense for the social criticism with which both texts ultimately conclude. Moreover, Dickens continuously employs irony in his sketches to make his criticism all the more scathing, for example when he refers to the office lads' "consciousness of [...] the receipt of seven shillings a week", which "comes to their aid" in preventing them from purchasing the pastry. The "amusement" (Dickens 1994: 170) which Boz claims to wish to give his readers thus sounds increasingly cynical as he focuses again and again on the depiction of the misery of those less fortunate within the spectacle of the city.[78]

However, Dickens himself can also be considered a prime example of the writer's integration into the workings of the market, on the lines of Mr Spectator; he incessantly walked the streets of London, especially when plagued by bouts of insomnia, and openly admitted to the compulsiveness of this habit, so that rumor has it that Dickens was the role model for Poe's 'man of the crowd' (see Roob 2018: 248; see Rachmann 1975: 49–51).[79] Dickens, who produced an immense output during his fifty-eight years of life, managed to successfully sustain himself as well as his family by means of writing. His novels, usually published as individual chapters in journals and other serial publications, were extremely popular and were often marketed through reading tours and "semidramatic readings by gaslight" (Alexander 2013: 290). Therefore, it is all the more ironic that he should have written a regular column in his *All the Year*

---

[78] The claim that Dickens frequently includes empathetic depictions of the London poor which constitute clear instances of social criticism has also been made by Byerly (1999: 356), Lauster (2007: 187), Piggott (2012: 174–175), Sicher (2007: 45), and Tambling (2009: 41).

[79] See also Piggott (2012: 160): "Dickens' obsession with walking in the city and his own understanding of its importance to his production surely makes him a flâneur in the mould of Benjamin's Baudelairean writings."

Round magazine called "The Uncommercial Traveller", which centers on the persona of the eponymous 'uncommercial traveller' – as opposed to a commercial traveler whose travels are determined by his business – who works "for the great house of Human Interest Brothers" (Dickens 2000: 28). His walking, consequently, is "objectless, loitering and purely vagabond" (Dickens 2000: 119), yet at the same time, "it is one of [his] fancies, that even [his] idlest walk must always have its appointed destination" (Dickens 2000: 380), thus reflecting the overall ambivalence of the publication, which of course also depends on being bought by its audience. Hence, in the *Sketches by Boz* as well as "The Uncommercial Traveller" the flâneur's apparent disinterestedness is contaminated by political as well as financial interests.

This ambivalence is indicative of a friction present not only in Dickens's journalistic writings, but also in his novelistic work. While he continuously describes the city as a bleak and cruel place subjected to the all-encompassing mechanisms of capitalism and industrialization, he also seems to be fascinated by the subject itself and aestheticizes his depictions of nineteenth-century real and imaginary cities by means of powerful rhetorical devices.[80] Dickens's work thus seems to be torn between an affirmation of and fascination with the modern metropolis and a critique of the cruel living conditions it inflicts on its inhabitants. His journalistic writings are no exception, and likewise display this ambivalent attitude. The motivation for the walks of his flâneurs might thus very well be a simple reveling in the spectacle that is the city, but the motivation for his textual flânerie is political as well as financial.

This ambivalence then again aligns with the overall ambivalence of the trope of the flâneur itself. While the paradigm of flânerie might serve the purpose of affirming political or economic systems as well as the spectacle of the modern metropolis that might be associated with them – as is the case in the writings of Addison and Steele or the essays of Charles Lamb (see also Vila-Cabanes 2018: 48–50) – it might just as well function as a vehicle for social criticism – as can be seen in the poetry of William Blake, Mercier's *Tableau de Paris*, or Dickens's *Sketches by Boz*. Moreover, the aspect of a political motivation of flânerie becomes all the more present in counterdiscursive functionalizations of the trope in feminist or postcolonial responses to hegemonic strategies of 'othering'. An examination of Anglophone literature that uses flânerie to that purpose, such as, for example, the Sierra Leonean writer A.B.C. Merriman-Labor's *Britons Through Negro Spectacles* (1909), might prove particularly fruitful.

---

[80] See also Middeke (2012: 69): "No other Victorian writer has given that much life to the big industrial city, its dirt, its bad smells, its labyrinthine streets as Charles Dickens."

There is therefore a rich history of flânerie to be found in British literature, although it is worth emphasizing that the British flâneur originated a lot earlier than his French counterpart, at the beginning of the eighteenth century. A British tradition of flânerie is thus rooted in the beliefs and discourses of the Enlightenment and the ensuing focus on reason, rationality, and morality, whereas the French tradition carries the traces of the French Revolution and is later mainly associated with the aestheticism of the second half of the nineteenth century. Moreover, British flânerie's connection with the market is particularly marked and might be considered an even more fitting example for the analogy that Benjamin draws between the flâneur and the commodity. Ultimately, this comparison highlights another, more general aspect in the tradition of flânerie, namely that flânerie is an international phenomenon that transgresses borders and cannot be reduced to its existence in any individual national literature.[81]

However, in all of the traditions delineated above – as well as in other national literatures – a number of structural as well as thematic characteristics recur throughout the centuries which can be usefully drawn on for the description of a heuristic model of what could be called the aesthetics of the flânerie text.

2.6 Synopsis: The Aesthetics of the Flânerie Text

In her PhD project, Vila-Cabanes argues that flânerie literature might be classified as a genre of its own due to its continuous existence throughout several historical periods (2018: 26–28), drawing on a quote by Aragon who refers to flânerie as "a formula of which literature furnishes us with several examples" (Aragon 1987: 224). While Vila-Cabanes refrains from attempting to delineate any such genre due to the fact that, according to her, "pleading for a distinct genre could result in the exclusion of texts which are essential for the study of the reception of the type both as a literary and a social phenomenon" (2018: 28), I think the formula to which Aragon refers could be said to recur in a few structural characteristics that follow from the aimless movement of the flâneur and surface in most, though not all, flânerie texts, and could be assembled into a heuristic model of the paradigm of the flânerie text.

---

[81] The transgression of the border between French and British culture is even engrained in the tradition of French flânerie itself due to the adoption of dandyesque self-stylizations during the French 'anglomania' mentioned above.

2.6 Synopsis: The Aesthetics of the Flânerie Text — 67

My description of what might be called the flânerie text is based on Neumeyer's minimal definition of flânerie as a mode of perception which involves aimless strolling through the space of the city. On a thematic level, the flânerie text is thus always set in a metropolis and features the mode of perception described by Neumeyer. This aimless strolling could be performed by the narrator or the protagonist, or it could occur when the overall structure and content of the text gives the impression of an aimless walk through the city, as is the case in texts like Benjamin's *One-Way Street*.[82]

On a structural level, a specific form follows from the thematic characteristics of flânerie since flânerie texts usually feature an episodic form or constitute a part of a series. This feature becomes especially manifest in serial publications like *The Spectator*, "The Uncommercial Traveller", or the *Tableau de Paris*, which mirror the ephemeral character of the city by means of a series of short sketches or essays that function as 'snapshots' of the city. Yet, the episodic form appears not only in journalistic writings, but also in poems, as is the case with Baudelaire's *Parisian Scenes*, each of which contains an episode of its own. In narrative texts, the structural focus on an accumulation of small episodes often also results in a reduction of plot, as can be seen in many of the novels I analyze in this book, but even more in one of the prime examples of literary flânerie – James Joyce's *Ulysses*. One could even assume that this tendency to seriality and the tying together of individual episodes brought forth by a demand for continuous consumption as one of the central characteristics of modernity already implies Jean-François Lyotard's 'postmodern knowledge' and its focus on heterogeneity and plurality (Lyotard 1984). This specific structural property might thus also heighten a text's focus on the particular.

The last characteristic pertains to the thematic as well as to the structural level and can be described in terms of Benjamin's observation that the flâneur "stands on the threshold" (Benjamin 2006: 40). Flânerie texts feature transgression in a variety of ways. While the characteristic of transgression might be found in any kind of literature, there are genres, such as, for example, Gothic literature, which are particularly prone to the display of transgression. The flânerie text can in my opinion be counted among them. First of all, the concept of transgression is intrinsic to the act of walking since walking constantly creates as well as transgresses spatial boundaries. At the same time, walking also offers a new perspective with every step that is taken by the individual, which might result in the co-presence of different perspectives on the city within one single text and thus in

---

[82] See Rummel (2012: 74) for a conceptualisation of this structural dynamic into a "cultural and literary practice" in British Modernist literature.

transgression on a thematic level. Transgression then becomes all the more likely if this walking is undertaken in an aimless manner. Moreover, flânerie texts frequently cross generic as well as medial boundaries. While Baudelaire's prose poems in the *Parisian Scenes* combine poetic forms with features of prose writing, flânerie texts like Addison and Steele's *Spectator*, for example, might cross the border between the fictional and the factual or, as is the case with the writings of Benjamin, the line between literature and philosophy. The boundary between text and image is also frequently crossed in flânerie texts through the inclusion of either overt or covert intermediality. Lastly, the history of the trope as such proves the flâneur as well as the flânerie text to have an ambivalent character whose functionalizations elude any precise classification.

Those characteristics, together with a strong emphasis on flânerie as material practice throughout the second half of the twentieth century, Benjamin's reflection on the 'death of the flâneur', and a reconceptualization of flânerie as *techne*, then form the basis for contemporary flânerie texts' new focus on a negotiation of ethical subjecthood. Here, the 'death of the flâneur' aligns with the 'death of the subject' as proposed by Michel Foucault, while at the same time forming a backdrop against which new forms of subjecthood can be illustrated. Those new forms, the so-called 'ethics of the self', were first advanced in the late work of Foucault and have since been systematized and expanded on in Judith Butler's conception of the ethical subject. Given their importance to my analysis, I shall therefore devote the next chapters to delineating Foucault's and Butler's approaches towards ethical subjecthood.

3 Michel Foucault's Ethics of the Self

Michel Foucault's work has become famous, almost notoriously so, for its central thesis of the so-called 'death of man', its proclamation that the subject is – contrary to a Cartesian concept of the subject – neither sovereign nor autonomous. Foucault's subject, by contrast, is not only dominated, but produced by discourses of power that largely determine what could be known or thought by it. Therefore, the subject depends on those very same discourses of power and cannot return to any kind of essentialist core or origin. Nevertheless, Foucault's examination of what he has identified as 'technologies of the self', undertaken in individual essays as well as his studies on the *History of Sexuality*, seems to re-evaluate this thesis. Those technologies of the self

> permit individuals to effect by their own means or with the help of others a certain number of operations on their own bodies and souls, thoughts, conduct, and way of being, so as to transform themselves in order to attain a certain state of happiness, purity, wisdom, perfection, or immortality. (Foucault 2000a: 225)

The practice implies a conception of subjecthood according to which the subject is at least partially autonomous and therefore capable of transforming itself according to its own wishes. What here seems to constitute – at least partly – a direct contradiction to his earlier claims about the 'death of man' is, according to Foucault himself, nothing more than a shift in focus that might involve some minor adjustments but that does not abandon his former findings entirely:

> If one wants to analyse the genealogy of the subject in Western civilization, one has to take into account not ony [sic] techniques of domination but also techniques of the self. One has to show the interaction between those two types of self. When I was studying asylums, prisons, and so on, I perhaps insisted too much on techniques of domination. [...] I would like, in the years to come, to study power relations starting from techniques of the self. (Foucault and Sennett 1982: 10)

Foucault locates the basis for his analysis of those techniques of the self in ancient Greek culture and its *technē tou biou*, the practice of leading a good life. The techniques of the self then not only form the object of Foucault's study as an important nexus at the historical intersection between changing epistemes of subjectivity, but also serve as a possible example for a new non-normative and postmodern type of ethics. While his writings on the history of sexuality descriptively retrace the genealogy of a moral experience in which the subject modulates and reigns over its desire and thus emphasize the processual quality of concepts of subjectivity – that is, the fact that the subject itself is historically variable – the interviews and essays that Foucault produced at that time also assign a value to those ancient techniques, implying that they might constitute an alternative to the traditional Cartesian subject (Schmid 2000: 10). Yet, Foucault specifies that ancient Greek morality should not therefore be conceived of as an ideal, but rather as an inspiration for alternative modes of subjectivity:

> Trying to rethink the Greeks today does not consist of setting off Greek morality as the domain of morality par excellence which one would need for self-reflection. The point is rather to see to it that European thinking can take up Greek thinking again as an experience which took place once and with regard to which one can be completely free. (Foucault 1990: 249).

In order to become viable for the twentieth and twenty-first centuries, the mode of subjectivity displayed in ancient Greek dietetics, or health theory, then has to be re-interpreted, problematized and potentially adjusted to contemporary societies and culture.

Moreover, the quote implies a differentiation between ethics and morality central to poststructuralist ethics and also present in Foucault's late work. What he is not trying to construct is any kind of normalizing universal morality (Best and Kellner 1991: 64).[83] Instead, his definition of ethics is based on the ancient Greek term *ethos*, meaning 'habit' (see Butzer 2009: 221), and is used in order to refer to any kind of attitude (see Waldow 2013: 53) or form that an individual might develop in relation to their surroundings as well as to themselves.

Thus, ethics are for Foucault predominantly political: he refers to the main focus of his late work as "politics as an ethics" (Foucault 1984a: 375) and describes ethics as "the deliberate form assumed by liberty" (Foucault 1988: 4), which implies that liberty itself is expressed through the particular form of ethics he suggests. The difference between an *ethos* and any kind of normative morality lies in its position with respect to social and political norms, to which the late-Foucauldian subject is not passively subjected but which it can question via individual forms (Schmid 2000: 225). The aforementioned attitude manifests itself in the form that individuals give themselves based on, and continually tested by, reflection on that very form (Schmid 2000: 225). Yet, although this 'new' subject might be partially autonomous with respect to the norms aiming at its subjection, it still has to participate in those very same structures and is still "discursively and socially conditioned" (Best and Kellner 1991: 64). Hence, according to

---

[83] Although Foucault often doesn't distinguish between morals and ethics in his writings, quotes like the one given above suggest that this distinction is implicit in his writings on ethics and is often described as such in secondary literature (see e.g. Waldow 2000; Best and Kellner 1991).

Foucault's conception, a certain interdependence exists between technologies of domination – that is, normative and moralistic technologies – and the techniques of the self – that is, techniques by means of which subjects put themselves into a relationship toward their selves and thus form nodes of resistance (Schmid 2000: 256). While those subjects are still subjected to discourses of power, those discourses are not invariable, but can be changed by means of practices of resistance (Waldow 2013: 55).

The practices of resistance then do not create a new, sovereign subject; they only protect the subject against being subjected to discourses of power "quite so much" (Foucault 2003a: 265). Instead of rooting those practices of resistance in any essentialist conception of what the subject actually *is*,[84] Foucault suggests a subjectivity that only resides in the form that an individual molds their life into, as well as the process of reflecting on that form. A fitting example of this attitude manifests itself in what Foucault calls a 'pessimistic activism'; that is, an activism that is pessimistic because it does not assume that an ideal situation is ever within reach, but that at the same time does not draw the conclusion that every political action is therefore essentially pointless. This kind of activism is not normative since it does not construct any idealistic norm, but rather assumes that temporally limited guidelines might be revised at any moment (Schmid 2000: 257–258). Those guidelines are "nevertheless not something that the individual invents by himself. They are patterns that he finds in his culture and which are proposed, suggested, and imposed on him by his culture, his society and his social group" (Foucault 1988: 11) – that is, even in the practices of the self and their performance of resistance the individual ultimately depends on already existing patterns produced by discourses of power. In order to account for his re-conceptualization of subjectivity, Foucault then coins the term 'aesthetics of existence' which clarifies further how this subjectivity could be understood.

---

84 In "On the Genealogy of Ethics", Foucault refers to this loss of foundation or origin as the precise problem of contemporary revolutionary movements: "Recent liberation movements suffer from the fact that they cannot find any principle on which to base the elaboration of a new ethics. They need an ethics, but they cannot find any other ethics than an ethics founded on so-called scientific knowledge of what the self is, what desire is, what the unconscious is, and so on" (Foucault 2000f: 255–256).

3.1 The Aesthetics of Existence

The term 'aesthetics', in the 'aesthetics of existence', already implies the paradoxical situation of a subject that balances a subjection to aesthetic norms or values with the disruptive, creative and potentially revolutionary character of art. For Foucault, aestheticism means, first and foremost, the ability to transform oneself and thus to fashion oneself into a particular form (see also Schmid 2000: 281). The life of the individual is thus turned "into an *oeuvre* that carries certain aesthetic values and meets certain stylistic criteria" (Foucault 1992: 10–11). Those stylistic criteria resonate with Nietzsche's demand "[t]o 'give style' to one's character" (Nietzsche 2001: 163; see also Schmid 2000: 260) and thus emphasize the individualistic character of the aesthetics of existence (Schmid 2000: 235).[85] The individual style then cannot become the basis for any generally binding system of norms, but is only valid in relation to the personal choice of the individual and as regards the particular existence of that individual (Schmid 2000: 235). This restriction of the validity of any individual ethical style of existence recurs in the relations that Foucault draws between the ethics of ancient Greece and their contemporary appropriation: "It is important to point out the proximity and the difference, and, through their interplay, to show how the same advice given by ancient morality can function *differently* in a contemporary style of morality" (Foucault 1990: 247; my emphasis). When adopting an ethical style to suit the individual needs and circumstances of any existence, the relation to another style or another aesthetics of existence can thus only ever be one of similarity but never one of identity.

This style has to be personally chosen by each individual, taking into account historical and biographical experiences, recent problems, risks of normalization and restrictions of the individual choice of others. The aesthetics of existence thus affirm the liberty of the individual who freely chooses the form and the *hegemonikon* – that is, the governing principle that they want to establish for themselves – of their lives. This choice cannot be entirely arbitrary, but has

---

[85] Interestingly, Foucault refers in this context to Baudelaire's description of the dandy in "The Painter of Modern Life" in order to illustrate what he calls the 'attitude of modernity' which entails an active process of self-formation. Here, he also mentions the flâneur, yet dismisses him as an apt model for the performance of this particularly modern attitude. Foucault however ignores the fact that Constantin Guys, the eponymous 'painter of modern life', is in fact according to Baudelaire "the perfect idler" (Baudelaire 1972: 399), and identifies him with what would rather be called a gawper who does nothing beyond gawking at his surroundings. Given Baudelaire's combination of dandyism with flânerie, flânerie might then very well form part of the dandy's 'aesthetics of existence'.

to be based on a thorough reflection on the individual's past and present context, thus drawing on another aspect of the aesthetics of existence which is its relation to the production of knowledge.[86]

Although Foucault rejects any conception of the subject that is based on knowledge about the inner being or the essence of this subject, he does not exclude knowledge itself from his ethics of the self. On the contrary, he uses the term 'technologies of the self' in order to refer to the practices of the self that he analyzes in his late writings, thus indicating an interplay between *techne* and *logos* – that is, between techniques and knowledge (Schmid 2000: 282). What he aims at, is merely the discarding of "certain calcified and boring forms of knowledge" (Foucault 2018: 169; see also Schmid 2000: 283), that is, any kind of knowledge that is not open to revision or that claims to be absolute. Foucault's conception of the aesthetics of existence's relationship to truth and knowledge is closely linked to his reflections on the Enlightenment insofar as he aims to translate into an ethos the Enlightenment's emphasis on searching for new truths:

> I have been seeking, on the one hand, to emphasize the extent to which a type of philosophical interrogation – one that simultaneously problematizes man's relation to the present, man's historical mode of being, and the constitution of the self as an autonomous subject – is rooted in the Enlightenment. On the other hand, I have been seeking to stress that the thread which may connect us with the Enlightenment is not faithfulness to doctrinal elements but, rather, the permanent reactivation of an attitude – that is, of a philosophical ethos that could be described as a permanent critique of our historical era. (Foucault 2000c: 312)

What Foucault envisions as consonant with an aesthetics of existence is thus rather the practice of critique as a constant criticism of existing discourses of power (Waldow 2013: 59) and an interest in a transformation of existing truths.

Moreover, the kind of knowledge that is of importance for the aesthetics of existence is always a knowledge of particularities. It does not claim any absolute validity for itself, but only ever refers to particular situations and contexts to which it has to be actively applied (Schmid 2000: 284). The knowledge of the aesthetics of existence is a practical knowledge that is concerned with the practical application of its content to particular situations (Schmid 2000: 283). What is more, this knowledge is gained by means of experience and perception and is thus in the literal sense of the word 'aesthetic' (Schmid 2000: 284). Alluding to western metaphorizations of knowledge through the symbol of the eye, this aesthetic knowledge is often described by Foucault in terms of visuality. Thus,

---

86 See for entire paragraph Schmid (2000: 288–289).

he refers to a "a new way of looking" (Foucault 2000b: 327) that needs to be developed in the aesthetics of existence, to a "certain form of attention, of looking"[87] (Foucault 1985: 32; my trans.) when describing the care of the self that creates the aesthetics of existence or, in his introduction to *The Use of Pleasure*, to a transformation of "one's way of looking at things" (Foucault 1992: 11) when engaging with the aesthetics of existence. The aspect of a material perception of particular situations is thus stressed and knowledge is linked to a predominantly material approach towards perspective as well as experience. It is not just a knowledge that is supposed to be tied to practice, but one that can be challenged by changes of experience and modifications of perception.

A Foucauldian aesthetics of existence thus entails three main characteristics: 1) the aspect of stylization that involves a conscious modification of the life of the individual by the individual, who thus expresses their very own 'style of existence' 2) the aspect of personal choice that emphasizes the liberty of the subject of the aesthetics of existence and thus the subject's partial autonomy from existing discourses of power and 3) the aspect of reflexivity that ensures reflection and revision of the form that the individual has chosen, which is based on a conception of knowledge and truth as historically variable and perspectival.[88]

The aesthetics of existence are then closely linked to the so-called 'care of the self', a term that Foucault uses to refer to the whole array of the techniques of the self in antiquity. The care of the self can be understood as being based on the aesthetics of existence as well as producing them (Schmid 2000: 280) and derives from the Greek term *epimeleia heautou*. The care of the self describes the form of the Foucauldian subject and thus describes the subject itself because the Foucauldian subject only manifests itself as form. Thus, the care of the self aims at the aesthetics of existence as a result, but also needs those aesthetics and their characteristic of personal choice as its foundation (Schmid 2000: 280). In the care of the self, the individual develops a relationship towards themselves and forms and transforms this self thus contributing to the aspects of stylization as well as of reflexivity.

The care of the self takes place via the techniques of the self, which have to be understood as methods of searching (Waldow 2013: 73) in an always incomplete process of the formation of the self; that is, those techniques often contribute to the individual's formation as well as to reflection on its formation and on the practices that have been forming it so far. Those practices range from tech-

---

[87] "bestimmte Form der Aufmerksamkeit, des Blicks."
[88] I am adopting this framework from Schmid (2000: 280).

niques of writing, to correspondence and conversation, to the bodily act of strolling. In the following, I shall present a selection of the techniques of the self whose analysis figures most prominently in Foucault's work in order to illustrate the various ways in which the three main characteristics of the aesthetics of existence – the form, the personal choice and the reflection on/of the form – might occur within actual practices.

3.2 The Techniques of the Self

As mentioned above, the techniques of the self can be understood as methods of searching by means of which subjects seek to transform themselves. This description already implies that the individual subject might not be able to foresee the full outcome of the application of those technologies (otherwise it might be judged a sovereign subject) but also implies that those technologies follow from the intention to transform oneself. In the definition quoted at the beginning of this chapter, Foucault points out that those technologies are supposed "to effect [...] a certain number of operations on [the individual subjects'] bodies and souls, thoughts, conduct, and way of being" and thus emphasizes the connection between thought and an extralinguistic reality that those practices shape. The techniques that he analyzes are rooted in ancient Greek dietetics and involve not only practices such as writing or conversation but also bodily activities such as gymnastics (Foucault 2000e: 99) or strolling as well as ascetic exercises through which individuals prove to themselves that they can endure situations they dread, such as poverty or famine. The body thus plays a vital part in those practices of the self and offers "sensuous modes of access to the truth" (Waldow 2013: 73; my trans.)[89] – that is, an ethos – in the practice of those techniques of the self. I will next delineate three different dimensions of Foucauldian techniques of the self, focusing on their relation to writing, truth and experience and the ways in which the 'aesthetics of existence' are implicated in each of those dimensions.

3.2.1 Writing the Self

Among the ancient techniques of the self involving practices of writing, Foucault analyzes two meditation techniques, the *hypomnêmata* – a kind of notebooks –

---

[89] "sinnliche [...] Zugangsweise zur Wahrheit."

and the correspondence with a friend, in his essay "Self Writing". The *hypomnêmata* as well as the process of writing them down constitute, according to Foucault, an important moment in the "subjectivation of discourse" (Foucault 2000d: 210). They form a preliminary stage to what Foucault terms 'ethopoietic writing' and serve the purpose of collecting individual thoughts and relevant advice. Their content consisted of "quotes [...], extracts from books, examples and actions that one had witnessed or read about, reflections or reasonings that one had heard or that had come to mind" (Foucault 2000d: 209). Yet, those contents should not "be thought of as a memory support" (Foucault 2000d: 210), but were rather supposed to serve as a basis for further exercises, meditations and "conversing with oneself and others" (Foucault 2000d: 210). They should be at the disposal of the individual in relevant situations and become "part of ourselves" (Foucault 2000d: 210). The purpose of these practices lies in the appropriation of another kind of speech, in the interaction of the writer with him- or herself as well as in the potential transformation of the self in response to a recognition of individual inadequacies. They contribute to the formation of the self especially due to the following three characteristics: "the limiting effects of the coupling of reading with writing, the regular practice of the disparate that determines choices, and the appropriation which that practice brings about" (Foucault 2000d: 211). The quote points out not only that what is appropriated is limited and ordered, but also that the recording of the rules and reflections in the *hypomnêmata* is initially rather arbitrary and results in idiosyncratic combinations, which makes it different from any kind of coherent text. The formation of the self thus also contains a moment of arbitrary combination of materials that is not tied to the discourse of a single philosopher, but becomes disseminated in the process of combination and reflection through the recipient. This reception, moreover, is not a hermeneutic act of interpretation that aims at the penetration of the meaning intended by the speaker of the sentence:

> It does not matter, says Epictetus, whether one has read all of Zeno or Chrysippus; it makes little difference whether one has grasped exactly what they meant to say, or whether one is able to reconstruct their whole argument. The notebook is governed by two principles, which one might call "the local truth of the precept" and "its circumstantial use value". (Foucault 2000d: 212)

Writing at the same time insures against what Foucault describes as the "deficiency of *stultitia*" (Foucault 2000d: 211), meaning a "state of mental agitation, distraction, change of opinion and wishes and consequently weakness in the face of all the events that may occur" (Foucault 2000d: 211–212). This kind of deficiency might be produced by "endless reading" (Foucault 2000d: 211), while the disparate appropriation of what has been read by means of writing creates a subject that is capable of acting according to the internalized writings. Foucault even mentions a "*corpus*" (Foucault 2000d: 213) that is the result of the process of writing. This corpus is "not [...] a body of doctrine" (Foucault 2000d: 213) but "the very body of the one who, by transcribing his readings, has appropriated them and made their truth his own" (Foucault 2000d: 213). Moreover, he claims that "writing transforms the thing seen and heard 'into tissue and blood' (*in vires et in sanguinem*). It becomes a principle of rational action in the writer himself" (Foucault 2000d: 213). The practice of writing therefore serves a double function. On the one hand, writing engrains regulations and fragments of discourse in the writer and therefore transforms truth into ethos. On the other hand, writing as an individual process of composition disseminates meaning and partially frees the subject from oppressive overarching structures that might otherwise be internalized. Moreover, the *hypomnêmata* exemplify the three characteristics that can be attributed to the aesthetics of existence: the fact that the subject freely chooses from texts it has encountered relates to the aspect of personal choice while the engraining of those fragments of discourse in the subject contributes to the aspect of formation, or the subject as form, and the aspect of reflexivity surfaces – among others – in the juxtaposition of different texts in individual combinations that might lead to new interpretations of those texts.

The second ancient technique that Foucault analyzes in "Self Writing" is the correspondence between friends via written letters. This technique is, on the one hand, quite similar to the *hypomnêmata* and, like those, serves the appropriation of certain principles and rules, since it influences the individual in a similar way as the *hypomnêmata* due to the effect that the act of writing has on its sender as well as the effect that "the act of reading and rereading [has] on the one who receives it (Foucault 2000d: 214). The help that one offers to another person makes it possible to practice and prepare oneself for similar situations in one's own life and thus introduces certain rules and norms into the life of the individual, contributing to the formation of the self (Foucault 2000d: 215).

At the same time, the correspondence is significantly different from the *hypomnêmata*, since it not only assists in processes of "subjectivation of true discourse, its assimilation and its transformation into a 'personal asset'" but it also constitutes an "objectification of the soul" (Foucault 2000d: 216–217), because the letter also has the function of presenting one's life to another person by exposing the writing subject to the gaze of the receiver (Foucault 2000d: 216). By means of this letter, the writer becomes directly present to the receiver, "present with a kind of immediate almost physical presence" (Foucault 2000d: 216). This presentation is strictly honest and authentic and does not aim at transmitting a specific image of oneself to the reader. Quite the contrary: Foucault claims that

> Through the missive, one opens oneself to the gaze of others and puts the correspondent in the place of the inner god. It is a way of giving ourselves to that gaze about which we must tell ourselves that it is plunging into the depths of our heart (*in pectis intimum introspicere*) at the moment we are thinking. (Foucault 2000d: 217)

Yet, this introspection does not constitute the "decipherment of the self" (Foucault 2000d: 217) – as would be the case in Christian approaches to introspection – but rather "an opening one gives the other onto oneself" (Foucault 2000d: 217) and can according to Foucault be counted among the earliest examples of descriptions of the self (Foucault 2000d: 217). The purpose of those writings was decidedly the "account of one's relation to oneself" (Foucault 2000d: 217), in which what was reported mostly comprised the "interferences of soul and body (impressions rather than actions) [...] and leisure activity (rather than external events)" (Foucault 2000d: 217), thus preferring the everyday to the extraordinary (Foucault 2000d: 217). Foucault connects this to the practice of examining one's conscience, in which the individual remembers the preceding day in order to identify potential misbehavior (Foucault 2000d: 219). The correspondence thus forms an equivalent to this examination since it exposes the writing self to the gaze of the other, in order to search one's conscience. Foucault mentions in this context that a central aspect of the correspondence consists in "bringing into congruence the gaze of the other and that gaze which one aims at oneself when one measures one's every-day actions according to the rules of a technique of living" (Foucault 2000d: 221). According to this conception of the correspondence, it is important that the friend be conceived of as an "*alter ego*" if the advice given by the writer of the letter with reference to his own life is to be useful to the receiver (Butzer 2009: 227). Thus, the correspondence is, first and foremost, a technique of the self whose primary aim is to have an effect on the self of the writer (Butzer 2009: 227).

The three main characteristics of the aesthetics of existence can therefore also be found in the correspondence: while the appropriation of rules and the examination of the coincidence of the letter writer's life with those rules suggest the formation of the subject as well as the personal choice of those rules, the aspect of examination via the act of writing constitutes an act of reflexivity, thus creating a 'reflection', an image of the self in scripture that is different – due to the process of reflection that accompanies this image – as well as similar to the self, and thus enables the subject to reflect on its own process of transformation. This concept of correspondence as a "metaphor for the self" (Schmid 2000: 310; my trans.) is highly reminiscent of poststructuralist theses on scripture like Derrida's concept of *écriture* in that it emphasizes the reflexive – and therefore metaphorical – character of writing. Both of the techniques that Foucault analyzes with regard to the writing of the self thus draw heavily on the deferring and disseminating quality of scripture, which implies that deconstruction and deferral of meaning might be two of the main instruments of reflexivity (and by extension resistance) in the techniques of the self.

However, Foucault also refers to the significance of individual others in the techniques of the self – others who can add to the reflexivity of the 'aesthetics of existence' in parrēsiastic practices of truth-speaking.

3.2.2 Reflexivity and Truth-Speaking

Indeed, scripture is not the sole source of reflexivity that Foucault mentions in his studies on the techniques of the self. Another vital part is played by personal conversations with a friend or mentor, which figure most prominently in his writings on the practice of *parrēsia*, so-called truth-speaking, that he identified as occurring on different levels in ancient Greek society.[90]

According to Foucault, truth is "a system of ordered procedures for the production, regulation, distribution, circulation, and operation of statements" (Foucault 2002b: 132). It is therefore, as Michael Ruoff argues, "the product of a discourse whose aim it is to justify certain ways as well as rules of behavior" (Ruoff 2018: 262; my trans.), and is closely linked to power itself. For Foucault, "the production of truth entails […] the construction of areas in which the practice of true and false can be regulated and valid at the same time" (Foucault 2005: 34; my trans.). Notions of truth might thus, historically speaking, range from the judgment of God to more modern-day concepts of proof, specialization, and subjects competent to speak the truth in a certain area, and thus necessarily also include norms according to which statements can be rendered false or judged to be lies.

Foucault's reflections on *parrēsia*, however, introduce a tension in his work that has its origin in the problematic paradox created between truthfulness as a value in his later writings and his earlier thesis that truth has to be understood as a mere construction. While he emphasizes the constructed character of truth and its alignment with power in his earlier writings, in his late work on the concept of *parrēsia* he stresses the importance of truthfulness as a value. Here, he assigns a much more positive value to the significance of truthfulness in political contexts as well as in processes of self-subjectification. One of the problems he was implicitly addressing in those texts can be located in the problematic conclusions that might be drawn from a constructivist approach towards truth

---

[90] Parts of this chapter have already been published in Riedelsheimer and Ries (2021).

with respect to any kind of morality. In short: the assumption that truth might be a mere construction could also foster ethical relativism.[91]

'Speaking the truth' can occur on different levels: the political level, at which an individual stands up either to tyranny or to the *demos* in democratic societies, and the personal level, at which *parrēsia* is used instrumentally in techniques of self-formation in which the truth about an individual is told to this individual by one of his or her friends or in which the individual questions him- or herself about his or her relation to the truth (see Foucault 2019: 15). In the first case, of political *parrēsia*, the subject takes up a critical position with regard to an existing truth and thus re-defines its relationship towards the truth. This practice involves reflection on present circumstances, the (trans-)formation of the self by means of the active influence that the individual exerts on existing discourses of power and the personal choice that becomes especially visible in Foucault's observation that parrēsiastic individuals might face an imminent threat of death when resisting discourses of power (Foucault 2019: 65).[92] Political *parrēsia* is then another example of the 'subjectivation of discourse' because the subject here quite literally seizes the discourse by adding its own perspective. This 'subjectivation' will influence the subject in a two-fold way: while its position within discourses of power might change due to its challenging of said power, the subject might just as well change the discourses that determine subjectivity within an existing society. In any case, the subject will be transformed by this practice. Closely related to this political *parrēsia* is the personal *parrēsia* in which the subject forms itself in relation to the truth – that is, in an active process that tries to align words and works of the subject while at the same time reflecting on this particular truth (Schmid 2000: 273). The last group of examples that Foucault mentions in his lectures on the practice of *parrēsia* consists of different types

---

91 As Thomas Flynn observes, the charge of ethical relativism was not unique to Foucault's brand of poststructuralist thought: "Foucault was facing an issue that many have regarded as the Achilles' heel of Marxism and structuralism alike: the moral implications of their theories of history and society. Do they lead to a sterile amoralism, rendering inconsistent any viable moral theory?" (Flynn 1987: 225).

92 This observation refers both to a metaphorical level on which the subject faces its death on the level of discourse, and also to what might be called an autobiographical level on which Foucault's writings on the death of the subject counteract traditional theories while at the same time accepting that this implies his own death as a subject. However, Foucault points out that this 'threat of death' might just as well refer to the actual death of this subject as is the case in the example of Plato who was facing his actual death when standing up to the tyrant of Syracuse.

of personal conversations in which a friend or mentor[93] gives advice to the subject or confronts the subject with a truth that it was not aware of until that point. The aspects of reflection and transformation figure prominently in those practices since they emphasize Foucault's general stipulation with regard to techniques of the self that they "arm the subject with a truth it did not know, one that did not reside in it" (Foucault 2000e: 102). He particularly points out that

> It was a generally accepted principle that one could not attend to oneself without the help of another. Seneca said that no one was ever strong enough on his own to get out of the state of *stultitia* he was in. "He needs someone to extend him a hand and pull him free." (Foucault 2000e: 97–98)

Most importantly, "[t]he *parrēsia* of a friend, [...] prevents the care of the self from succumbing to the flightiness and expediency of egotism" (Gros 2019: xvii) and thus does not allow the subject to remain within an entirely subjective discourse.

The subject's reflection therefore occurs not only in those practices in which the subject reflects on its form or in which a written self is produced, thereby observing themselves as an 'other', but equally in the confrontation with an actual other that makes the subject aware of a truth that it has not been cognizant of until that point. This aspect of personal *parrēsia* then mirrors political *parrēsia*: in the same way that the truth produced by discourses of power can be challenged by the subjectivation of discourse through the individual, individual truth can be challenged by the discourses of other individuals and thus contribute to the (trans-)formation of the subject.

In all the cases of *parrēsia* mentioned above, the individual puts him- or herself in a relation to the truth and therefore participates in what Foucault terms 'games of truth.' What is striking in Foucault's account of *parrēsia* is that the different variants of *parrēsia* result in a somewhat double-edged concept: whereas the subject can directly influence the games of truth, it is also subject to the truth of others and therefore granted an autonomy whose boundary can be marked by the discourse of others. Thus, a precarious balance is created between subjectivity and objectivity (or rather intersubjectivity) in productions of truth. Moreover, according to this conception, truth cannot be found out or discovered, but is created in an active process that is never quite finished. While Foucault therefore does not provide any definition of what truth actually *is* (Flynn 1987: 227), he clearly assigns a value to the concept of truthfulness in his writings on subjec-

---

[93] Nevertheless, the difference between friend and mentor already indicates the transition to the technologies of domination since the mentors might already imply a much more hierarchical relationship.

tivity and truth, proposing an alternative to the traditional Cartesian conceptions of subjectivity, one that involves truthfulness as an ethos on several levels. The notion of an absolute truth in discourse is thus discarded and replaced by truthfulness as ethos (Gros 2019: xvii) – that is, as an active performance or a habit that at the same time affirms the value of truthfulness.

The positive evaluation of truthfulness and *parrēsia* becomes particularly evident when one considers that for Foucault the whole practice of critical philosophy is rooted in the various manifestations of *parrēsia* that he describes in his lectures on this topic (see Foucault 2019: 224; Gros 2019: xix) and is emphasized in the description of the philosophical level of *parrēsia*. Foucault focuses here in particular on the philosophical *parrēsia* that is embodied in the life and words of the Cynics. For them, philosophy becomes a way of life and is to be understood as a "visible performance of truth" (Schmid 2000: 276; my trans.). The questioning of norms is directly translated into the individual life and thus forms a 'style of existence'. While the famous example of Diogenes living in a barrel reduces life to its bare essentials and thus questions societal norms of what could be considered life's necessities, Foucault also mentions examples that are strikingly reminiscent of contemporary political performance art, such as an instance in which Diogenes presents a horse with a laurel wreath during the Olympics for a fight it has won against another horse, thus questioning the norms according to which athletes are awarded a prize after winning a competition (see Foucault 2019: 171). Yet, the focus of the Cynics does not reside in introducing any new kind of morality or norm but only in problematizing already existing norms and thus sparking discussion on their possible transformation. It is in this sense that Foucault's thought can likewise be described as a kind of *parrēsia* or an aesthetics of existence that constantly questions existing truths and focuses on the possibility of thinking 'differently', thus aiming at a constant transformation of itself (Schmid 2000: 276). One of the most striking examples might be the re-birth of the subject in his late work that can be seen as a continuation of his previous work yet at the same time shows his thought undergoing a transformation from an emphasis on the technologies of domination to an emphasis on the technologies of the self.

This process is also described by Foucault in terms of actual 'experience', which constitutes the third dimension of the 'aesthetics of existence'.

3.3 The Subject of Experience

The aspect of transformation looms particularly large in the concept of experience that Foucault describes in his conversation with Duccio Trombadori. According to Foucault,

> in the course of their history, men had never ceased constructing themselves, that is to shift continuously the level of their subjectivity, to constitute themselves, in an infinite and multiple series of different subjectivities that would never reach an end and would never place us in the presence of something that would be "man." Man is an animal of experience, he is involved *ad infinitum* within a process that, by defining a field of objects, at the same time changes him, deforms him and transfigures him as a subject. (Foucault 1991: 123–124)

The quote suggests a direct link between the processual, variable quality of the subject and the concept of experience. Mankind is subject to constant change and a human can therefore be described as an animal of experience, that is, on the one hand an object that is constituted by the discourses to which it is subjected and at the same time continuously transformed by a process which it enters partly intentionally, as seems to be suggested by the phrase "men had never ceased constructing themselves". This process occurs whenever the subject places itself in relation with itself.

Furthermore, Foucault adds that experience is "neither true nor false: it is always a fiction, something constructed, which exists only after it has been made, not before; it isn't something that is 'true,' but it has been a reality" (Foucault 1991: 36). Although "[a]n experience is [...] something one has alone", it cannot "have its full impact unless the individual manages to escape from pure subjectivity" (Foucault 1991: 40) and it "must be linkable, to a certain extent, to a collective practice and to a way of thinking" (Foucault 1991: 39). As Anke Haarmann points out, this experience can hardly be considered to be outside the realm of power (1995: 105). Fittingly, in his introduction to *The Use of Pleasure*, Foucault defines experience as "the correlation between fields of knowledge, types of normativity, and forms of subjectivity in a particular culture" (Foucault 1992: 4). Here, 'experience' describes the nexus between those three aspects and is the prerequisite for recognizing oneself as a subject (Foucault 1992: 4) and thus the condition for any kind of formation of the subject (Waldow 2013: 76).

The underlying tension in this term is further emphasized by the fact that Foucault refers to what Haarmann calls 'disciplinary experience' in *Madness and Civilization*. There, experience is also that which preconditions our perspective onto the real and thus influences our perception of the real world; 'experience' therefore becomes a term that oscillates between subjection to power and potential transformation (Haarmann 1995: 105). While Foucault refers to his project as "an analysis of the 'games of truth,'" the games of truth and error through which being is historically constituted as experience" (Foucault 1992: 6–7), implying that being is turned into experience by discourses of power, experience might just as well become the gateway through which prediscursive being influences discourses. Moreover, by actively entering processes of self-constitution, the individual might also partake in the constant transformation of subjectivity by affirming a processual form of subjectivity.

Among the experiences that Foucault names, two different types seem to be predominant: textual experiences and political experiences in which the subject is transformed through witnessing political events. The textual experiences Foucault describes come about through practices of writing and reading, so that reading or writing a book can result in a transformative experience for the individual (see Foucault 1991: 41–42). The political experiences derive from one's interaction with an extralinguistic reality. Here, Foucault refers to his immediate experience of student revolts in Tunisia in May 1968, which he describes as a "true political experience" (1991: 134). In both cases, knowledge formation and ideology still play a role, but they are checked by reflection as well as deferral. In the case of the Tunisian upheavals, Foucault points out that they were loosely based on Marxist philosophy, but that the protesters did not aim at any profound exegesis of Marx's works, so the revolts entailed a deferral of his ideology. In his works, Foucault therefore reflects on historically verifiable data from a different vantage point and thus engages in a transformative experience.

The term 'experience' therefore shares its ambivalence with the term 'subject' in Foucault's work and likewise gains a double-edged quality that envisages the possibility of subjection as well as resistance/transformation. As Haarmann (1995: 105) notes, Foucault seems to repeatedly defer his definition of experience by implying another kind of experience, one belonging to the partly autonomous subject that serves as a valuable alternative to the Cartesian subject. Yet, it is precisely this deferral that blurs the border between autonomy and subjection as well as between discursive experience and prediscursive being or counter-discursive subjectivity and leaves open the question as to when the technologies of the self become too much infiltrated by technologies of domination. This tension becomes especially evident if we juxtapose the following two quotes:

> People do revolt; that is a fact. And that is how subjectivity (not that of great men, but that of anyone) is brought into history, breathing life into it. A convict risks his life to protest unjust punishments; a madman can no longer bear being confined and humiliated; a people refuses the regime that oppresses it. That doesn't make the first innocent, doesn't cure the second, and doesn't ensure for the second the tomorrow it was promised. Moreover, no one is obliged to support them. No one is obliged to find that these confused voices sing

better than the others and speak the truth itself. It is enough that they exist and that they have against them everything that is dead set on shutting them up for there to be a sense in listening to them and in seeing what they mean to say. A question of ethics? Perhaps. A question of reality, without a doubt. All the disenchantments of history won't alter the fact of the matter: it is because there are such voices that the time of human beings does not have the form of evolution but that of history, precisely. (Foucault 2002a: 452)

There is an irony in those efforts one makes to alter one's way of looking at things, to change the boundaries of what one knows and to venture out a ways from there. Did mine actually result in a different way of thinking? Perhaps at most they made it possible to go through what I was actually thinking, to think it differently, and to see what I had done from a new vantage point and in a clearer light. Sure of having travelled far, one finds that one is looking down on oneself from above. The journey rejuvenates things, and ages the relationship with oneself. I seem to have gained a better perspective on the way I worked – gropingly, and by means of different or successive fragments– on this project, whose goal is a history of the truth. (Foucault 1992: 11)

The first quote, an excerpt from Foucault's essay "Useless to Revolt?", emphasizes what he called "pure subjectivity", the individual experience that still infiltrates the technologies of domination, no matter how massive their impact. The second one, by contrast, taken from the introduction to *The Use of Pleasure*, highlights the continuities between Foucault's earlier works and his study of forms of subjectivity. It not only shows that Foucault here continues his practice of seeing something from "a new vantage point", but also that the 'reality' he describes has remained the same and that what he describes does in fact coherently follow from his analysis of discourses of power and, what is more, does not assume that the subjectivity he describes here is entirely free from subjection.

This tension resurfaces in the practices and concepts described above. Thus, the aesthetics of existence feature techniques of formation which are then checked by active attempts at reflection and transformation – apart from the fact that the aspect of transformation is already implicit in the act of formation. The *hypomnêmata* aim at instilling given principles in the subject, yet combine this aim with the freedom of choice and the potentially disseminating quality of *écriture*. Foucault's reflections on the genealogy of *parrēsia*, in turn, create a balance between truthful statements and the truthfulness of a critique based on performances that are in themselves fictitious, and his remarks on experience locate the concept in between a resistant subjectivity and the dynamics of power.

Hence, the ethics of the self occupy an ambivalent position within Foucault's oeuvre. They cannot be entirely separated from the technologies of domination, yet a closer look at this form of subjectivity which offers an alternative to the Cartesian subject might reveal ways of not being governed 'quite so much'. If each form of subjectivity plays a part in the correlation between epistemes, power and the subject, then a different form of subjectivity will influence this correlation and create new experiences. In this context, *The Use of Pleasure*, in particular, is entirely self-referential. The text describes the transformation of the ethics of the self into the hermeneutics of the subject and in so doing brings into focus the mutability of subjectivity; analogously, the 'aesthetics of existence' are based on the possibility of the (trans-)formation of the subject. Therefore, the ethics of the self in Greek and Roman antiquity can offer an example of alternative subjectivities, but they have to be adapted to the twenty-first century. The text itself is likewise a technique of the self because according to Foucault, writing this text – or any of his other texts – transformed his self (Foucault 1991: 38), and here he implicitly also refers to the transformation of conceptions of subjectivity that the text actively creates by bringing them into focus. Moreover, it brings the self into a relationship with itself by focusing on modes of subjectivity. Thus, a deferral is created in Foucault's work as a whole that starts from the subjection of the subject and moves towards the resistance of the subject. *The Use of Pleasure* then represents Foucault's own transformation and offers this transformation to its readers. The techniques of the self he describes can on this basis become a collection of tools which are not subject to the sovereignty of the author but can be re-interpreted and related to political agendas by the readers: "If people want to open them and use this or that sentence, this or that idea or analysis as a screwdriver to short-circuit, dismantle or blow up systems of power, maybe including those systems of power from which my books orginated – well, all the better" (Foucault 1976: 53; my trans.).[94]

The textual analyses that I undertake in this book focus on the abovementioned characteristics of the ethics of the self and consider the literary texts to be examples of a possible interpretation of the Foucauldian ethics of the self. Those examples bring palpability to the concept by transferring it to the concrete materiality of the city and relating it to political discourses while at the same time reflecting on the possibilities of resistance within those discourses. Flânerie then concentrates different activities into a bundle of intersecting techniques of the self that allow for the formation of and the reflection on a new ethical subject that resurfaces in their textualization.

Nevertheless, I also hold that the flânerie texts I analyze contribute to a sedimentation of the recognition of the human condition of precariousness and relationality which – although implied in Foucault's writings – is only explicitly

---

[94] "Wenn die Leute sie aufmachen wollen und diesen oder jenen Satz, diese oder jene Idee oder Analyse als Schraubenzieher verwenden, um die Machtsysteme kurzzuschließen, zu demontieren oder zu sprengen, einschließlich vielleicht derjenigen Machtsysteme, aus denen diese meine Bücher hervorgegangen sind – nun, umso besser."

named and conceptualized in the work of Judith Butler. Butler further systematizes and expands on the Foucauldian notion of the subject by crystallizing it into the concept of performance – with all of the ambivalences that the term entails – and rooting it more firmly in processes of signification. Especially in their late work Butler focuses on the negotiation of the ethical implications of this view of subjectivity which ultimately result in a call for the development of an "egalitarian imaginary" (Butler 2020: 28). I will therefore turn next to an overview of Butler's interpretation of Foucault and the concept of the precarious.

4 Judith Butler's Precarious Subjects

Like Foucault's, Butler's writings can be located in the field of critical philosophy and are therefore just as much "condemned to dispersion, dependency and pure heteronomy" (Foucault 2003a: 263). What is more, they directly respond to the societal conditions from which they emerge and are therefore continually updated in the course of Butler's work, precisely because they engage with a constantly changing social environment (see also Redecker 2011: 15). For my analysis, I will employ several aspects of Butler's conceptualizations of subjecthood that occur at different stages within their work and have proven to be central to their concept of subjectivity; among these, I shall focus especially on issues of the materialization of discourse, the melancholia of the subject, resistance as a form of 'promiscuous obedience', the overall precariousness of the subject and the creation of a post-sovereign subjectivity.

4.1 Discourse and Materialization

An early adaptation of Foucault's theses on a non-essentialist conception of the subject can already be found in Butler's seminal work *Gender Trouble: Feminism and the Subversion of Identity* (1990). Here, Butler argues that gender only materializes by means of a constantly repeated categorization within a matrix of intelligibility that consists of societal norms and thus lacks any ontological basis. This classification of human beings into the categories of 'man' or 'woman' occurs, on the one hand, by means of speech acts – such as the declaration "It is a boy!" or "It is a girl!" after the birth of a child – which effectively influence the body through a framework of norms that correlates with the matrix of intelligibility and is validated by it. On the other hand, the classification takes place by means of speech acts and performances in which the subject repeats those norms in a citational manner. Gender is thus, according to Butler, always already an "effect of discursive practices" (Butler 1999: 24). One consequence of this is that the distinction between 'sex' and 'gender' which is often used in feminist theory becomes invalid, since Butler basically dissolves 'sex' into 'gender' (Bublitz 2010: 107).

Butler's theses concerning the discursive materialization of bodies are based, first and foremost, on their definition of performativity, which derives from John L. Austin's speech act theory as introduced in his lecture published under the title *How to Do Things with Words*. Performative speech acts are, according to Austin, those instances of speech that enact what they name. Those kinds of enunciation do not describe an extralinguistic reality but perform an action. For this action to be performed successfully, the speech act has to correspond with certain conventions. Those conventions are of a societal nature and are determined by the society within which they are valid. An exemplary case of this kind of speech act could be found in conventional marriage ceremonies during which a priest or justice of the peace performs the act of joining two people in marriage by means of the words "I hereby declare you husband and wife!" The success of this action then always depends on the obedience to the corresponding conventions, yet by creating what it names, language actively participates in the creation of an extralinguistic reality. Consequently, Butler refers to those speech acts as "'dramatic' and 'non-referential'" (Butler 1997a: 404). While the description of such speech acts as 'non-referential' relates to the points mentioned above, the adjective 'dramatic' adds the idea of a theatrical performance to the concept. This aspect then implies not only the deliberate deception of the 'as-if' but also a connection to the performance of theatrical or ritualistic actions – and thus to actions that are designed in order to be repeated.

The description, moreover, entails the possibility of the embodiment of language as well as the symbolic quality that the body can acquire so that performance can be understood as the embodied manifestation of performative speech acts (Bublitz 2010: 23). Those speech acts are, according to Butler, preceded by a "matrix of power" (Butler 1993: 83) that assigns a (variable) signified to those utterances and thus divides society up into different 'normal' or 'abnormal' roles and therefore into what Butler calls 'livable' and 'non-livable' lives.

Performativity then only creates the effect of materiality, which originates from the repeated citation of norms. In contrast to Austin's concept, Butler's performances do not constitute single and intentional acts, but rather a "reiterative and citational practice, by which discourse produces the effects it names" (Butler 1993: 2). Performativity then disguises the historicity of an action as well as its relationship to conventions, which it actually repeats (Bublitz 2010: 24). Butler refers to this process as 'materialization' and thus emphasizes the inseparable connection between discourse and matter. For Butler, there is no such thing as prediscursive matter. Matter is only constituted at the same time as discourse. Discourse then organizes things and thus assigns them the "status of the real" (Bublitz 2010: 24; my trans.). Like knowledge, truth is then just an effect of discourse. As problematic as this might sound in the light of twenty-first-century discourses about fake news and so-called post-factuality, it needs to be seen in the context of the Foucauldian approaches towards truth mentioned in chapter 3. Like Foucault, Butler does not imply that everything is equally 'untrue' if seen from a different perspective but rather emphasizes that truth uncontaminated by the influence of power-laden discourses cannot be obtained. Whenever we examine matter in order to obtain any kind of truth about it, our truth will already be influenced by the discourses that shape our perception of matter. Moreover, Butler's theses focus on the realm of the social and the kind of 'absolute' truths that might be taken for granted within this sphere such as gender-specific attributes and the conclusions that might be drawn from these attributes, thus deliberately taking a political stance against gender essentialisms. Those theses then tie in with Foucault's aversion to any definition of 'the human' and primarily serve the function of securing humans in general against normalizing definitions that force them into anything that might be considered their 'natural' behavior.

4.2 Sovereign Melancholia and Resistance as "Promiscuous Obedience"

Based on these theses, Butler then develops their theory of subjectivity, which they elaborate in detail in their 1997 work *The Psychic Life of Power: Theories in Subjection*. In this text, Butler aims at delineating the effects of discourse within the psyche of the subject and at proving them to be primarily structured through power. Drawing on Foucault, they conceive of the subject not just as being subjected to the workings of discourse and thus degraded by it, but even more as being produced by it in the first place. It is only the power of discourse that creates the subject since the formation of the subject is always already tied to the individual's social existence and thus to the matrix of power that manifests itself as a matrix of intelligibility. The idea that results from this thesis is paradoxical: the subject is already subjected at the moment of its creation since it is only produced through discourse; at the same time, the subject turns against power as an effect of power itself due to a reflexive 'revolt', a 'turning around' in the original sense of the word, of the subject. Butler agrees here with Foucault who would see the freedom of the subject as itself also an effect of power and would understand the resistance of the subject first and foremost as part of a game of power (see also Bublitz 2010: 81). According to Butler, "resistance [then] appears as the effect of power, as a part of power, its self-subversion" (Butler 1997b: 93). Since power can, just like the language by means of which it is executed, be deferred, the formation of subjects who look at themselves reflexively and can thus form themselves influences the performative formation of power and becomes resistance. In this situation, the subject can influence discourses of power, but cannot control this influence due to the decentralized structure of discourse itself. This concept of resistance is strongly reminiscent of Foucault's ethical subject. Just as in Foucault's conception of sub-

4.2 Sovereign Melancholia and Resistance as "Promiscuous Obedience" —— 91

jectivity, Butler's subjects form themselves and can choose this form from the options discourse offers. In the process, subjects reflectively turn towards themselves and thus become nodes of resistance. Nevertheless, the resistance of the Foucauldian subject seems to be based on a more intentional act of reflection and choice than that of Butler's subjects, which instead have resistance ingrained into their very existence. While both Foucault and Butler assume that there are subjects who are 'more' and subjects who are 'less' resistant,[95] for Butler resistance seems to be a quality that to some extent adheres to every subject.

In their concept of subjectivity, then, Butler focuses first on the links between the psyche and the social sphere, since the realm of the psyche is for them an effect of power as well, and thus formed by social norms. What they want to show is the primary bond between subject and power and the psychic form that the subject takes in the process.

Drawing on the work of Louis Althusser, Butler refers to the concept of the 'appeal' which is made by the sovereign power of the state and to which the subject reacts by 'turning around'. Butler then argues against this idea that the subject is always already subjected to the power of the state and thus does not just accept this power in its moment of turning around since it is only inaugurated by that very same power (which is in Butler's case discourse itself). Althusser's concept, by contrast, would assume that the subject as well as the conscience of the subject already exist prior to the appeal of the power of the state. Moreover, Butler follows the Foucauldian concept of power in which power in modern societies is not articulated by means of the centralized power of a sovereign, but consists of a complex constellation of forces whose origin is finally uncertain (see also Bublitz 2010: 86–87). Hence, subjects cannot free themselves from the discursive power that produces them and resistance is only possible within the workings of power.

Subjects are then formed in the repeated, reflexive turn towards themselves that ties them at the same time to their subjection and determines the idea of the 'turn' as the central element of their constitution. The psychic institution of a subject's conscience then only originates from this foundational moment as a representative of power within the psyche of the subject which forces subjects to reflect on themselves. The original turn is only recognizable as a trace within

---

[95] Although the constant deferral of the boundary between those who are more and those who are less resistant implies that this distinction is not as clear-cut as the shift effected from Foucault's earlier to his later writings might suggest, the emphasis that he places on the techniques of the self as a starting point for new conceptualizations of subjectivity in the twentieth and twenty-first centuries also implies that his ethical subject is actually 'more' resistant – and therefore desirable to develop – than the traditional Cartesian one.

the subject. The psyche then becomes the institution within the subject that controls it and that subjects the body to the requirements of society and forms it accordingly. Yet, the body itself is not prior to the psyche, but is only brought into being – that is into social existence – as a "powerladen schema" (Butler 1997b: 90) through the psyche.

The subjection to the norm remains hidden from the consciousness of the subject in this. The unconscious itself is then just as much an effect of that power; it cannot be understood as an antagonist to it. Butler explains this process by referring to melancholia as defined by Sigmund Freud in his essay on "Mourning and Melancholia"[96] and thus traces the power-laden form of the unconscious. According to Butler, the subject coalesces into a sedimentation of relationships that are supposed to substitute for lost relationships of desire. This "sedimentation of relations of substitution over time" (Butler 1997b: 169) becomes the being of the self. The loss of those options or modes of desire that are excluded through the workings of discourse and power is relegated to the realm of the repressed. As lost desires, they are moved to the prediscursive unconscious and thus cannot be articulated (Butler 1997b: 170). At the same time, they are melancholically – that is, as threats of dissolution – integrated into the subjects who unconsciously establish relationships of substitution in order to satisfy themselves as well as the discourse that grants their existence. "Melancholia", according to Butler,

> rifts the subject, marking a limit to what it can accommodate. Because the subject does not, cannot, *reflect* on that loss, that loss marks the limit of reflexivity, that which exceeds (and conditions) its circuitry. Understood as foreclosure, that loss inaugurates the subject and threatens it with dissolution. (Butler 1997b: 23)

Yet, melancholia also concerns the original loss of sovereignty that the subject undergoes in the process of subjection (Redecker 2011: 97). Here, subjects deny precisely their subjection as ungrievable loss of their own sovereignty. In affirming their own sovereignty, they re-perform the original loss and divide themselves by forming themselves. It is from this formation, which only ever

---

[96] Freud defines melancholia as a deviant form of mourning, in which the subject does not work through a loss but denies it. In order to keep up with this denial, the ego internalizes the lost object and identifies with it. Yet, the attitude towards the lost object – which has now become a part of the self – turns out to be ambivalent. Reproaches towards the lost relationship are integrated into the self and create an ambivalence within the subject (see Freud 1969: 427–446).

manifests as an obedience to discourses of power, that the resistance of the subject derives.

Nevertheless, Butler also deviates from the Freudian concept of melancholia by pointing out that in the stages following this first loss of sovereignty in their conception of subjectivity no melancholic identification with the lost object – as Freud postulates it – occurs. The object rather becomes the vehicle of an oppositional and distinguishing identification (Redecker 2011: 99). Moreover, the discourse of power is not translated evenly into the subject. Thus, the social and psychic manifestations of power are not identical since power passes through several spirals of repetition due to its incorporation into the subject and is thus split and transformed (see also Redecker 2011: 99). During this process, options of false appropriation and decontextualization of norms are created within the subject: "If conditions of power are to persist, they must be reiterated; the subject is precisely the site of such reiteration, a repetition that is never merely mechanical" (Butler 1997b: 16). Alongside the performativity of subjects and thus their turn towards language, is created the resistance of the subject, which is the condition of the subject's primary alienation within the realm of the social (Bublitz 2010: 92). Since errors of translation might – or must – occur in the subject's reflexive turn towards power and can thus enter discourse through processes of subject formation, the subject can be called resistant. Butler thus seems to put special emphasis on the possibility of unintentional resistance which basically derives from a deferral of norms in processes of subjection.

Those theses are taken up again in Butler's meditations on the possibility of protest in their work *Antigone's Claim: Kinship Between Life & Death*, which was published in 2000. Options for protest reside, according to Butler, in what they call a "[p]romiscuous [o]bedience" (Butler 2000: 57) in which the subject obeys norms ambiguously and thus creates options of destabilization and deconstruction of those norms. Protest then occurs alongside subjection, which then again cannot be circumvented due to its constitutional function with regard to the subject. It is precisely through the performative repetition of norms that space for difference is created, which in turn makes the constructed character of the norm visible by means of its deconstruction. The autonomy that the subject might obtain within this concept thus remains restricted. At the same time, subjects are not subjected to norms in any mechanical or foreseeable way since difference is always already inherent to repetition.

Yet, protest does not remain without consequences for the subject and ends, in the case of Antigone which Butler analyzes in *Antigone's Claim*, with the resistant subject's death. This is also where Butler's critique as well as their political agenda – which is here not concerned with the psychic structure of the individual, but with the norms that form the precondition for Antigone's death – are located (see also Redecker 2011: 107). Butler emphasizes that Antigone's death can be directly deduced from those norms which on the one hand are the precondition for her existence as a subject, but which on the other hand assign a life to her that is unlivable due to the fact that she originated from incest, and thus predetermine her death:

> Her fate is not to have a life to live, to be condemned to death prior to any possibility of life. [...] Is it perhaps the unlivable desire with which she lives, incest itself, that makes of her life a living death, that has no place within the terms that confer intelligibility on life? (Butler 2000: 23)

The desire that Butler refers to here seems to have two signifieds. On the one hand, there is Antigone's own desire which, according to Butler, is based on her desire for her brother Polyneices. On the other hand, the "unlivable desire with which [Antigone] lives" seems to consist of the incestuous desire of which Antigone is the product as daughter of Oedipus and Jocasta and which assigned this unlivable position to her. Antigone is not aware of the loss of her desire since it has been relegated in terms of repression to the prediscursive unconscious and can thus not be articulated linguistically. Antigone herself as well as her desire remain 'unintelligible' and thus 'unlivable'. Her life is thus also determined to be 'unlivable' and she is doomed to death.

4.3 Precarious Subjects

In their later works, Butler turns towards ethical questions and moves from the concept of the melancholic subject towards an ontological 'fiction' of precariousness and the concept of post-sovereign subjectivity associated with it.[97] They approach this concept, first of all, by drawing on the significance of the experience of mourning for the subject and the idea of the primary dependence of the subject on an other, whose loss would be responsible for the experience of mourning. This loss is accompanied by uncertainty and disorientation so that mourning causes a process of transformation the result of which remains opaque to the subject and thus causes a feeling of uncertainty:

> Perhaps, rather, one mourns when one accepts that by the loss one undergoes one will be changed, possibly for ever. Perhaps mourning has to do with agreeing to undergo a trans-

---

[97] In this, Butler's deferral of forms of subjectivity performs the constant transformation of subjectivity that Foucault sees as essential in the ethics of the self.

formation (perhaps one should say *submitting* to a transformation) the full result of which one cannot know in advance. (Butler 2004: 21; original emphasis)

This conscious act of "submitting to a transformation" is according to Butler an attitude that is constitutive of the concept of ethical subjectivity that they develop. In the attachment of the subject to an other, the primary vulnerability – what Butler calls 'precariousness' – of the subject manifests itself as *conditio humana*. Only a 'post-sovereign' subjectivity which does not remain trapped in the affirmation and performance of its own sovereignty is capable of exercising different options for the construction of identity and can thus open those options for others whom the subject constitutes as well. Thus, the subject gains options of freedom and becomes – like the Foucauldian ethical subject – resistant to discourses of power.

Additionally, Butler links their observations on the discursive formation of identity to the confrontation with individual people and thus frees them from their rigid anchoring in the melancholic primal scene. In *Undoing Gender* (2004) they argue that subjects continuously disseminate and transform their identity in the encounter with individual others or rather that this identity is transformed by others. Here, Butler links the thesis that self-knowledge can only be gained by referring to a norm that has been made by others and that is only represented through others with the process of transference in which the individual re-creates its own story by means of a projection of earlier encounters onto the present other. Thus, the already existing identity of the individual can be constantly disseminated by means of the alterity of every other:

> We might see this as the confession at the core of psychoanalytic practice: the fact that we always show something more or different than what we mean, and that we hand this unknowing part of ourselves to another to return to us in ways that we cannot anticipate in advance. […] Moreover, the self in its priority is not being discovered at such a moment, but becoming elaborated, through speaking, in a new way, in the course of conversation. In these scenes of speech, both interlocutors find that what they say is to some extent beyond their control but not, for that reason, out of control. If saying is a form of doing, and part of what is getting done is the self, then conversation is a mode of doing something together and becoming otherwise; something will be accomplished in the course of this exchange, but no one will know what or who is being made until it is done. (Butler 2004a: 173)

Butler calls the subject that results from this conception "ecstatic" (Butler 2004a: 20) since it is located outside itself. What is noteworthy in this context, is that especially sexuality and gender, which might be considered to be elements that are the most 'proper' to the self, become vehicles for transformation and thus constitute "*modes of being dispossessed*" (Butler 2004a: 19; original emphasis; see also Redecker 2011: 122). This 'dispossession' is evaluated positively by Butler when they state that it is precisely this sociality which forms the basis for "a field of ethical enmeshment with others" (Butler 2004a: 25) and emphasize that this situation is always more desirable for the subject than isolation which would be the price that the subject would have to pay in order to gain the absolute security of the sovereign subject.

Butler further elaborates on this concept in their 2005 text *Giving an Account of Oneself* by focusing on the scene of appellation as a model for the primary dependency of the subject on an other and the integration of the other into the subject resulting from it. Here, Butler initially emphasizes the narrativity of the self which manifests itself in the event of dialogic exchange and stresses the analogy to processes of self-justification – of *Giving an Account of Oneself* – which is central to this narrativity. This justification already takes many normative expectations into account and is consciously as well as unconsciously structured. Nevertheless, the actual 'life' of the subject can never be reduced to this representation, but can only ever be understood as that which supersedes every attempt at explanation (Butler 2005: 43). Subjectivity is thus marked by a state of non-representable exposition (Butler 2005: 39) which can be understood as prediscursive due to its 'non-representability'. In this, Butler creates a deferral with respect to the model that they created in *The Psychic Life of Power*, in which they linked the production of the subject much more directly to the norm and the incorporation of the law (Butler 2005: 15). By now deferring the mediation of the norm to the plurality of scenes of appellation, Butler also transfers the reference of the primary melancholia of the subject – and thus of its primary subjection – to other subjects to which this subject is attached, while only the subsequent turns of the subject are directed towards discourses of power. Here, Butler adheres to a discontinuity between norms and the actual other which contains the potential to question the norm by means of continuous desires of recognition:

> If and when, in an effort to confer or to receive a recognition that fails again and again, I call into question the normative horizon within which recognition takes place, this questioning is part of the desire for recognition, a desire that can find no satisfaction, and whose unsatisfiability establishes a critical point of departure for the interrogation of available norms. (Butler 2005: 24)

Thus, the subject is primarily constituted through the other and is forced to refer to discourses as well as the norms that are transmitted by those discourses as the medium of his or her recognition. Yet, it is because the attachment of the subject to others precedes those discourses that resistance becomes possible in the first place and can thus result in an outcome different from the case of Antigone. In this context, Butler also refers to the work of Emmanuel Levinas and his concept of the 'face' of the other which confronts us with an unconditional and inescapable ethical demand to respond. In contrast to Levinas, Butler points out that even the face of the other is always already discursively mediated and thus cannot be entirely extraneous to discourse, although they also assume a certain excess of mutual attachment beyond discursive influence. Similar to Levinas, Butler employs the term 'responsiveness' which is opposed to a term like 'responsibility' and is supposed to refer to a responsibility beyond justification, since anything that is located in the realm of justification would imply the accountability of the subject.[98]

In their essay collection *Precarious Life: The Powers of Mourning and Violence* (2004), Butler coins the term 'precarious life' in the context of 9/11 and its aftermath and thus refers to life as primarily endangered and vulnerable. Here, the term 'precariousness' first and foremost emphasizes the danger of dehumanization as an inevitable framework of war. Alongside their discussion of the subject's primary dependence on the other, the concept of precarious life then already implies a moral and ethical request. In this context, Butler explicitly draws on Foucauldian theses on the formation of ethical subjects and the concept of an 'aesthetics of existence'. According to Butler, post-sovereign subjects form themselves with reference to a certain number of codes, rules and norms and can thus also develop a critical attitude towards norms present within a society (Butler 2005: 16–17). Subjectivation then does not just consist of a subjection to a certain norm, but rather surfaces as a reference to that norm which can just as well result in a denial of said norm:

> The injunction compels the act of self-making or self-crafting, which means that it does not act unilaterally or deterministically upon the subject. It sets the stage for the subject's self-crafting, which always takes place in relation to an imposed set of norms. The norm does not produce the subject as its necessary effect, nor is the subject fully free to disregard the norm that inaugurates its reflexivity; one invariably struggles with conditions of one's own life that one could not have chosen. If there is an operation of agency or, indeed, freedom in this struggle, it takes place in the context of an enabling and limiting field of constraint. (Butler 2005: 18–19)

The freedom of subjects is thus on the one hand limited by the norms to which they need to refer in order to be intelligible to those who constitute the subject through their own responsiveness. On the other hand, the freedom of subjects is secured by means of a process of selection which does not demand the subjec-

---

[98] See also Levinas (2005: 305) who describes responsiveness as a "response without a question". See for entire paragraph also Redecker (2011: 129).

tion of the subject to the norm in any univocal way: discourse delineates what constitutes the framework of what can be 'said', that is, performed by the subject, yet within this framework subjects can form themselves according to their own wishes (Bublitz 2010: 102). Thus, the precarious is according to Butler the ontological[99] basis of the subject and determines the responsiveness of the subject, which precedes the subject's formation through discourse and functions as the condition for the necessity of subjects to make themselves understood by others. Discursive norms and moral guidelines are always only subordinate to this primary dependence of the subject and need to be adjusted to it; the opportunity to do so is given to subjects through their freedom to assume a specific attitude towards those norms. What is more, Butler even distributes the process of the recognition of the subject into different encounters and thus enables the subject to constantly re-perform this relation of recognition in the encounter with several, different others.

What can then be considered to be problematic and potentially violent is according to Butler the "melancholic background [of our] social world, if not [our] First-Worldism" (Butler 2004b: 46), by means of which the limits of what could be called 'human' are determined. Drawing on the experience of mourning, Butler coins the term 'ungrievable lives', which refers to those lives that are not included in the norm that constitutes what can be considered to be 'human' and thus can or cannot be mourned.[100] Consequently, and necessarily, one way to protect the lives of others can thus be found in the resistance to norms and discourses as well as in making visible what constitutes the framework within which what is 'human' is defined, as Butler explains in their 2009 text *Frames of War* in relation to the publication of the Abu Ghraib pictures (Butler 2009: 78). Moreover, the primary dependence on the other requires that one be attentive to this relationship by responding to the other in a non-violent way. On the one hand, Butler thus once again engages critically with the effects of social norms and demands foregoing the assumption that one can have understood an other entirely, since doing so would transmit norms that would force an un-

---

99 The term 'ontology', however, is rather problematic in this context since Butler repeatedly points out that their thesis on the primary dependency of the subject is supposed to form a "counter-fantasy" (2020: 44) and a "different story" (2020: 40) with respect to the primary conditions of human beings. Thus, Butler explicitly distances themself from the authority of ontological concepts.

100 As examples of those 'ungrievable lives' Butler names homosexuals dying of AIDS in the 1980s, who had been excluded from the discursive norm due to their sexual orientation, as well as the deaths of Palestinians or Iraqis caused by the war on Iraq or the conflicts in the Middle East.

attainable yardstick onto the self-formation of the other (Redecker 2011: 131). In an even more general way, Butler assumes that every subject of whom moral sovereignty is requested, falls prey to 'ethical violence' since this kind of request of complete accountability supersedes the options of the non-sovereign subject.

> My account of myself is partial, haunted by that for which I can devise no definitive story. I cannot explain exactly why I have emerged in this way, and my efforts at narrative reconstruction are always undergoing revision. There is that in me and of me for which I can give no account. (Butler 2005: 40)

In this sense, any totalizing definition of the other would exert violence since it would damage the subject's self-formation which is non-sovereign and in a process of constant revision. For the same reasons, Butler judges even moderately critical judgement to be problematic since it assigns something to the other which does not deserve to be recognized and separates others from themselves as if this quality could only ever pertain to the other and never to oneself (Redecker 2011: 131). In terms of possible solutions, Butler does not recommend refraining from judging others entirely, but to take the "rhetorical condition" (Butler 2005: 50) in every moral situation into account and to refer to it by formulating any kind of recognition as an open question instead of a definitive allocation (Butler 2005: 43). In doing so, one recognizes "the limits of acknowledgment itself" (Butler 2005: 42) according to Butler, and in terms of ethics this recognition needs to be unattainable in itself so that it causes an infinite process of recognition which centers on the desire for recognition instead of its granting:

> So if there is, in the question, a desire for recognition, this desire will be under an obligation to keep itself alive as desire and not to resolve itself. "Oh, now I know who you are": at this moment, I cease to address you, or to be addressed by you. (Butler 2005: 43)

The open question allows for an infinite continuation of the process of recognition and represents recognition as an incomplete process, thus taking the primary dependence of the subject on an other into account.

Furthermore, Butler points out that even if the subject falls victim to violence the primary dependence of the subject needs to be considered. Any kind of redemptive action, by contrast, aims at the restoration of one's own sovereignty which has been lost due to the violent action of the other and thus denies the subject's own primary vulnerability (Redecker 2011: 133). Consequently, Butler argues, with regard to the United States' 'war on terror':

> In recent months, a subject has been instated at the national level, a sovereign and extra-legal subject, a violent and self-centered subject; its actions constitute the building of a

> subject that seeks to restore and maintain its mastery through the systematic destruction of its multi-lateral relations, its ties to the international community. It shores itself up, seeks to reconstitute its imagined wholeness, but only at the price of denying its own vulnerability, its dependency, its exposure, where it exploits those very features in others, thereby making those features "other to" itself. (Butler 2004b: 41)

The precariousness of the subject, its non-sovereignty, is turned into the 'uncanny' *sensu* Freud, a repressed part of the self which has to be met with aggression in order for it to remain repressed. This uncanny part which is actually a part of the subject itself is thus relegated to the identity of the other by means of a counter-attack to maintain the sovereign identity of the subject. Sovereignty can in this case only be emphasized by exposing the vulnerability of others and by locating this quality in the other, who is opposed to the self. In this way, the status of the other is at the same time transformed or manipulated and the violence of the subject towards the other legitimized by processes of dehumanization.

Hence, the question arises: what alternatives can be found to this kind of behavior? If denying one's vulnerability leads to a spiral of violence which causes more injuries, then an exit strategy to this constant repetition of violence could consist in a certain reconciliation with one's own vulnerability. Thus, the basis for non-violent action could, according to Butler, be found in a practice of self-dispossession which reminds subjects of their own vulnerability and at the same time protects those one loves (Butler 2009: 176). Nevertheless, Butler uses here the term 'struggle' in order to refer to this practice: "In this sense, non-violence is not a peaceful state, but a social and political struggle to make rage articulate and effective – the carefully crafted 'fuck you'" (Butler 2009: 182). This struggle then becomes "a certain ethical practice, itself experimental, that seeks to preserve life better than it destroys it" (Butler 2009: 177). The explicit utterance – "to make rage articulate" – sustains the connection of the scene of appellation, as opposed to the extinction of the other by means of violence, and thus holds on to the dependence of the subject on the other even if subjects find themselves in situations in which it might be tempting to deny this connection (Redecker 2011: 135). This situation is very much linked with fear for oneself as well as with the confrontation with one's aggression, yet also offers the opportunity to recognize one's primal state of vulnerability and thus to disrupt the circle of violence by means of a different kind of repetition. Nevertheless, the attitude which is necessary for this kind of recognition has to be made possible in relation to social norms, since subjects can only ever draw from a pool of norms which constitute the framework of what can be said. In this context, the medium of discourse which produces those norms and which becomes manifest via different media (such as text, image or film), is itself significant.

Butler also expands on the idea of the articulation of resistant rage and a 'militant pacifism' in her most recent publication, *The Force of Nonviolence* (2020). Here, they argue that it has to be acknowledged that human relationships are freighted with ambivalence and that the primary dependency on an other might imply love as well as aggression, or rather that love itself is ambivalent and might equally contain a destructive potential. Therefore, subjects have to be aware of the fact that their actions might be imbued with this potential for violence. The identification that "the solidarity of sentiments" which Butler calls for entails is thus an "ambivalent bond [...]" which has to be "mindful of the affirmative and destructive potentials that follow from this vexed relation" (Butler 2020: 171).

Likewise, norms have a two-fold and at times paradoxical function. On the one hand, they enable violence to affect those individuals who do not submit to the norm, on the other hand, they can work in favor of subjects if they are turned into a normative request. Thus, Butler also emphasizes that their theses on ethics cannot lack a normative dimension:

> The point is not to accept a general relativism. The task, rather, is to track and expose the oscillation of frameworks within which naming practices take place. [...] While I take seriously Benjamin's claim that we have to think critically about how such justificatory schemes are established before we use them, I also think that we are obligated to make decisions that commit us to certain frameworks. (Butler 2020: 139–140)

Here, Butler concludes their reading of Benjamin's essay "The Critique of Violence" by highlighting the necessity for establishing norms according to which 'violence' can be differentiated from 'non-violence', thus forming the basis for the authority and power of law. At the same time, Butler demands that the frameworks which offer definitions of violence and non-violence be constantly "track[ed] and expose[d]" in terms of a critical reflection and constant questioning of the conditions of one's normativity.

Consequently, Butler also seeks to establish an "egalitarian imaginary that apprehends the interdependency of lives" (Butler 2020: 203). Thus, the ontological fiction of precariousness would be installed as a norm – a process that Butler actively supports by means of their work – and a utopian system could emerge which judges all lives equally grievable and therefore ensures that they are also equally well protected. Similarly, Butler explicitly points out in *Undoing Gender:* "But there is a normative aspiration here, and it has to do with the ability to live and breathe and move and would no doubt belong somewhere in what is called a philosophy of freedom" (Butler 2004a: 219).

Nevertheless, the question remains as to how those normative aspirations could be distinguished from problematically violent social norms. In this context, Eva von Redecker draws in her introduction to Butler's oeuvre on the Foucauldian term "disciplinary normalization" (Foucault 2004: 89) when delineating what a problematic or potentially violent norm could look like. In cases of disciplinary normalization, normativity along with societal power divides people up into the categories of 'normal' and 'abnormal' depending on their submission or resistance to a norm (Redecker 2011: 137). Only if conforming to a norm – such as the norm of one's sex – is an individual assigned the attribute 'human'. Deviations from that norm turn into 'unlivable lives'. By means of parodic subversion – "promiscuous obedience" – such a division into 'normal' and 'abnormal' can be avoided and positions of subjectivity can be multiplied.

At the same time, Butler assumes that subjects cannot, due to their primary dependence on others, find a form of freedom in a kind of self-realization that is recognized by others, but only ever in forms of critical self-dispossession since only then are they not forced to deny their own vulnerability by means of a constant affirmation of their sovereignty. Here, Butler demands an active decomposition of the self which relativizes the aspiration to sovereignty and transforms the self – in a similar way to how mourning would do so. This request, of course, aligns with the principle of transformation or reflection in the Foucauldian 'aesthetics of existence'. The willingness to engage in a transformation of the self, according to Butler, manifests itself, on the one hand, in 'promiscuous obedience', by means of which subjects submit themselves to norms only to disseminate them, and, on the other hand, in moments of self-dispossession, which explicitly acknowledge one's own precariousness. This transformation can thus never remain external to subjects by only appropriating what is useful for them, but always assumes that the subjection to a norm will change the subject, who accepts those changes without knowing the results beforehand. That any moral practice thus always becomes a self-transformative practice Butler explains with an explicit reference to Foucault:

> Foucault gives us an indication of what he means by virtue in the introduction to *The Use of Pleasure: The History of Sexuality, Volume Two*. At this juncture he makes clear that he seeks to move beyond a notion of ethical philosophy that issues a set of prescriptions. Just as critique intersects with philosophy without quite coinciding with it, so Foucault in that introduction seeks to make of his own thought an example of a non-prescriptive form of moral inquiry. In the same way, he will later ask about forms of moral experience that are not rigidly defined by a juridical law, a rule or command to which the self is said mechanically or uniformly to submit. The essay that he writes, he tells us, is itself the example of such a practice, "to explore what might be changed, in its own thought, through the practice of

a knowledge that is foreign to it." Moral experience has to do with a self-transformation prompted by a form of knowledge that is foreign to one's own. (Butler 2002: 216)

For Butler, subjectivity then also includes the willingness to question the knowledge that one has about oneself and thus to constantly broaden and transform one's identity. In this context, they also draw on Foucault's method of 'experimenting with foreign knowledge' and execute this practice in their reading of Gloria Anzaldúa's *Borderlands/La Frontera* (Redecker 2011: 139). In their observations on Anzaldúa's work Butler combines both Anzaldúa's and their theoretical concepts in a way that leaves it open which parts of Butler's representation of Anzaldúa are their own and which pertain to the work Butler writes about. Thus, both are transformed in the process and the text performs what it advocates:

> She [Anzaldúa] is asking us to stay at the edge of what we know, to put our own epistemological certainties into question, and through that risk and openness to another way of knowing and of living in the world to expand our capacity to imagine the human. She is asking us to be able to work in coalitions across differences that will make a more inclusive movement. [...] The unitary subject is the one who knows already what it is, who enters the conversation the same way as it exits, who fails to put its own epistemological certainties at risk in the encounter with the other, and so stays in place, guards its place, and becomes an emblem for property and territory, *refusing self-transformation, ironically, in the name of the subject*. (Butler 2004a: 228; original emphasis)[101]

As becomes clear especially in the last part of the quotation, Butler does not specify which of the reflections on the unitary subject have been taken from their own and which from Anzaldúa's work or if both just coincide in their opinions. Butler's writings here demonstrate how self-dispossession via scripture as well as via a 'foreign knowledge' might work and presents their readers with a written subject – that is, Butler themself – into whom 'foreign knowledge' has been inscribed and thus incorporated into the subject.

The principle of self-dispossession is then essential for the concept of an ethical subject: on the one hand, because it opens up possibilities for the subject

---

101 Nevertheless, as Redecker (2011: 140) points out, one might question in what way Anzaldúa, whom Butler refers to as "Chicana, Mexican, lesbian, American, academic, poor, writer, activist" (Butler 2004a: 228), actually constitutes that much of a 'foreign knowledge' for Butler since three quarters of those attributes could also be assigned to Butler; furthermore, the concepts of subjectivity that both writers develop seem to be very similar. Redecker refers in this context to shared aims that have to be pursued in coalitions which overcome differences (2011: 140) and sees the selection as an expression of forming such a coalition.

due to a pluralization of options of performance – by means of a simple broadening of knowledge as well as the questioning of one's identity – and because it prevents any occurrence of any kind of "disciplinary normalization", and, on the other hand, because it forms the condition for any practice of non-violence by means of this state of 'ecstasy' in which subjects potentially recognize their condition of vulnerability.

Another practice of self-dispossession could be found in the concept of flânerie as a *techne* that willingly accepts giving up one's sovereignty in the interaction with the city and thus aims at the possible transformation that this entails. In this, the interaction with individual others encountered in the city's crowds has the potential to become a 'gateway to the precarious' since it bears the possibility of deferral of what has already been engrained in the subject. Moreover, the subject can directly influence – although not determine – these transformations by means of individual performances that defer the norms offered by society. Hence, especially Butler's emphasis on the significance of the other in processes of subject formation is an important addendum to the Foucauldian 'aesthetics of existence' which include the other in the techniques of the self, but are not centered around it. In the following, I will give a brief overview of the ways in which Foucault's and Butler's approaches can be brought to bear on the analysis of contemporary flânerie texts and will accordingly present a more detailed account of my overall thesis.

5 Synopsis: Ethical Subjects and the Flânerie Text

In the following case studies, I will show how flânerie texts take a belated 'ethical turn' between the end of the twentieth and the start of the twenty-first century by becoming a vehicle for the negotiation of manifestations of the ethical subject due to their ambivalent position between the materiality of the everyday and the transcendence of reflection.

This assumption is based on a link that can be established between the coincidence of several lines of tradition in the history of the trope and Foucault's and Butler's concepts of ethical subjectivity. The trope of the flâneur is from its very beginnings a very diverse and ambiguous concept that oscillates between poles of acceleration and deceleration as well as anonymity and individuality, but also between the realms of the fictional and the factual as well as the literary and the philosophical. This ambiguity is mirrored in Benjamin's meandering paradoxical remarks on the flâneur as a socio-historical phenomenon as well as a literary trope. While no unified concept of the flâneur could be extracted from Benjamin's writings, some of his observations can nevertheless be assembled into what could be called a 'continuum of strolling', that is, a continuum that ranges from poles of absolute deceleration to absolute acceleration. Whereas Benjamin links those two poles to different stages of the incorporation of the flâneur into the dynamics of the market, he also implies that the flâneur's attempts at performing sovereignty are always already illusory since this sovereignty was undermined in a variety of ways from the start. Moreover, Benjamin also suggests a different type of flânerie that could be understood as a kind of *techne* centered on giving up one's own sovereignty in relation to the objects of observation.

Due to Benjamin's Marxist agenda, he embeds the flâneur in a complex framework of subjection, resistance, and sovereignty which paves the way for materialist reconceptualizations of flânerie and can therefore be understood as a central nexus between the diverse history of the trope of the flâneur and post-sovereign concepts of subjectivity. This becomes especially clear if seen from the perspective of materialist approaches towards the city that employ the interpretative lens of spatial theory to reinterpret walking in terms of performance – that is, as a kind of embodied speech act situated within the city's 'matrix of intelligibility' as has been shown by Michel De Certeau. An aspect that has widely been neglected in research so far is the intermediality of flânerie texts that is deeply rooted in the history of the trope. In the context of a discourse analytical approach towards flânerie, intermediality can become an interesting tool in unveiling the flâneur's subjection to different modes of perception.

As discussed in chapter 2.5, a difficulty in examining flânerie within Anglophone literature lies in the relative absence – apart from a few exceptions – of individual studies on the history of the trope in an Anglophone context, despite the plethora of examples that could be found in British, American and the New English Literatures. However, it can be argued that because the trope of the flâneur originated almost a century earlier in Great Britain than it did in France, this attests to the possibility of different modes of flânerie in different cultural environments. As a consequence, the tradition of the strolling spectator in Great Britain is rooted in the mental framework of the Enlightenment and a corresponding concern with morality and reason, thus embedding the flâneur in a more normative setting. Furthermore, Benjamin's analogy between flâneur and commodity fits the tradition of British flânerie exceptionally well, since publications like Addison and Steele's *Spectator* or the work of Charles Dickens prove his central thesis of the subjection of the flâneur to capitalism on an aesthetic as well as a socio-historical level. But there is also a tradition of a socio-critical flânerie in Anglophone literature that contributes to the socio-critical strand in the history of the trope in general. The chapter then once more proves that the flâneur is prone to the transgression of borders since the phenomenon is indeed international. Nevertheless, my study focuses on the French and German tradition of flânerie as being the most influential in the development of the trope and therefore sees examples from these two traditions as the central points of reference in its conceptualization of flânerie.

Several aspects that recur throughout the centuries in the tradition of flânerie could then be assembled to delineate a heuristic model of what could be called the flânerie text. The trope's overall resistance to classification and the deconstruction of binary oppositions resulting from it, as well as the episodic form of flânerie literature, its metropolitan setting and emphasis on particularity might be seen as the principal characteristics of the flânerie text. Along with new developments in the tradition of flânerie, like the emphasis on flânerie as a material practice sparked by Benjamin's historical-materialist analysis, these characteristics form the breeding ground for new variations of the flânerie text that lend themselves particularly well to the metaphorization of ethical subjecthood in contemporary literature.

Conceptualizations of the ethics of the self or the ethical subject can first and foremost be found in the work of Michel Foucault. The Foucauldian turn towards ethics goes hand in hand with a new focus on alternative conceptions of the subject on which Foucault's non-normative approach towards ethics is based. He describes this new ethical subject in terms of an 'aesthetics of existence' which centers on reflexivity, self-formation, and personal choice and which can be achieved as well as performed through various techniques of the self such as practices of writing, parrēsiastic speech, or textual as well as political experience. Those techniques might not only be accompanied by bodily activity, but also by writing practices that envision self-formation in terms of writing as a material practice that combines formation with transformation and difference. Foucault's main emphasis lies on the care of the self as a "practice of freedom" (1988) that aims at the continuous formation and transformation of an attitude in the subject. The Foucauldian ethical subject thus primarily serves the function of resistance, although, due to Foucault's constant practice of deferral in his writings, it remains unclear where exactly effective resistance starts.

While this problem remains in Butler's reconceptualization of Foucault's theses, Butler also systematizes his suggestions into a more coherent concept of subjectivity that Butler develops throughout their work. Like Foucault, Butler describes the subject as being subjected to but also produced by discourses of power whose matrix of intelligibility forms the framework by means of which identity can be established. Yet, since every repetition of a norm prescribed by the matrix of intelligibility also entails a deferral of this norm, the subject is always already potentially resistant, with various degrees of resistance possibly resulting from different degrees of deferral. Moreover, Butler points out that subjects tend to repress their own state of subjection in a melancholic internalization of the always already lost state of sovereignty. Yet, the subjection to discourses of power is only secondary and only follows from every subject's primary dependence on others that can be described in terms of the precariousness of the subject. In order to successfully perform a sovereignty that has actually never existed for the subject, and thus to integrate it into one's identity, vulnerability then needs to be located in the other – and only in the other – by means of discursive or physical violence towards an other. According to Butler, any approach towards performances of non-violence thus has to situate its starting point in the acknowledgement of one's own state of precariousness.

Butler's and Foucault's takes on the ethical subject thus differ especially in their attitude towards normativity. Although both concepts are based on the dynamics of formation and transformation that Foucault suggests, they vary in the amount of emphasis that they put on freedom and normativity, respectively. Foucault places a deliberate emphasis on the non-normativity of his concept of the ethical self; as a result, it can only be gleaned by means of an individual interpretation of his rather eclectic comments on the ethics of the self, so that any kind of normative claim can only be arrived at through an analysis of the sedimentation of certain aspects in his writings. Butler's work, by contrast, contains a "normative aspiration" in her explicit demands for a practice of non-violence and the recognition of one's primary state of vulnerability while simultaneously aiming at a pluralization of performance options through the continuous practice of critique.[102]

The textual analyses I undertake in my study focus on the abovementioned characteristics of the ethics of the self and consider the literary texts to be examples suggesting possible interpretations of this open and ever-transforming concept. Those examples bring palpability to the concept by transferring it to the concrete materiality of the city and relating it to political discourses while at the same time reflecting on the possibilities of resistance within those discourses. Flânerie texts then crystallize different activities into a bundle of intersecting techniques of the self that allow for the formation of and the reflection on a new ethical subject that resurfaces in the textualization of the practice of flânerie. While the texts I analyze present flânerie as a Foucauldian technique of the self, the practice also serves to demonstrate the overall precariousness of the subject and can be understood as an ambivalent pathway to acknowledging the precariousness of one's self. Moreover, by translating the practice of flânerie into text, the novels also juxtapose various individual interpretations of ethical, post-sovereign subjecthood and thus create ever new variations of Foucault's as well as Butler's takes on the ethical subject.

In this context, some characteristics as well as stages of development in the history of the trope of the flâneur have to be particularly emphasized. First of all, resistance figures prominently in the history of the flâneur due to the flâneur's deliberate counterposition to discourses of utility and profit. Especially the characteristic of aimless motion emphasizes this aspect since it implies a mode of walking that lacks an immediate purpose. While walking itself has often been conceptualized as a crossing of boundaries and has therefore been described as a practice of resistance, the aimlessness of the flâneur's walks puts a specific emphasis on the resistant quality of walking. Second, the material aspect of walking that has been brought into focus by new interpretations of flânerie like Guy Debord's situationist psychogeography or the findings of the spatial turn locates the subject within the palpable materiality of the city. Third, the encounter with the crowd further supports a new interest in a negotiation of ethical questions since it already posits the flâneur opposite an other and therefore highlights issues of relationality. And lastly, as has already been pointed out

---

[102] This, however, should not be understood as a clear-cut distinction between their approaches that projects Butler's ethical writings as entirely 'normative' and Foucault's as entirely 'non-normative', but only as a difference in emphasis despite the congruities between the philosophers.

5 Synopsis: Ethical Subjects and the Flânerie Text — 109

in the context of walking as a constant crossing of boundaries, the flâneur "stands on the threshold" so that his strolls often effect a deconstruction of binary oppositions which then might form part of the processual, performative identity of the strolling subject. Additionally, a crossing of medial boundaries can become a form of resistance through the reflection of the flâneur's sensory perceptions by means of the defamiliarization of the structural principles of a specific medium.

The concept of a post-sovereign, ethical subject then fits the aesthetics of the flânerie text exceptionally well. Butler's as well as Foucault's approaches take as their starting point questions of resistance in a world framed and produced by discourses of power. Building on Benjamin's analogy between flâneur and commodity, the trope of the flâneur turns into a symbol of every individual's subjection as well as resistance to the workings of power. Additionally, the aimlessness of flânerie as a *techne* potentially opens the subject up to its transformation either by exposure to a new perspective on the city due to its aimless strolls through the metropolis or by the confrontation with the other as a representative of the crowd. In this, the materiality of the city takes on an ambivalent role. While it adapts the subject to the workings of power, as Benjamin states with reference to Marx, flânerie as a material practice might equally become a means of self-formation. By turning the body into a sign in the midst of the jungle of signifiers that is the city, a flâneur transmits a message through the performative act of strolling and thus flânerie as material performance becomes a means of resistance. Since materiality and signs coalesce in the text of the city, it is particularly apt for performances of resistance. Due to the flâneur's constant transgression of boundaries, a performative deferral of norms might occur, and through his aimlessly wandering perspective onto the city hegemonic discourses can be disseminated into a variety of perspectives. Lastly, the encounter with the crowd which can be dissolved into individual others forms the basis for reflections on the relationship between self and other. In particular, the focus on the representation of the crowd in earlier flânerie texts is now turned into a reflection on the sovereignty and precariousness of interpretation, while at the same time negotiating the ultimate dependency of the precarious subject.

While all those aspects belong to the level of plot, the textualization of this plot adds an additional level of reflection that might further contribute to the formation of ethical subjects according to the Foucauldian criterion of reflexivity in novels with homodiegetic narration. Formal features can thus be turned into a means of reflection and self-reflexivity will surface both on the level of *histoire* as well as the level of *discours*.

Moreover, flânerie texts' focus on the particular – manifest in their episodic form – and simultaneous appeal to totality – which is implied not only by the exemplary status of the flâneur as a representative of the individual subject in the history of the trope, but also by a tendency in contemporary city texts to envision the city as a representation of the world itself – are both evident in contemporary flânerie texts' balancing of the general with the particular, which serves to negotiate between the particularity of Foucault's approach towards non-normative ethics and the general norms deduced from Butler's theses on the precarious as human condition. By juxtaposing a focus on general questions of philosophy like truth or ethics with an episodic form that emphasizes the importance of difference and particularity and that has the potential of a constant deferral of the norm, the texts therefore negotiate between normative and non-normative approaches towards ethics, thus performing the overall aim of critique.

The flânerie text thus becomes a medium of critique as it has been envisioned by both Foucault und Butler. By drawing on contemporary political contexts while at the same time suspending any appeal to factuality, in its negotiation of ethical subjecthood it turns into a medium between an extra-linguistic reality and a philosophy that reflects in an abstract way on questions of a much more general nature such as truth, freedom and good and evil, thus illustrating a characteristic of literature in general. The texts refrain from creating any factual knowledge; nevertheless, they disrupt our normativity and partake in ever new transformations of the subject in the form of an 'aesthetics of existence', while simultaneously emphasizing the overall precariousness of the subject.

The first text I analyze below, Ian McEwan's *Saturday*, serves to explicitly differentiate sovereign from post-sovereign subjecthood. Although it presents a protagonist who ticks all the boxes of the norm of the westernized sovereign subject, the novel also suggests the possibility of developing a post-sovereign subjecthood to the reader. This analysis thus describes a limit case against which the other readings can be compared; at the same time, it begins to explore the potential inherent in the specific structure of the flânerie text.

6 The End of Flânerie? The Sovereign Subject and Precarious City Life in Ian McEwan's *Saturday*

As was pointed out in chapter 3, in his later writings Foucault juxtaposes the techniques of the self with the techniques of domination that he described in his earlier works. At the same time, he does not specify where the border between the techniques of domination and the techniques of the self might be located (see Best and Kellner 1991: 67) and explicitly dissolves this boundary when stating that "[p]erhaps at most they [his studies of the techniques of the self] made it possible to go through what I was actually thinking, to think it differently, and to see what I had done from a new vantage point and in a clearer light" (Foucault 1992: 11). Butler's translation of the techniques of the self into the concept of performance does not solve the problem either, since Butler does not specify at which point a performance crosses the boundary between resistance and the affirmation of power structures. While this border cannot be clearly marked on a theoretical basis, I suggest that Ian McEwan's novel *Saturday* presents a counterpoint to the examples of flânerie as a technique of the self that I will discuss in the remainder of my study. In *Saturday*, flânerie becomes a vehicle for the depiction of techniques of domination and the multiple ways in which the sovereign subjectivity that those techniques of domination project endangers the shared human condition of precariousness. While any potential construction of post-sovereign subjectivity on the level of plot remains questionable, the plethora of intertexts that the novel alludes to establishes a flânerie text that escapes any fixed interpretation and therefore explicitly challenges the sovereignty of the reading subject.

6.1 A Flâneur without Flânerie: Henry Perowne as Benjaminian 'Man of the Crowd'

Ian McEwan's *Saturday* is not a text that employs flânerie in any traditional sense of the term.[103] Nevertheless, the novel implicitly refers to classic flânerie texts like Virginia Woolf's *Mrs Dalloway* or James Joyce's *Ulysses* by describing

---

103 Parts of this chapter have already been published in Ries (2020).

one single day in the life of its protagonist, the neurosurgeon Henry Perowne.[104] On this particular day, 15 February 2003, Perowne's car collides with that of the petty criminal Baxter and thus starts a cycle of violence which culminates with Baxter invading Perowne's house and taking Perowne's family hostage. Despite this, Perowne not only saves Baxter's life but he also decides to ensure further treatment and care for Baxter. The novel ends with Perowne returning to his home and his family and reflecting on notions of vulnerability and precariousness.

The opposition between Perowne and Baxter is particularly striking because it represents various diametrically opposed principles. Perowne, on the one hand, is nothing if not successful in every aspect of his life: he works as a neurosurgeon in a hospital in Westminster not far from his rather opulent and safely guarded home; he is married to an equally successful lawyer; and is father to an aspiring poet (Daisy) and a promising blues musician (Theo). Baxter, on the other hand, who is only presented to the reader through the eyes of Perowne, seems to spend his days in dubious establishments and to keep himself afloat by means of petty crime. First and foremost, their opposition is determined by social class. Moreover, while Perowne is depicted as being in the best of health, Baxter appears to suffer from Chorea Huntington's disease, the first symptoms of which have already become discernible at the time the story takes place. Relations of power between the two characters are therefore uneven from the very beginning and they remain so throughout the novel.

As is the case with *Mrs Dalloway* and *Ulysses*, *Saturday* is above all a text about a city and its inhabitants and thus centers largely on the description of London. Yet, *Saturday*'s London is a palimpsestic city composed of an abundance of reference texts that add an infinite number of layers of meaning to the depiction of the city as well as to the story of its protagonist (see Groes 2009: 113; Riedelsheimer 2020: 158).[105] Those reference texts disclose a perspective onto the city that conflates past and present and depicts London and its inhabitants as strongly influenced and formed by the past. Modernist literature in particular is most emphasized among those texts through the many ways in which *Saturday*'s plot as well as the topics treated in the novel are informed by *Ulysses* and *Mrs Dalloway* as well as other works of the period. Yet, while flânerie can be found in Joyce's and Woolf's novels as a mode of metropolitan ex-

---

104 For an extended discussion of the many ways in which *Saturday* quotes Woolf and Joyce see e.g. Groes (2009: 104–108) as well as Adams (2012: 550–565), Head (2007: 192), Currie (2007: 129 and 132).
105 For a comprehensive list of texts implicitly alluded to or explicitly referred to by the novel see Groes (2009: 102).

perience, it seems to have disappeared from McEwan's London. I argue that although Henry Perowne does not qualify as a flâneur in any 'classical' sense, even if a broad definition such as Neumeyer's minimal definition is applied,[106] *Saturday* still counts as a contemporary flânerie text: Perowne can, in fact, be likened to Benjamin's 'man of the crowd' owing to the (temporal) continuum that is opened up between him and a character like Leopold Bloom, so that while Perowne might not be a flâneur himself, he stands for what would have become of the flâneur in a twenty-first-century city.

The text establishes this temporal continuum by means of the marked reference to *Mrs Dalloway* and *Ulysses*, thereby likening Henry Perowne to Clarissa Dalloway as well as to Leopold Bloom. On the one hand, Perowne is likened to Leopold Bloom walking the streets of Dublin in an often aimless manner, on the other hand, his is clearly different from Bloom's ambulatory practice. Thus, whereas Bloom would still qualify as a flâneur, Perowne clearly does not. He can, however, be linked to Benjamin's notion of the disappearance of flânerie due to the transformation of the flâneur into the 'man of the crowd' since the way that *Saturday* draws on earlier flânerie texts associates Perowne with what would become of the flâneur after being incorporated into the crowd. Perowne is thus a hyperbolic version of Benjamin's passers-by whose perception has been trained according to the demands of capitalism. In the nineteenth century, according to Benjamin, those walking in the city's streets and among its crowds developed a consciousness that reacted to the shocks experienced by the individual in the crowd owing to the necessity of adapting to the demands of traffic; Perowne's car has a similar function for him: "Shamelessly, he always enjoys the city from inside his car where the air is filtered and hi-fi music confers pathos on the humblest details – a Schubert trio is dignifying the narrow street he's slipping down now" (McEwan 2006: 76). Driving through the city by car is thus an extension of the situation which Benjamin describes as constitutive for the citizen of the modern metropolis – and therefore for the end of the flâneur as a counterpoint to the crowd. According to Benjamin, citizens of modern-day metropolises keep to themselves and thus produce what Benjamin, drawing on Engels, refers to as "the unfeeling isolation of each within his private concerns" (Engels, qtd. in Benjamin 2006: 88), which describes the citizen's capability of excluding anything from their perception that could distract them

---

106 Although he does display a rather contemplative mood when driving through the city, his movements are never aimless but follow a tight schedule. See also Ganteau (2014: 224; original emphasis): "[...] Leopold Bloom's wanderings have lost some of their aimlessness in moving down to hyper-active, hyper-focused Henry Perowne, more a postmodern *stalker* in a sense, than a modernist *flâneur*."

from making their way through the city (see Benjamin 2006: 88). Similarly, his car protects Perowne from the polluted air outside and its hi-fi music system even glosses over the more profane aspects of the city. The noise of the metropolis has now been transformed into the "Schubert trio [...] dignifying" everything that Perowne perceives in London and simultaneously blocks out what might be more worrying about city life so that nothing remains to disturb the 'preponderance of visual activity'. What is more, contrary to the pedestrian flâneur, the automobile needs a prefabricated pathway – the street – which aligns it with the rest of the crowd of cars and the citizens driving them and therefore turns its driver, like Benjamin's 'flâneur, who is not a flâneur anymore', into a twenty-first-century 'man of the crowd'. Perowne is thus mostly immune to anything in the city that could harm or transform him as long as he is inside his car. Due to the temporal continuum that the novel opens up by means of the references to *Ulysses* and *Mrs Dalloway*, Perowne can be understood as an even more accelerated – given the fact that the 'man of the crowd' is already an accelerated version of the flâneur – version of what becomes of the flâneur as soon as he has been incorporated into the crowd. The novel hence evokes the tradition of flânerie without employing flânerie on the level of content.

In this, Perowne also bears traces of Bauman's 'postmodern flâneur' who is formed according to capitalism's demands of efficiency and consumption and lives his life according to the prescribed templates of success. As mentioned above, Perowne leads a hyperbolically perfect life that ticks all the boxes of what might be deemed the markers of success in western societies. The focal point of his performance as sovereign western subject lies in Perowne's profession, which determines his mode of thought and is not only responsible for his financial success, but is also the place where he encountered his wife and therefore indirectly also the basis for his successful family life. Since "work [is] the ultimate badge of health" (McEwan 2006: 24) and thus the ultimate marker for a successful performance of the norm, Perowne fulfils his "obligation [] to be useful" (McEwan 2006: 11) in capitalist society.

Contrary to some scholars, I do not think that Perowne could be considered an "'Everyman'" (Detmers 2008: 371) since most people, even in the western world, do not own a chateau in France (see also Riedelsheimer 2020: 159, fn. 116), but rather the hyperbolic expression of the norm or the ideal that might function as the motivator for the norm to be fulfilled by others. Like Bauman's 'postmodern flâneur' who has formed himself according to the ready-made images he received as a constant flow on television (2015: 155), Perowne has constructed his identity as the epitome of sovereign western subjectivity. Consequently, Perowne sees his world like a twenty-first-century Candide – as the 'best of all possible worlds' – when driving through the city in his car:

6.1 Henry Perowne as Benjaminian 'Man of the Crowd' — 115

> He listens to the Schubert trio sweetly fade and swell. The street is fine, and the city, grand achievement of the living and all the dead who've ever lived here, is fine too, and robust. It won't easily allow itself to be destroyed. It's too good to let go. Life in it has steadily improved over the centuries for most people, despite the junkies and beggars now. The air is better, and salmon are leaping in the Thames, and otters are returning. At every level, material, medical, intellectual, sensual, for most people it has improved. The teachers who educated Daisy at university thought the idea of progress old-fashioned and ridiculous. [...] In Daisy's final term he went to an open day at her college. The young lecturers there like to dramatise modern life as a sequence of calamities. It's their style, their way of being clever. It wouldn't be cool or professional to count the eradication of smallpox as part of the modern condition. Or the recent spread of democracies. In the evening one of them gave a lecture on the prospects of our consumerist and technological civilisation: not good. But if the present dispensation is wiped out now, the future will look back on us as gods, certainly in this city, lucky gods blessed by supermarket cornucopias, torrents of accessible information, warm clothes that weigh nothing, extended life-spans, wondrous machines. This is an age of wondrous machines. Portable telephones barely bigger than your ear. Whole music libraries held in an object the size of a child's hand. Cameras that can beam their snapshots around the world. Effortlessly, he ordered up the contraption he's riding in now through a device on his desk via the Internet. [...] But for the professors in the academy, for the humanities generally, misery is more amenable to analysis: happiness is a harder nut to crack. (McEwan 2006: 77–78)

Strikingly, Perowne links the "happiness", which he assumes to be the primary marker of a twenty-first-century human condition, to an excess of consumption. The western sovereign subject is elevated to the position of a "lucky god[]" due to the existence of "supermarket cornucopias, torrents of accessible information, warm clothes that weigh nothing" and the kind of "wondrous machines" that the western world has become accustomed to in the twenty-first century. Only the "extended life-spans" do not quite fit in with this pattern, but instead serve to connect Perowne himself, as a doctor, with those accomplishments of civilization. The juxtaposition with the humanities' critique of capitalism and Perowne's riposte implying that they want civilization to be "wiped out" constitutes what will later on be referred to as a state of "happiness cut with aggression" (McEwan 2006: 79), that is, an aggressive stance towards anyone who questions Perowne's evaluation of these 'happy times'. Like Clarissa Dalloway,[107]

---

[107] During her walk to the flower shop at the beginning of Woolf's novel, Clarissa Dalloway reflects on life in London in the following way: "For Heaven only knows why one loves it so, how one sees it so, making it up, building it round one, tumbling it, creating it every moment afresh; but the veriest frumps, the most dejected of miseries sitting on doorsteps (drink their downfall) do the same; can't be dealt with, she felt positive, by Acts of Parliament for that very reason: they love life" (Woolf 2000: 4). It goes without saying (and is also emphasized

Perowne is not capable of imagining a life that is different from his own and therefore projects his own perception onto the rest of the world. Interestingly, neither Mrs Dalloway nor Perowne constitute classical examples of flânerie and the restriction of their movement aligns with a restriction of perspective, while their individual performances of normality ensure their status as sovereign subjects. Nevertheless, he is not yet the kind of 'postmodern flâneur' that Bauman envisions, who mostly refrains from movement itself and rather observes the images moving around him. As Bauman remarks (2015: 155), streets are to be avoided by the 'postmodern flâneurs' of late capitalism, probably because their immediate materiality bears the potential of resistance. Consequently, not all seems to be lost with regard to a possible transformation of Perowne.

If anything, Perowne can only ironically be linked to certain characteristics of the flâneur in the way that he combines work and leisure. While the nineteenth-century flâneur pretends to be idle, he is actually working and collecting material for his writings. Perowne's day of leisure, by contrast, is strictly organized, thus mimicking a regular workday. Whereas the flâneur performs idleness in order to deceive others, Perowne seems to refer to Saturday as his day off in order to deceive himself about still being somewhat idle, but at the same time gives in to capitalist society's demand for constant productivity. Therefore, Henry Perowne can be interpreted as a continuation of Benjamin's 'man of the crowd' who marks the end of flânerie as a practice of resistance. This continuation, moreover, aligns with Bauman's concept of postmodern *flâneurisme*, although it still leaves open the possibility of resistance and change.

6.2 Technologies of Domination in *Saturday:* The Flâneur as Sovereign Subject

The connection to Benjamin's 'man of the crowd' and his performance of sovereignty that is actually tied to the subjection to discourses of power is further emphasized through *Saturday*'s narrative situation. The novel features a heterodiegetic narrator with a fixed internal focalization on Henry Perowne who tells the story as it takes place; that is, the time of narrating deviates from the more common type of subsequent narration (see Genette 1980: 218–220) due to the narrative being written in the present tense. According to Genette, narrating in the present tense emphasizes either the *discours* or the *histoire* (see Genette 1980:

---

by focalization on other characters) that the "frumps" and "most dejected of miseries" to whom Dalloway refers do not "love life" in the way that she envisions it.

219) and in this case, it could be interpreted as an indicator of the interdependence between the workings of discourses of power and those discourses' dependency on the performance of individual subjects.[108] Thus, the novel starts with the narrative voice's remark that "[s]ome hours before dawn Henry Perowne, a neurosurgeon, wakes to find himself already in motion, pushing back the covers from a sitting position, and then rising to his feet" (McEwan 2006: 3). On the one hand, the quote emphasizes that Perowne and his consciousness are only created by the *discours* which not only wakes him up, but literally brings him into existence.[109] On the other hand, since the *discours* relies on its focalization on Perowne, its existence depends just as much on Perowne being conscious, which becomes discernible in the second sentence: "It's not clear to him when exactly he became conscious, nor does it seem relevant" (McEwan 2006: 3). This sentence explicitly refers to the border line between sleep and wakefulness at which the subject does not yet consciously perceive their surroundings. The narrative starts as soon as this boundary is unequivocally crossed and it ends with Perowne going back to sleep approximately twenty-four hours later: "There's always this, is one of his remaining thoughts. And then: there's only this. And at last, faintly, falling: this day's over" (McEwan 2006: 279). Moreover, the novel's frequent integration of stretches of free indirect discourse further foregrounds the interdependence between narrative voice and focalizer by means of the "double-edged nature" (Rimmon-Kenan 2002: 117) of free indirect discourse itself, which voices the speech of the narrator along the character's speech or thought. This specific narrative situation allows for drawing an analogy with the interdependence between subject and discourse. While, in order to come into existence, discourses of power rely on subjects to actively produce and perform them, the subjects themselves are – quite paradoxically – produced and formed by those very same discourses.

Here, especially the connection between Perowne's consciousness, which constitutes the medium for the narration of the story, and his profession as a neurosurgeon along with his constant reflections on the human brain, create the impression of a centered subject which is 'conscious' of itself (see also Detmers 2008: 370). At the same time, the heterodiegetic narrative voice emphasizes that this consciousness is in fact filtered through a *discours* that is not its own. The subject Henry Perowne is thus not only produced by a given discourse of power, but this discourse even constructs him as a sovereign subject that has

---

[108] See also Riedelsheimer's comments on the function of simultaneous narration in *Saturday* (2020: 169).
[109] This is again highlighted by the self-reflexive comment that "[i]t's as if, standing there in the darkness, he's materialised out of nothing, fully formed, unencumbered" (McEwan 2006: 3).

been formed according to norms of sovereignty within a given society. Perowne's consciousness is therefore structured according to evaluations of the discourse of power and every written account of this consciousness is also designed according to the rules of the discourse/*discours*.

His position as a sovereign subject is repeatedly affirmed throughout the text. Not only does he imagine himself to be remembered as a "lucky god[]" in the example mentioned above, but this self-conception of absolute sovereignty is already alluded to at the beginning of the novel: "They cross towards the far corner of the square, and with his advantage of height and in his curious mood, he not only watches them, but watches over them, supervising their progress with the remote possessiveness of a god" (McEwan 2006: 13). Here, Perowne observes two women – or at least he presumes them to be women – crossing the square in front of his house while he stands at the window. The *discours* seems to allow him to compare himself rather unironically to a god, a point further emphasized by his being located on a higher level than them, physically and professionally, since he assumes them to be nurses.[110]

What is more, performances of sovereignty seem to 'come naturally' (more or less) to Perowne during his first encounter with Baxter:

> But here on University Street it's impossible not to feel that play-acting is about to begin. [...] He is cast in a role, and there's no way out. This, as people like to say, is urban drama. A century of movies and half a century of television have rendered the matter insincere. It is pure artifice. [...] Someone is going to have to impose his will and win, and the other is going to give way. Popular culture has worn this matter smooth with reiteration, this ancient genetic patrimony that also oils the machinations of bullfrogs and cockerels and stags. And despite the varied and casual dresscode, there are rules as elaborate as the *politesse* of the Versailles court that no set of genes can express. For a start, it is not permitted as they stand there to acknowledge the self-consciousness of the event, or its overbearing irony: from just up the street, they can hear the tramping and tribal drums of the peace mongers. Furthermore, nothing can be predicted, but everything, as soon as it happens, will seem to fit. (McEwan 2006: 86–87)

Perowne's evaluation of his upcoming conflict with Baxter is strikingly ambivalent. On the one hand, he openly admits that the situation between them is "pure artifice" and that he has been "cast in a role". On the other hand, the quote also

---

[110] See McEwan (2006: 12): "nurses surely, heading home, though this is a strange time to be coming off shift". Interestingly, the quote also implies that the assumption that the two "figures" (McEwan 2006: 12) could be nurses returning from their shift, is not as plausible as it might seem from Perowne's thoughts on the matter and could just as well be interpreted as Perowne's projection that ties in particularly well with his overall self-assessment as a sovereign subject in this scene.

roots the behavior of both adversaries within affirmations of male sovereignty in the animal world and therefore evokes a biological and essentialist justification for their actions, which would provide further evidence for Perowne's claim that "there's no way out". Nevertheless, this claim is almost immediately refuted by his reflection on a set of "rules [...] that no set of genes can express", thus creating ambivalence. The justification of an affirmation of patriarchal hegemony through the masculine gene pool is thus explicitly shown to be discursively formed and therefore potentially changeable. This is further highlighted by the assessment that "nothing can be predicted" – which implies the possibility for change – and the contradictory statement that "everything, as soon as it happens, will seem to fit". Whereas the quote proves that Perowne is perfectly aware of the fact that he and Baxter only perform prescribed roles during their encounter, he does not seem to realize that this also means that there actually is a "way out of" the role in which he has been "cast". Moreover, he even adds an essentialist explanation for his performance of sovereignty. The ambivalence of the quote, however, foregrounds that a breach of rules would be very much possible for Perowne as well as for Baxter.[111]

Yet, Perowne's insistence on participating in the cycle of violence that those performances of sovereignty quite necessarily produce further highlights the various levels on which sovereignty can be performed (see Gauthier 2013: 20). In the ensuing encounter with Baxter, he, for example, reflects on the link between activity and sovereignty by remembering that "[i]t's important not to be passive. It has to be his move" (McEwan 2006: 89) and he highlights the connection between education and sovereignty by drawing on a lexicon that places him in a position that is intellectually superior to Baxter's (see McEwan 2006: 89). What is more, Perowne insists on exchanging the insurance details which would probably protect him from having to pay any compensation to Baxter, not because the insurance company would pay for the damage (after all, this would still imply that Perowne would have to deal with the dreaded "paperwork" [McEwan 2006: 89]), but rather because Baxter would probably not want to have any contact with representatives of juridical institutions – at least, this is what might cause his reluctance to accept the exchange of insurance details (see McEwan 2006: 91). This deliberately performed sovereignty triggers an exertion of physical violence on Baxter's side which then results in an actual

---

111 Furthermore, Perowne, the 'postmodern flâneur' of television, apparently extracted those rules from popular culture, which paradoxically has "rendered the matter insincere". Art and popular culture are therefore assigned an ambivalent function: while they contribute to the production of norms, they might also emphasize the artificiality of those norms and thus offer a gateway to their deferral.

attack on Perowne's physical integrity (see McEwan 2006: 92). Consequently, Perowne next uses the interpretation of medical signs as a tool in order to re-establish himself as a sovereign subject[112] and reads Baxter's behavior as being symptomatic of Huntington's disease (see McEwan 2006: 91–94; see also Nunius 2009: 259), a diagnosis that is, though not necessarily wrong, not confirmed by any other character in the novel. By drawing on the scientific and medical discourses that assigned him his authority as a doctor, Perowne manages to expose Baxter's sickness to his subordinates and thus to flee the scene of the accident. In this, Perowne's diagnosis draws its authority from his reference to medical discourses as well as from his overall authorization by the discourse of power. Although his role as a doctor is questioned by his inappropriate outward appearance – "Dressed as a scarecrow, in mangy fleece, his sweater with its row of holes, his paintstained trousers with a knotted cord" (McEwan 2006: 86) – the Mercedes S 500 that Perowne drives supports his identity as carrier of the discourse. The norm is applied to Baxter by means of a devastating judgment when Perowne announces that "'[y]our father had it. Now you've got it too'" and indeed, "[h]e has the impression of himself as a witch doctor delivering a curse" (McEwan 2006: 94).

However, Perowne's putative sovereignty is placed in question by the novel on several levels, and indeed, according to Butler, such sovereignty can never represent the actual situation of the subject, thus raising the question of whether or not this confrontation with his own state of precariousness will incite a change of perception in Perowne himself.

6.3 Precarious City Life: Ambiguous Transformations

In *Saturday*, city life and life in general are repeatedly marked as precarious and this shared condition is then contrasted as well as combined with the characters' performances of sovereignty. Yet, whether or not the confrontation with one's precariousness leads to a transformation of subjectivity remains ambiguous in the novel.

First of all, *Saturday* contrasts Perowne's explicit performance of sovereignty with an emphasis on the precarious condition of human life by means of the recurrence of topics like illness (see, for example, McEwan 2006: 8–10, 142 and

---

[112] In fact, Perowne repeatedly tries to establish himself as a sovereign reading subject (Nunius 2009: 259–260) by interpreting and evaluating the events taking place around him. See also Winterhalter (2010: 346), who already sees the first scene of the novel as an instance of reading.

182), aging (see McEwan 2006: 21, 104–105), and terrorism (see e.g. McEwan 2006: 16, 180–181 and 277), all of which serve as existential threats to human life. Although Perowne tries to maintain his performance of himself as a sovereign subject, he is actually *subjected* to the constant affirmation of this supposed sovereignty in an analogous way to the flâneur in Benjamin, who is subjected to performing a seemingly sovereign practice of observing the market while actually being already drawn into the workings of capitalism. This becomes especially clear in the cycle of violence that starts between Baxter and Perowne after their cars collide.

Perowne's car functions as a symbol as well as a protector of his sovereignty. It is only in the filtered atmosphere of the car that he experiences the city unencumbered. As soon as this car is damaged in the accident, Perowne feels that "[s]omething original and pristine has been stolen from his car, and can never be restored, however good the repair. [...] His car will never be the same again. It's ruinously altered and so is his Saturday" (McEwan 2006: 82). Although he has only experienced a minor accident and although his car is only slightly damaged, Perowne perceives it as being "ruinously altered" since what has been actually taken from his car is his illusion of invincibility and absolute sovereignty while driving through the streets of London. As soon as this illusion is broken, it can "never be restored, however good the repair". As a consequence, Perowne's level of aggression rises:

> Above all, there swells in him a peculiar modern emotion – the motorist's rectitude, spot-welding a passion for justice to the thrill of hatred, in the service of which various worn phrases tumble through his thoughts, revitalised, cleansed of cliché: just pulled out, no signal, stupid bastard, didn't even look, what's his mirror for, fucking *bastard*. [...] He feels he's been left behind. (McEwan 2006: 82; original emphasis)

Paradoxically then, although Perowne seems to be at least partly aware of the precariousness of human life on a material level due to his profession as a doctor – which constantly confronts him with the frailty of human life – as well as his age, his self-concept is also based on the assumption of the sovereignty of the subject which is reflected in his repeated self-envisioning as a god. In order for this paradoxical self-concept to be maintained, he has, of course, to constantly re-affirm it, especially when it has been questioned by sudden reminders of his own precariousness. This occurs soon after the accident in the squash match between Perowne and his colleague Jay Strauss, which turns into another instance of "urban drama" for the sake of Perowne's self-perception as a sovereign subject to be reinforced by means of performance.

In the squash match, Perowne's feelings of vulnerability merge with his construction of an identity that either marks him as a 'winner' or a 'loser' depending on the outcome of the game. Already before they start to play, Perowne "suddenly feels his own life as fragile and precious" and he muses that "[h]is heart will be even more vulnerable after that punch [that he received from Baxter]" (McEwan 2006: 102). During the game, the thought of Baxter returns and throws Perowne off balance when "[h]e sees the pathetic figure of Baxter in his rear-view mirror" at the moment that "the ball floats off the front wall towards him" (McEwan 2006: 104). The image of the mirror in connection with Baxter is especially telling in this context since the text repeatedly constructs Perowne and Baxter as a pair of doubles and thus suggests that Baxter represents some repressed content of Perowne's psyche, such as their shared condition of precariousness. This is emphasized not only by the cycle of violence that highlights the similarity in both characters' performances of sovereignty, but also through the novel's intertextual reference to Robert Louis Stevenson's novella *Strange Case of Dr Jekyll and Mr Hyde*, which undermines Perowne's unabashed belief in progress and in his own superiority.[113] While the juxtaposition between Dr Perowne, who belongs to the upper-middle class, and Mr Baxter, a representative of the lower classes with a propensity for violence and petty crime, might already indicate the allusion to Stevenson's novella, the reference is all the more striking given how Baxter is described as seen from the perspective of Perowne. Indeed, internal focalization on Perowne reveals how he repeatedly compares Baxter to an ape when, for example, he refers to Baxter's "general simian air" (McEwan 2006: 88) or his "vaguely ape-like features" (McEwan 2006: 97). Similarly, Stevenson's Edward Hyde is often described as sharing characteristics with apes due to the novella's overall degenerationist borrowings (see, for example, Stevenson 2003: 37). The reference to *Strange Case of Dr Jekyll and Mr Hyde* might thus imply that despite their obvious differences Perowne and Baxter might be more alike than they seem to be from the outside (see Ries 2020: 17). While Perowne assumes that "guilt is certainly an element" of the "rising unease" and "feeling of disquiet he can't yet define" (McEwan 2006: 102) after the encounter with Baxter, the image of him receding in Perowne's rear-view mirror suggests a very different kind of haunting that is based on Perowne's constant attempts to repress the recognition of his own vulnerability, which is repeatedly brought back to him by the memory of Baxter.

The fact that Perowne, as a result of his lack of concentration, loses points in his squash match with Strauss sends him further into a downward spiral and

---

[113] For an extensive analysis of possible allusions to *Strange Case of Dr Jekyll and Mr Hyde*, see Bar-Yosef (2020).

foregrounds the performative nature of his construction of identity. Soon his insecurity turns into self-hatred:

> Why has he volunteered for, even anticipated with pleasure, this humiliation, this torture? It's at moments like these that the essentials of his character are exposed: narrow, ineffectual, stupid – and morally so. The game becomes an extended metaphor of character defect. Every error he makes is so profoundly, so irritatingly typical of himself, instantly familiar, like a signature, like a tissue scar or some deformation in a private place. (McEwan 2006: 106)

His deficiencies in this particular game are directly translated into the "essentials of his character", an assumption that seemed to have been looming behind his celebration of the splendid times in which he is living and to which he contributes. Losing in a simple game of squash thus already classifies Perowne among the 'losers' who exist outside the norm of success and perfectionism – that is, those he associates with "character defect[s]" and "deformation". Consequently, "[t]here is only one thing in life he wants. [...] He has to beat Jay Strauss" (McEwan 2006: 107). In order to achieve this goal and thus re-convince himself of his own sovereignty, Perowne is – quite paradoxically – willing to risk his own health when both players "[o]blivious to their protesting hearts, [...] hurl themselves into every corner" (McEwan 2006: 113). The quote therefore emphasizes how a discourse of power that assigns subject positions only to those who prove to be sovereign, actually subjects precarious individuals to potentially dangerous behavior. And because there is in fact nothing at stake in this contest, the non-referentiality of the two men's performance and absurdity of their clash is especially marked.[114] It so happens that the actual result of the game is temporarily suspended due to the men's disagreement over the last score, which allows Perowne to feel morally superior to Strauss by giving in to his claim that the last serve has to be repeated; Strauss then manages to win the game (see McEwan 2006: 116–117).

In the course of the novel, Perowne then struggles to regain a feeling of sovereignty, yet does not quite manage to do so until the cycle of violence that started with his encounter with Baxter comes to a head with Baxter intruding into Perowne's house. At the end of the novel this cycle of violence seems to be suspended – Roland Weidle for example speaks of the "final happy ending" (2009:

---

[114] The scene dovetails nicely with the "Oxen of the Sun" chapter in *Ulysses* since it also features doctors performing an empty fight for sovereignty (see Joyce 1986: 314–349). Yet, whereas those doctors only form the backdrop against which the sacred acts of creation – of human life as well as of art – take place in Joyce's novel, the lack of any such act in *Saturday* again highlights the meaninglessness of Perowne and Strauss's struggle.

67) of the novel – when Perowne saves Baxter's life in the operating room, yet this scene as well as his plan to care for Baxter for the rest of his life can be interpreted ambiguously (see Nunius 2009: 270–271; Gauthier 2013: 19) and betray his continuous performance of sovereignty even in decisions concerning the realm of morality. The following quotation is particularly striking:

> [B]y saving his life in the operating theatre, Henry also committed Baxter to his torture. Revenge enough. And here is one area where Henry can exercise authority and shape events. He knows how the system works – the difference between good and bad care is near-infinite. (McEwan 2006: 278)

Perowne's plan not only performs sovereignty once again, but also contains the possibility of exerting unlimited power over Baxter and is therefore also potentially violent (see Cornier Michael 2014: 232). The last sentence can therefore be interpreted ambivalently since it indicates the possibility of consigning Baxter to a facility that Perowne associates with "good [...] care" just as much as one that is associated with "bad care". In any case, it does not include any independent decision on Baxter's side or any consideration of Baxter's wishes on Perowne's part. Moreover, the quote implies that Perowne's decision to save Baxter's life already carries an ambivalent connotation since it could just as well be interpreted as an instance of revenge.

Strikingly, Perowne's particular 'revenge' bears even more markers of sovereignty. When operating on Baxter he finally manages to regain his status of authority in the realm of his profession as a doctor. Once again, he performs an action whose sole purpose is apparently to reinstate his sovereign identity when he "places his finger on the surface of Baxter's cortex" (McEwan 2006: 255) without any necessity to do so (see Riedelsheimer 2020: 166). As Martin Riedelsheimer points out, Perowne is now in "a situation where his opponent is quite literally under his thumb" (2020: 167) and consequently returns to a position of "'magical' authority" (2020: 166).

This ties in with what Riedelsheimer, drawing on Eaglestone, refers to as Perowne's "metaphysics of comprehension" (2020: 160–167; Eaglestone 2004: 184) – that is, Perowne's particular system of categorical thought that reduces "the world around him to familiar categories and reject[s] everything that does not fit these categories" (Riedelsheimer 2020: 161). More often than not, this approach gets problematically close to a biologically deterministic[115] twenty-first-

---

[115] On Perowne as representative of essentialist discourses of power, see also Heidi Butler (2011: 102).

century version of Social Darwinism that separates humanity into those who have what it takes to fulfill the norm and those who do not.

> Perowne, the professional reductionist, can't help thinking it's down to invisible folds and kinks of character, written in code, on the level of molecules. It's a dim fate, to be the sort of person who can't earn a living, or resist another drink, or remember today what he resolved to do yesterday. No amount of social justice will cure or disperse this enfeebled army haunting the public places of every town. So, what then? Henry draws his dressing gown more closely around him. You have to recognise bad luck when you see it, you have to look out for these people. Some you can prise from their addictions, others – all you can do is make them comfortable somehow, minimise their miseries.
> Somehow! He's no social theorist and, of course, he's thinking of Baxter, that unpickable knot of affliction. (McEwan 2006: 272)

The final link back to Baxter already signals the problematic slide that Perowne effects in his analysis of societal non-normativity. The reductionist conclusion that he draws is mostly based on the assumption that since there are neurodegenerative diseases that are inscribed into human DNA, every kind of deviation from societal norms has to derive from "invisible folds and kinks of character, written in code, on the level of molecules". This argumentation, which is more than a little logically flawed, then leads him to the assumption that "[n]o amount of social justice will cure or disperse this enfeebled army" and consequently absolves him from any reflection on potential social injustice and the measures that might have to be taken against it. What is more, the statement already implies a hierarchy which denies the genetically 'underprivileged' any possibility of changing their circumstances. Necessarily, even Perowne's societal solution of the problem of various kinds of precarity affirms the sovereignty and moral superiority of those who "look out for these people". As a consequence, he continues his performance of sovereignty and decides to take care of Baxter by ensuring that "the system" will "draw him in securely before he does more harm" (McEwan 2006: 278).

Perowne's musings at this late point in the novel thus put into question whether he has transformed into a post-sovereign subject or rather negate that this is the case. On the one hand, his attitude towards the war on Iraq has changed from being vaguely supportive or at least ambivalent about it (see McEwan 2006: 73) to realizing that his "appetite for removing a tyrant" has disappeared at the end of the novel due to the "way consequences of an action leap away from your control" (McEwan 2006: 277); that is, his stance on this issue has explicitly been influenced by his experience of vulnerability. On the other hand, at no point in the novel does Perowne question that he is perfectly capable of sovereign and successful interpretations of both events and social dynamics despite the many occasions on which his blatant misreading of an experience becomes apparent. Whereas he is perfectly aware of the fact that material existence is vulnerable, he does not recognize that signification and interpretation might be just as precarious. Even though the fact that his opinion about the war on Iraq has changed implies that he might revoke other assessments as well, he seems not quite to have reached this point at the end of the novel. Consequently, the ending of *Saturday* has been interpreted ambiguously, both as attesting the human capability to develop empathy towards others as well as testifying to the ways in which empathy can be turned into just another means of domination, therefore denying the possibility of the development of post-sovereign subjectivities. Yet, the novel might in fact offer its readers a gateway to this specific kind of precariousness through its performance of a particular kind of flânerie.

6.4 Precarious Interpretations: Strolling through the Memory Space of Literature

Although it has been argued that Perowne can be seen as a modern-day flâneur (see Pleßke 2014: 293), I would suggest that flânerie takes place on a different level in McEwan's novel, one that becomes apparent when compared to how flânerie functions in *Mrs Dalloway*. Similar to Henry Perowne, Clarissa Dalloway does not qualify as a flâneuse. Yet, in Woolf's novel *histoire* and *discours* combine to produce what could be called flânerie on a formal level. It is in fact the heterodiegetic narrator who strolls aimlessly and moves from one focalizer to another while the *histoire* of the novel offers the environment of the city within which this movement occurs. This does not hold true for *Saturday* where the narrative voice remains solely focalized on Perowne. However, while the readers only get to know Perowne's perspective on the events, the plethora of reference texts with which his narrative is juxtaposed, ranging from the aforementioned *Strange Case of Dr Jekyll and Mr Hyde* to Joyce's short story "The Dead" (see Ganteau 2014: 223–238) and Matthew Arnold's poem "Dover Beach", forms a memory space that puts Perowne's point of view into various other perspectives (see Winterhalter 2010: 351). If intertextuality is understood in the sense of Renate Lachmann as a quality pertaining to texts that reflect spaces of memory, but at the same time partake in memory spaces, then *Saturday* itself becomes a flâneur who strolls through the memory space of literature which is, on the one hand, represented by the apparent intertextuality of the novel, but on the other hand, is also referred to as a basis for this intertextuality.[116] Insofar as *Saturday* takes up the manifold reference texts it encounters on its rambles through the memory space of literature, it represents this space at the same time that it moves through it. The city of London becomes the palpable representative of this movement through memory space, yet in this representation it also changes it, producing its own memory space, similar, but not identical to the one it represents. According to Lachmann, a text creates places or concrete architectures that it imagines, like cities, landscapes, or houses, which suggest its participation in the mnemonic art, or culture of remembrance, at the same time that they hide it.[117] In the same way that the textual city of London refers back to the memory space that it represents, yet hides it at the same time, Perowne's movement through the city refers back to flânerie, yet also hides the flânerie of the text itself. Nevertheless, the question remains as to whether the way the text moves through the memory space of literature really qualifies as flânerie, particularly with respect to this movement's aimlessness. In order to prove my point that *Saturday*'s movement can be called flânerie, I will take a closer look at the different effects that intertextuality generates in the novel.

First of all, as has already been mentioned, the text cites a countless number of reference texts. It is framed at the start by an epigraph from Saul Bellow's *Herzog* and at the end by Matthew Arnold's "Dover Beach", which is quoted in its entirety. The plot is to a large extent modelled on *Mrs Dalloway* with Henry Perowne standing in for Clarissa Dalloway running errands for a party that is to take place at his house in the evening, a party that is eventually invaded by a segment of the city's population that has so far been excluded from Perowne's realm of perception in a similar way that Clarissa Dalloway's party is invaded by the news of Septimus Warren Smith's suicide (see Adams 2012: 553–554). Whereas a large number of intertextual references are explicit, the text also alludes implicitly to many other reference texts that can only be identified by the way that passages, topics, or formal structures are directly or indirectly

---

116 See Lachmann (1997: 16): "Intertextuality and memory architecture should therefore be conceived in relation to each other. The text traverses memory spaces and it settles into them, but it also represents this mnemonic space."
117 See Lachmann (1997: 15): "Yet the text also sketches out the places it imagines, the cities or landscapes, houses or concrete works of architecture that suggest a cryptic participation in mnemonic art. [...] The memory image is invisible, but from its concealed position it can act as the generator of a manifest imagery developing within a text. Although literature as an art of memory draws from a fund of images supplied by mnemotechnics, it exceeds this field to the extent that it exteriorizes the inside of memory and thematizes the relation of inside and outside as such."

quoted by the novel (see also Riedelsheimer 2020: 159). The reader's act of interpretation by means of the reference texts therefore can be said to become aimless in that it is dependent on the individual reader's knowledge and recognition of these other texts hidden in the narration. The freedom of any individual's act of interpretation of any text is thus reinforced by the immense number of reference texts in *Saturday*. Although the novel refers to numerous intertextual references explicitly or implicitly in a very obvious way, it is precisely this practice that implies that there are always more reference texts hidden in the novel than those already detected by the reader.

Moreover, those texts often add an additional layer of meaning to Perowne's own perspective on the events, as we have seen with regard to the intertextual reference to *Strange Case of Dr Jekyll and Mr Hyde*. Yet, since the novel refers to many such texts that might add new layers of meaning to every single moment in the unfolding of events, meaning multiplies and is dispersed through the plethora of reference texts (see also Riedelsheimer 2020: 168). The beginning of the novel offers a good example of this pluralization of meaning. The whole scene in which Perowne opens the window and looks out onto the square echoes the opening scene of *Mrs Dalloway* when Clarissa Dalloway steps out of her house and remembers standing at the French windows in the morning at Burton (see Woolf 2000: 3). Perowne is thus likened to Clarissa Dalloway in this first scene, yet it has also been argued that the scene echoes the beginning of Kafka's *The Metamorphosis*, in which case Perowne would be likened to Gregor Samsa waking up transformed into an insect (see Kafka 1995: 67; Groes 2009: 103). Whereas Perowne is thus compared with a character – Clarissa Dalloway – who is fully ensconced in society, he is at the same time likened to Gregor Samsa, who has undergone a transformation that will cut him off from society. The meaning that the two reference texts confer on the scene is thus contradictory and the matter becomes even more complicated if one considers how the scene also echoes the first stanza of Arnold's "Dover Beach" (see Riedelsheimer 2020: 178; Winterhalter 2010: 354) in which the speaker is also standing at a window and listening to the waves "bring the eternal note of sadness in" (McEwan 2006: 281). Moreover, the next scenes suggest that the novel follows the sequence of chapters in *Ulysses* in reverse, with the first scene referring to Molly Bloom's stream of consciousness in the bedroom.[118] The first scene is thus re-written by

---

[118] *Saturday*'s opening scene is followed by a chat that Henry Perowne has with his son Theo in the kitchen, which is reminiscent of Bloom and Stephen Dedalus talking in the kitchen of the Blooms' house in the penultimate chapter of *Ulysses* (see Joyce 1986: 544–607); his quarrel with Baxter in front of the night-club can be linked to the ending of the "Circe" chapter in *Ulysses*, when Stephen is beaten up by English Privates (see Joyce 1986: 485–497); and the squash

the palimpsestic structure of reference texts that not only add, but also disperse meaning.

In a way similar to *Mrs Dalloway*, *Saturday* therefore employs the three central characteristics of flânerie named by Neumeyer. First of all, it takes place within the space of a city. This space represents the memory space from which the reference texts have been taken at the same time that it hides it in the palimpsestic construction of London. Second, the text itself strolls through this memory space and thus moves through a crowd of reference texts which resurface in different ways in the narrative. Yet, this movement becomes aimless – and this is Neumeyer's third characteristic – due to the dissolution of any fixed meaning effected by the plethora of reference texts. This flânerie thus decenters the author as well as the reading subject and therefore makes them non-sovereign.

While this could – at least according to poststructuralists – be said of any text, *Saturday* also takes up the topics of sovereignty and precariousness on the level of content. Whereas the actual reading subject is thus by means of the marked intertextuality of the novel ripped of his or her sovereignty, Perowne repeatedly tries to establish himself as a sovereign reading subject (Nunius 2009: 259–260) by interpreting and evaluating the events taking place around him. Moreover, interpretation is for Perowne a tool for performing sovereignty, as occurs in his confrontation with Baxter where he reads Baxter's behavior as symptomatic of Huntington's disease (see McEwan 2006: 91–94; see also Nunius 2009: 259). Nevertheless, it is especially his supposed sovereignty with regard to interpretation that is put into question in the course of the events of the novel by means of the numerous situations that Perowne misreads on this particular Saturday, most notably his misconception that Arnold's "Dover Beach" is one of Daisy's poems (see also Riedelsheimer 2020: 174). While the novel thus points out how the performance of sovereignty, the denial of one's own vulnerability and the ensuing exertion of violence are connected, it also thematizes the precariousness of interpretation in particular.

The novel therefore implies that it is not possible for Perowne to find a way out of his performance of sovereignty, but *Saturday*'s marked intertextuality emphasizes the workings of *écriture* and thus decenters the writing as well as the reading subject. This ultimately creates a non-sovereign reading subject that must stay "at the edge of what we know" (Butler 2004a: 228) about the novel.

---

game between Perowne and his colleague Jay Strauss can, as mentioned above, be compared to the "Oxen of the Sun" chapter which also centers around a meaningless competition between doctors for sovereignty (see Joyce 1986: 314–349).

Moreover, by strolling through the memory space of literature new perspectives based on the juxtaposition of Perowne's perspective with the reference texts that criticize his actions or at least put them in a different perspective are brought into focus. Thus, while Perowne is not able to develop a post-sovereign subjectivity, the readers still might, since the text itself makes the precarious visible as a category that is shared by Baxter and Perowne even though Perowne is unable to acknowledge this. Since Perowne functions as a mirror image of the norm of sovereignty, *Saturday* places this norm in question on the level of content and at the same time creates non-sovereign writing and reading subjects. Indeed, the mass of reference texts opens up an infinite process of interpretation that inhibits any kind of closed interpretation of the novel by its readers (see Riedelsheimer 2020: 181). *Saturday* thus takes up – by way of its reference to a countless number of other texts and especially to *Mrs Dalloway* – the tradition of flânerie and links it to contemporary ethical questions, opening a pathway for the formation of an ethical, post-sovereign subject.

Moreover, *Saturday* highlights how technologies of the self can be turned into technologies of domination by tying subjecthood to impossible performances of sovereignty and by explicitly delineating how those performances rely on and contribute to continuing cycles of violence since they demand that subjects locate precariousness in the other. Perowne's perspective on society could then best be described in terms of what Foucault refers to as "disciplinary normalization" (2004: 89); that is, a link between normativity and societal power that causes norms to be potentially violent. Establishing sovereignty as a strict norm that needs to be fulfilled in constructions of subjectivity exerts violence against the subject as well as against the other. This norm of sovereignty occurs in *Saturday* in terms of unambiguous interpretation, professional, material, and familial success, and overall competition, all of which contribute to Perowne's performance of sovereignty. In order to secure this sovereignty, Perowne has to compete with others who become precarious as soon as they are less successful than he is.

The difference with respect to the other novels discussed here is, however, decisive. Transformation by means of flânerie is denied on the level of the *histoire* since there is no actual flâneur left to stroll through the fictional London. Material experience and the experience of the dissemination of meaning seem to be separated and can only be reconciled in the act of reading. Indeed, Perowne's world is hyperbolically deterministic. While he enthusiastically follows the rules as the perfect sovereign subject of twenty-first-century capitalism, the only time he dares to resist those rules by driving down a street he is not supposed to use, he is immediately punished through the encounter with Baxter and thus runs the risk of becoming associated with vulnerability and precariousness. His reflections on social injustice, moreover, can only be called dystopian and resistance only occurs in the form of "phantom texts" (Ganteau 2014) that might only be recognized by those already well-versed in literary history. Interestingly enough, any kind of aimless movement – in the sense of not being subjected to a prescribed route – in this reading only takes place in an abstract imaginary realm while the movement through the city on the level of *histoire* is strictly limited. The way in which flânerie here works as a gateway to the post-sovereign can therefore only be found on an imaginary level. Consequently, it remains in question whether – and how – a connection is even possible between a flânerie on the level of content that confronts the subject with its own precariousness, and the development of this very subject into a post-sovereign one, since the concept of a post-sovereign subjectivity relies strongly on the specific application of the disseminating quality of *écriture* to matter and to relationships between actual people. While the possibility of the construction of a post-sovereign subjectivity on the part of the reader exists, the novel lacks any negotiation of post-sovereign subjectivity on the level of plot and therefore marks the limit of flânerie as a technique of the self. Indeed, the text lacks any positive evaluation of post-sovereign subjectivity and thus offers no orientation for the construction of subjectivity; instead, it focuses on the critique of technologies of domination. Whereas the city can still form a gateway to the precarious here, this confrontation only occurs in the form of the shock that ultimately precipitates the development of what Simmel called the "blasé attitude" (1971: 330) and what, in the novel, is translated into performances of sovereign subjectivity, that is, of being protected from precarious city life.

The two novels I will analyze next, Siri Hustvedt's *The Blindfold* and Teju Cole's *Open City*, by contrast, showcase two very different variants of the Foucauldian 'aesthetics of existence', with both ultimately engaging in the practice of critique that results from the 'aesthetics of existence' of their protagonists and that becomes manifest in the novels themselves. There, strolling as well as writing are turned into techniques of the self which contribute, as methods of searching, to the individual's 'aesthetics of existence'. Moreover, both novels tie in with the political counter-discourses of feminist and postcolonial criticism and therefore also exemplify how flânerie can become a self-reflexive performance of resistance.

7 Flânerie as Technique of the Self

7.1 Precarious Flânerie in Siri Hustvedt's *The Blindfold*

Siri Hustvedt's novel *The Blindfold*, which was published in 1992, is the oldest among the texts discussed here and was the author's first novel. The text comprises four individual stories, all of which take place in New York and center around the graduate student Iris Vegan, who also functions as the novel's autodiegetic narrator. Each of the stories describes an encounter with one or two other characters[119] that negotiates dynamics of subjection and power, usually, yet not exclusively related to issues of gender. Irritatingly, the temporal structure of the novel is not chronological so that the narrated time actually starts in chapter four, which also offers the framework within which the other three chapters can be situated: chapter one narrates events that have taken place after those described in chapter two, but before those narrated in chapter three, thus creating the impression of a "time-warp" (Knirsch 2010) in which the heroine is caught. Moreover, Hustvedt's novel showcases a variety of instances of the 'return of the repressed' and has therefore also been classified as an example of the so-called 'urban gothic' (see Dallmann 2009: 270), a genre that focuses on the uncanny quality of human relationships in the alienated cities of modernity. The characters frequently indulge in acts of voyeurism as well as psychological, discursive and physical violence, with Iris often reflecting the violence with which she is confronted by the male characters.

What is more, *The Blindfold* self-consciously transgresses the border between fictional and autobiographical writing since the novel's protagonist Iris not only shares several biographical details with the author – such as her post-graduate time at Columbia University, her rural origins or the fact that both lived in poverty during their time in New York (Hicklin 2019: n. pag.)[120] – but also shares her name, although read backwards.[121] By establishing such an allusive relationship between author and protagonist without trying to create an autobiographical pact *sensu* Philip Lejeune (1994), the novel gives the impres-

---

[119] Johanna Hartmann, for example, argues for a triangular relationship in each of the chapters (see Hartmann 2016: 87).
[120] See also Hustvedt's remark in her essay "Yonder" that "she [Iris] and I aren't the same person, but she's close to me" (1998: 32).
[121] Hustvedt's debut novel hence shows a characteristic trait of her whole oeuvre in which she continuously investigates modes of de- and reconstructing the self under (post-)postmodern conditions (see Tappen-Scheuermann 2012: 161).

sion that Iris could be interpreted as an alter ego of the author, or, and this is where my argument takes its start, that the protagonist undergoes a transformation throughout the novel on the level of plot which then results in the text itself, yet which also extends to the practice of writing this very text and the act of identity-formation it entails.[122]

In the following, I would like to show how this transformation takes place within the novel's *histoire* and how it is linked to Iris's specific practice of flânerie. In a second step, I will argue that the practice of telling one's own story is already linked to a process of healing as well as to the formation of the protagonist's self in the novel, which entails flânerie as one of its central constituents and which then recurs in the act of narration as a variant of writing the self. Iris's transformation, then, revolves around a staple of ethical discourse, namely the question of whether humans are intrinsically violent. Throughout the text, Iris's narration deconstructs the binary opposition between an essentialist stance that asserts humanity's predetermination to violence and the idea that violence is always inscribed on humans from the outside. The narrative thus frees the protagonist from the assumption that mankind is intrinsically violent and at the same time mimics practices of deconstruction that Iris also acts out on the level of the *histoire*. Those practices are, in turn, linked to the recognition of the primarily precarious state of the subject, which is emphasized by means of various intersubjective encounters in the novel. Moreover, the novel openly affirms the precarious non-sovereignty of its protagonist through formal features like minor instances of unreliability and the anachronistic temporal structure of the narration and by doing so showcases the formation of a resistant, yet

---

[122] This practice is highly reminiscent of James Joyce's *A Portrait of the Artist as a Young Man*, which also presents emancipation in terms of the fictionalization and narrativization of the self featuring a protagonist whose biography resembles that of the author without establishing an autobiographical pact (see Riquelme 2007: 366–381). Interestingly, the two novels share quite a number of similarities: Iris's boyfriend Stephen has not only the same first name as Joyce's protagonist, but also shows an interest in Friedrich Nietzsche whose ideas have often been associated with Joyce's work. Moreover, both novels interweave modes of visual and scriptural representation in their discussion of the production of the self, as the title of Joyce's novel already indicates. Like *The Portrait of the Artist*, *The Blindfold* could therefore certainly also be read as an autobiographical novel, that is, "as a fictional text, in which the reader presumes a certain identity between the protagonist and the author of the text on the basis of resemblances he/she means to have seen" (Missinne 2019: 464), although the autobiographical element is much stronger in Hustvedt's recent work *Memories of the Future* (2019), which treats the same time period in Hustvedt's life, yet features a narrator who is situated closer to the author due to her name being indicated by the letters S.H. In my analysis, I will therefore focus on the aspect of subject-formation and identity construction in general, which could also be integrated in a reading of *The Blindfold* as an autobiographical novel.

non-sovereign subjectivity. In the following, I shall therefore argue that flânerie connects three central facets of the novel: the deconstruction of binary oppositions, the recognition of one's own state of precariousness and the violent claim to sovereignty which might result from this recognition. Yet, flânerie is also translated into Iris's unique form of self-writing by means of which the writing subject (trans-)forms itself and affirms a primary state of vulnerability. Iris's particular brand of flânerie, however, needs to be seen in the context of the history of the flâneuse, which I will briefly outline next.

7.1.1 Streetwalking the Metropolis: The Female Gaze and the City

The title of this section, which is borrowed from Deborah Parsons' seminal monograph *Streetwalking the Metropolis: Women, the City, and Modernity*, indicates the problematic status of women in the public space of the city. As Janet Wolff argues in her essay "The Invisible Flâneuse", in the nineteenth century, the heyday of flânerie, "the public sphere [...] despite the presence of some women in certain contained areas of it, was a masculine domain" (1989: 142).[123] Academic discussion of the phenomenon of the so-called flâneuse tackles the issue on two levels, corresponding with the flâneur's double existence on the streets as well as on the page: the flâneuse as a (potential) socio-historical phenomenon and the sociological, philosophical and literary discourse concerning the phenomenon of flânerie and the experience of modernity to which it is linked. In both cases, research on the flâneuse, first and foremost, notes her absence. As Wolff points out, the public domain was usually conceived of as the realm of masculinity. This is affirmed not only by discourses which assigned a positive value to an association between women and the domestic sphere, such as the Victorian ideal of the 'Angel in the House', but even more so by historical sources proving that women without male company were actually banished from public spaces like cafés or restaurants (Gomolla 2009: 41).[124] Since unaccompanied women on the streets of the city were then in general deemed

---

[123] See also Vila-Cabanes, who points out that the flâneur was a "usually male" figure in the nineteenth century (2016: 15) and Gomolla (2009: 43).
[124] Another instance attesting to gendered separation in the public sphere can be found in women initially not being allowed on the upper level of omnibuses since it was considered unseemly for them to climb the narrow stairs that led up there (see Belenky 2019: 17–18). Benjamin (2002: 432) also refers to this exclusion.

unseemly,[125] female writers like George Sand who actually did indulge in flânerie decided to hide their femininity and dressed in men's clothes in order to be able to participate in metropolitan life (Wolff 1989: 148).

The socio-historical absence of the flâneuse was transferred to and perpetuated by the sociological analysis and representation of public space in the nineteenth and early twentieth centuries (Wolff 1989: 151). The classic writings on the phenomenon of modernity, like Baudelaire's "The Painter of Modern Life", Simmel's "The Metropolis and Mental Life" or Benjamin's works on Baudelaire as well as the *Arcades Project*, indeed focus predominantly on a male experience of modernity. The women who appear in those texts are mostly marked as deviations from the feminine norm. Prominent examples referred to in this context are prostitutes, lesbians, old women or murder victims (Wolff 1989: 148). As the discourse about modernity suggests, women who walk the streets of the nineteenth-century city might be perceived as deviant from the norm and therefore also run the risk of facing the consequences of this deviation.

Since the connection between observation, voyeurism and the space of the city is central to the history of the flâneur, feminist criticism has envisioned the flâneur as an embodiment of the male gaze. As Griselda Pollock argues, "the gaze of the flâneur articulates and produces a masculine sexuality which in the modern sexual economy enjoys the freedom to look, appraise and possess" (1988: 79). By turning the flâneur's observations into text, the male gaze is translated into patriarchal discourse that further consolidates the partition into male subject and female object. If the female object is then charged with the expectation of the male gaze, she turns into a prostitute, thus perpetuating a socio-historical normativity according to which female presence on the streets of the city is highly problematic and potentially deviant.

The perpetuation of the patriarchal discourse's objectification of the female stroller can be exemplified in the analogy between the flâneur and the prostitute, which has been emphasized by Susan Buck-Morss as a central analogy in Benjamin's work (1986: 120).[126] Benjamin employs the image of prostitution in order to further emphasize the state of commodification in which the flâneur finds himself. The intoxication which the flâneur experiences as commodity had already been 'tested' by prostitutes: "They tried the secrets of the free market: in this respect, commodities had no advantage over them" (Benjamin 2006: 86). Yet, the analogy between flâneur and prostitute is a telling one if seen from

---

125 As Carola Lipp points out, it was at times even considered to be problematic for women to look out of the window (1986: 21).
126 See Buck-Morss (1986: 104): "In commodity society all of us are prostitutes, selling ourselves to strangers."

the point of view of gender relations in the city. Like the flâneur, the prostitute needs to rely on practices of lounging and sauntering in order to make herself approachable by potential customers who could thus more easily differentiate between her and other women. The process of self-commodification is in both cases linked to the practice of leisurely strolling through the streets, yet the difference between the two reinvokes common gender stereotypes: while the flâneur is selling his mind, the prostitute is selling her body. The comparison moreover excludes the possibility of an actual female flâneur or flâneuse who might also indulge in flânerie as a mode of textual production instead of a commodification of her body.[127] What is more, it implies that the female stroller searches for the 'male gaze'. Whereas invisibility and anonymity are paramount for male flâneurs who use flânerie in order to collect material, the comparison between flâneur and prostitute does not grant this privilege to women whose appearance on the streets of the metropolis is always linked to exposure. Hence, the privilege of anonymous observation is only granted to men, whereas women cannot escape the fact that they are the object of this kind of observation (see, for example, Forna 2018: 1). The analogy between the flâneur and the prostitute therefore further consolidates the separation of the female, private space of the house from the male, public space of the street.

Consequently, the prostitute does not belong to the 'heroic' roles that Benjamin assigns to the modern subject since she only serves to further illustrate the aspect of commodification. Those roles are instead almost exclusively reserved for males, such as the categories of "[f]lâneur, apache, dandy and ragpicker" (2006: 125). The only woman to be grouped with those roles is the lesbian woman[128] who, for Benjamin, is, in a rather problematic equation of sexual orientation with sexual identity, equivalent to "the androgyne" (2006: 119) and therefore also connoted as masculine.

Yet, as the inclusion of the lesbian woman as well as the equation between flâneur and prostitute also imply, discourse about the metropolis and its subject is from the start infused with aspects of femininity so that the flâneur is also charged with feminine characteristics, as the analogy with the dandy, for example, suggests (see Parsons 2000: 24). What is more, Baudelaire was already envisioning women as observers in the city and is therefore used by Parsons as a

---

127 See also Elizabeth Wilson (1992: 107): "We might say that, as unpleasant as it may be to live out your life as a hack writer, it is worse to sell your body." Nevertheless, Wilson's stance towards the status of women in the city is a bit more nuanced than Wolff's. Thus, she, for example, points out that the city also offered a number of opportunities to women such as a wider range of jobs as well as alternative housing than in rural areas.
128 See Benjamin (2006: 119): "The lesbian is the heroine of *la modernité*."

source when tracing "the beginnings of the conceptual idea of a *flâneuse*" (2000: 24). The internal tensions inherent to the trope of the flâneur could therefore also be interpreted as contributing to the gradual development of the flâneuse (see also Parsons 2000: 38–39). In this context, particularly interesting for the analysis of flânerie in *The Blindfold* is a point made by Parsons who, drawing on Mary Ann Doane's reflections on female masquerade's potential for resistance (see Doane 2000: 248–256), emphasizes the significance of masquerade within Baudelaire's representation of femininity (2000: 25–26). Here, she does not refer to practices of cross-dressing which only aim at hiding the flâneuse's actual gender, but to the creative agency implicit in any kind of masquerade as an intentional construction of identity:

> The male observer is denied possession of the woman because he is only presented with certain façades, fragments of her identity put on display. She too is thus an artist, and through the masquerade of femininity does not so much objectify herself and see herself through the eyes of the male, as construct herself and present herself as she wants to be seen. (Parsons 2000: 26)

Although the border between 'objectifying oneself' and 'constructing oneself' might be more blurry than Parsons suggests, her claim ties in with Butler's concept of the potential of "promiscuous obedience" which could also entail active practices of masquerade.

A too simplistic perspective on the situation of the flâneuse, however, can be challenged not only on the level of textual reflections on flânerie, but also by taking into account a socio-historical situation that was both more nuanced and undergoing changes throughout the century, with women entering public spaces in various ways. Firstly, gendered restrictions mostly applied to women of the middle and upper classes, while working-class women had no other option than navigating the city streets on their own in order to go to work or to buy groceries. Yet, precisely because they defied gender restrictions in doing so, femininity (and even humanity) was often denied to them in contemporary representations which characterized them as "violent, wild and bestial" (Wilson 1992: 104). As Françoise Barret-Ducrocq points out, "[t]heir carelessness, their frivolity, their audacious impudence are tirelessly catalogued. These indomitable, intoxicated furies seem to fear nothing and nobody" (Barret-Ducrocq 1991: 31).

Secondly, the city was not only a place of restrictions for the female gender, but also one of opportunities that far exceeded the opportunities of women in rural areas. Thus, women's independence increased in cities due to "a wider choice of alternative forms of financial support (that is, paid work) and a wider range of alternative housing than in the rural areas" resulting, for example, in higher divorce rates (Wilson 1992: 103).

Additionally, women's situation improved in the course of the nineteenth century so that its second half saw a gradual adaptation of the public sphere to women's needs. Eating establishments began making "special provisions to ensure that women felt comfortable there" (Thorne 1980: 41), such as employing female staff or offering ladies-only dining rooms. This change was linked not only to the "growth of white-collar occupations for women" (Wilson 1992: 101), but also to the rise of the department store which offered a public space in which women's presence was deemed socially acceptable without their being accompanied by a man (see Wilson 1992: 101; Dinter 2019: 117; Nava 1996: 53). Like their male counterparts, potential flâneuses could there indulge in strolling and looking at the goods on display as well as the crowd, so that "[t]he department store may have been, as Benjamin put it, the flâneur's last coup, but it was the flâneuse's first" (Friedberg 1993: 37). While those innovations certainly offered more opportunities to women, they nevertheless also indicate the overall problem: the public sphere was still largely reserved for men, with only gradual adjustments being made to alter this situation towards the end of the nineteenth century (see also Wilson 1992: 90).

With the constant advance of women's liberation movements, possibilities for women's access to the public sphere increased, yet were also anxiously supervised by patriarchal discourse "characteriz[ing], examin[ing] and theoriz[ing them] into one or more male-authored stereotyped pathological states" (Parsons 2000: 43). At the turn of the century, several tropes had been developed from those images which persisted in the predominantly masculine discourses of the time and ensured women's status as a "possessable object" (Parsons 2000: 43). Nevertheless, as Parsons convincingly argues, women's growing access not only to the streets themselves, but also to the discourses about those streets allowed for "an alternative perception of women's presence in the city" (Parsons 2000: 43) due to the ambiguities involved in their description.

While women thus did enter the public sphere in the course of the nineteenth and twentieth centuries, their status has remained to a considerable extent problematic throughout the second half of the twentieth and into the start of the twenty-first century. Although they are not explicitly banned from public spaces, objectification persists, as ongoing discussions about sexual harassment and the discourses supporting a still existent 'rape culture' show (see also Wilson 1992: 110). As feminist projects like Hollaback!'s prominent campaign "10 Hours of Walking NYC as a Woman" or academic publications like Rebecca Solnit's *Men Explain Things to Me* prove,[129] women's status on the streets remains

---

[129] See, for example, Solnit's chapter on "The Longest War" (2014: 19–40).

precarious. *The Blindfold* therefore employs the image of the flâneuse and the tensions that arise from women's situation on the streets of the metropolis as a central metaphor around which more general reflections regarding power, identity, gender and violence revolve.[130]

7.1.2 Flânerie as Resistance in *The Blindfold*

Feminist topics pervade Hustvedt's whole oeuvre: she exposes gender-biased prejudices in the art world in her 2014 novel *The Blazing World*, rewrites the history of sexual difference in *The Summer Without Men* (2011: 146–154) and subjects the male gaze to her own observation in her 2016 essay collection *A Woman Looking at Men Looking at Women*. As the title of the last work already indicates, her critique often engages reflections on gender-specific vision and perspective and the influence that a male gaze and discourse exerts on women.

The motif of the male gaze and its link to patriarchal discourses of power, which subject and define female gender, recurs throughout *The Blindfold*. Every chapter (except – arguably – the third) centers around Iris's interaction with one or two male characters, in which a strong emphasis is put on aspects of vision. In the first chapter, Iris works for the reclusive Mr. Morning who tasks her with the description of several everyday objects that once belonged to a woman named Sherry Zalewski, who was murdered in Mr. Morning's apartment building. The project aims at "the evocation of a mental image of Sherri Zalewski" (Hartmann 2016: 108) which is supposed to result in his "seeing [her] face" (Hustvedt 1993: 29). Mr. Morning's attempted 'resurrection' of the dead woman involves his specific take on practices of 'objectification' by creating his own image of her through dead objects and thus forming her identity through these objects. During their whole collaboration, Mr. Morning remains an ambiguous character, whom Iris at times even suspects to be the murderer of Sherri Zalewski although this is never affirmed in the novel. An atmosphere of threat already pervades Iris's first encounter with Mr. Morning when he "without any apparent reserve" looks at Iris, "taking in [her] whole body with his gaze" (Hustvedt 1993: 11), and throughout their association the dynamics of looking at and concealing things represent an underlying struggle for power between them. Therefore, when she finally demands to hear the truth about his relationship to Sherri Zalewski, a request made indirectly via a tape recording, the scene is framed by practices of observation: while Mr. Morning retreats to his living

---

130 Parts of the argument in this chapter have already been published in Ries (2020).

room in order to listen to Iris's recording, she does not "close the door to the kitchen", but instead "let[s it] stand open slightly and put[s] [her] eye to the crack" (Hustvedt 1993: 34). As soon as Iris deviates from the usual script, her gaze is met by Mr. Morning's who "look[s] sharply in [her] direction" and by doing so forces her to "shut the door" (Hustvedt 1993: 34). As the scene indicates, power is on the side of Mr. Morning for several reasons: he is the potential murderer of Sherri Zalewski and therefore poses a possible threat to Iris as well, and as her employer he has the power to withhold money from Iris should she fail to follow his rules.

The dynamics of vision are linked to both characters' attempts at constructing other people's identities. While both engage in the mutual as well as separate construction of the identity of Sherri Zalewski, Iris also tries to get a grip on Mr. Morning's actual relationship to the murder victim and actively constructs her own image of his identity throughout the first chapter. She ultimately fails to find proof of her suspicions, however, and as a result Mr. Morning's identity remains ambivalent.

The triadic relationship between vision, power and identity becomes even more palpable in the second chapter of the novel which focuses on Iris's relationship with her part-time boyfriend Stephen and his friend George, "an artist who [takes] photographs" (Hustvedt 1993: 42). The interrelation between discourses of power, vision and representation crystallizes here in a picture of Iris taken by George, a portrait in which Iris appears fragmented and dissected. While Iris is deeply disturbed by the picture, George decides to add it to an upcoming exhibition where he plans on coupling it with the picture of a woman having a grand mal seizure whom he photographed without her permission. At the same time, talk of Iris's picture seems to circulate through her social sphere with changing descriptions of its content so that Iris is at times even confronted with questions about her assumed nudity in the picture – although she did not actually pose in the nude. The representation of George's male gaze thus keeps re-constructing Iris's identity until she retreats into her flat and avoids further social contact.

Iris's encounter with Dr. Fish, the male character in the third chapter of the novel, in turn, is directly linked to institutional discourses of power. As a neurologist, Dr. Fish is not only related to those medical authoritative discourses which have been one of the focal points in Foucauldian analyses of power, but he also works in a field that is located at the intersection between mind and body. In Iris's account of being treated by Dr. Fish dynamics of vision and discourses of power overlap. After suffering from severe migraines including hallucinations, temporary loss of vision and extreme nausea for several months, Iris decides to consult Dr. Fish, "who was known in New York as the 'Headache Czar'"

(Hustvedt 1993: 93). Whenever Iris then tries to describe her symptoms and her illness to Dr. Fish, the doctor 'translates' her narration into medical discourse by condensing her detailed descriptions into two or three words of medical jargon, thus classifying her illness and prescribing medication (see also Bein 2016: 229).[131] In so doing, Dr. Fish explicitly replaces Iris's discourse with his own and at the same time subjects her to an authoritative discourse of power. While this approach might have been helpful had it actually contributed to a process of healing, subsequent events emphasize the violence already inherent in Dr. Fish's reductive account of Iris's narration: the treatment he prescribes does not help and finally leads to Iris checking into the hospital. Moreover, during the sessions leading up to this point Dr. Fish's discourse is linked to his visual apprehension of Iris, as he constantly evaluates her appearance in positive terms: "Every week, I went to Dr. Fish, and every week, I looked better to him, less pale, less drawn, less tired" (Hustvedt 1993: 94). His male gaze might not be sexually charged, but it is linked to the production of his discourse of power which creates 'truth' concerning Iris's state of health and even leads her to adapt to Dr. Fish's erroneous evaluation, concealing her actual condition: "With Dr. Fish, I was always cheerful. I joked about my nerves. I smiled even when the headache raged and I had to hide my trembling hands by clasping them tightly together" (Hustvedt 1993: 94). The doctor's gaze therefore serves to prove the success of his treatment which would further ensure his position of power within medical discourse. Consequently, when Iris's health fails to im-

---

131 Although Dr. Fish's actions are probably perfectly justifiable in terms of his profession, Iris's account of her first appointment at Dr. Fish's already proves how reductive his approach is: "'It started last August,' I said. 'I was walking home from the library on Broadway, and I remember that the street looked different to me, very clear and beautiful, and I felt incredibly happy. I even said to myself, "I've never been happier than I am now." 'Yes,' he said, and fingered his bald head. I could see that Dr. Fish was restless, and although I wanted to explain that the feeling of completeness, of perfection, was essential to the story, I rushed on. 'But as soon as a I stepped inside my apartment, I felt a tug on my left arm, just as if someone had yanked it hard. I lost my balance and fell down. I was so dizzy and sick to my stomach that I didn't get up for a long time. While I was sitting there on the floor, I saw lights, hundreds of bright sparks that filled up half the room, and after they disappeared, I saw a big, ragged hole in the wall. That hole scared me to death, and the strange thing was that I didn't experience it as a problem with my vision. I really thought that a part of the wall was missing. I don't know how long it lasted, but after the hole was gone, the pain started.' Dr. Fish picked up the microphone. 'The patient suffered a scintillating and a negative scotoma'" (Hustvedt 1993: 92–93). Not only does Dr. Fish thus simply ignore several of Iris's physical symptoms like the pain or the nausea, he entirely excludes any psychical and emotional components which might be indicated by the different emotions that Iris mentions throughout her story.

prove he seems to lose interest, since "Dr. Fish was a man who loved successes" (Hustvedt 1993: 92).

Finally, the fourth chapter focuses on Iris's relationship to her professor Michael Rose, with whom she has an affair and who epitomizes the representation of discourses of power in the novel by not only being in a position of power over Iris as her professor as well as employer when she starts working for him as an assistant, but also by holding an institutional position of power and therefore directly participating in the production of orders of knowledge as "an aging academic star" (Hustvedt 1993: 119) at Columbia University. The relationship between Iris and Professor Rose is laden with power struggles ranging from Rose's failed attempt at intimidation during their very first encounter to their debates regarding their conflicting interpretations of the fictive novella *The Brutal Boy* to a bet concerning their familiarity with the streets of New York City. Those struggles culminate in one final scene in which Rose tries to rape the blindfolded Iris after having lost the bet with her. The scene illustrates the nexus between power and vision: not only is Iris deprived of her vision by the eponymous blindfold, but this blindness is directly linked to Rose's desire for her: "Again I went for the scarf and again he stopped me, saying, 'No, not now. I want you blind, just this once'" (Hustvedt 1993: 203). While their sexual interaction starts off as a performance of conquest and subjection, in which Iris willingly assumes the passive role of the subjected, the role-playing turns into reality when Rose pins Iris onto the bed despite her attempts at freeing herself and finally slaps her across the face and calls her a "Witch" (Hustvedt 1993: 204). The ability to see the other is thus directly linked to power, desire and potential violence whereas blindness is related to subjection and passivity.[132]

Hence, the connection between (discursive) power and vision is emphasized throughout the novel and resurfaces again in Iris's attempts at resistance against the (mainly patriarchal) power structures to which she is subjected. A central resistant practice can be identified in Iris's flânerie. As Caroline Rosenthal argues, Iris uses flânerie, which she deliberately engages in as performance, as a mode of resistance against the male gaze:[133] on her walks through the mostly nocturnal New York Iris dresses up as a man and renames herself Klaus (Rosenthal 2016:

---

[132] However, blindness is ambivalently connoted in the novel since it is also the condition under which she proves her mastery of the New York streets to Rose.

[133] Tellingly, Iris integrates the act of cross-dressing into her daily life only after her apartment was robbed and a female student who was living in the same building was raped in the elevator. The narration suggests that wearing the suit is a direct reaction to those events when Iris states that "[n]ot long after the rape, I started wearing the suit" (Hustvedt 1993: 163; see also Tappen-Scheuermann 2012: 168; Dallmann 2009: 267; Jameson 2010: 424).

55). The name Klaus is taken from the German novella that Iris has been translating for Professor Rose. While her disguise functions at first predominantly as a mask for Iris, flânerie also turns into a technique of the self by means of which she actively (trans-)forms herself:

> For me Klaus remained a young man, despite the fact that those who knew me as Klaus never mistook me for a boy. The gap between what I was forced to acknowledge to the world – namely that I was a woman – and what I dreamed inwardly didn't bother me. By becoming Klaus at night I had effectively blurred my gender. The suit, my clipped head and unadorned face altered the world's view of who I was, and I became someone else through its eyes. I even spoke differently as Klaus. I was less hesitant, used more slang and favored colorful verbs. (Hustvedt 1993: 169–170)

The quote powerfully delineates the interaction between Iris's imagination and the reaction of those around her: while she explains at the beginning of the excerpt that those she encounters recognize her as a woman so that wearing the suit does not automatically 'transform' her into a person identified as male, her clothes do seem to fulfil this function for herself and for those who see her from a distance on the streets.[134] Her disguise first and foremost influences her self by altering the way in which she is perceived by others (Hartmann 2016: 92), which then also leads to Iris's change of habitus. Thus, the suit further inscribes onto Iris the ambivalent gender that it lends to her and perpetuates this inscription until the border between male and female genders has successfully been deconstructed when she states that "[t]he suit effectively blurred my gender." Flânerie becomes a technique of the self for Iris by means of which she inscribes onto herself an ambivalent gender that, through her exposure to the eyes of others, allows her to be perceived partly as male and partly as female. By taking up the role of the flâneur, Iris appropriates a piece of cultural text and turns it into a performance of resistance.[135]

Moreover, the practice of flânerie leads directly to a temporary improvement of Iris's health; while Iris's encounters with Mr. Morning as well as Stephen and

---

[134] See, for example, her comment that "in the dark, people think I'm a man" (Hustvedt 1993: 164).

[135] See also Hustvedt's reflection on writing *The Blindfold* in her essay "Being a Man": "It has never occurred to me until now that taking on a masculine position as a survival technique has roots in my own family, that in the suit Iris lives out the duality and uncertainty of my dreams, and that when she reinvents herself as a male character she is finally able to imagine her own rescue" (Hustvedt 2006: 101).

George are almost immediately followed by severe bouts of migraine,[136] flânerie alleviates her symptoms and seems to have a healing effect on her: "I needed Klaus, and despite my sense that I had fallen again, the walks at night did me good, cleared my head" (Hustvedt 1993: 181). Flânerie also enables Iris to meet people who, despite the ambiguity expressed by her looks – an ambiguity that places her outside of societal norms – remain responsive and in so doing affirm her as a subject: "Again I found people unruffled by my eccentricity" (Hustvedt 1993: 181). Going to bars she would normally have avoided and talking to the strangers she encounters there, opens up new performance options for Iris outside of the matrix of intelligibility in which she has been located so far. Those encounters confirm the actual plurality of her identity, illustrating Butler's point that identity formation reoccurs in each individual encounter with an other (see section 4.3). Nevertheless, she is also well aware of the fact that this kind of recognition is limited to her nightly walks and cannot be transferred to the sphere of her social peers; she therefore avoids entering bars where she might encounter Columbia students (Hustvedt 1993: 166). The kind of primary responsiveness that Butler calls for, and which Iris experiences during her nightly visits to the bars, is thus denied to her within the social sphere to which her identity as Iris belongs.

The limited value of this particular type of flânerie as a continuous performance of resistance is further problematized in the novel through its link to performances of sovereignty. By adopting a stereotypically masculine sovereignty whenever she dresses up as Klaus, Iris inscribes a claim to sovereignty in herself which at first secures her from taking up more passive roles. Consequently, her flânerie enables her to win her bet against Rose about her being able to walk blindfolded back to her flat in New York City. Since her nightly walks inscribed the space of the city into her, Iris is now able to inscribe herself into the city and to claim her sovereignty over Rose when it comes to their familiarity with the streets of New York (Hustvedt 1993: 210–211). While this scene only repeats a power struggle that permeates Iris's whole relationship with Rose and is a direct reaction to his constant attempts to dominate her, the performance of sovereignty which accompanies her flânerie also takes more problematic forms.

While Iris's flânerie seems to be tied to a performance of masculinity in general, the novel also suggests that the norms which she adopts have been explicitly derived from two other characters in the novel: her acquaintance Paris, and

---

136 See, for example, Iris's reaction to her picture in Stephen's bedroom (Hustvedt 1993: 66–67) or her remark that "[i]n July Mr. Morning came along for whom I wrote reports, another story altogether, but by the time I left him, I was desperate for money again, and the headaches started [...]" (Hustvedt 1993: 178).

the fictional Klaus, the so-called 'brutal boy'. The inscription of Klaus is evident not only from the fact that Iris uses his name when changing into her role as flâneuse/flâneur, but also from the fact that she seems to copy his misdemeanors directly, since nocturnal flânerie is one of Klaus's favorite acts of resistance:

> Then one night, the boy leaves the house and once in Krüger's city, designated only by the letter S., he celebrates his freedom. He is happy just to walk where he should not walk and see what he should not see, finding odd streets and peering through the windows of closed shops and lit saloons. The night is a chaos of sights and smells and sounds, and the child becomes a tiny voyeur of the city's secrets, a hidden witness to street brawls and soliciting prostitutes. (Hustvedt 1993: 135–136)

Klaus's flânerie is characterized by the traditional anonymity and voyeurism of the trope as well as a resistance to the norms that have been imposed on him, since he "walk[s] where he should not walk". Similarly, Iris's flânerie takes place at night, resists social convention and is based on the denial of her visibility and exposure on the streets as a woman:

> The nights were dangerous. I walked where I shouldn't have walked alone, but my recklessness pleased me. I sang loudly in the darkness, whistled at strangers, and once, I wrote NEVER MIND in huge letters on a wall with spray paint I had bought specifically for that purpose. (Hustvedt 1993: 181)

As her act of "whistl[ing] at strangers" or the slogan "NEVER MIND" – which explicitly expresses a detached attitude towards anything that might potentially threaten her[137] – indicate, Iris's practice of resistance is linked to a demonstrative affirmation of sovereignty. Yet, the inscription of the 'brutal boy' ultimately tilts towards the potentially physically violent when Iris tries to steal a police officer's gun while attending a strip club (Hustvedt 1993: 74–75). By adopting the 'brutal boy's' norms of resistance, Iris also runs the risk of subscribing to a performance of the hidden violent impulses which Klaus embodies.

But Iris's performance of flânerie also seems to be heavily influenced by her acquaintance Paris whose practices of cross-dressing as well as of changing one's identity by means of a change of name she adopts. Iris meets Paris, an in-

---

[137] Iris actually uses this slogan to ward off reminders of her vulnerability on several other occasions: "I had to handle it myself, and discovered that if I lay in bed and chanted, repeating over and over the little incantation 'Never mind,' I could dampen the pain considerably. I chanted a lot in those days. When I looked at the list of books I was supposed to know and felt the panic rise in my chest, I chanted. Each time the hospital sent a bill, I chanted" (Hustvedt 1993: 181).

famous New York art critic, for the first time at a friend's Halloween party. He functions in various ways as an embodiment of the city's carnivalesque opportunities of disguise and anonymity. Not only does Paris defy gender norms with respect to his outward appearance,[138] but his whole identity revolves around the concept of disguise. Thus, he introduces himself to Iris by openly announcing the artificiality of his identity:

> "My name's Paris," he said. "Just Paris?" I said. "No last name?" "No, that's it," he said. "It used to be something else, but I banished it." "Just like that?" He took a step toward me, lifted his chin, and lowered his voice. "Went to court, had the judge toss out the old and bring in the new. Legal magic. Since then I've been Paris, just Paris." "What was your old name?" "That's a secret," he said, [...]. (Hustvedt 1993: 125)

The scene explicitly emphasizes the fluidity of identity resulting from identity-formation's reliance on signification. As Paris does not reveal his actual name, his identity remains hidden and is at the same time marked as being entirely artificial because it is made up of signifiers – such as the name as a central indicator of identity – that can be exchanged at any time. Whereas gender is already marked as a social construct by Paris's "promiscuous obedience" to gender norms, his change of name highlights how new meaning can be added to the identity of a person through the addition of new signifiers. Paris, as a character, therefore functions as an embodiment of a poststructuralist denial of essentialism and the resulting fluidity of identity. However, he also symbolizes the flip side of a deconstructivist dissolution of binary oppositions which manifests itself in an ethical relativism to which he openly admits at the end of the novel (see also Versluys 2003: 104; Marks 2014: 88). His attitude becomes especially clear in his reaction to Iris's narration at the end of the text, when he says, "there aren't any rules, not really. Who makes them? God? I think you're interested in dirt, in a hint of cruelty" (Hustvedt 1993: 220). His fluid identity, moreover, allows him to secure his performance of dominance and sovereignty and is rooted in a denial of his relations to others. Therefore, when Iris refers back to the relational tie of friendship which is the only reason she could open herself up to him in the first place, he denies that any such thing ever existed:

> "I can't believe it. An hour ago you were the sympathetic friend, oozing charity. Who the hell are you now?" "I don't know why you're so excited. I had a little fun with you, so what?" "Paris, I trusted you enough to tell you. We've been friends." He looked at me with blank eyes. "Bullshit," he said without raising his voice. "I've been convenient, a dis-

---

[138] See Hustvedt (1993: 124): "'That's Paris', she said. 'Who's he supposed to be?' 'Nobody,' she said. 'He always looks like that.' 'He's wearing make-up.' 'As usual.'"

traction once in a while, but not someone to be taken seriously, hardly a leading man. I'm too short, remember?" He turned the glass in his hand and shrugged. (Hustvedt 1993: 218–219)

The quote fits Butler's argument about performances of sovereignty being based on the experience of vulnerability. While Paris needs to deny his friendship with Iris in order to secure his position of sovereignty by ridiculing her experiences, the motivation for this denial of their friendship seems to be based on a primary feeling of inferiority and subjection, of being "hardly a leading man". His behavior in this scene moreover echoes a rumor about his being responsible for the suicide of an artist whom Paris promoted at first only to slam his work in a review later on (Hustvedt 1993: 124), thus proving his status of sovereignty.

Along with Paris's affirmation of a fluid identity, several of the acts that Iris commits during her strolls through the nocturnal city seem to adopt his ethical relativism as well. The slogan 'Never mind', for example, expresses not only a denial of her own vulnerability, but just as much a rejection of moral boundaries which she also performs in her acts of vandalism and rebellion. Like Paris, she denies her connection to others in order to gain moments of sovereignty when she, for example, decides to answer a passer-by's question in "gibberish" following an impulse to which the man reacts by displaying "a moment of fear before he hurried away" (Hustvedt 1993: 170).

Hence, flânerie becomes a problematic performance of resistance in *The Blindfold*. Triggered by reminders of her own vulnerability as a woman on the streets of the city, Iris takes up norms from three different sources and defers them in their application. First of all, dressing as a – somewhat dandyesque – man inscribes into her norms of masculinity which then further materialize in Iris's body when she cuts her hair (Hustvedt 1993: 167), changes her dialect (Hustvedt 1993: 164) or keeps losing weight so that her body looks more and more masculine (Hustvedt 1993: 176). As a result of being "transformed" (Hustvedt 1993: 164) through the suit, Iris also turns into a flâneur; she thus reports, about the night in which she wears the suit for the first time, that "[m]y wanderings began that same night and lasted all summer" (Hustvedt 1993: 164). Most importantly, this transformation involves both poles of the trope's ambivalent tension between seeing and being seen. In order to become a flâneur, Iris first has to be perceived by others as a man so that she knows that she will be safe and 'invisible' – as opposed to the kind of exposure and visibility that she would have to face as a woman. During her flânerie she then indulges in anonymous observation and voyeurism just as much as the flâneur would and therefore performs a new kind of 'male gaze' when admitting that she was "looking at everyone and everything, indulging myself in long stares" (Hustvedt 1993:

164).¹³⁹ This norm interlocks with the norm offered by the 'brutal boy' and extends the implied violence of this intrusive kind of observation to the abovementioned acts of social rebellion. Moreover, both inscriptions – that of the 'brutal boy' as well as that of masculinity – tie in with the deconstruction of binary oppositions – the deconstruction of gender norms through Iris's acts of cross-dressing and the deconstruction of norms of morality through her acts of (potential) violence – already performed by Paris, and thus further blur traces of origin.

What all three norms – or clusters of norms – have in common is the fact that their effects on Iris resist any essentialist notion of a 'true' self.¹⁴⁰ Iris's performance of masculinity, which starts out as fiction and masquerade, seems to awaken a second identity in Iris which she feels was already present in her. Accordingly, she describes her experience of becoming Klaus in the following way:

> The midwestern accent I had worked hard to lose returned during my nocturnal wanderings, something I still find odd. The voice just came. I made no effort, and because of this, I felt my speech was neither theater nor delusion, or at least no more than any other talk is. I was that boy. Where he came from, I didn't know. Klaus had been constructed long ago in an underground place I couldn't reach. (Hustvedt 1993: 170).

While this quote acknowledges Klaus as an intrinsic part of Iris, this masculine identity is never defined as her 'true' identity in the novel. At the same time, the fact that she has the feeling that Klaus actually is a part of her implies that the kind of female identity which she expresses in her encounters with Stephen, George and Rose is likewise not a representation of her 'true' self. In the same way that the suit blurs her gender for those whom Iris meets on the streets, the trope of flânerie blurs her gender identity as a character in the novel and deconstructs the binary opposition between male and female (see also Rosenthal 2016: 56; 2017: 87). Whether there is any such thing as a preexisting gender identity in Iris, or whether her feeling that Klaus constitutes a preexisting part of her actually derives from a sedimentation of norms which for her turns into truth, remains unclear. The contested relationship between authenticity and theatrical performance is emphasized in Iris's remark that she "felt that [her] speech was

---

139 While Iris also commits acts of voyeurism outside of her periods of flânerie, as the beginning of the novel – which does not coincide with the beginning of the narrated time – indicates when she reports having "watched the neighbours from [her] bed" (Hustvedt 1993: 9; see also Hartmann 2016: 86), it is only her particular brand of flânerie-while-being-dressed-as-a-man that enables her to take this habit to the streets.

140 This has also frequently been noted in research on *The Blindfold*, although most critics evaluate Iris's 'loss' of her 'true' self rather negatively (see Versluys 2003: 104; Rohr 2003: 94; Jameson 2010: 424).

neither theater nor delusion, or at least no more than any other talk is", by means of which she implies that any kind of conversation might be considered 'theater' or rather that performance is the norm in social interactions.

Nevertheless, Iris's flânerie not only deconstructs an essentialist notion of the self, but also opens her up to her own precariousness as well as that of others. During her walks through the city Iris meets an unhoused man and at first, similar to the violent impulses mentioned above, feels an urge to physically harm him. She describes the scene as follows: "I bent over him, holding my breath to shut out the stench. I stood up and felt it – a desire to kick him. It overwhelmed me. My body grew rigid and there was a tingling sensation in my foot" (Hustvedt 1993: 171). Yet, after she looks at him a second time and recognizes his evident need for protection she frees herself from the desire to hurt the man:

> I remember I closed my eyes. I swayed from the waist. I forced myself to look at him again. He was abject, gruesome. Keep yourself away, I said. You'll hurt him. And then I noticed his hand. He was curled up in the fetal position with one hand over his crotch. The protective gesture made me wince. I covered my open mouth. Then I took a dollar of my tip money and tucked it into his shirt pocket. (Hustvedt 1993: 171)

The turning point in Iris's desire to kick him can therefore be situated in the moment she looks at the position of the man, which points out his precariousness symbolically. Iris reacts in a direct, bodily way to the recognition of his precariousness. Although she tries at first to keep herself from hurting him by talking to herself, it remains doubtful whether this strategy would have succeeded if the specific position of the man had not caught her attention. She identifies with the precariousness that his posture displays by wincing as if in pain and decides to give him money instead. Although her act of charity might still contain sovereignty since she is to some extent still positioning herself above the man, Iris is not intent on exerting unlimited power over him – as Henry Perowne, for example, does with Baxter – or aiming at securing her own sovereignty in some other way.

In conclusion, flânerie is ambiguously connoted throughout the novel. While it functions as a liberating act of resistance against the male gaze, it also forms a gateway to a violent affirmation of Iris's sovereignty and – through her identification with Klaus as well as the anonymity of the metropolis – supports the exertion of violence. In both cases, Iris's flânerie actively deconstructs the notion of a true self and emphasizes the performative character of any construction of identity.[141] Nevertheless, it is also during her strolls that Iris is not only confirmed as a subject outside of social norms of intelligibility, but also confronted with the precariousness of others and thus reminded of her own state of primary vulnerability. Finally, this ambiguity is mirrored in the ambivalent evaluation of vision and the gaze in the novel which might constitute an act of violence – as is the case with George's picture of Iris and its circulation in Iris's social environment – but might also become a gateway to recognition and empathy – as is the case in Iris's encounter with the unhoused man.[142] Consequently, the ambivalence of the human gaze, which also constitutes flânerie's main mode of perception, repeats the ambiguity of flânerie itself.

7.1.3 The Logic of "War and Struggle": Discourse, Power and *parrēsia* in *The Blindfold*

While many analyses of Hustvedt's novel focus on its representation of a postmodernist loss of self in the alienating environment of the city,[143] I hold that the novel can instead be interpreted as a manifestation of the active, processual creation of Iris as a post-sovereign subject who escapes the circularity of violence suggested on the level of plot. Even though the ending of the novel, with Iris fleeing from Paris's flat like a "bat out of hell" (Hustvedt 1993: 221), might project a rather bleak outcome for her, the narration, which explicitly affirms Iris as a narrating I telling her own story with increasing coherence, implies that the narrating I undergoes a healing process while writing the story. Most importantly this

---

[141] See also Meeks (2019: 202), who argues that Iris gains a "resistive peace" by losing her identity.
[142] For a similar argument regarding the ambivalence of gazes in *The Blindfold*, see also Marks (2014: 104).
[143] See e.g. Rohr (2003: 94), Versluys (2003: 104) or Flieger (1997: 107). Those analyses would then situate *The Blindfold* within a canon of postmodern city texts that focus on the alienation and disorientation of the individual in the postmodern landscape of the twentieth-century metropolis, such as Paul Auster's *New York Trilogy* (1987), Jay McInerney's *Bright Lights, Big City* (1984) or Bret Easton Ellis's *American Psycho* (1991). I would argue, by contrast, that *The Blindfold* already forms part of an ethical turn following the postmodernist void of signs and already aims at developing new techniques and practices of subjectivity against the backdrop of the postmodern city's palimpsestic excess of signification. This can best be seen in the doubling between Iris and Paris, which juxtaposes Iris with her uncanny doppelgänger Paris and thus suggests that Paris's lack of meaning, which is further emphasized by the abundance of shiny surfaces in his flat (see Hustvedt 1993: 216), constitutes a repressed part of Iris which she overcomes when cutting off further contact with him in the end.

story ultimately combines Klaus and Iris into a complex and ambivalent identity which defies a normative matrix of intelligibility and remains "at the edge of what we know". One of the central aspects of this identity is the reflection on a possible human predetermination to violence which is implied by concepts like the early Foucauldian notion of the logic of "war and struggle" (Foucault 2003b: 18). Iris's narration and the trope of flânerie in particular deconstruct the binary opposition between a possible human predetermination to violence and the possibility that violence is always inscribed on humans from the outside so that the novel participates in the creation of a non-violent imaginary. Significantly, this deconstruction also results in the construction of a non-sovereign subjectivity that becomes manifest on the level of content as well as on the level of form in the novel and therefore affirms the precarious as a norm of subjectivity.

As was already implied in the previous section's focus on vision and the male gaze, each of Iris's encounters is permeated by mechanisms of subjection and resistance. Whereas subjection is usually at first performed by the male characters, Iris's practices of resistance often copy the dominance displayed by her male counterparts.[144] Thus, the narrated time of the novel already starts with a power struggle between her and Rose. When entering Rose's office, Iris extends her hand to Rose, while he refrains from taking it in a decisive gesture of power (Hustvedt 1993: 119). It is only when Iris does not withdraw her hand, but her fingers start to tremble, that Rose decides on shaking it. Tellingly, during this encounter both steadily stare at each other.[145] Here, Iris's resistance only originates from Rose's gesture of dominance and constitutes a direct reaction to it. Iris therefore performs sovereignty and directly mirrors Rose's attitude. Her act of resistance is then a direct repetition of a norm already performed by Rose. Hence, Iris's act of resistance copies a kind of sovereignty which in the text is at first mostly represented with a male connotation.

Those dynamics of subjection and a resistance which essentially mirrors the sovereignty displayed in the initial acts of subjection resurface throughout the novel. When she feels betrayed by Paris, for example, after telling him her story, Iris attempts to subject him:

> "What's your real name?" I said. He sat in the chair without moving. I've hit a nerve, I said to myself. "The name your parents gave you. What is it?" He didn't even blink. "Maybe it's Fred?" "No, it isn't." "Arnold," I said. "Arnold's cute. Abe, Alfred, Abner. My God, there are thousands of possibilities. Buddy, Bert, Bertrand, Brian, Billy, Buster, Caleb, Curtis. That's

---

[144] This is of course also reflected in the above-mentioned dynamics of vision.
[145] See Hustvedt (1993: 119): "I stared at him and he continued to gaze at me."

nice." The names soared through my head. "Let's forget the alphabet," I said, my hysteria rising. "Dickie, Dick, Rick, Ricky, Prick." The invective pleased me. [...] "Maybe there's a 'junior' attached to your name. Bob junior, a little Jim. You're a junior, aren't you?" I looked at him. (Hustvedt 1993: 219)

Supported by an interchange of gazes – "He didn't even blink" and "I looked at him" – the scene depicts a power struggle between Iris and Paris during which Iris tries to (re-)gain sovereignty after having been hurt by Paris. In order to subject him, she not only insults him by means of names like "Prick" or the sexual innuendo of the name "Dick", but also draws directly on discourses of power by alluding to Paris's deviant lack of height which locates him outside of the norm of masculine sexuality: she suggests names which emphasize his small size as well as a potential inferiority resulting from it such as "Bob junior, [...] little Jim" or the general comment that "You're a junior, aren't you?"

Ultimately, Iris's performance as Klaus, which leads to her adoption of several norms of masculine sovereignty as a consequence of her resistance to the male gaze, condenses the circularity of violence implied by the dialectics of the gaze, and the concomitant dynamics of subjection and resistance, into the central image of the text: the ambiguous doubling between the imaginary character of Klaus, the fictional brutal boy, and Klaus Krüger, Iris's – at first equally imaginary – second self.

The association between the two characters raises one of the central questions of the novel that ties in with the aforementioned focus on a deconstruction of essentialist concepts of self: whether or not humans are intrinsically violent. While the text seems to suggest on the one hand that the exertion of violence is inscribed into Iris by means of her performance as Klaus Krüger and is thus not representative of intrinsic desires within Iris, but prescribed by specific norms, it also implies that her reading of *The Brutal Boy* only activates feelings that have been present within Iris since her childhood, although this option is – as I argued above – further problematized by the novel.

Nevertheless, this question does not only arise on the level of interpretation, but is explicitly brought up by Iris herself within the novel's *histoire* when, while teaching the novella and focusing on its reference to the possibility of an intrinsic compulsion of humans to violence, she exclaims: "Who is Klaus?" (Hustvedt 1993: 211). At the same time, reflections on humankind's possible predetermination to violence – which could for example be based on an essentialist connection between humans and violence – occur repeatedly in Iris's conversations with Rose. During those talks, the professor often emphasizes that he considers himself to be driven by 'evil' or a wish for the exertion of violence:

Then he grabbed my upper arms with his hands and shook me, not hard but firmly. "You want to hear the truth?" he said. "Goodness aside. I'm going to make you run. You're going to hate me before we're through." (Hustvedt 1993: 193)

Rose's essentialist approach to evil is explicitly affirmed by him in a discussion with Iris during which he reminds her to differentiate between 'goodness' and 'truth' and points out that evil could just as well be congruent with the truth:

He looked at me. "You mustn't confuse virtue and the truth. The two are very different." The words took hold, and my mistake jarred me. "Virtue is a moral quality distinct from what's true," he said. I nodded. "So that evil can be the truth." "Of course." (Hustvedt 1993: 192)

Interestingly, Rose's distinction between the categories of truth and morality does not seem to apply to his own essentialist conception of evil. While he criticizes Iris for her more or less unintentional equating of the categories of 'virtue' and 'truth',[146] Rose himself insists on a basic distinction between the two categories, although he does not claim this kind of distinction for the differentiation between truth and evil. Whereas Iris asks him whether "evil can be the truth", Rose sees this option as self-evident when he answers "[o]f course".

Rose and Iris's fixation on the topic is epitomized by their shared metaphorical child, the translation of the novella *The Brutal Boy*. Reasons for the eponymous boy's invincible brutal drives are ambiguous in the novel. Thus, the text starts in the following way: "Klaus was a good boy, [...] [h]e was ten years old, did well in school, was obedient, kind, and loyal" (Hustvedt 1993: 134). Since Klaus is obedient, discourses of power seem to have been successfully inscribed in him, so that his brutal impulses could also be interpreted as a reaction to the force of repression. This interpretation is supported by the ending of the novella when Klaus's brutal drives return after a morning spent being especially obedient: "He has endured the rigors of a starched collar and a long church service" (Hustvedt 1993: 137). The second quote emphasizes the violent force of discourses of power more explicitly by pointing out that Klaus "has endured the rigors of a starched collar". The trope of the 'evil child', however, rather suggests the opposite, namely that Klaus's violence represents humankind's original predetermination to violence. Therefore, while the reasons for Klaus's brutal drives remain unexplained at the level of the novella's story, it offers proof for both interpretations: the possibility that violence is inscribed on humans from the outside and the possibility that humans are intrinsically predetermined to violence. *The Bru-*

---

146 See Hustvedt (1993: 192): "I've often felt that ideas of goodness, of the truth, have to be unbending, absolute, or everything falls apart."

tal Boy thus metafictionally repeats the central question of *The Blindfold*. Both texts implicitly pose the question of whether humans are predetermined to violence by juxtaposing an essentialist conception of evil with the possibility of violence as representative of the way 'evil' is inscribed into humans from the outside.

This question remains equally unsolved in the novel. As has been argued above, Iris's behavior as Klaus already problematizes an essentialist conception of self. Her narration then combines the experience of Klaus's brutal drives being inscribed into Iris with the memories of a young Iris who likewise seems to have experienced a desire to hurt others. However, the question remains of why she, unlike the 'brutal boy', has not acted on those desires so far. Moreover, those memories are marked as potentially unreliable. The narration itself therefore exemplarily deconstructs the difference between the possibility of humankind's predetermination to violence and an inscription of violence from the outside by dissolving the opposition between inscription and intrinsic motivation through Iris. Here, seemingly authentic memories are framed by processes of translation, transformation and deferral as Iris's first account of her translation of *The Brutal Boy* exemplifies:

> I snapped the book shut and looked out my window. The snow had stopped. It's an odd little work, I thought, slight and strange but good enough to translate, a gruesome comedy really. I began the next morning, searching for English words to mirror the German, and the effort changed the story for me. As I transcribed Klaus's fantasies, I had an uncanny feeling of intimacy. Brief but vague memories surfaced and then were gone. I was in the Webster Municipal Library, standing beside another little girl I didn't know. It was hot. She had a red face. It must have been summer. I wanted to shake her. That was all. I remembered nothing else, but the vision was provocative and brought with it a feeling of mild distress. To the extent that my text grew, the German one disappeared, and I claimed the new narrative. It's mine, I said to myself, my reinvention. I'm making it. And so I struggled over the sentences, polishing them until they seemed perfect and I recall that once when I paused from the translation to go to the bathroom, I caught a glimpse of myself in the mirror and was taken aback. I was grinning like a half-wit. Good God, I thought, you don't even look like yourself. (Hustvedt 1993: 138)

As the quote implies, the process of translation is marked by the occurrence of various changes not just in the novella but also in Iris, so that "the effort [to find the right tone for the translation] changed the story for" her. She points out that she "claimed the narrative" and "reinvent[ed]" it until the process of transformation seemed to extend to her as well: she sees herself in the mirror and recognizes that by now she "do[esn't] even look like [her]self". Embedded in those ongoing dynamics of change is Iris's "vague memor[y]" of the little girl in Webster's Municipal Library that is then linked to the context of *The Brutal*

Boy and therefore creates "an uncanny feeling of intimacy" in Iris. Although the link that is established between Iris's memory and *The Brutal Boy* seems to suggest that there is in fact an intrinsic motivation for violence in Iris, the actual context of the memory remains unclear. What is more, the scene's focus on processes of inscription and transformation explicitly suggests that in translation as well as interpretation (of memories, for example) changes might occur that affect the result of the interpretation. Iris's memory itself might therefore have been changed when it is triggered by this new context.

Her account of the process of translating the novella similarly blurs the line between possible insights into a 'true' self and an inscription of new norms from the outside by mixing authentic memories with imagination and therefore further emphasizing how the inscription of Klaus possibly transforms Iris's notion of self. For example, "[b]rief but vague memories surfaced and then were gone" when Iris translates the story, which suggests that she had impulses of brutality when she was a child as well (Hustvedt 1993: 138). However, only a few pages later Iris recounts the following episode which also takes place while she is translating the novella:

> That evening I sat down to work on the novella again. The boy is leaving the house. The passage was troubling. I rewrote it several times. He pulls on the heavy door, dreading noise, feels the night air, and slips out into the street. I changed the verbs, the adjectives. Each time I did it over, I saw Klaus going through the door into the street. I looked up from the book and my mind wandered. I remembered a white nightgown my mother gave me when I was seven. I had forgotten it. Then I imagined myself pushing open the door to my parents' house and stepping outside. I felt my bare feet on wet grass. I saw the lights from Webster a mile away. Wee Willie Winkie runs through the town, I thought. Upstairs and downstairs. In the fantasy I peeked into a window but then stopped myself. Don't look. Go home. I remembered the sound of Professor Rose's voice from the other side of the door. I bent down to hear the words, but they were monstrous, and I suppressed the daydream. Then I spoke sternly to myself. Keep your distance, I said, your sense of irony. You're losing your grip, confusing one thing with another. Buck up. This little speech was an attempt to save myself from what had, in effect, already happened. (Hustvedt 1993: 143–144)

While working on the novella, Iris starts to link her memory of the white nightgown to Klaus's story and imagines herself wandering through her own hometown when she was a child. Whereas she clearly differentiates between memory and fantasy at first, her recollection of Rose's voice already seems to be mixed up with imagination when she describes his words as "monstrous" and remarks that she had to suppress "the daydream". In the appeal to herself following this experience, the speech acts she uses convey an ambivalent message: on the one hand, she reminds herself to keep her distance, on the other hand, she states that she is "losing [her] grip" and "confusing one thing with another", thus affirming and potentially perpetuating this state of confusion. Consequently, she admits in the end that this confusion has already taken place. Memory and imagination therefore seem to have been mixed up already, so that the passage deprives especially those recollections which occur during the translation of *The Brutal Boy* of their authenticity. The impression that Iris actually had any primary urges to brutality when she was a child that might only have been brought to the surface now is thus challenged by her potential unreliability with regard to those childhood memories. The inscription of norms allowing for a potentially violent behavior, however, also problematizes the norm of a non-violent core of the self and therefore denies any essentialist concept of the self.

Likewise, Iris's memory of having always been "prone to terrible fantasies" seems to be triggered by her performance of Klaus (Hustvedt 1993: 170). Yet, the examples that Iris mentions differ from her actions as Klaus in terms of the direction that the violence acted out in them takes: for Iris, "[s]eeing a steep staircase, for example, instantly prompts a vision of falling. On a roof or balcony, I feel tempted to throw myself over the edge" (Hustvedt 1993: 170). The violence here is clearly directed at herself whereas the "perverse impulses" (Hustvedt 1993: 170) which she experiences as Klaus are always directed at others, like the abovementioned man she meets on the streets or the unhoused man she encounters during another nightly walk. Hence, the inscription of Klaus changes Iris's fantasies and impulses and does not simply reproduce something that already exists, although the novel also leaves open the question of whether the selection of "terrible fantasies" that Iris describes is entirely arbitrary, so that it could still be possible that when mentioning those fantasies she is also referring to a propensity for violence against others.

Deconstructing the binary opposition between internal predetermination and inscription of violence from the outside ultimately gives Iris an ambivalent identity as regards this issue and thus contains the potential to free her from the idea of being predetermined to violence. Constructing herself as an opaque subject *sensu* Butler by implying that the subject at least *might* not be predetermined to violence seems to have a potentially liberating effect on Iris.[147]

---

[147] The opacity of the subject is further emphasized in the negation of other essentialisms. As has already been mentioned above, Iris's flânerie deconstructs the binary opposition between man and woman, yet this deconstruction is repeated in Iris's relationships with men in the novel: while Iris and Stephen follow stereotypically gendered patterns of behavior in their relationship, with Iris longing for more intimacy and commitment and Stephen partly committing to her and partly rejecting her, those stereotypes change to the opposite in her relationship with Rose, in which he loses his stereotypical male sovereignty due to his jealousy regarding Iris

The construction of this kind of subjectivity that is located outside of the matrix of intelligibility is preceded by a complex process of healing on the level of plot which can be understood as a combination of Foucauldian techniques of the self which involve bodily activities like flânerie together with practices that appeal to Iris's psyche as well as the recognition of one's precariousness. Thus, Iris's medical history implies that for her, healing on the basis of an entirely neurological therapy, that is, one based on observations concerning the biological essence of humans – in this case the nervous system – is not possible, but that medicine instead needs to rely on methods that appeal both to the body and to the mind. Dr. Fish's famous 'cocktail' of pills, the composition of which is based on the classification of symptoms, is not able to alleviate Iris's headaches or cure her migraines (see Hustvedt 1993: 229), but what finally helps Iris to get better is a mixture of imagination (see Bein 2016: 230), the recognition of one's own precariousness, the constitution of the self by means of talking to oneself, telling one's own story and the performance of flânerie.

Hence, Iris's cure seems to have its starting point in her recognition of her own precariousness when she identifies with the demented Mrs. O, with whom she shares a room in the hospital. Mrs. O represents everything that is 'other' to the norm.[148] Not only does she remain a mystery to the people who surround her and therefore defies intelligibility, but she also resists the restraints that she is subjected to by the hospital. Along with the fact that she seems to look extremely fragile, she functions as a symbol of human precariousness in the novel. Not only is she entirely dependent on others to feed, protect and care for her, but she is also deviant from the norm. In an extreme way, she exemplifies the precarious resistance of every human individual with regard to discourses of power. Consequently, Iris perceives her as an uncanny presence since, to her, she represents the return of her own repressed precariousness. Nevertheless, Iris feels compelled to identify with Mrs. O and answer her when she calls out to Iris, addressing her as 'Eleanor', Mrs. O's own name.[149] Her exclamation "I'm

---

while she sovereignly takes her liberties and does not experience the feeling of lacking something which she experienced with Stephen.

148 See also Dallmann (2009: 272; my trans.): "Symbolically, Mrs. O can be read as a character who illustrates the fortune of those who try to evade the scopic regime, in which patriarchal structures of power are embedded." – "Symbolisch kann Mrs. O als Figur gelesen werden, die das Schicksal derer illustriert, die versuchen, sich einem skopischen Regime zu entziehen, in das patriarchale Machtstrukturen eingeschrieben sind."

149 Yet, the scene also has a violent connotation, since although Iris does become responsive to Mrs. O, she also takes over her identity. Consequently, Mrs. O then disappears from the action of the novel (see Hustvedt 1993: 114).

here!" simultaneously affirms Iris's own existence as a subject and has a direct effect on her bodily sensations: "I called her as if she was far away, and as the sound of my voice came from me, it was as if a wind had blown through my body, opening my lungs and throat" (Hustvedt 1993: 112). Afterwards, she lies down and "beg[ins] to breathe very deeply and slowly". The next morning Iris notices the outside world again, for the first time, when she realizes that it is snowing. According to Mrs. M, another of Iris's neighbors, this has already been happening for days without Iris noticing (Hustvedt 1993: 115).

Yet, it is not only Iris's recognition of her own precariousness that causes her gradual improvement, but also a first attempt at telling her own story. After the incident with Mrs. O, a psychotherapist is sent to her who asks about her life, her family and her studies. In this conversation, which has a calming effect on Iris, she further consolidates her own discourse and the constitution of her self (Hustvedt 1993: 113). Shortly afterwards, Iris decides to discharge herself from the hospital.[150]

The next step in Iris's process of healing aligns an act of *parrēsia* with a performance of sovereignty and therefore partly represses the precariousness she had previously acknowledged. Nevertheless, this performance is a direct consequence of her constitution of a self which is forced to become resistant due to the inadequacy of the medical as well as economic discourses of power to which it is subjected. Thus, Iris's parrēsiastic act of discharging[151] herself from the hospital already constitutes a performance of resistance with respect to the medical authorities. At that very moment, however, Klaus begins to resurface in her actions. When faced with a huge bill for her 10-day stay at the hospital,[152] she decides to

---

150 See Hustvedt (1993: 179). Although Iris leaving the hospital and her encounter with Mrs. O are not directly linked to each other by the novel, she mentions in the fourth part of the story that she discharged herself from the hospital after ten days. The incident with Mrs. O only happens after eight or nine days and when describing Mrs. O for the first time, Iris points out that "She was the secret – the paralysis and the frenzy – but I didn't understand that until the very end" (Hustvedt 1993: 95).

151 I refer to this act as parrēsiastic since Iris explicitly speaks out against Dr. Fish's medical discourse of power by discharging herself from the hospital. That this was in fact the right decision is confirmed by later developments in the novel. On the practice of *parrēsia* see section 3.2.2.

152 The scene powerfully alludes to the deficiencies of the US healthcare system when Iris reacts to the presentation of the bill by simply referring to the bad status of her health: "Dr. Fish, whom I had hardly seen, was annoyed, but I pulled my frail carcass out of the bed, dressed, and tottered out to the desk in the hospital lobby. 'I'm signing out,' I told the woman there. After I gave her my name, she presented me with a bill for $2,038.46 and asked me to pay it before I left. My university insurance had covered eighty percent of the bill. This was the remaining sum. [...] She was speaking to me, explaining hospital procedure, telling me what had to be

eat the document and later explains that she had turned into Klaus again: "It was Klaus who ate the bill, after all, and silly as it was, there's a lot to be said for it" (Hustvedt 1993: 181). Her turn towards resistance continues when, only a few days later, she once again starts dressing up as Klaus and strolling through the streets of New York. As Iris says, "the walks at night did me good, cleared my head" (Hustvedt 1993: 181). Additionally, she constantly recites to herself, using the phrase 'Never mind' – which she will later write as graffiti on a wall one night during her strolls through the city – whenever she is faced with anything that might cause her distress (see Hustvedt 1993: 181). In both cases, those acts contribute to her process of healing.

This process is only interrupted by Iris's sudden encounter with Professor Rose while sitting in one of the bars she often frequents. After this point in the story, her migraines are no longer mentioned and seem to be at least partly healed; what has happened thus far therefore suggests the negation of a process of healing which only focuses on bodily symptoms and biological mechanisms. By contrast, the novel depicts an alternative process of healing which consists of a complex and individual combination of different elements: the simple affirmation of one's existence along with the acknowledgment of one's precariousness; the telling of one's story; parrēsiastic resistance against authorities, in which the self stands by itself; self-directed speech; and, lastly, flânerie. Flânerie, however, carries an ambivalent connotation in the novel and reinforces strands of sovereignty in Iris's resistance that were already partly present before and therefore her flânerie becomes potentially violent.

Iris's further development is characterized by a complex and twisted itinerary which also exemplifies the contingency and temporally limited success of the techniques of the self. As soon as Iris encounters Professor Rose, for instance, she transforms again and abandons her nightly strolls and, by extension, her resistant techniques of the self. Yet, while she at first reintegrates feminine traits into her outward appearance and personality, her performance as Klaus has in fact further inscribed an inclination towards resistance into her. As was already mentioned above, her relationship with Rose differs from her former gender-stereotypical relationship with Stephen, with Iris now showing stereotypically masculine traits and Rose behaving in a stereotypically feminine way. Moreover, Iris also develops new techniques of the self in her first attempts at coming to terms

---

done. The bill was in my hand, and I studied the numbers. Stupidly I began to ponder the forty-six cents. I can pay that, I thought. Yes, that can easily be paid. The change was in my pocket. 'Are you all right?', said the woman. I looked at her. She was lovely. Her skin was nearly black. I stared at it, then gazed down at the bill. 'I'm sick,' I said to her finally, explaining myself to her simply" (Hustvedt 1993: 179–180).

with her potential for violence when she argues against Rose's equation of evil with truth; that is, she aims at influencing discourses of power – represented by Rose – that contribute to shaping a general conception of human subjecthood. Resistance recurs in her bet with Rose concerning her ability to walk the streets of New York blindfolded and in her physical resistance to his attempt at raping her. As a whole, the relationship represents Iris's flirtation with power itself. During the affair she is resistant yet at the same time drawn towards power, until in the end Rose leaves her. The ending of their relationship juxtaposes Iris's ambivalence with Rose's desire to comprehend and, consequently, subject her:

> Still he didn't turn to look at me. "When I found you, Iris, again, in that bar, you were like a lost boy, a haggard, wild-eyed kid, a little crazy, too. Do you think I've forgotten about that? I think about it all the time."
> "You saved me from perdition, is that it?"
> "No, this might be worse than that. I don't know. What I mean is that I've seen you, really seen you, and what I've seen isn't simple or small. It's complex, ambivalent, mysterious, and it's driven me crazy." (Hustvedt 1993: 208)

Although there already seems to be attraction between the two early on in their acquaintance, they only start having an affair after Rose has seen Iris as Klaus, which turned her into a mystery to be solved by him. After the attempted rape Rose breaks up with Iris because, he says, they will "turn [themselves] into monsters, [...] Or at least [he] will" (Hustvedt 1993: 209). While he blames this problem on their individual dynamic, Iris, by contrast, recognizes that there is a pattern which both of them follow:

> "Sometimes I feel that what we do and what we say is just a repetition, that's [sic] it's all happened before," I said.
> "Déjà vu," he said, his voice flat.
> "No, not that, not identical – vaguely the same, like we're trapped in a pattern or an idea that we can't give up, that leads us by the nose…" (Hustvedt 1993: 207)

Although Iris does not become more specific in her analysis of their problems, her remarks are very much reminiscent of Butler's concept of the repetitive performance of social norms since she points out that "what [they] do and what [they] say is just a repetition" that is "not identical", but rather "vaguely the same", in the same way that the performance or repetition of social norms always entails difference. Nevertheless, she cannot convince Rose of her evaluation and the conclusion that "[t]his is a crisis that can send [them] into a new world" (Hustvedt 1993: 210). The final scene once again demonstrates Iris's ambivalent relationship with power itself in the novel. While her attempt at escaping their compulsion to repeating existing social norms – that is, the mysterious feminine riddle to be solved by the rationalizing male subject – constitutes a new manifestation of resistance by unveiling the discursive power structure that forces them to repeat the same behavior over and over again throughout the novel, the fact that she uses her analysis in order to miraculously resurrect her relationship with Rose and is therefore willing to simply forget the physical violence she has just experienced suggests that she still succumbs to power.

The last scene in the novel then suggests a repetition as well as a transformation and thus leaves open the question as to whether Iris has actually changed by this point. As happens at the end of the novel's first chapter, when Iris flees from Mr. Morning, here she escapes from the flat of her former friend Paris, with whom she severed all ties after he dismissed her suffering (see Hustvedt 1993: 220). While the scene creates the impression of a circular structure, her decisive turning away from Paris also implies that she lets go of several ideas that he represents such as the ethical relativism which Paris openly espouses as well as the complete disguise of one's identity. Hence, the ending is still ambivalent with respect to the possibility of Iris's transformation and is also evaluated differently in secondary literature on the novel.[153]

Nevertheless, while the plot of the novel remains ambivalent with regard to the outcome of Iris's possible transformation by means of a combination of the several techniques of the self she practices, the novel's *discours* shares several characteristics with those practices and implies further that Iris actually transforms herself by means of writing the novel. First and foremost, on the level of the *discours*, the autodiegetic narrative voice of the novel constitutes an equivalent to Iris's affirmation of her own existence when she calls out "I'm here!" during her encounter with Mrs. O. At the same time, the text depicts Iris as a fragile and vulnerable character, which establishes a parallel with her identification with Mrs. O by means of which she confirms her own vulnerability. The telling of one's own story which takes place in her talk with the psychiatrist corresponds to the overall theme of the novel. Moreover, Iris deconstructs discourses of power that prescribe gender stereotypes, parameters for the differentiation between sickness and health as well as seemingly irrefutable metaphysical truths, in her account of herself, similarly to the way she uses her flânerie as a means to deconstruct gender stereotypes and constellations of power. Flânerie then forms a fundamental basis for Iris's partial recovery precisely because it demonstrates how the connection between deconstruction and the social environment

---

153 Thus, Versluys (2003: 103) and Rohr (2003: 94) agree that Iris does not evolve during her time in New York and gets rather lost in the destructive mechanisms of the city. Hartmann (2016: 81) and Reipen (2014: 108), by contrast, see a gradual development towards emancipation taking place in Iris.

in practices of performance can constitute a central technique in the liberation from discourses of power.

At the same time, flânerie also serves to remind Iris of the precariousness of others, as occurs in her encounter with the unhoused man. Flânerie then already indicates another turn in Iris's process of recovery which is also represented as well as performed by the text itself: in her interaction with the man Iris overcomes her desire for violence – which has been inscribed into her by flânerie up until this point – due to her acknowledging and empathizing with his precariousness. Similarly, her identification with the precarious Mrs. O prompts her to renounce her sovereignty. Finally, her rejection of Paris, which constitutes the ending of the novel, seems to align with taking an ethical stance that repudiates performances of sovereignty and establishes protecting the vulnerability of others as an ethical value. Moreover, Iris's reaction seems to question her previous development and thus indicates a transformation 'at the cost of her life'.[154] Turning away from Paris simultaneously means turning away from one of her last attachment figures, and also from a role model – as is, for example, indicated by Iris's practice of cross-dressing – which can be interpreted as another instance of resistance.

Acknowledging the precariousness of others and deconstructing binary oppositions finally combine in the text itself. Iris's rejection of deconstruction for the sake of ethical relativism and the affirmation of one's sovereignty – as exemplified by Paris – manifests itself in the deconstruction of the binary opposition between an essentialist belief in mankind's predetermination to violence and an inscription of violence from outside. While Paris uses his fluid identity in order to

---

[154] This precarious transformation is emphasized by two ambivalent images at the end of the novel. On the one hand, Iris disappears in the end into the black hole of the New York Subway. While this image certainly suggests death, that is, the 'cost of her life', and thus corresponds with the questioning of her previous way of life as well as her partial process of healing up to this point due to her ethical decision, it also carries a positive connotation since being without vision can also be linked to Iris winning the bet against Rose and her ability to move through the city in this way (Reipen 2014: 107–108; see also Meeks [2019: 205], who interprets the black holes in Iris's vision as instances of escape). Moreover, walking blindfolded through the city implies finding new means of orientation which are linked to the senses of touch and hearing and which indicate an escape from the potentially violent dialectics of looking and being looked at. On the other hand, Iris compares her flight with the emergence of a "bat out of hell" (Hustvedt 1993: 221) and thus creates the image of a birth scene. Since the idiom alludes to the superstition that bats are associated with the occult and therefore originate in hell, the expression – which concludes the entire novel – stresses the way in which Iris has become accustomed to the struggles for power in the city, yet at the same time now renounces her participation in those dynamics.

remain untouchable, the deconstruction of binary oppositions of predetermination and inscription contains an ethical impetus, which does not define humans as being predetermined to violence and therefore opens up the possibility of the formation of ethical subjects. The act of turning away from Paris is repeated in this specific kind of deconstruction which takes place by means of the presentation of the narration and has an effect on the speaker's representative on the level of action and thus implicitly also on the narrator herself. The process of healing at which it aims is already represented on the level of plot in Iris's recovery from her migraines. The text now adds its own technique of writing the self to Iris's pool of techniques of the self.

As the structure of the novel implies, writing the self contributes to Iris's recovery from her experiences in New York City. While the first three chapters do not follow any kind of chronological sequence, but represent single, fragmented impressions, the narrator manages in the last chapter to put those events in the right order so that a coherent, yet mobile self can be formed.[155] It is then especially the formal feature of the representation of time in the novel – with the first three anachronistic chapters culminating in the coherent narrative in the fourth chapter – that suggests Iris's successful transformation towards her recovery. Flânerie, as the first long-term practice which Iris adopts on this path, already contains central elements of the following process of recovery, but is also ambivalently connoted since its manifestations depend on the role model that Iris uses for her flânerie as technique of the self. Iris's particular brand of flânerie here contains traces of the sovereign-yet-subjected conception of the flâneur sketched out in Benjamin's writings on Baudelaire, yet it also alludes to the

---

155 Nevertheless, as Christian Knirsch points out in his essay on "The Issue of Chronology in Siri Hustvedt's *The Blindfold*", there are still some discrepancies with regard to chronology to be found in Iris's account even in this fourth chapter (2010: n. pag.). In his argument, Knirsch focuses mostly on the fact that Iris seems to be an unreliable narrator with regard to the exact beginning of her migraines. Thus, he rightly argues that while Iris tells Dr. Fish that "[i]t started last August" (Hustvedt 1993: 92), she also mentions in the fourth chapter that right after her encounter with Mr. Morning in July 1980 "the headaches started" (Hustvedt 1993: 178). Nevertheless, she seems to be prone to hallucinations and fainting even before that, when she collapses in Stephen's bedroom already in May 1980 or when she tells right at the beginning of the fourth chapter that she was losing consciousness "every once in a while" (Hustvedt 1993: 121) in the fall of 1978. The actual beginning of her migraines thus seems to remain in the dark, yet the situation doesn't seem to be as dramatic as Knirsch suggests. While it is certainly correct that Iris describes her first full-blown fit as having taken place in August, her account also implies a gradual development of this particular timespan which led to her admission to the hospital with the headaches starting in July and being joined by hallucinations in August. Her narration thus circles around the beginning and development of her migraines and demonstrates another approach towards telling the story of her illness.

concept of flânerie as *techne*, for which especially giving up one's sovereignty is of utmost importance. Flânerie, on the one hand, serves Iris as a practice of adopting the sovereignty that had hitherto been reserved to male characters; on the other hand it also serves as a gateway to an encounter with the precariousness of one's self as well as that of others and can therefore lead to the formation of an ethical self that accepts the precariousness of one's own self as well as that of others and takes this precariousness into account in its own actions.

The self which Iris expresses by means of her narration is then a decidedly precarious one. Not only is Iris a vulnerable character, but she also admits to the limitations of her own perspective and thus refrains from a sovereign stance with respect to the depiction of other characters. Consequently, Iris has repeatedly been deemed an unreliable narrator in secondary literature on the novel (see, for example, Dallmann 2009: 241; Meeks 2019: 206; Knirsch 2010: n. pag.; Flieger 1997: 89). However, I suggest that Iris's particular 'unreliability' rather serves to emphasize the subjectivity of the individual's perspective – exemplified in the novel's problematization of vision – as well as the constitution of a subject that is located outside a normative matrix of intelligibility – exemplified in the problematization of the boundary between madness and sanity in *The Blindfold*. Antje Dallmann, for example, bases her classification of Iris as an unreliable narrator on her description of Iris as a 'mad woman'. Yet, at no point in the narration does the novel indicate that parts of her account of her time in New York might be untrue due to her, at times, non-normative behavior.[156] Quite the contrary, Iris's behavior often mirrors that of other, equally 'mad' characters and therefore questions the existence of a clear-cut boundary between madness and sanity. Moreover, the novel problematizes the reliability of vision or rather the meaning that can be assigned to visual phenomena in various ways; this is first discernible in a scene where Paris asks Iris to describe Giorgione's painting *The Tempest*

---

[156] The discrepancy between Iris and actual unreliable narrators becomes clear when a common framework like Ansgar Nünning's 'check-lists' of unreliable narration (1998: 28, 30 and 31) is applied to the novel. Even though Iris's world view might differ from the perspective of some of her readers and therefore fulfils the criterion of deviating from individual conceptualizations of normativity, her narration does not fit textual criteria such as "linguistic signals of expressivity", "syntactic signs indicating a high degree of emotional involvement" or an "explicit thematization of the narrator's credibility" (Nünning 1998: 28; my trans.). Among all the textual features that Nünning names, only the "verbal utterances [...] of other characters" (Nünning 1998: 28) which might at times contradict Iris's evaluation of situations could be detected in Hustvedt's novel. Yet, since those evaluations often occur in the realm of aesthetics or in a much more problematic way on the level of ethics – for example, the ethical relativism to which Paris, but also Stephen and George subscribe – those characters would not serve as reliable narrators either.

based on her memory of it. While Iris is able to remember the minutest of details, and states, for example, that "[t]he most delicate foliage grows in front of her [that is, the woman in the picture], and it makes a pattern on the pale skin of her leg without hiding its shape" (Hustvedt 1993: 151), she forgets the man who is clearly visible in the picture. According to Paris, Iris blanked out the man because he constitutes a double of the spectator of the painting so that she identified with him and basically "entered the picture [...] completely" (Hustvedt 1993: 152). As Paris's analysis indicates, it is not Iris's memory which is unreliable in this context, but rather her perception of the painting, which seems to have been inaccurate from the start. Yet, the novel also implies that visual representation and, even more so, its reception, might be unreliable or at least polyvalent. This idea is most prominently emphasized in Iris's reaction to the photograph that George takes of her and the differing reception of it by George, Stephen and Iris. When confronted with the picture for the very first time, Iris does not recognize herself in it (Hustvedt 1993: 62). Later on, she describes it as "ugly" (Hustvedt 1993: 63) and "horrible" (Hustvedt 1993: 69). Stephen, by contrast, admires the mystery that it evokes for him and is constantly drawn to it (Hustvedt 1993: 69), while George sees it as one of his "studies in counterpoint" (Hustvedt 1993: 86) and intends it to form part of a juxtaposition between suffering and ecstasy. Hence, it is not the image itself which is unreliable but the meaning that is assigned to it. The unreliability of vision therefore occurs via its mediation so that this theme emphasizes how vision needs to be translated into signs in order to become meaningful. In this, the novel stresses the presence of the unreliable in the presumably self-evident and therefore ties in with a Foucauldian resistance to the fixity of certain images in discourses of power. Vision, as has been argued above, is closely linked to power; placing it in question by means of the juxtaposition of George's, Stephen's and Iris's perspectives on the picture thus relativizes the power of fixed images.

In Hustvedt's novel *The Blindfold*, literature disrupts existing orders of knowledge. By means of the deconstruction of several binary oppositions and the narrator's admittedly limited perspective, the novel refrains from constructing a new sovereign perspective, but openly announces the protagonist's process of searching. By combining various techniques of the self it negotiates possibilities for the creation of an ethical post-sovereign subject. In this, the novel emphasizes how performance in the form of masquerade can align with practices of resistance so that individual fictions acquire the potential to alter social normativity. Moreover, *The Blindfold* highlights how the post-sovereign subject's techniques of the self rely on practices that affect the mind as well as the body. However, the post-sovereign subject's ideal realm seems to be the written text itself whereas instances of an affirmation of one's precariousness or attempts at protecting the precariousness of others on the level of plot cannot quite escape the risk of including performances of sovereignty. Resistance, furthermore, seems to rely on performances which, at least partly, include a mimicking of sovereign power, or as Butler puts it, "a carefully crafted fuck you", before turning towards the development of post-sovereign performances.

7.2 Precarious Truth-Speaking in Teju Cole's *Open City*

Teju Cole's 2011 novel *Open City* can in many ways be interpreted as an equivalent to Hustvedt's *The Blindfold*. Not only do both works feature an aimlessly strolling protagonist who bears a striking resemblance to the author but whose identity is clearly distinguished from that of their creator by means of a different name, but they also include an abundance of intertextual references to literature and other media as well as a focus on reflections on power and resistance.[157] The affinity between the authors is further underscored by the fact that Hustvedt contributed a foreword to one of Cole's latest publications, the essay collection *Blind Spot* (see Hustvedt 2016b). Nevertheless, while Hustvedt focuses on issues of feminist resistance, Cole's novel centers mostly on topics associated with postcolonialism, decolonization and cosmopolitanism. And whereas *Open City* places much greater emphasis on the negotiation of questions regarding truth-speaking (*parrēsia*) and the construction of truth in the twenty-first century, *The Blindfold* only touches those issues in passing. As discussed below, both texts' approaches towards a negotiation of the formation of ethical subjects is based on their portrayal of flânerie as a technique of the self and a specific form of self-writing. In Teju Cole's *Open City*, flânerie becomes a technique of the self that contributes to a parrēsiastic 'aesthetics of existence' which negotiates the different values of the ideal of objectivity and the necessity of taking a subjective stance within political discourse. The novel centrally problematizes the norms that determine truth and falsehood in our everyday lives as well as political discourse, and negotiates the connection of truth and (discursive) power discussed by Foucault. Moreover, it affirms the ontological 'fiction' of precariousness within concepts of subjectivity.

---

[157] As Margaret DeRitter points out, Cole and his protagonist (and autodiegetic narrator) Julius both "grew up in Nigeria, live[] in New York, [have] a broad range of interests [and, ...] are about the same age" (DeRitter 2011: n. pag.). Like Julius, Cole moved to the US for college at the age of seventeen (DeRitter 2011: n. pag.). Moreover, he openly admits to playing with the autobiographical dimension of the novel as a way of "provok[ing] readers into thinking about fiction a little bit differently" (Cole, qtd. in DeRitter 2011: n. pag.).

The story of Cole's novel centers on the Nigerian psychiatrist Julius who, during his last year of training at Columbia University, develops a habit of wandering aimlessly around New York City. Julius is depicted as being extremely well-read – in fact, reviewers[158] and scholars[159] alike have judged him a bit too well-read – and interested in a wide array of topics ranging from literature, art and music to politics and history. During his walks he engages with his surroundings by drawing historical connections, reflecting on political as well as philosophical issues, and by talking to the inhabitants of the city. While his attempts at finding "the line that connected [him] to [his] own part in these stories" (Cole 2011: 59) remain fruitless at first when he tries to unearth his own past by reuniting with his grandmother during a trip to Brussels, he ultimately reconnects with a different part of his past in the second half of the novel when he encounters Moji, the sister of one of his school friends in Nigeria, who now also lives in New York. Moji's unveiling of Julius's past, however, brings a rather unexpected issue to the surface since she accuses him of having raped her when he was 14 and she 15 years old. To this accusation Julius seems not to react at all, whether on the level of *histoire*, or on the level of *discours*, which he also occupies as the autodiegetic narrator of the novel. Several months pass after Julius's account of the conversation with Moji and no further mention is made of the incident before the novel closes after just one more chapter and further meditations on Mahler's *Lied von der Erde* and Manhattan bird-life. By means of this plot twist, Julius's narration, which seemed to tend towards an ideal of objectivity, is revealed to be a subjectively inflected discourse of power, similar to the hegemonic discourses of western history that his counterdiscursive unearthings of colonial history had seemed to challenge. Its reflections on the relationship between power, truth and historiography (also) link the novel to the tradition of postcolonial flânerie, discussed in the next section.

7.2.1 Traveler, Migrant and Nomad: The Triple Dilemma of the Postcolonial Flâneur

While travelogues and journals have always formed part of the tradition of flânerie, the specific condition of the postcolonial flâneur is a phenomenon that

---

[158] See e.g. Giles Foden, who refers to Julius as an "intellectual show-off" (Foden 2011: n. pag.).
[159] See e.g. Gabriele Rippl, who points out that the information Julius gives concerning a theatre he encounters in Brussels largely coincides with the corresponding article on Wikipedia and therefore resembles an entry in a lexicon rather than a spontaneous association (Rippl 2018: 279). See also Vermeulen (2015: 97) and Elze (2017: 98) for similar remarks.

is firmly rooted in the events and mindsets of the late twentieth and early twenty-first centuries and that is tightly linked to questions of migration, hybridity and alienation. The central issue of the postcolonial flâneur revolves around different modes of mobility in the twentieth and twenty-first centuries that can best be exemplified in the heuristic models of the roles of the traveler, the nomad and the migrant as delineated by Tim Cresswell (1997: 362). The traveler's mode of movement is always a privileged one, and is "clearly marked by issues of gender, class, ethnicity and culture" (Cresswell 1997: 361; see also Clifford 1992: 105), since only those who can afford to travel for pleasure or adventure actually do so. The migrant, by contrast, is situated in a subordinated position with regard to power structures and characterized by a diasporic experience of longing for home, either in the past or in the future (see Cresswell 1997: 362); that is, they are still orientated towards a given place. The nomad, in turn, is constantly on the move and therefore "has no *place* in which meaning and identity can rest" (Cresswell 1997: 362) although they might be subjected to disciplinary structures which constantly try to put them into place.

The latter two types in particular have frequently been employed by postmodern and postcolonial theoretical frameworks to represent the corresponding forms of subjectivity (see also Cresswell 1997: 361–367). Thus, Edward Said sees postmodern subjectivity reflected in the metaphor of the migrant, with the state of exile constituting the norm for subjects in the postmodern era (1994: 403), while Deleuze and Guattari locate resistance in the metaphorical figure of the nomad (1986: 29), and Zygmunt Bauman links the image of the nomad with that of the flâneur to describe the overall structure of late-capitalist identities (1994: 154). In these latter two approaches, the culturally inflected subjectivity of the nomad has thus been appropriated by western philosophers in order to represent a supposed universal condition of postmodernity (see Clifford 1992: 110). This comparison draws on the mobility and consequently fluid identity of the nomad, which makes the image a fitting one to reflect postmodernism's free-floating signifiers and circulation of capital. However, not only is the appropriation of the non-western character of the nomad itself problematic, but the assumption that there is anything like a universal freedom of movement and mobility ignores a social reality permeated by power structures that either prevent a large part of the world's population from access to such movement or that force them into performing it – mobility in terms of freedom of movement is a privilege that is much more likely to be granted to westerners than to non-westerners, whereas populations that are forced into mobility tend to be located in the Global South. The utmost form of mobility, represented by the metaphor of the nomad in the theoretical frameworks mentioned above, is in actuality caught between the power structures reflected respectively in the figures of the migrant and the traveler, between those forced to become mobile due to their subordinated position within geopolitical structures of power and those choosing freely to be mobile for a certain amount of time due to financial privilege.

Consequently, the hybrid identity of the migrant is quite different from the fluidity of the travelling western subject of the twentieth and twenty-first centuries (see McLaren 1997: 158), since the former is marked by the experience of diaspora and an unequal distribution of power. As Shohat and Stam argue,

> A celebration of syncretism and hybridity per se, if not articulated with questions of historical hegemonies, risks sanctifying the *fait accompli* of colonial violence. For oppressed people, even artistic syncretism is not a game but a sublimated form of historical pain, which is why Jimi Hendrix played the "Star Spangled Banner" in a dissonant mode, and why even a politically conservative performer like Ray Charles renders "America the Beautiful" as a moan and a cry. As a descriptive catch-all term, "hybridity" fails to discriminate between the diverse modalities of hybridity: colonial imposition, obligatory assimilation, political cooptation, cultural mimicry, and so forth. Elites have always made cooptive top-down raids on subaltern cultures, while the dominated have always "signified" and parodied as well as emulated elite practice. Hybridity, in other words, is power-laden and asymmetrical. (1994: 43)

Given this asymmetrical distribution of power with regard to hybridity, one central difference can be located in the matter of choice. Cultural hybridity which contains the mark of the oppressed is always limited by this very mark: the hybridity itself has not been chosen, but has been forced upon the oppressed and is, therefore, radically different from postmodern freedom. The three exemplary modes of mobility mentioned above – the nomad, the migrant and the traveler – thus illustrate the different power-laden modes of hybridity. For the traveler, hybridity is freely chosen and derives from financial privilege, which allows for developing a multifaceted, hybrid identity infused by the influences taken up by travelling all over the world. The nomad, by contrast, might be born into this condition of mobility, yet is not forced from their place due to geopolitical events. The migrant, in turn, is compelled to leave their place due to famine, war or economic reasons. Hence, while the nomad's hybridity seems to be 'naturally' given, the migrant's hybrid identity always carries the trace of expulsion and longing.

In instances of postcolonial flânerie, the hybridity of figures like the nomad and the migrant seems to match the hybridity of the flâneur who is usually located between the inside and the outside, the public and the private domain, subjection and resistance. As mentioned above, for Bauman, under the conditions of postmodernity the nomad and the flâneur even coalesce into constituting postmodern subjectivity *par excellence*. Flânerie itself is now an activity that is freely chosen by the individual. The flâneur's hybrid status between the public and the private, between being part of the crowd yet always remaining outside of it, is his own choice. But it is worth remembering that Benjamin's class-based reflections on the figure of the flâneur had already introduced the dynamics of subjection and resistance into the discourse on flânerie. The motif of the flâneur thus has long featured a link between mobility and the reflection of structures of power.

Accordingly, the postcolonial flâneur is located in an area of tension between the different aspects of mobility and hybridity represented by the nomad, the migrant and the traveler and highlights issues of (post)colonial oppression and violence due to their particular cultural hybridity. Alexander Greer Hartwiger (2016: 5–7) points to a variety of rather disparate characteristics of postcolonial flânerie that have been mentioned within academic discourse on the phenomenon. The term occurs already in Adebayo Williams's 1997 essay "The Postcolonial *Flâneur* and Other Fellow Travellers: Conceits for a Narrative of Redemption", which alludes to the possibility that the postcolonial flâneur "might undo the master narrative of globalization and resituate it within the context of colonial projects" (Hartwiger 2016: 6) and thus emphasizes the resistant aspect of postcolonial flânerie (Williams 1997: 836). Simon Gikandi, by contrast, highlights the privileged situation of the flâneur and puts him in direct opposition to what Homi K. Bhabha calls 'the unhomely' – those whose mobility and resulting hybrid identity have not been a matter of choice (see Gikandi 2010: 22). The postcolonial flâneur is thus an insider as well as an outsider since he also attends "the haunts of the leisured postcolonial class, at book launchings, galleries and symposiums" (Gikandi 2010: 22).[160] For Lisbeth Minnaard the "postcolonial flâneur emphatically pursues moments of encounter and interaction in an urban contact-zone that has clearly been touched by the transformative effects of globalization" and ultimately "aims at relation, despite difference(s)" (2013: 90). Minnaard's flâneur is thus not necessarily a figure of resistance, but rather acknowledges the "complicated histories shaped by colonialism in an era of globalization" (Hartwiger 2016: 6).

The postcolonial flâneur, according to Hartwiger, therefore can be said to combine the resistant perspective mentioned by Williams with Gikandi's observation that postcolonial flânerie always involves the flâneur's privilege to be admitted to every part of a city. Hartwiger defines the postcolonial flâneur as "the figure whose critical gaze provides a way to read the legacies of colonialism, oppression, and exploitation back into globalization and the economic, social, and political frameworks that shape the global city" and who creates a "contrapuntal

---

[160] That flânerie could also be understood in terms of colonial sovereignty and the wish "to participate in the popular sense of empire" has also been suggested by Rob Shields (2015: 74).

reading" of the city that juxtaposes hegemonic perspectives with marginalized ones (Hartwiger 2016: 7).

This account dovetails with Cecile Sandten's description of the postcolonial or diasporic flâneur; she argues that those flâneurs "explore history as well as their own identity; they are men who contemplatively observe their surroundings in the context of a postcolonial setting and are at the same time part of an in-between- or underworld" (2012: 363; my trans.).[161] The male gaze to which Sandten alludes implies a certain amount of sovereignty and mastery, whereas her reference to the 'underworld' implies a connection to subordination and resistance from below. Moreover, the link between postcolonial flânerie and Said's concept of 'contrapuntal reading' has also been established by Willi Bolle (1994: 379–388) who, drawing on Benjamin, analyses examples of non-eurocentric flânerie in Latin American literature, thus reversing the flâneur's gaze which is now directed from the periphery towards the center. Rolf Goebel likewise bases his approach on Benjamin's "fragmentary theory of the *flâneur* as the privileged personification of geographic dislocation, cultural transgression, and conceptual reconfiguration", yet reconceptualizes flânerie into the self-reflexive activity of the western traveler, suggesting that "[i]n the *flâneur*'s subjectivity, instances of cultural and historical hybridity acquire self-reflexive significance for the interpretation of modernity" (Goebel 1998: 378; see also Goebel 2001).[162] The postcolonial flâneur could then be said to be frequently poised between privilege and oppression and thus might give rise to reflections on intersectionality. While privilege can be associated with the biracial heritage of a flâneur or their return from diaspora – which has instated a westernized perspective or sovereignty in the strolling subject – it might also derive from the flâneur's class or gender and thus create friction between different markers of identity.

The abovementioned approaches point to several other characteristics adapted from the tradition of flânerie to support the postcolonial endeavor. Due to the critical aim of the postcolonial flâneur, this new variation on the motif takes up the flâneur's aptitude for walking back "into a vanished time" (Benjamin 2002: 416) in order to unearth the history of the oppressed, which has been veiled by hegemonic discourses. Additionally, postcolonial flâneurs might draw on techniques of montage that are tightly linked to the flânerie text's focus on the particular and thus create a polyphonic image of the multi-

---

[161] "Sie graben in der Geschichte und ihrer eigenen Identität; sie sind Männer, kontemplativ-beobachtend im Kontext eines postkolonialen *setting* und gleichzeitig Teil der Zwischen- oder Unterwelt."
[162] See also Carol Dell'Amico (2005: 11) who argues in the context of postcolonial flânerie that "any given flâneur text must be scrutinized for any number of negotiations."

cultural city in the twentieth and twenty-first centuries (see also Sandten 2012: 357). Lastly, the analogy drawn by Benjamin between the flâneur and the commodity acquires a special relevance if seen in the light of twenty-first-century globalization and its constant flow of goods and people. This issue is taken up by postcolonial flânerie texts in various ways (see Hartwiger 2016: 7; see Sandten 2012: 357), indicating, for example, a cleavage between the unhindered flow of commodities and travelers and the laborious movement of the migrant.

The postcolonial flâneur, as understood in most of the publications mentioned above, is therefore particularly apt to tie in with the Foucauldian notion of the aesthetics of existence as a critical lens that aims at uncovering the power dynamics which impose order on the city, and by extension the entire globe. They are hybrid characters that function as personifications of the power-laden liminal space of displacement, yet, at the same time, perform a post-sovereign subjectivity that takes the limitation of the subject's perspective into account. As we shall see in relation to Cole's novel, the postcolonial flâneur is located in a field of tension between the supposed universal characteristics of postmodern subjectivity and the culturally inflected distribution of power that he represents.[163]

7.2.2 Representation and Knowledge-Formation in *Open City*

In *Open City*, issues of truth, power and historiography, which are central to postcolonial reflections, are negotiated by means of Julius's representation of the city as well as that of others. This is powerfully illustrated by a scene in the middle of the novel where Julius's perspective onto New York is doubled, overlapping with his memory of a detailed model of the city that he once saw at the Queens Museum of Art (see Cole 2011: 150). This memory is then intertextually linked to Jorge Luis Borges's short story "On Exactitude in Science", a literary forgery which fictionally mimics factual historiography – and hence bears a resemblance to the way Cole's novel plays with the border between fact and fiction,

---

[163] Fittingly, *Open City* has often been associated with discourses of cosmopolitanism (see Elze 2017; Hallemeier 2014; Oniwe 2016; Vermeulen 2013 and 2015) and Afropolitanism (see Neumann and Rippl 2017; Gehrmann 2015; Fongang 2017), with publications tracing the manifold ways in which Cole's novel critically reflects on a too optimistic cosmopolitanism that ignores global dynamics of power, as well as the ways in which it negotiates basic tensions of Afropolitanism, which combines the cultural hybridity of the twenty-first-century migrant with their African roots and therefore projects an identity that is fluid and at the same time firmly rooted in the individual subject's African heritage.

7.2 Precarious Truth-Speaking in Teju Cole's *Open City* — 173

given its autobiographical borrowings. Borges's story describes a fictional kingdom where a map is created on a 1:1 scale which then covers the whole kingdom and is later discarded due to its impracticability (see Borges 1989: 225). The story, which has become a staple of postmodernist discourse,[164] illustrates the unbridgeable gap between signifier and signified within representation and the resulting lack of exactitude in science which needs to rely on signification in order to communicate its findings. In *Open City*, the whole nexus of the inadequacy of representation, the ideal of objectivity and exactitude and the impossible bird's-eye view on the city of New York are then further linked to the topic of the 9/11 attacks:

> But as we broke through the last layer of clouds and the city in its true form suddenly appeared a thousand feet below us, the impression I had was not at all morbid. What I experienced was the unsettling feeling that I had had precisely this view of the city before, accompanied by the equally strong feeling that it had not been from the point of view of a plane.
>
> Then it came to me: I was remembering something I had seen about a year earlier: the sprawling scale model of the city that was kept at the Queens Museum of Art. The model had been built for the World's Fair in 1964, at great cost, and afterward had been periodically updated to keep up with the changing topography and built environment of the city. It showed, in impressive detail, with almost a million tiny buildings, and with bridges, parks, rivers, and architectural landmarks, the true form of the city. The attention to detail was so meticulous that one could not help but think of Borges's cartographers, who, obsessed with accuracy, had made a map so large and so finely detailed that it matched the empire's scale on a ratio of one to one, a map in which each thing coincided with its spot on the map. The map proved so unwieldy that it was eventually folded up and left to rot in the desert. Our view from the plane, as we banked over Queens itself, brought all of that back to mind, and in this case it was the real city that seemed to be matching, point for point, my memory of the model, which I had stared at for a long time from a ramp in the museum.
>
> On the day I had seen the Panorama, I had been impressed by the many fine details it presented: the rivulets of roads snaking across a velvety Central Park, the boomerang of the Bronx curving up to the north, the elegant beige spire of the Empire State Building, the white tablets of the Brooklyn piers, and the pair of gray blocks on the southern tip of Manhattan, each about a foot high, representing the persistence, in the model, of the World Trade Center towers, which, in reality, had already been destroyed. (Cole 2011: 150–151)

First and foremost, the passage demonstrates how the novel itself is structured. *Open City* presents itself to its readers as an (ostensibly) aimless collection of impressions which mainly stem from Julius's rambles through the city. Those impressions then trigger further associations and reflections in Julius which are linked to the visual impression at hand and create the continuous image of "lay-

---

[164] See e.g., Umberto Eco (1995) or Jean Baudrillard (1994).

ers and layers of ideas that exist in the world" (Cole, qtd. in DeRitter 2011: n. pag.) or the postmodern concept of the city as a "palimpsest" (Cole 2011: 59; see also Hartwiger 2016). The meaning of those associations, however, has to be supplied by the reader whose interpretation depends on individual contexts and pre-existing cultural knowledge. Although Julius frequently adds his own opinions on what he observes, he just as often refrains from doing so and might even switch from one political position to another depending on his interlocutors. The reader is often left with a web of references which seem to ask for disentangling.

Yet, this particular passage is telling on the level of content as well. Julius remembers his fascination with the model's "meticulous" "attention to detail" which induced him to stare at it "for a long time from a ramp of the museum". The bird's-eye view that he adopts in this situation as well as in the situation triggering this memory, alongside the emphasis on detail, is reminiscent of an ideal of objectivity[165] that is reflected in Julius's own representation of the city, characterized by a detached attitude towards people and topics and a similarly meticulous attention to detail.

At the same time, the mention of Borges's story already implies that this ideal can never be reached. While Julius experiences an actual bird's-eye view over the city from the plane, the association with the model of the city at the Queens Museum of Art simultaneously indicates that this perspective is just as inaccurate as any other since the model misrepresents the city by still including the towers of the World Trade Center. The Borgesian reference further points out that reaching the ideal itself would not result in any useful representation of the city. The juxtaposition between an attempt at absolute objectivity and the subsequent reminder that this attempt can never actually reach its goal mirrors the novel's overall trajectory on the level of plot: Julius's seemingly objective and neutral perspective onto his surroundings is eventually countered by the inclusion of Moji's story which unveils Julius's own blind spot and thus uncovers his actual subjectivity. This tension between the affirmation of the ideal of objectivity and the simultaneous reminder of its status as an ideal that can never be adequately reached is central to the novel as a whole.

The visual aspect of this passage is key, since it links the topic of knowledge acquisition – as this link has traditionally been established in western thought – to visual perception. As Borges's story suggests, science depends on visual perception and representation so that the ideal of omniscience and totality becomes

---

[165] This might already be indicated at the beginning of the novel when Julius marvels at the perspective that the migrating geese might have onto the city (see Cole 2011: 4).

associated with an all-encompassing perspective like the bird's-eye view. Nevertheless, the symbol of the eye itself, which is associated with visual perception, at the same time indicates subjectivity since human – as well as avian – vision is necessarily restricted on a physiological level and can never actually achieve the ideal of omniscience.

Moreover, the fact that this nexus is coupled with an allusion to the events of 11 September 2001 might also speak to a false sense of superiority or the repression of any notion of vulnerability. The topic of 9/11 recurs repeatedly in *Open City* and forms one of the main issues in a debate at the center of the novel, between Julius and two Moroccan Muslims he meets on a trip to Brussels, a debate which focusses on the construction of western discourses of power and knowledge (see Cole 2011: 117–129).

Lastly, the whole scene is reminiscent of a thesis that Jean Baudrillard brings up in his seminal monograph *Simulacra and Simulation* (1981). Here, Baudrillard argues that

> If once we were able to view the Borges fable in which the cartographers of the Empire draw up a map so detailed that it ends up covering the territory exactly [...] as the most beautiful allegory of simulation, this fable has now come full circle for us, and possesses nothing but the discrete charm of second-order simulacra. [...] It is the real, and not the map, whose vestiges subsist here and there, in the deserts which are no longer those of the Empire, but our own: The desert of the real itself. (Baudrillard 1994: 1)

According to Baudrillard, the relationship between the real and representation has changed during the twentieth century. The remnants of representation that had been discarded in the desert are now turned into the last vestiges of the real which have been abandoned in a desert full of representation. In a similar way, the real city takes the place of the map in Julius's analogy and the model that of the Empire itself since "in this case it was the real city that seemed to be matching, point for point, [his] memory of the model". Julius's detached attitude towards everything that he encounters seems to mirror a twenty-first-century society's exaggerated emphasis on representation.

The aerial scene in *Open City* thus implies that 9/11 as a notion of the real has to be repressed in the representation of the city while Julius's focus on the memory of the representation instead of on an observation of the actual city as seen from above suggests that he buys into this dynamic. The end of the novel, as we will see, seems to appeal to its readers to give up a detached attitude and take a stance, thus entering the real.

Nevertheless, this example emphasizes what has already been mentioned above: extracting any kind of meaning from Julius's observations always relies on an individual interpretative trajectory, and on whatever pre-existing knowledge is projected onto the text, since the novel's web of references usually offers starting points for a variety of interpretations.[166] The text itself thus mirrors not only Julius's distancing approach towards what he encounters but also the eponymous 'open city' which allows for any kind of interpretation due to its palimpsestic nature (see also Vermeulen 2013: 52). The text is, however, the product of Julius's performance of flânerie by means of which "New York worked itself into [Julius's] life at walking pace" (Cole 2011: 3) and which is later on translated into a special case of self-writing through which Julius forms himself, but also performs a parrēsiastic act of critique that problematizes existing norms of knowledge production and truth-speaking. The following section therefore analyzes the first of those two steps, Julius's flânerie as a technique of the self.

7.2.3 Flânerie as Technique of the Self in *Open City*

In the first place, flânerie serves as a technique of the self that is supposed to have a therapeutic effect on Julius[167] and thus is used by him to improve his life. According to him, the walks formed a "counterpoint" (Cole 2011: 3) to his days at the hospital and functioned as a "reminder of freedom" (Cole 2011: 7). At the beginning, Julius suggests a binary opposition between the hospital as "a regimen of perfection and competence" and his flânerie during which "[e]very decision [...] was inconsequential" (Cole 2011: 7), yet this opposition is somewhat dissolved when he mentions trying to sort his encounters and experiences after returning home and thus implies that the order of his workplace infiltrates the aimless and inconsequential experience of his strolls.[168] Moreover, the walks are also supposed to break the isolation and monotony of Julius's evenings (see Cole 2011: 6) – usually spent reading and listening to foreign radio stations – although they don't seem to quite succeed in fulfilling this function since "the impress of these countless faces did nothing to assuage [his] feelings of isolation" (Cole 2011: 6).

---

166 See also Vermeulen's contention (2013: 51–52) that *Open City* mainly aims at making legible the traces of history in an imperfect and incomplete way without assuming that any great cosmopolitan resolution can come from literature's intervention.
167 See Julius's remark that "The walks met a need: they were a release from the tightly regulated mental environment of work, and once I discovered them as therapy, they became the normal thing, and I forgot what life had been like before I started walking" (Cole 2011: 7).
168 See also Gamso (2019: 68) who argues that "Julius' fitful attempt to reassemble the day's encounters might thus be reconceived as an [sic] wish to make knowledge [...]".

Those first descriptions already indicate the ambivalence of Julius's flânerie which combines typical characteristics of the tradition of flânerie with other influences like Julius's psychiatric practice or his conversations with his mentor Prof Saito. The characteristics build on the full range of a western history of flânerie. First of all, he emphasizes the aimlessness of his walks (see Cole 2011: 3, 7, *et passim*) and thus fulfils Neumeyer's basic criteria of aimlessly strolling through the space of the city. Second, he repeatedly encounters crowds of people, although he does not always engage with them. Already the very first pages of the novel describe his encounter with the crowd as an experience of intoxication and excessive demand, "as though someone had shattered the calm of a silent private chapel with the blare of a TV set" (Cole 2011: 6). Later on, he flees from the accelerated crowd of the New York Marathon (see Cole 2011: 8), observes African-American crowds in the "Harlem nights" (Cole 2011: 18) or watches crowds of business people on Wall Street (Cole 2011: 47). Thirdly, as in *The Blindfold*, there is a clear focus on visuality during Julius's walks. Thus, he points out that "[w]alking through busy parts of town meant I laid eyes on more people [...] than I was accustomed to seeing in the course of the day", or that on coming back from his walks he "rehearsed in the dark the numerous incidents and sights I had encountered while roaming" (Cole 2011: 6).[169] Nevertheless, contrary to *The Blindfold*, *Open City* does not exclusively focus on visual sensory impressions but juxtaposes its paradigm of visuality with the paradigm of auditory impressions by means of which Julius "encounter[s] the streets as an incessant loudness" (Cole 2011: 6) and which manifests itself in his numerous conversations with the inhabitants of New York and Brussels. Fourthly, Julius often walks back "into a vanished time" (Benjamin 2002: 416) while strolling through New York and Brussels, uncovering not only the hidden parts of the city's history and the hidden traumata of its inhabitants, but also his own discarded memories of his childhood in Nigeria.[170] In this, the city often simply serves as a trigger for his recollections, for example when he sees a blind man in the subway and then starts reflecting on Yoruba beliefs regarding physical disabilities (Cole 2011: 24–25) or when the sight of the Statue of Liberty leads him into ruminations about immigration and slavery (Cole 2011: 54–55). Lastly, the novel itself takes up the typical structure of a flânerie text in which the text mirrors not only Julius's subjectivity, but also the city itself. The text as well as its

---

[169] See also Briana Finocchiario (2019: 1) who compares the narration resulting from those visual impressions with Impressionist paintings.
[170] See e. g. also Miller (2015: 199): "Julius [...] is preoccupied with New York's past. At times he looks at New York as if he were an archaeologist" or Vermeulen (2013: 47) who, drawing on Rebecca Walkowitz (2006: 158), refers to the "'Benjaminian gaze'" that the novel establishes.

narrator prefer the particular over the general and thus create an image of the city that represents it in its diversity, complexity and particularity, yet this also entails refraining from taking a too straightforward political stance.[171]

Julius, his narrative and the city can thus be described in terms of the central metaphor of the 'open city' which, as is pointed out in Julius's conversation with his acquaintance Dr Maillotte, designates a city that surrenders to invading powers in order to be saved from bombardment (see Cole 2011: 97). Julius's detached attitude, which distances him from any continuous political commitment on the level of the novel's *histoire*, echoes the political attitude of the 'open city' since more often than not Julius does not react to or comment on racist, homophobic or antisemitic comments.[172] This indifference then recurs on the level of the *discours*, which juxtaposes different political attitudes or ideas, but refrains from commenting on them any further. Julius's narrative therefore represents the openness of the city which can function simultaneously as a motor for oppression and resistance. On a thematic level, the novel then fulfils the flânerie text's criterion of transgression. The episodic form of the novel, moreover, supports its thematic diversity since – due to the massive reduction of plot[173] – it implies that all scenes are equally important and all opinions are equally valuable.[174] This is further emphasized by the more or less equal length of the twenty-one individual chapters.

Besides such traditional characteristics of the flâneur, Julius's individual performance of flânerie involves other influences which derive from his personal and professional background. Thus, the practice of psychiatry seems to loom

---

[171] Julius's lack of more explicit political opinions has frequently been referred to in the secondary literature. See e.g. Elze (2017: 101), Fongang (2017: 138) and Neumann and Rippl (2017: 168, 2020: 218)

[172] This is especially the case in his conversations with Dr Maillotte who revels in stereotypical thought when pointing out that many Nigerians "are arrogant" and juxtaposing them with Ghanaians who "are much calmer, easier to work with" (Cole 2011: 88) or is openly homophobic when referring to a homosexual acquaintance of hers as "a complete faggot" (Cole 2011: 92). Yet, Julius's indifference here becomes also obvious in his talk with Farouq who – despite his often differentiated and nuanced approach towards other political topics – also indulges in anti-semitism when he describes the Jewish population in Morocco and remarks that "[t]hey look just like us, though, of course, they do better in business. I think sometimes that maybe I should become a Jew, just for professional reasons. I'll be able to get everything done" (Cole 2011: 124).

[173] See also Elze (2017: 95–96) who draws a connection between Julius's "distrust in causes" and the novel's reduction in plot, "as it is precisely the joining of a cause that would create perceivable social semantic spaces to be bridged by the dynamics of action and plot."

[174] Nevertheless, the notion of surrender to which the term 'open city' is linked also implies the ethical problem that such an approach might constitute.

large during his strolls since the memories he unearths often refer to collective or individual trauma (see also Neumann and Rippl 2017: 169; see Elze 2017: 102), as is the case when his spontaneous talks with Prof Saito bring up the topic of Japanese internment during the Second World War (see Cole 2011: 13–14), or when his visit to a bookstore prompts a brief summary of one of his patients' accounts of the slaughter of Native Americans (see Cole 2011: 25–26), or when the sight of Battery Park reminds him of the American banking system's involvement with slavery (see Cole 2011: 162–163). Yet, the ability to do this seems to be derived not only from Julius's work as a psychiatrist, but also from the conversations with his mentor Prof Saito who taught him "the art of listening [and...] to trace out a story from what was omitted" (Cole 2011: 9). Interestingly, Julius points out that he learns this art by means of practice when he recalls that Prof Saito did almost all the talking in their conversations.

That he applies this ability later on during his strolls through the city is suggested by numerous encounters during which he listens to the stories that his interlocutors tell him. His kind of flânerie thus deviates from typical examples of flânerie – like Baudelaire's *Parisian Scenes* or Hessel's *Walking in Berlin* – which mainly rely on the visual perception of the city and thus often involve instances of projection, an aspect that is reflected in Benjamin's remark that the flâneur only seemingly escapes from his own isolation: "by filling the hollow space created in him by such isolation with the borrowed—and fictitious—isolations of strangers" (Benjamin 2006: 88). Julius's flânerie is different because it puts an additional emphasis on listening to the city rather than just observing it and thus increases the chances of defying projection and changing one's perspective onto the other. The textualization of Julius's flânerie then reflects on his sensory perception of the city and marks the limits of various "sensuous modes of access to the truth".

Thus, visuality is problematized as a subjective, yet still valid paradigm in the production of truth, whereas auditive perception is validated as a necessary addendum to this paradigm in order to arrive at a polyphonic, albeit still limited, representation of the city. In this, it is not only the gaze which is connoted as potentially violent, but even more so the construction of meaning which follows the gaze and which only leads to more projection by means of reflection. Quite fittingly, Benjamin draws on Georg Simmel to elaborate on the consequences of a "preponderance of visual activity":

> People had to adapt themselves to a new and rather strange situation, one that is peculiar to big cities. Simmel has provided an excellent formulation of what was involved here. "Someone who sees without hearing is much more uneasy than someone who hears without seeing. In this, there is something characteristic of the sociology of the big city. Inter-

personal relationships in big cities are distinguished by a marked preponderance of visual activity over aural activity. [...]." These new situations were, as Simmel recognized, not pleasant. (Benjamin 2006: 69)

The metropolis is thus especially disconcerting to the individual because they can see others, but might not talk with them. This, according to Benjamin, creates a moment of suspense for the citizen who is confronted with the image of his fellow citizens but does not have any information regarding this image, which in turn leads him to projecting ideas onto the other and thus suspecting the other of criminal activities (Benjamin 2006: 69).

While projection is already associated with a feeling of distress in Benjamin, *Open City* expands on the potential for violence that might become aligned with the citizen's alienated relationship towards others and the projection it entails. As the epigraph to the first part of the novel – "Death is a perfection of the eye" (Cole 2011: 1) – implies, the eye as well as the whole paradigm of visuality, present in *Open City* in a variety of manifestations, is associated with death and violence. Visuality here repeatedly becomes an instrument in the exertion of violence or is used as a metaphor for the exertion of violence. Thus, Farouq, a Moroccan with whom Julius talks in Brussels about the way African-Americans are stereotyped in the US, draws the following conclusion: "They are victims of the same portrayals as we are" (Cole 2011: 119). To which Julius answers: "The same portrayal [...], but that's how power is, the one who has the power controls the portrayal" (Cole 2011: 119).[175] In this, the process of stereotyping is referred to as a portrayal and is directly linked to the term 'power'. The quote implies two things: first, those portrayals do not constitute truthful representations, but contain, just like the projections of the citizen of the metropolis in Benjamin, a simplification of what is represented; second, this simplification entails a moment of violence with regard to another subject which subsumes them under an inadequate generalization.

Similarly, projection seems equally inevitable in Julius's perception of others during his strolls. Thus, when he encounters a marathon runner while wandering through the city, he quickly starts to create an image of the man:

> At Sixty-second Street, I fell in with a lithe man with graying sideburns who carried a plastic bag with a tag on it and was visibly exhausted, limping on slightly bowed legs. [...]. Eventually, I asked him whether he had just finished the race and, when he nodded and smiled, congratulated him. But, I began to think, after twenty-six miles and 385 yards,

---

[175] Interestingly, this stereotyping is linked to visual representation on TV since Khalil asks Julius: "The American blacks [...] are they really as they are shown on MTV: the rapping, the hip-hop dance, the women? Because that's all we see here" (Cole 2011: 119).

he had simply collected his bag, and was walking home. There were no friends or family present to celebrate his achievement. I pitied him, then. [...]. At the street in front of the opera houses, I bid him goodbye and began myself to walk faster. I imagined his limping form receding as I pressed ahead, his wiry frame bearing a victory apparent to none but himself. (Cole 2011: 15)

Julius's perception of the man is at first determined by his outward appearance. He notices his limping, exhaustion and grey hair. The following reflections then do not only refer to the bodily deficits of the man, but also his seeming social isolation and lead to Julius pitying the man. Yet, his opinion changes as soon as Julius situates the activity of the marathon runner within its historical context:

> The first man who ever ran a marathon had died instantly, and small wonder: it is an act of extreme human endurance, still remarkable no matter how many people now do it. And so, turning around to look at my erstwhile companion, and thinking of Phidippides' collapse, I saw the situation more clearly. It was I, no less solitary than he but having made the lesser use of the morning, who was to be pitied. (Cole 2011: 15–16)

Due to his reflections, Julius's perspective changes radically – and literally, since he is "turning around to look at" the man. Nevertheless, the reference to the paradigm of visuality – "I *saw* the situation more clearly" – already implies the continuing 'limitation of the gaze'. Thus, Julius changes his opinion regarding the marathon runner to be pitied, yet this does not prevent him from believing that one of the two strollers has to be pitied – in this case, Julius himself. Reflection – which of course carries the semantic traces of the paradigm of visuality – then does not lead to an objectivization of the gaze, which can never be entirely objectivized, but rather to a re-evaluation of the projection already taking place.

Flânerie, therefore, always seems liable to remain associated with projection, yet as Julius's conversation with his acquaintance Farouq, about the Moroccan writer Tahar Ben Jelloun, proves, flânerie also has the capacity to produce an especially 'authentic' and, thus, potentially truthful account of the city. Here, the link between stereotypical portrayal, writing, power and flânerie is further negotiated when Farouq argues that "he [Ben Jelloun] writes out of a certain idea of Morocco. It isn't the life of people that Ben Jelloun writes about but stories that have an oriental element in them. His writing is mythmaking. It isn't connected to people's real lives" (Cole 2011: 103).

Farouq criticizes the way Ben Jelloun creates stereotypes of life in Morocco, the "certain idea of Morocco" which is disseminated through Ben Jelloun's texts and which contributes to proliferating the orientalized image of his native country without representing the 'actual' life of Morocco's population. As a counterexample, Farouq names the writer Mohamed Choukri who unlike Ben Jelloun has never left Morocco and thus has, according to Farouq, never lost contact with the Moroccan population: "He was raised on the street and he taught himself to write classical Arabic, but he never left the street" (Cole 2011: 104). The place of contact is essential here, and it draws an immediate connection with flânerie, since for Farouq it is on the street that the encounter between a writer and his objects of representation takes place. While the scene between Julius and the marathon runner shows that the flâneur is always at risk of projection and thus of creating stereotypical images when he comes to write about what he has seen, the quote implies a twofold coding of flânerie in the novel according to which the 'man of the street' who is in close contact with the population might be able to produce a more truthful account.

Moreover, Julius's flânerie offers an equivalent to Farouq's concept in its connection with Benjamin's theses on the recuperation of the past by means of flânerie when his conversations with strangers juxtapose different perspectives onto the colonial history of New York and Brussels and therefore produce an image of those cities based on the narratives of the people 'on the street'. This rediscovery of the past occurs by means of the memories of those whom Julius encounters during his strolls and who confront him either with their own stories or with parts of history of which Julius did not seem to be aware before. Thus, Julius extracts the past from the auditory perception of the city and partly re-assigns the status of subjects to the objects of his narration by lending them the ability to talk within the report of the flâneur. Only recording the actual speeches of the objects of representation can liberate them partly from their status as objects and turn them into subjects within the *discours* of an other. As Moji's accusations imply, conversation and its representation within the narrative open Julius's discourse up for counter-discourses which might break through the subject's projection or at least undermine it. A possible exit from one's own projection – which can only ever be temporary, as the scene with the marathon runner implies – becomes then possible through the medium of speech, but remains always fleeting since it congeals into an 'image' as soon as any definite opinion is formed.[176] This tension is reflected in Julius's oscillating between direct and in-

---

[176] Yet, this analysis is not supposed to suggest that Cole's novel makes a general statement about humankind's potential for intersubjective communication. The text rather emphasizes Julius's subjective perspective, which also manifests itself in the construction of the text and Julius's retrospective evaluation of the events. On a structural level, the text thus repeats Julius's problematic suggestion of the possibility of an objective observation of the city, which always remains stuck within a subjective perspective, yet at the same time does not exclude the possibility of partially gained knowledge and a corresponding transformation of the subject.

direct speech whenever he incorporates the discourse of another character into his narration.[177] The paradigm of the auditory is thus always caught up in visuality within *Open City*, and consequently remains linked to reflection as well as to the construction of meaning, just as much as Julius's gaze onto the stories of New York's and Brussel's respective populations remains subjective.

Scripture, or the medium of written speech, then seems to constitute an approach towards a more 'objective' gaze onto the city, since it draws a connection between the medium of spoken language and the medium of the visual image. This is explicitly pointed out in Julius's ruminations on bedbugs. The creatures become "visible only in speech" (Cole 2011: 173) so that knowledge about their existence can by means of scripture's potential of dissemination become accessible to a broad mass of recipients (see also Vermeulen 2015: 99)[178] or can be communicated in individual conversations as is the case with Julius and Prof Saito. The expression "visible only in speech" mixes visual with auditory perception and transfers the counterdiscursive potential of the medium of speech into visuality so that it becomes linked to visuality's propensity for projection. This might indicate the reformulation of a staple of deconstructivist theses about scripture, namely that a text, as soon as it is received – that is, as soon as it has made things visible – runs the risk of its meaning being deferred and changed by means of its insertion into a new context. Oscillating between discourse and counter-discourse thus becomes a structural principle in *Open City*.

Flânerie then becomes a technique of the self which offers various "sensuous modes of access to the truth", yet – and this will be the next step in my argument – by means of its translation into the flânerie text it also becomes a parrēsiastic technique which negotiates different notions of truth and truthfulness and questions existing approaches towards truth and truth-speaking. In so doing, Cole's flânerie text functions as a means of reflection on the form that Julius gives himself in his performance of flânerie and actively transforms Julius's identity.

---

[177] This is further elaborated on in the sections below on *parrēsia*, truthfulness and unreliable narration.

[178] Correspondingly, what is repressed as well as what is past also becomes visible when the flâneur lends the ability 'to talk to him' to objects, buildings and memorials in the city by recollecting information that he had read previously or that he collects from inscriptions or information boards; that is, the visual paradigm is positively evaluated here.

7.2.4 Truthfulness and *parrēsia* in *Open City*

The novel expands on its reflections on different modes of perception by means of an additional focus on truth and truth-speaking. It approaches this topic through Julius's double role of uncovering truth by giving a voice to oppressed discourses and simultaneously engaging in such oppression in his own narration.[179] The ensuing tension between Julius's resistance to discourses of power and his perpetuation of such discourses is instrumental in highlighting a paradox ingrained in the notion of truthfulness if seen through a Foucauldian lens. On the one hand, truth for Foucault immediately depends on discursive power, which can be considered a relativist understanding of truth, while on the other hand in his late work Foucault admits to the necessity of truthfulness as a value that manifests itself for example in the practice of *parrēsia*. In the character of Julius, the novel juxtaposes these two notions of truthfulness when, faced with the accusation of rape against him, Julius simply remains silent on the issue and so prevents the reader from gaining any insight into the events. By rendering the facts of the case inaccessible in this way, the narrative marks its own opacity and directs readers' attention to the mechanisms of discursive power inherent in Julius's narration and, in a wider sense, in any instance of the production of truth, a power that, as the novel also shows, somewhat paradoxically can only be countered by acts of truth-speaking. The novel thus highlights a central conundrum in our relationship towards the truth: while objectivity forms a necessary ideal in any production of truth, this ideal can neither be obtained by subjects nor would a truth that has not been subjectivized be of any use since it lacks a relationship to the subject.

As has been mentioned above, subjectivization of discourse is marked in the novel by means of the critique of the paradigm of visuality. While visuality is still emphasized as a viable mode of access to the truth, it is also problematized due to its intrinsic restriction of perspective. Narrative as an extension of this restriction and subjectivization of discourse is juxtaposed with the plurality of discourse represented by an auditive paradigm which aims at an ideal of objectivity, yet can only ever produce intersubjectivity – that is, a plurality of subjective perspectives. This link between the production of truth, its material preconditions and its critique is negotiated in *Open City* by means of the novel's employment

---

[179] Parts of the argument of this chapter have been published in Riedelsheimer and Ries (2021). I am very grateful to Martin Riedelsheimer for pointing out to me Phelan's category of 'underreporting' as well as Lamarque's remarks on the 'opacity of narrative'.

of unreliable narration and the problematization of its autodiegetic narrator Julius.

To begin with, Julius's account seems to be nothing but truthful within the fictional world of the novel. As a psychiatrist, he is assigned a position as a competent subject speaking the truth within the discourse of his profession of clinical psychiatry. Moreover, his flânerie often takes the form of a rigorously objective collecting of data – Rebecca Clark (2018: 194), for example, points out that "[e]verything and everyone that Julius encounters seems to be leveled out into information" – and Julius thus performs several norms that function as markers for speaking the truth in the twenty-first century, such as aiming at an ideal of objectivity as well as giving very detailed historical information on the sites he visits. In this, his tone is mostly neutral and distanced, projecting disinterested observation (see Steckenbiller 2018: 5; Elze 2017: 86), and his detailed descriptions cause a stretching of narrated time that suggests precision in his reporting, which creates the impression that Julius's main interest lies in a punctilious representation of facts. As Clark puts it, "[t]he sweeping range of knowledge – or at least abundance of factoids – that Julius recalls at a moment's notice as he aimlessly wanders the city seems to mimic a bird's-eye view, a privileged perspective that can pan out to see, read, and map the whole, from a subject position of disinterested omniscience (or at least omni-vision)" (2018: 186). Within the logic of the fictional world Julius thus seems to engage in or at least mimic factual speech.

An example that entails several of those markers of truth can be found in Julius's account of V., one of his patients whose book he encounters in a bookshop during one of his strolls:

> At around ten, I entered a bookshop, [...], and as I went in I remembered a book I had wanted to look at for a long time: a book of historical biography by one of my patients. I found it quickly—*The Monster of New Amsterdam*—and settled in among the quieter stacks to read it. V., an assistant professor at New York University and a member of the Delaware tribe, had based the book on her doctoral dissertation at Columbia. It was the first comprehensive study of Cornelis Van Tienhoven. Van Tienhoven had been notorious as a seventeenth-century *schout* of New Amsterdam, [...]. He had arrived in 1633, as a secretary for the Dutch East India Company, but as he climbed up the social ladder, he became known for his many brutal acts, notable among them a raid he led to murder Canarsie Indians on Long Island, after which he had brought back the victims' heads on pikes. [...] V.'s book made for grim reading. It was full of violent events, and in the endnotes were reprinted the relevant seventeenth-century records. (Cole 2011: 25–26)

In this excerpt, Julius's narration conforms to several norms necessary for the production of truth: first, the information on Van Tienhoven that Julius includes in his narration is very detailed, including exact dates and verifiable historical facts. Second, since this information seems to be drawn directly from an academic book, it is bolstered by the authority of academia, which is even further emphasized when Julius explicitly refers to the sources at the end of the book, as proof of the truthfulness of the information given by the narrator as well as by V. herself. Moreover, the quotation shows how Julius's practice of flânerie is tightly linked to his work, a realm in which he actually is in the position of a subject competent to speak the truth: only due to the fact that V. is his patient is Julius led to include the narration of the hidden collective trauma of the Canarsie Indians in his narrative of New York. As mentioned earlier, Julius either encounters sites in the city that prompt him to uncover lesser-known parts of the city's history or he meets people who tell him stories of individual as well as collective trauma in several complementary scenes. Those traumata then run counter to what might be considered white discourses of power: the stories that Julius reveals usually belong to ethnic minorities, whose narratives of trauma form counter-discourses to white hegemonic discourses about New York. In juxtaposing the received truths of the majority with conflicting voices from the margins, this narrative practice already implies the constructed character of any notion of an absolute truth (see Hartwiger 2016: 16). Thus, there is no single absolute truth about the city that determines its identity; instead, the city's identity is constantly re-created throughout the text. Julius's narration therefore aligns with a Foucauldian notion of truth that rejects the concept of an absolute truth and assumes that the construction of truth is always linked to the workings of power. At the same time, it performs as well as emphasizes the ideal of objectivity (or at least intersubjectivity) by checking hegemonic discourses with more marginalized voices.

Nevertheless, the novel doesn't stop at simply producing a postcolonial counter-discourse to the implicit hegemonic discourse of power but shows Julius adopting a problematically relativist stance towards ethics that might follow from constructivist notions of truth and that Foucault was accused of supporting. This becomes clearest in a passage in which Julius discloses his personal beliefs and self-image twenty pages before the end of the novel. In this scene Julius commits to his own brand of ethical relativism[180] and even extends this self-image to his potential readership:

> Each person must, on some level, take himself as the calibration point for normalcy, must assume that the room of his own mind is not, cannot be, entirely opaque to him. Perhaps

---

[180] See also Li (2018: 67) who refers to Julius as "committing [an] ethical lapse as he is in many ways 'isolated from all loyalties'" as well as Neumann and Rippl (2017: 169) and Gamso (2019: 72–73).

this is what we mean by sanity: that, whatever our self-admitted eccentricities might be, we are not the villains of our own stories. In fact, it is quite the contrary: we play, and only play, the hero, and in the swirl of other people's stories, insofar as those stories concern us at all, we are never less than heroic. [...] We have the ability to do both good and evil, and more often than not, we choose the good. When we don't, neither we nor our imagined audience is troubled, because we are able to articulate ourselves to ourselves, and because we have, through our other decisions, merited their sympathy. (Cole 2011: 243)

Hence, according to Julius, not only can every individual judge for themselves whether they perceive their actions to qualify as 'good' or 'evil' but the option of anyone identifying as 'evil' is excluded entirely, which leads to the problematic conclusion that no matter how bad an action might be it won't register in one's image of oneself, because "we are able to articulate ourselves to ourselves" and can therefore justify any action to ourselves. Julius thus uncovers his own purely relativist stance towards the truth – since the truth about the identity of the individual remains entirely subjective – and combines it with a relativist stance towards ethics – since according to his point of view we can always reinterpret our own actions as justified (see also Neumann and Rippl 2020: 232–233).

Such an apparent relativization of truth as an absolute concept, and possibly even the implicit rejection of searching for any truth as a value, can also be found elsewhere in Julius's narration, including at the level of narrative discourse itself. One example where extratextual historical factuality is abandoned is the episode in which Julius narrates his encounter with Pierre, a Haitian shoeshiner he meets in the underground part of Penn Station. In rendering his conversation with the shoeshiner, Julius almost entirely surrenders the narrative voice to Pierre's first-person narrative, which is mostly presented in free direct speech (Cole 2011: 71–74). Pierre claims that he left Haiti together with his employer, a Mr. Bérard, "when things got bad there" (Cole 2011: 71–72), due to what he calls "the terror of Boukman" (2011: 72). This places Pierre's life in the context of the Haitian revolution of 1791, in which Dutty Boukman was a leader of the enslaved Haitians who fought for their freedom, a temporal frame that is further implied when Pierre claims that after Mr. Bérard's death, in New York, he bought freedom for himself and his sister (2011: 73; see also Elze 2017: 100). As the rest of Julius's narrative is set in the years 2006 and 2007, this would make Pierre over 200 years old, a clear deviation from the realism and historical factuality the novel seems to pursue up to that point.

Taken by itself, this break with factuality is difficult to assess, particularly since it is not Julius who seems to deviate from the truth. By surrendering the narrative voice to the shoeshiner, Julius himself assumes the role of a neutral narrative medium, a task he fulfils by rendering Pierre's narration without any notable intrusion – and above all without any evaluation, conforming with the ideal of disinterested objectivity he seems to pursue elsewhere. Even when Pierre departs from what is possible within the conventions of realism and thus from any possible historical factuality, Julius still seems to be within the parameters of the truthful as far as his own narrative is concerned: after all, he listens to and records the shoeshiner's story in the same way he does his patients' or those of other characters he meets on his walks through the city. Yet, although he proves to be a precise commentator on historical facts elsewhere, he either does not recognize the obvious contradictions in the shoeshiner's account or willfully ignores them, thus leaving open the question of whether the narrator's evaluation of events can be trusted at all. In this way, the novel points out how common norms of truth only form part of an overall construction of truth that does not ensure that the speaker who obeys those norms actually speaks the truth. In this case, it is precisely Julius's detached attitude that becomes part of the problem because he does not challenge Pierre's account.

While in first-person narration truthfulness is commonly assumed to be a given and deviations are subsumed under the label of unreliable narration, this is not quite applicable to Julius here. As the narrator in this case does not provide any comment on the narrative he renders (that is, Pierre's story), but only seems to record it faithfully, the 'lie', if it may be so termed, is Pierre's. However, while Julius in this case does not produce a false statement himself, his lack of any comment on Pierre's story nevertheless tears open a gap in the narrative that may cause the unwary reader to be deceived. As a consequence of this evaluative gap, a 'gapped truth'[181] – one where it is entirely unclear who has violated the norm of truthfulness at this point – is created in the narrative of *Open City*. This then points towards the difficulty of rendering truth in narrative, or, following (early) Foucault, to the way in which discursive mechanisms are essential in the construction of what is considered to be true.

A similarly gapped version of the truth, albeit at a much more personal level for the narrator, occurs when Julius's acquaintance Moji confronts him at the end of the novel and tells him that when they were both teenagers he had raped her (2011: 244). While this sudden revelation certainly lets Julius's moral evaluation appear doubtful, it is in particular his response that seems problematic with regard to the status of truth in the novel. For the narrator remains silent on the issue and consequently prevents not only Moji but also the reader from gaining any insight into his reaction to this accusation – a behavior that distinctly echoes the shoeshiner episode. Instead, he leaves the party and goes home, upon which

---

[181] See also Weymann-Teschke who refers to the fact that Julius "frequently leaves gaps in his story" (2018: 205).

the chapter, the novel's penultimate, ends. The last chapter is set in autumn, leaving a conspicuous temporal gap of several months from the night of the party, which was in May (2011: 232), and never returning to the rape. On the one hand, this lack of any direct reaction on Julius's part does not seem to constitute an outright case of lying. Rather, Julius seems to have taken to heart Philip Sidney's claim that lying depends on an affirmation of facts (2012: 1068) and therefore avoids the lie by not speaking on the matter at all and thus not 'affirming' anything. On the other hand, there is something about this narrative non-engagement that rings entirely false. There is a cleavage between Julius's actions as a character who makes uncovering hidden trauma his business and his stance as a narrator who remains silent on and so engages in repressive discourse – again an evaluative gap opens up in Julius's narrative, only this time the gap concerns a rather more personal story than the vaguely political narrative of Pierre the shoeshiner.

The reporting, interpreting or evaluating that the narratee is offered by Julius is minimal, reluctant and gapped. While Moji's accusation is presented by the narrator, the rhetorical construction of the narrative gives the impression that this reporting occurs only hesitantly. Thus, Julius mentions his unwillingness to go to the party in the first place (Cole 2011: 231) and the chronology of his accounts of the party is oddly shuffled, with a lengthy description of his leaving the party and walking home inserted before the confrontation with Moji is reported, as if the narrator's intention were to defer or avoid this reporting. Further, the way in which the accusation itself is subtly framed in Julius's reporting suggests that only a minimal account of Moji's claims is presented. Julius renders Moji's allegation in indirect speech and in a strongly summarized version – the "probably six or seven minutes" (2011: 244) she spends presenting her version of events are condensed to just about one page of text and so reduced to a minimum – the ultimate effect of which is that the victim's voice is broken in the prism of the voice of the accused who wields the narrator's control of the narrative. Crucially, Julius's account only allows Moji direct speech[182] when she turns to the present and accuses him: "You'll say nothing, she said. I know you'll say nothing. I'm just another woman whose story of sexual abuse will not be believed" (2011: 245).

Moji indeed correctly anticipates what happens next: during and after reporting the confrontation with Moji at the party, Julius says nothing about the

---

[182] As Clark (2018: 193) as well as Pieter Vermeulen (2013: 48) point out, Julius directly incorporates other characters' speech in his own narration without separating the discourses of other characters from his own by means of quotation marks.

truth or falsity of her claim that he had "forced [himself] on her" (2011: 244) or about his reactions, both cognitive and emotional, to such an accusation. This means there is no overt evaluating or interpreting of Moji's claim on offer. The only evaluative statements Julius makes do not pertain to the veracity of the accusation but to the way in which Moji presents it and possibly to her own conviction of its truth, since he admits that "[s]he had said it as if, with all of her being, she were certain of its accuracy" (2011: 244).

There is then little in Julius's narration that allows either the narratee or the reader to make an informed decision on what truly happened and to what extent Julius is guilty. Hence, there is little to be inferred from Julius's silence beyond a general sense of discomfort with the situation, expressed in his reluctance to present a fuller version of the events – unless, that is, one were to infer an admission of guilt from Julius's silence on the matter. Overall, Julius's lack of a reaction to Moji's claim seems to be an extreme case of what Phelan calls "underreporting", a type of narration that "occurs when the narrator tells us less than he or she knows" (2005: 52). Although Phelan stresses that "[n]ot all underreporting [...] constitutes unreliability" (2005: 52), but only the omission of "salient" (2005: 52n) information that cannot be expected to be inferred by the narratee or reader, Julius may still be considered unreliable by these standards, as the ellipsis in his narrative cannot be filled with any certainty. However, it is not at all clear whether this makes the narrator unreliable, since declaring Julius unreliable would rely on the problematic notion that 'not speaking' is equivalent to 'not speaking the truth'. Ultimately, the lack of information provided by Julius makes it extremely difficult to decide on his reliability in this case, since the gap that is thus created remains impossible for the reader to fill.

Nevertheless, although Julius seems to give himself up to the interpretation of the readers by not commenting on Moji's accusations at all and therefore to turn himself into a precarious subject, his previous statement that everyone takes themselves as their "calibration point for normalcy" and that "neither [h]e nor [his] imagined audience will be troubled" if he does not "choose the good", betrays his actual conception of sovereign subjectivity. The function of Julius's underreporting as a rare case of unreliable narration is then precisely to indicate that he negates the scene of appellation which is according to Butler at the center of every construction of identity. The reason why he does not have to counter or even to react to Moji's account lies, as Julius himself points out, in the fact that for him her accusation does not register in his identity. Necessarily, she experiences his reaction as particularly painful because it denies the primary state of interdependence and precariousness that she has been reminded of by his assault. This is made explicit by Moji herself:

> Afterward, she said, her eyes unwavering from the bright river below, in the weeks that followed, in the months and years that followed, I had acted like I knew nothing about it, had even forgotten her, to the point of not recognizing her when we met again, and had never tried to acknowledge what I had done. (Cole 2011: 244)

Julius's non-reaction on the level of *histoire* as well as on the level of *discours* clearly marks vulnerability and precariousness as 'other' to himself and, therefore, implies that he is a sovereign subject, superior to the precarious and vulnerable other represented by Moji.

Moreover, in remaining silent, Julius pushes the ideal of a disinterested objectivity to the limit, pretending to act as a non-involved reporter of the accusation against him. The implicit denial of his own investedness that this behavior suggests thus indeed appears as an act of "torturous deception" (2011: 244). For a human being (and by extension for a realistically conceptualized character) it seems impossible not to react to claims that must rattle their entire social existence: the mimetic illusion of a life-like narrator is clearly broken here. Paradoxically, Julius's subjectivity is unveiled by his apparent insistence on a disinterested objectivity that aims at veiling his subjectivity, yet actually counters his seemingly objective account. Julius's seeming objectivity thus clashes with the fact that he, like any subject, inevitably must have a subjective perspective on the issue because he is personally involved in it. After all, this is a narrative which – as much as it might aim at an ideal of objectivity – is still based on processes of selection and subjective framing. Moreover, objectivity is linked with the relativist stance towards the truth as well as towards morality which Julius refers to in his introduction to Moji's story, and as such, it is unveiled as masking subjectivity anyway because it serves as the basis for his subjective moral evaluation of himself. Ultimately, Julius's attempt at strict disinterested objectivity seems to blur any access to truth just as much as any radically subjective take on the truth might.

The most prominent function of this narrative gap is therefore to highlight the problems with the notion of truth in narrative in the first place. As Julius observes with regard to his own profession as a psychiatrist:

> As physicians [...] we depend, to a much greater degree than is the case with nonmental conditions, on what the patient tells us. But what are we to do when the lens through which the symptoms are viewed is often, itself, symptomatic: the mind is opaque to itself, and it's hard to tell where, precisely, these areas of opacity are. (Cole 2011: 238)

This is equally true for readers of narrative. In a concept that seems to be echoed by Julius here, Peter Lamarque has called this the "opacity of narrative" (2014).

For Lamarque, the opacity of narrative ensues because the mode of presentation of a narrative is inextricably entwined with its content:

> Rather than supposing that narrative descriptions are a window through which an independently existing (fictional) world is observed, with the implication that the very same world might be presented (and thus observed) in other ways, from different perspectives, we must accept that there is no such transparent glass – only an opaque glass, painted, as it were, with figures seen not *through* it but *in* it. (Lamarque 2014: 3; original emphasis)

It is then the narrative perspective itself that constitutes an integral part of the narrative in the first place (see Lamarque 2014: 11). The lens, be it that of the narrator of a (fictional) narrative or that of the narrator of a personal story of illness, as would be the case with Julius's patients, in this sense is indeed symptomatic of what it depicts. In a similar vein, the Foucauldian notion of truth might be considered one of opacity: any access to truth is only possible through the prism of power, which means that truth is opaque in so far as it rests in and on discourses of power.[183]

In *Open City*, this is thematized precisely through the narrative gaps and through the way in which the narrator frames these omissions. It is typical of first-person narration that the narrator who reports the events also frames them as a character involved in them – the events thus reported become inseparable from the narrator's perspective and mode of presentation. Julius's 'underreporting' emphasizes the aspect of selection in the production of truth. Moreover, the selective perception of visuality is here emphasized by this specific kind of unreliable narration which foregrounds the opacity of narrative. While any narrative is opaque, Julius's personal investment in Moji's story inevitably makes the mechanisms of the narrator's framing more transparent. He introduces readers to Moji's accusation immediately after musing on the relative nature of normalcy and on how "we are not the villains of our own stories":

---

[183] Interestingly, Cole himself refers to Édouard Glissant's reflections on the term 'opacity' in his essay on "A True Picture of Black Skin" in *The New York Times Magazine* (2015: n. pag.) and suggests that what Nicholas Gamso calls an "ethic of opacity" (2019: 60) is performed in the work of Black photographer Roy DeCarava. DeCarava engaged in photographic techniques which instead of compensating for the fact that cameras were often calibrated according to a white norm embraced the opaque effects produced by the camera's representation of the dark skin of his subjects and by doing so regranted value to Blackness itself. Nevertheless, by transferring this "ethic of opacity" onto the personal encounter between Moji and Julius and by extension, Julius's narration, the novel stresses how it could just as well be turned into an instrument of power if performed by those who are not marginalized, but instead are already in a subject position competent to speak the truth within a given discourse.

> And so, what does it mean when, in someone else's version [of a story], I am the villain? I am only too familiar with bad stories – badly imagined, or badly told – because I hear them frequently from patients. I know the tells of those who blame others, those who are unable to see that they themselves, and not the others, are the common thread in all their bad relationships. There are characteristic tics that reveal the essential falsehood of such narratives. But what Moji had said to me that morning [...] had nothing in common with such stories. She had said it as if, with all of her being, she were certain of its accuracy. (Cole 2011: 243–244)

Although he overtly acknowledges Moji's claim to truthfulness, by distancing her story from the "bad stories" of his patients – where notably Julius does not seem to distinguish between "badly imagined" and "badly told" – in a subtle way he expresses his doubt, finally relegating her story to the fictional realm of the 'as if'. What is more, Julius goes on to wield his discursive power as a narrator in rendering Moji's accusation in a summarized, "clinical" (Clark 2018: 196) version, initially in indirect speech. As a consequence, he regulates the way in which her claim is presented and implicitly sets the benchmark for any evaluation of it as true or false, or, in this case, relegates it to the status of the unclear and possibly made up. This marks a stark contrast to the way he gives voice to the suffering elsewhere in the novel – in particular to the way in which he almost entirely surrenders his narrative voice to the Haitian shoeshiner. As opposed to Pierre's, Moji's voice is only presented in free direct discourse briefly, at the end of the passage. Hence the initial full brunt of her accusation is defused in the detachedness of indirect speech. What Julius's presentation of Moji's story makes clear, then, is that all along – not just after admitting to a relativist stance towards truth – as a narrator he has been covertly in control of what passes as truth in his narrative, even when no indicators for unreliable narration mark his discourse as problematic. It is the inevitable opacity of any narrative that is thus exposed in the way Julius presents Moji's accusation.[184]

The point of the narrative here is that an absolute notion of truth and violent discursive power are just as much entangled as are violence and a radically relativist stance towards truth, or, in other words, that an absolute subjectivization of discourses of truth is equally violent as their absolute objectivization.[185] Moreover, objectivity can never be obtained by a singular voice which would only ever veil its own subjectivity by claiming to be entirely objective. Quite the contrary,

---

184 See also Miller (2015: 203) who claims that in this passage Julius "is talking about his profession but he is also talking about himself."
185 See also Katherine Hallemeier who argues that Julius's "frequent incorporation of other's stories into their own can be read as admirably worldly, problematically passive, or both" (Hallemeier 2014: 241–242).

objectivity or rather intersubjectivity can best be achieved by the polyphony of voices that is implied by the juxtaposition of Julius's narrative with Moji's accusation (although this accusation still forms part of Julius's narrative or his discourse of power). The question that the novel here poses is whether an alternative to those two opposing ends of a spectrum – the relativist stance towards truth and the absolute notion of truth – can be found. Foucault suggests such an alternative in the orientation towards truthfulness in his techniques of the self. This orientation is exemplified in the practice of *parrēsia*, which in turn, according to Foucault, forms the basis for the "critical tradition of philosophy in our society" (Foucault 2019: 224). Indeed, this relationship is reflected in Cole's novel, where Moji's accusation against the narrator qualifies as an act of *parrēsia* both on a personal and on a 'political' level. It constitutes an act of personal *parrēsia* because Moji tells Julius the truth about himself and thus might contribute to his formation of self by means of the techniques of the self – if only Julius were interested in any such practice. This personal *parrēsia*, "[t]he *parrēsia* of a friend, [...] prevents the care of the self from succumbing to the flightiness and expediency of egotism" (Gros 2019: xvii). It is therefore usually employed in order to keep the subject from taking him- or herself as "the calibration point for normalcy" and does not allow for an entirely subjective construction of identity.

Yet, Moji's narrative qualifies just as well as an act of political *parrēsia*, since she is well aware of the political position that she puts herself in by accusing Julius of rape. Political *parrēsia* often entails an imminent threat of death to the subject speaking the truth, whether the truth-speaker's actual death or their death as a speaking subject due to being silenced by the discourse of power (Foucault 2019: 43). Thus, Moji is fully aware of Julius's discursive power to remain silent and is also aware that her own victimized position is one that "will not be believed" (Cole 2011: 245). This means that she knows that by speaking her truth she deprives herself of her own subject position: she is aware of the fact that she risks her death as a speaking subject. Moreover, the scene creates an analogy with the relationship between hegemonic discourses and counter-discourses that Julius created throughout his narrative and now thrusts him into the position of being faced with a counter-discourse to the (narrative) discourse of power that he produces as autodiegetic narrator. While Julius quite openly announces that his discourse constitutes an act of performance that among other things serves his own construction of identity – "we play, and only play, the hero" – Moji's narration then forms a counter-discourse, created by her own parrēsiastic act, to Julius's narrative of the heroic subject. This act forms an example of truth-speaking in which the subject puts herself into a relation with the truth and where the presence of her subjectivity thus unmasks the impossibility of the objectivity of the discourse of power.

Whether Moji's *parrēsia* actually becomes such a counter-discourse or whether it is cancelled out and not believed then depends on the reader and their evaluation of her narration. Readers who set themselves in a relationship towards the truth and therefore take into account the possibility that Julius might be an unreliable narrator would – in a retrospective reassessment of the narrative (see Clark 2018: 183) – start tracing back the story for factual evidence and might be faced with Julius's particular art of 'framing' his story and using his discursive power for his own means. Moji's act of *parrēsia* therefore can start an analysis of the workings of power within the discourse of the narrative text itself on behalf of the reader. In other words, what the novel projects and the reader ultimately engages in is the work of critique as suggested by Foucault:

> The critical ontology of ourselves must be considered not, certainly, as a theory, a doctrine, nor even as a permanent body of knowledge that is accumulating; it must be conceived as an attitude, an ethos, a philosophical life in which the critique of what we are is at one and the same time the historical analysis of the limits imposed on us and an experiment with the possibility of going beyond them *[de leur franchissement possible]*. (Foucault 2000c: 319)

Here, Foucault demands that the kind of philosophy he envisions focus on uncovering the discourses and workings of power that structure our systems of knowledge, allowing us to reflect on the ways we can escape the limits that those systems impose on us. Similarly, in *Open City*, the reader's investigation of Julius as a possibly unreliable narrator unmasks the workings of power in the novel and at the same time makes visible the limits of knowledge and truth within this particular narrative – as well as within narrative in general.

7.2.5 Parrēsiastic Aesthetics of Existence: Truthfulness and Critique in *Open City*

The specific parrēsiastic critique of the novel thus seems to rely on two stages in Julius's aesthetics of existence. The first is a conscious attempt at self-transformation that manifests itself in Julius's flânerie, which forms a counterpoint to the order and regulation at his workplace and creates a disorienting experience for him. By means of this practice, Julius is confronted with perspectives other than his own and forms himself according to the ideal of objectivity which in this case involves a constant changing of perspective and a polyphony of voices and opinions. Hence, flânerie challenges Julius's 'blind spots' by confronting him with ever new perspectives onto the city and ever new narratives about its history whenever he starts talking to other people; in this sense, his account could be said to become at least 'more' objective. This is, for example, the case when Julius visits a night club in Brussels and assumes that all the other people in the club are Congolese until the bartender informs him that most of them are from Rwanda:

> I had arrived in Brussels with the idea that all the Africans in the city were from the Congo. I knew the colonial relationship, I had a basic understanding of the history of the slave state there, and that had dislodged any other idea from my head. But then I went out one night to a restaurant and club on rue du Trône, a place called Le Panais. I spent the evening alone at my table, drinking and watching the young Congolese, all dressed up, fashionable, flirting with each other. The women wore afros or hair weaves, and many men wore long-sleeved shirts tucked into their jeans and looked particularly African, like recent arrivals. The music was hip-hop and the average age was twenty-five or thirty. It was a scene such as one would see in any city in Africa, or in the West: a Friday night, young people, music, liquor. After almost three hours, I paid for my drinks and was about to leave, and that was when the bartender came to talk to me. He asked where I was from, and we had a brief conversation; he was himself half-Malian and half-Rwandan. But what about the crowd, I wanted to know, were they all Congolese? He shook his head. Everyone was Rwandan. (Cole 2011: 138–139)

As the quote implies, the city always contains a potential for disruption that resides in its relationality, predominantly represented by the auditory paradigm in *Open City*. The notion of disruption then recurs in Julius's narration, which bears the imprint of his walks. As mentioned above, *Open City* is a typical flânerie text in that it prefers the particular to the general, and as such produces a polyphonic image of the cities it depicts. Flânerie, then, can certainly be understood as a technique of the self that transforms Julius, as can be seen in the thematic lack of order of his narrative, which reflects the disruptive quality of his walks.

However, even though Julius's account seems to be often jumbled on the level of content, it is at the same time rather well-structured and coherent on the level of form. The story is subdivided into two parts, each of which features an epigraph alluding to the overall theme of the part. Moreover, although the novel does start *in medias res*, the time frame is clearly indicated and remains – except for the inclusion of Pierre – coherent throughout the narration.[186] In this, Julius's narrative is decidedly different from Iris Vegan's techniques of writ-

---

[186] The paradoxical quality of Julius's narration as simultaneously disparate and well-arranged is reflected in Julius's practice of imposing order onto his experience of strolling: as soon as he arrives home, he starts sorting what he has seen during his walks and in this way merges the regulation that he tried to escape with his practice of strolling (Cole 2011: 7).

ing the self in *The Blindfold*. While the form of Hustvedt's novel suggests that the actual practice of writing transforms and stabilizes the autodiegetic narrator by means of its increase in temporal coherence, Julius's narration does not change in form at any point. Instead, his possible transformation by means of the text is only located within the moment of reception. Like his flânerie, writing might have a deconstructive and disruptive quality, yet this does not seem to register in Julius's concept of self during the process of writing.

Quite the contrary, this self is in fact *constantly* fleeting and therefore showcases a subject that takes continuous transformation as its only norm. Thus, the text creates a multifaceted image of Julius in which he stars twice as a heroic lifesaver (see Cole 2011: 145 and 195–196), multiple times as the voice of the oppressed, once as an "outraged American" (Cole 2011: 120), once as the only person of color at a concert in Carnegie Hall (see Cole 2011: 252) and once as a rapist. The narration thus constantly re-creates Julius's identity and the reader's perspective onto him. Yet, as has been mentioned above, since Julius assumes that neither he nor his "imagined audience" will be "troubled" whenever he deviates from "choosing the good", he himself does not seem to regard the state of his own identity as precarious. Therefore, Julius's concept of self is safe precisely because of scripture's deconstructive function since Julius's taking himself as "the calibration point for normalcy" is rooted in a constructivist belief in ethical relativism. While for Iris her practice of self-writing becomes another means of transformation and communicates a new sense of self that is both non-sovereign and increasingly stable, Julius's narration at best postpones this transformation to the moment of reception.

Yet, there remains the question of why Julius includes Moji's account into his narrative in the first place and why he apparently deems it necessary to frame it and increase the level of mediation by recounting her accusations in indirect speech, thus implying that he does not really assume that his moral integrity depends solely on his own evaluation. Moji's story is put at the end of Julius's narration, after he has already established himself as a positive character on various occasions, and this in particular suggests that his narration is indeed based on some kind of recognition of the precariousness of his own identity. Moreover, as criticism has aptly shown,[187] the real audience's judgement usually clashes with the judgement of Julius's "imagined audience". Although Julius denies it, it is precisely the fact that the audience is troubled by Moji's account and that she points towards the violence of his silence on the matter which establishes the subjectivization of discourse as a value and which potentially does transform Ju-

---

187 See e.g., Gamso (2019: 74).

lius's identity.[188] While Julius's flânerie then seems to emphasize the value of an objectivization of discourse, the narration itself by means of this objectivization returns to the simultaneous necessity of a subjectivization of discourse.

Hence, the flânerie text links the personal to the political by establishing a connection between Moji's personal counter-discourse and the numerous postcolonial counter-discourses voiced throughout the novel. Indeed, the inclusion of her account seems to derive from the value of an objectivization of discourse that Julius has acquired during his aimless wandering. That the objectivization of discourse is actually established as a value becomes clear through the numerous counter-discourses that Julius lends his voice to in his narration, which would otherwise have remained oppressed by hegemonic white discourses of power. Simultaneously, the subjectivization of discourse is described as equally valuable since Julius uses the detached attitude associated with the objectivization of discourse as a means of violence against Moji.

The whole conundrum regarding the violent potential of a subjectivization of discourse and the equally problematic aspects of the passivity implied in an absolute objectivization of discourse is aptly summarized by Julius himself much earlier in the novel:

> A cancerous violence had eaten into every political idea, had taken over the ideas themselves, and for so many, all that mattered was the willingness to do something. Action led to action, free of any moorings, and the way to be someone, the way to catch the attention of the young and recruit them to one's cause, was to be enraged. It seemed as if the only way this lure of violence could be avoided was by having no causes, by being magnificently isolated from all loyalties. But was that not an ethical lapse graver than rage itself? (Cole 2011: 107)

Here, Julius reflects on the political dilemma of the twenty-first century by depicting a political landscape that has been ravaged by a "cancerous violence" and by alluding to the rise in affect that led to an increase in polarization in various countries of the western world.[189] Yet, the antidote to this sort of politics

---

[188] One might argue that Julius's account of Pierre's surreal narrative about slavery and the Haitian revolution might have already sparked readers' doubt, yet this problematic scene has not gained much attention in secondary literature so far and could be interpreted as an indicator of a western blind spot with regard to African American history.

[189] Julius brings up this idea repeatedly: "This was part of my suspicion that there was a mood in the society that pushed people more toward snap judgements and unexamined opinions, an antiscientific mood; to the old problem of mass innumeracy, it seemed to me, was being added a more general inability to assess evidence. This made brisk business for those whose speciality was in the promising of immediate solutions: politicians, or priests of the various religions. It

charged with affect, an increase in reflection and detachment from any kind of political leanings, might be just as problematic or even more so, and thus "an ethical lapse graver than rage itself". Which of those two values, a distanced approach towards political topics or the subjectivization of discourse, is to be rated the more important remains a question that remains unanswered throughout the novel.

This is all the more vexing since Julius seems to succumb to exactly this "ethical lapse" in the penultimate chapter: it is unclear if he changed his opinion on the matter, or if his unreliable and, therefore, untruthful performance serves the purpose of asking implicitly the question that Julius asks explicitly in the above quotation. In the latter case, he would thus move from political to philosophical *parrēsia* by staging his own unreliability in order to criticize existing norms and ideals in the production of knowledge. In the same way that Diogenes crowns a horse with a laurel wreath in order to question social values (see chapter 3.2.2), Julius employs his own 'style of existence' for the sake of critique. His underreporting thus becomes a means for questioning his own ideal of an objectivization of discourse. In this, Julius's account of himself is not 'truthful' in the sense of 'entirely honest', yet neither would this be the case with Diogenes's performance. The philosophical *parrēsia* of the Cynics aligns the words and life of the philosophical subject – hence Diogenes's living in a barrel – in a performance that asks a question. Similarly, Julius turns his life into a work of art – a novel – in order to ask a question concerning which value should be preferred in the production of truth: the ideal of objectivization of discourse or the equally necessary act of a subjectivization of discourse.

In this, the form and structure of the novel which makes its readers stroll through New York and Brussels as well as through Julius's self support the validation of both approaches towards the truth. In the same way that Iris transforms herself by means of the eyes of others when she walks through the streets of New York dressed as a man, Julius asks for an ethical judgement on his actions when including Moji's account in the written account of himself, and by explicitly not commenting on her accusations problematizes the different values regarding the construction of truth.

The narration itself then becomes parrēsiastic in the sense of the Cynics because it questions existing norms of knowledge production by establishing the two contradictory values of a subjectivization and an objectivization of discourse. For this to happen, the 'death of the subject' has to take place on two

---

worked particularly well for those who wished to rally people around a cause. The cause itself, whatever it was, hardly mattered. Partisanship was all" (Cole 2011: 28).

levels: on the one hand, the relativization of individual perspectives by means of the objectivization of discourse implies the death of the sovereign, omniscient subject and emphasizes the precariousness of the individual subject of knowledge; on the other hand, the inclusion of Moji's account necessitates the death of Julius as a reliable narrating subject whose moral evaluation can be trusted. On the surface, Julius is similar to Paris in Hustvedt's *The Blindfold*, yet while Paris simply decides to exist outside of any norm, Julius's parrēsiastic performance highlights the rupture in the normative system itself. Moreover, the active inclusion of Moji's account in fact is an instance of truthfulness and at least surrenders to the possibility of his death as a reliable narrating subject.

Julius's parrēsiastic narration thus constitutes a technique of the self that not only directly affects himself, but, like Iris's deconstruction of a human determination to violence, also challenges norms that might apply in constructions of subjectivity while at the same time emphasizing the precarious as a shared human condition. The flânerie text here becomes a medium which links not only the materiality of the city to the city as a signifier, but also truth with fiction since Julius's fictional performance seems to communicate a higher truth without being factual. Moreover, the fact that Julius shares some characteristics with his author Teju Cole seems to emphasize this link[190] while the novel's rootedness in historical fact as well as the political situation of the twenty-first century implies a connection between truth, fiction, performance, politics and history.

Additionally, *Open City*'s juxtaposition of the visual and the auditive paradigm to which different functions are assigned during Julius's flânerie ties the novel's paradoxical question to the material reality of sensory perception. Just as visual and auditive perception intersect in Julius's account of the city, the objectivization and subjectivization of discourse are checked by each other. In this analogy, visuality comes to stand for subjective discourse whereas an objectivization of discourse is represented by the auditive paradigm which recurs in the polyphony of voices in the novel. The juxtaposition of those paradigms and their connection to discourse formation is further reflected in the novel's use of direct and indirect speech and emphasizes the potentially problematic results of both

---

190 Cole even explicitly states in an interview that he wanted to invite reflections on fiction and fictionality: "'It's not offensive to me when people make the mistake that I am Julius [...]. I think it's an interesting tension. The fact that the confusion arises says something about the expectations we have about what a book is supposed to do. Maybe to a certain extent, this particular book is stymieing those expectations a little bit. In that I wanted to provoke readers into thinking about fiction a little bit differently, I think I succeeded. I'm quite happy with that aspect of it'" (DeRitter 2011: n. pag.).

approaches. Hence, the mostly indirect speech which Julius uses when summarizing Moji's account betrays his subtle framing and the way in which he subjectively influences the way she is portrayed in the novel. Although Julius seems to suggest otherwise, readers are confronted with his subjective perspective onto Moji. By contrast, the direct speech employed when Julius surrenders his narrative voice to Pierre, the Haitian shoeshiner, alludes to the auditive paradigm. Here, Julius turns into a recording device which uncritically copies what it perceives. What is missing in an objectivization of discourse is precisely the taking of a subjective critical stance and an evaluation of what is recorded. In both cases, however, the simultaneous application of the contrasting value ensures the problematization of the approaches mentioned above; that is, Moji's account can only be incorporated into Julius's narration if he at least to a minimal extent subscribes to the value of an objectivization of discourse, and Pierre's story is only problematic because his euphemistic[191] account of the history of slavery in the US is itself an example of an extreme subjectivization of discourse.[192] Thus, critique is tied to the material reality of the city and the limitations of the human senses. Reflection of the material form takes place by means of its representation in text.

Ultimately, *Open City*'s take on the Foucauldian ethical subject then ties in with the dilemma of the postcolonial flâneur; that is, Julius's flânerie can be located in-between the concepts of the traveler and the migrant, thus projecting a constant tension between sovereignty and subjection. First and foremost, he copies a practice prefigured in French literature of the nineteenth century and therefore aligned with colonial heritage and sovereignty. Second, Julius's flânerie relies heavily on his financial independence which allows him not only to fly to Brussels for four weeks, but also to not have to work more than one job, and so have free time to set out on his strolls. Third, part of his particular brand of flânerie derives from his profession as clinical psychiatrist, an area in which he is assigned a position as a subject competent to speak the truth, and therefore lends him the opportunity to create an authoritative discourse. The discursive power he wields in the narrative thus reflects the way he occupies a position of power in various areas in his life. Lastly, Julius manages to turn the flâneur's quick changes in perspective into a means of establishing a (seemingly) sover-

---

[191] Pierre never directly refers to himself having been enslaved, but only mentions at one point in his narrative that "[a]fter a while, [he] had enough money for [his] own freedom", yet remained in the household since "[s]ervice to Mrs. Bérard was service to God" (Cole 2011: 73).
[192] Interestingly, not only is Pierre's story problematically subjective, but its positioning after the Liberian refugee Saidu's story creates a political message that implies another subjectivization of discourse veiled by a seeming objectivization.

eign subjectivity based on the fluidity of his identity and his proclaimed ethical relativism which is in turn founded on a constructivist approach towards truth. By contrast, his flânerie also seems to be driven by the social isolation of the diasporic subject (see Fongang 2017: 138) and therefore carries the imprint of an unequal distribution of power that his walks back "into a vanished time" reflect as well. His sensitivity towards issues of power and marginalization and his unearthing of colonial trauma then suggest the perspective of the migrant who is aware of global structures of power precisely because he experienced them first-hand. Hence, Julius oscillates between a sovereignty partly based on his hybrid identity and the reflection of discourses of power and therefore represents the tension in which postcolonial flânerie is located.

By productively drawing on this ambivalence, *Open City* showcases flânerie as a technique of the self within Julius's parrēsiastic 'aesthetics of existence' that problematizes existing norms of truth-production. Moreover, the novel brings a central problem of the Foucauldian ethical subject to the surface: if transformation is the norm, the subject might run the risk of becoming altogether unreliable and irresponsible. And not only: if the subject is to undergo an ever-transforming form, it always runs the risk of dissolution. A Foucauldian ethical subject is thus constantly torn between the necessity of transformation and reflexivity and the truthfulness of formation itself. *Open City* then points out that a subject transforming too quickly or being dissolved in reflexivity and representation becomes a subject without responsibility. Nevertheless, the aspect of privilege and power is in turn dismantled through the textualization of Julius's flânerie, which carries the imprint of the reflexivity ingrained into him by means of strolling. The formal feature of 'underreporting' as a special case of unreliable narration highlights Julius's discursive power and functions as a self-critical comment.

Hustvedt's and Cole's novels therefore negotiate the ethical subject's boundary between constant transformation and the truthfulness of conversion and formation: the variations in form in *The Blindfold* seem to suggest that Iris actually transforms herself during the act of writing since she quite literally puts herself into a new form. In Julius's discourse, by contrast, transformation seems to become so much the norm that it no longer appears to register, but instead congeals into relativism. By turning himself into a work of art and staging his own unreliability and lack of moral responsibility, however, Julius self-reflexively problematizes his perspective and thus affirms the precarious as a shared human condition.

8 City Matters: Affect and Media in Precarious Performances of Subjectivity

Whereas the previous chapters examined the borders and frameworks within which a post-sovereign ethical subject could be located in contemporary flânerie texts, the following two chapters explore the material formation of subjects as foregrounded in two works. Trinidad-born Canadian writer Dionne Brand's novel *What We All Long For* (2005), which highlights the work of affects and emotions[193] in performances of post-sovereign subjectivity, and the Scottish author Robin Robertson's prose poem *The Long Take, Or a Way to Lose More Slowly* (2018), which reflects on mediality and perception in processes of subject formation.

8.1 Performing the City: Precarious Ethical Subjects in Dionne Brand's *What We All Long For*

Like *Open City*, *What We All Long For* engages with topics of postcolonialism, diaspora, migration, and cultural identity, but Brand adds a particular focus on the material and affective side of resistance. Those aspects are discernible throughout most of her work, which she has referred to as a practice that is based in "wanting to be wanted, to be understood, to be seen, to be loved" and that involves acts "of translation, of succumbing or leaning into another's body idiom" (Brand 2001: 193). This dialogic structure has variously been described as a "grammar of dissent" (Morrell 1994), "dialogic of difference" (Zackodnik 1995: 206) or "transwriting" (Walter 2003: 38) and surfaces in what could be called a "politics/poetics of 'drifting'" (Bernabei 2008: 111; Goldmann 2004: 13).

In *What We All Long For*, the polyphonic quality of Brand's writing is discernible on the level of form as well as content. In contrast to the two novels analyzed in the previous chapters, Brand's novel juxtaposes a heterodiegetic narrator, whose perspective oscillates between zero focalization and variable as

---

[193] Following Sara Ahmed's contention that the distinction between emotion and affect can only ever serve an analytical purpose (2004: 6), I understand 'affect' and 'emotion' as intricately entangled notions constantly merging into each other. For an excellent overview of the field of affect studies see Aragay, Delgado-García and Middeke (2021: 1–18).

well as multiple internal focalization,[194] with an autodiegetic narrator who participates in the action that is told through the heterodiegetic voice.[195] The story centers on five protagonists, four of which function as focalizers for the heterodiegetic narrator, whereas the fifth produces the autodiegetic narration with which the story of the other four is interspersed. All five protagonists are born of parents who have either immigrated to Canada or have moved to Toronto from other parts of Canada and represent the perspectives of various minorities living in the Canadian metropolis. The story of Quy, the narrator of the autodiegetic discourse, however, is decidedly different from the others' since he retrospectively narrates how he grew up after being separated from his parents as they escaped Vietnam after the outbreak of the Vietnam War.[196] The other protagonists, by contrast, were all born and raised in Toronto and mostly struggle with their status as second-generation immigrants, which leaves them torn between the cultural heritage represented by their parents and a more westernized identity.[197] As the narrator points out, "[b]reaking their doorways, they left the sleepwalk of their mothers and fathers and ran across the unobserved borders of the city, sliding across ice to arrive at their own birthplace – the city. They were born in the city from people born elsewhere" (Brand 2005: 20).

The individual background of the four characters is, however, very different and determined by different markers of race, class, gender, and sexuality. The cast of the heterodiegetic narrative includes Tuyen, Quy's younger sister, who was born in Toronto after her parents had already lived in Canada for several

---

194 This formal particularity has not been picked up by secondary literature on Brand's novel which usually describes the narrator of the Toronto-based chapters as "omniscient" (Birkle 2019: 70; Rosenthal 2011: 241; Ben Gouider Trabelsi 2010: 56; Langwald 2015: 360) or, rather irritatingly, as a first-person narrator due to a few segments in which the narrator could be characterized as overt (Garvey 2011: 766). By contrast, I would argue that the novel productively engages with the precarious boundary between zero and variable internal focalization and thus emphasizes the individual restriction of perspective in the city while only seldom switching to an actual zero focalization.
195 Interestingly, this is somewhat reminiscent of Charles Dickens's *Bleak House* (1852/1853) where the discourse of a heterodiegetic narrator with zero focalization is juxtaposed with the autodiegetic discourse of Esther Summerson, one of the main characters in the novel.
196 The discrepancy between Quy's story and the lives of the other four characters is even emphasized on the very material level of the text itself, where the heterodiegetic narrative is justified and the homodiegetic narrative is left-aligned so that it looks slightly battered and disarrayed at the edges (see Langwald 2015: 361).
197 The only character to be partly excluded from these dynamics is Jackie, whose Africadian parents moved from Nova Scotia to Toronto, so she does not actually count as a second-generation immigrant. Nevertheless, she still has to face struggles similar to those of other Black characters in the novel.

years; Carla, the daughter of an Italian mother and a Jamaican-Canadian father, whose mother committed suicide when Carla was only five years old; Oku, whose parents emigrated to Toronto from Jamaica; and Jackie, whose Africadian parents moved to Toronto from Nova Scotia. The four characters have known each other since high school where they bonded due to their shared situation of hybridity:

> They couldn't wait to get out of school, where they had very early realized, as early as grade three, that nothing there was about them. Their parents didn't understand anything. They abandoned them to the rough public terrain that they themselves couldn't handle but out of which they expected their children to emerge with good grades and well adjusted. So they settled in as mainly spectators to the white kids in class. (Brand 2005: 19–20)

Their relationships to each other are further complicated by romantic entanglements in which they suffer non- or only partly reciprocated love. Tuyen is madly in love with Carla and with varying degrees of explicitness tries to seduce her into reciprocating Tuyen's affections, although Carla repeatedly emphasizes that she is heterosexual. Oku, by contrast, is interested in Jackie, who does show sexual interest in him although she is in a relationship with a German-Canadian musician called Reiner, who, for Jackie, symbolizes the kind of security and upward mobility that Oku could not offer. The example of Jackie and Oku, in particular, shows how the construction of identity in *What We All Long For* is deeply entangled with affective relations and involves the circulation of affects and emotions between the characters.

In the following, I will show how Brand's novel condenses what has so far been discussed as individual techniques of the self into a panorama of a variety of different techniques performed by its protagonists. The novel foregrounds the work of emotions in processes of subject formation and showcases how flânerie, affects, and reflexivity interlock in different techniques of the self which the story juxtaposes with each other. Moreover, especially the discrepancy between Quy and the four other characters suggests that techniques of the self involve at least some kind of privilege that can only be found among those who do not have to fight for their immediate survival. His narrative also highlights Butler's concept of 'ungrievable lives' and contributes to the novel's overall meditation on the vulnerability and precariousness of human life and different manifestations of precariousness in the characters. This precariousness, the novel implies, can be approached through affective relations among individuals, while the power structures causing a heightened precariousness might at the same time be upheld through the constant circulation of affective value. Ultimately, the ambivalent trope of flânerie serves to negotiate a critique of ethical violence in Brand's novel that affirms precariousness as a shared human condition, yet at the same time problematizes the sovereignty implied in individual performances of responsibility.

8.1.1 The City as Fluid Materiality: Affects, Matter and Textuality in *What We All Long For*

The story of the five protagonists is told against the backdrop of the city of Toronto which could best be described in terms of what Nan Ellin calls the "walking city" (1996: 241; see also Rosenthal 2011: 228); that is, a city that is in a state of constant transformation and thus becomes increasingly unreadable due to "global flows of people, ideas, capital, and mass media" (Rosenthal 2011: 228).[198] However, Brand's take on the "walking city" emphasizes the transformative potential of cities as "intense" spaces, given her focus on the central nexus of the fluidity of signification and representation, the impenetrability of matter, and affect as a combining element between the two other characteristics that either increases the effects of materiality and subjection or actively contributes to processes of transformation. It is precisely this fluid materiality of the city that enables the production of subjects who acknowledge their own relationality and condition of interdependence with others.

Fluidity, in general, recurs in a variety of ways in the description of Toronto:

> It's like this with this city – you can stand on a simple corner and get taken away in all directions. Depending on the weather, it can be easy or hard. If it's pleasant, and pleasant is so relative, then the other languages making their way to your ears, plus the language of the air itself, which can be cold and humid or wet and hot, this all sums up into a kind of new vocabulary. No matter who you are, no matter how certain you are of it, you can't help but feel the thrill of being someone else. (Brand 2005: 154)

The passage contains several concepts that the novel frequently relates to the city of Toronto. First of all, there is a sense of disruption and chance in the idea that one can "get taken away in all directions" in this city. Second, identity is fluid since "you can't help but feel the thrill of being someone else", which is further linked to the notion of multiculturalism, alluded to by "the other languages making their way to your ears".[199] This fluidity is, however, dependent

---

198 See also Langwald (2011: 125), McKibbin (2008: 504) and Carrera Suárez (2008: 191).
199 This is of course already implied through the diverse cast of characters, yet is also openly announced at the beginning of the novel: "In this city there are Bulgarian mechanics, there are Eritrean accountants, Colombian café owners, Latvian book publishers, Welsh roofers, Afghani dancers, Iranian mathematicians, Tamil cooks in Thai restaurants, Calabrese boys with Jamaican

on the material forces of the weather which can make it "easy or hard" to be "taken away". At the same time, the passage once again subjects this dependency to the evaluation, that is, the interpretation, of the citizen, who might find the weather "pleasant", which "is so relative", so that interpretation and the fluidity of signs again seem to be the deciding factor. Yet, this thesis is countered by the beginning of the novel, which foregrounds the determining nature of the weather:

> This city hovers above the forty-third parallel; that's illusory of course. Winters on the other hand, there's nothing vague about them. Winters here are inevitable, sometimes unforgiving. Two years ago, they had to bring the army in to dig the city out from under the snow. The streets were glacial, the electrical wires were brittle, the telephones were useless. The whole city stood still; the trees more than usual. The cars and driveways were obliterated. Politicians were falling over each other to explain what had happened and who was to blame – who had privatized the snow plows and why the city wasn't prepared. The truth is you can't prepare for something like that. It's fate. Nature will do that sort of thing – dump thousands of tons of snow on the city just to say, Don't make too many plans or assumptions, don't get ahead of yourself. Spring this year couldn't come too soon – and it didn't. It took its time – melting at its own pace, over running ice-blocked sewer drains, swelling the Humber River and the Don River stretching to the lake. The sound of the city was of trickling water. (Brand 2005: 1)

Here, nature and, in particular, the weather, hold the city firmly in their grip. In the very first sentence of the novel, representation and signification are doubly devalued: the representation of Toronto's location is faithful to geographical standards, yet is deprived of any authority by the narrative voice who points out that "that's illusory of course" whereas "there's nothing vague about" winters in this city. Likewise, interpretation and evaluation are of no importance to the immediacy of the city's subjection to the workings of the weather since despite the politicians' attempts at explaining who caused the current situation, the narrator states that "[t]he truth is you can't prepare for something like that". Therefore, the citizens of Toronto are explicitly deprived of any state of sovereignty and reminded to not "make too many plans or assumptions".

The third aspect, the intermediary position of affect and its link to sensory impression, is emphasized with the arrival of spring and the concomitant return of the citizens to the public sphere:

---

accents, Fushen deejays, Filipina-Saudi beauticians; Russian doctors changing tires, there are Romanian bill collectors, Cape Croker fishmongers, Japanese grocery clerks, French gas meter readers, German bakers, Haitian and Bengali taxi drivers with Irish dispatchers" (Brand 2005: 5).

> Have you ever smelled this city at the beginning of spring? Dead winter circling still, it smells of eagerness and embarrassment and, most of all, longing. Garbage, buried under snowbanks for months, gradually reappears like old habits – plastic bags, pop cans – the alleyways are cluttered in a mess of bottles and old shoes and thrown-away beds. People look as if they're unravelling. They're on their last nerves. They're suddenly eager for human touch. People will walk up to perfect strangers and tell them anything. After the grey days and the heavy skies of what's passed, an unfamiliar face will smile and make a remark as if there had been a conversation going on all along. The fate of everyone is open again. New lives can be started, or at least spring is the occasion to make it seem possible. No matter how dreary yesterday was, all the complications and problems that bore them down, now seem carried away by the melting streets. At least the clearing skies and the new breath of air from the lake, both, seduce people into thinking that. (Brand 2005: 1–2)

Like the excerpt quoted at the beginning of this chapter, this quotation suggests that pleasant weather enables contact between the inhabitants of the city. This process is induced by sensory perception – the smell of the city at the beginning of spring or the auditory impression of the "trickling of water" mentioned in the previous quotation – as well as the affective circulation of "eagerness", "embarrassment" and, most of all, "longing". While the "fate" of nature had inhibited contact in winter, now "[t]he fate of everyone is open again" and the nice weather "seduce[s] people into thinking that" they can start "new lives" in the same way that "you can't help but feel the thrill of being someone else". In both cases, affects and emotions loom large and echo the decisive focus on the experience of longing that is already indicated in the novel's title.

Hence, in the city two different kinds of fluidity and chance collide: on the one hand, there is the fluidity of signs as markers of identity; on the other hand, matter, which potentially might offer more security than the arbitrariness of signification, is just as subject to chance and might change at any time as well. In this, the border between representation and matter is constantly crossed by emotions and affects which potentially connect people with each other, but which are similarly subject to a fluid materiality. This is also emphasized by the narrative voice at the beginning of the novel:

> Mornings are like that on the subway trains – everyone having left their sovereign houses and apartments and rooms to enter the crossroads of the city, they first try at not letting the city touch them, holding on to the meagre privacy of a city with three million people. But eventually they're disrupted like this. Anonymity is the big lie of a city. You aren't anonymous at all. You're common, really, common like so many pebbles, so many specks of dirt, so many atoms of materiality. [...] What floats in the air on a subway train like this is chance. People stand or sit with the magnetic film of their life wrapped around them. They think they're safe, but they know they're not. Any minute you can crash into someone else's life, and if you're lucky, it's good, it's like walking on light. (Brand 2005: 3–4)

The passage is strongly reminiscent of Butler's concept of the precarious subject which can be 'undone' by other subjects at any time due to its primary state of dependency. Thus, the "sovereign houses" where subjects might be able to maintain a more fixed and secure identity are juxtaposed with the "crossroads of the city" where "they're disrupted like this" since no one is truly anonymous in the city, and everyone could "crash into someone else's life" at any time. Disruption is then clearly linked to contact with other people, which is further emphasized by repeated references to human emotions and contact since contact with the city is described in terms of a "touch" and the very last sentence seems to hint at the experience of falling in love.[200] The city with its "meagre privacy" thus becomes a reminder of the precariousness of subjects since people are constantly affected by others with whom they might even form strong emotional relationships. Fittingly, Butler names love and mourning especially as gateways to the recognition of this primary state of dependence.

Crucially, anyone engaging in the practice of flânerie therefore cannot remain sheltered within their own anonymity here since, according to the narrator, "[a]nonymity is the big lie of a city". The characteristic invisibility of the flâneur that protects him from becoming actively engaged and that usually supports his practice of observation is a lot harder to achieve in the city depicted in Brand's novel. The material presence of the flâneur in the crowd might, instead, cause him to collide with other material presences at any time, establishing an affectively charged relation between individuals in the public sphere. By emphasizing the supremacy of the public aspect of cities over a privacy that can only be contained in houses and apartments the novel also engages with discursive formations of the public/private divide commonly negotiated in city texts since the nineteenth century. Like *Saturday*, *The Blindfold* and *Open City*, *What We All Long For* forms part of a new tradition of city literature that combines a postmodern excess of signification with the ethical turn's emphasis on relationality.

Butler's concept of subject formation can, however, be further applied to Brand's novel which emphasizes not only the fluidity of matter, but also the fixity of discourses of power linked to material markers of identity such as race or gender. The following section, therefore, will delineate how *What We All Long For* juxtaposes the supposedly open borders of the multicultural city with the rigid dynamics of power in Toronto.

---

200 The notion of the "magnetic film" ties in with the novel's overall theme of longing, thus highlighting the potential attraction individual subjects might exert on each other.

8.1.2 (Un-)Grievable Lives: Global and Local Structures of Power in *What We All Long For*

As each of the characters' individual stories shows, racial identity is deeply embedded in a force field of power in the novel. The postcolonial flâneurs in *What We All Long For* thus cannot be likened to the sovereign traveler briefly described in the previous chapter who freely decides on the fluidity of their own identity, but rather oscillate between feeling at home in a state of constant hybridity and being haunted by the diasporic entanglements of the migrant. In this, each of the five protagonists serves as an example of the heightened precariousness of minorities subjected to an inferior position due to sedimented histories of power.

Tuyen's struggle to escape the trauma and resulting responsibilities that her familial affiliations impose on her, for example, leads her to partly return to an affirmation of and subjection to hegemonic discourses of power. Although she and her brother Binh were born in Toronto after their parents had already emigrated from Vietnam, the whole family is caught in the continuous trauma of having lost the oldest son, Quy, during their flight. This trauma becomes intermingled with the other losses that her parents have experienced during the process of immigration: whereas Tuan, Tuyen's father, had been an engineer, and Cam, Tuyen's mother, a physician in Vietnam, they are forced into new professional identities by the city after their arrival in Toronto. Since after the initial hardships of immigration neither Tuan nor Cam find a job in their original profession, they give in to "the way the city saw them: Vietnamese food" (Brand 2005: 67), and open up a small Vietnamese restaurant although neither of them is able to cook particularly well. Their acceptance of giving up parts of their identity is explicitly linked to the experience of the loss of Quy when the narrative voice explains that "[a]fter the loss of Quy, it made a resigned sense to them that they would lose other parts of themselves" (Brand 2005: 66). As a consequence, Tuan and Cam seem to have developed a series of coping mechanisms that all center around the idea of possession as counteracting the continuous experience of loss. Thus, Cam, on the one hand, assures herself of being in possession of her own identity and being able to prove this identity by developing a rather extreme habit of wrapping things in plastic or, especially, laminating important documents because "she had a mad fear of being caught without proof, without papers of some kind attesting to identity or place" (Brand 2005: 63). Tuan, by contrast, seems to focus on keeping his own family close which leads him to constantly complain about Tuyen having moved out of the house. According to Tuan, family is defined by a shared identity, as he explains to Tuyen: "How you think a family works? Same house, same money, same life" (Brand 2005: 57). This is translated by her into the concept of possession when she reflects that "[s]he was his possession, like his whole family was" (Brand 2005: 56). Moreover, both parents collect more and more material possessions due to their "businesslike readiness to have all the world had to offer by way of things" (Brand 2005: 62).

Tuyen's parents' fulfilment of capitalist ideals regarding the accumulation of goods and possessions is, as the narrative voice indicates, rooted in their longing to get away from their immigrant identity:

> Tuyen's family is rich, newly rich. They have a giant house in Richmond Hill, where rich immigrants live in giant houses. Richmond Hill is a sprawling suburb outside of the city. It is one of those suburbs where immigrants go to get away from other immigrants, but of course they end up living with all the other immigrants running away from themselves – or at least running away from the self they think is helpless, weak, unsuitable, and always in some kind of trouble. They hate that self that keeps drawing attention, the one that can't fit in because of colour or language, or both, and they think that moving to a suburb will somehow eradicate that person once and for all. And after all the humiliations of being that self – after they've worked hard enough at two or three jobs and saved enough by overcrowding their families in small dour rooms and cobbled together enough credit – immigrants flee to rangy lookalike desolate suburbs like Richmond Hill where the houses give them a sense of space and distance from that troubled image of themselves. (Brand 2005: 54–55)

Accumulating financial value and performing an identity that displays one's purchasing power are Tuan and Cam's means of escaping their old immigrant identity, which they identify with a "helpless, weak, unsuitable" self "that can't fit in because of colour or language". The quote clearly demonstrates how the evaluation of a person as 'helpless', 'weak' or somehow 'unsuitable' is linked to markers of race and nationality and thus to material features that either cannot be changed or can only be changed slowly. Nevertheless, the move to Richmond Hill seems to work only partially since Tuyen's family now still forms part of a community of immigrants who tried to cope with their identity as immigrants in a similar way.

This new identity of immigrants who have been successfully integrated into Canada's economic system by giving in to the stereotypes that the country had on offer is precisely the identity that Tuyen herself tries to run away from. In this, she often oscillates between resisting the hegemonic white discourse, on the one hand, and assimilating to western performances of identity, on the other hand. Her resistance manifests itself, for example, in her rant against "[w]hite folks' culture" where she artfully connects the general concept of "the repetition of some old hackneyed images" with the metaphor of bleaching and corrosion:

> "[...] Jesus, I'm sick of Madonna. I can't understand how she can stand walking around in that body. It's the dried-out pupa sack of Marilyn Monroe. Every generation of Americans gets to fuck over Marilyn Monroe all over again. They get to batter her, to jerk off over her, and kill her. The main scary thing about that image is it all depends on bleach, the hair is bleached, the skin is bleached, the body is bleached. They get to corrode her in public. The eyes do damage to her body. [...] And Eminem is only Elvis Presley, another repetition. Like I have to say more?" (Brand 2005: 211)

Especially the comparison between Eminem and Elvis Presley is telling in this context since it implicitly alludes to the fact that both white artists copied artistic styles from Black musical culture – Rap music in the case of Eminem and Blues in the case of Elvis Presley – and became huge commercial successes by doing so. The context here further solidifies the metaphorical link between repetition and bleaching since Black artistic styles seem to have been 'bleached' by being performed (and thus repeated) by white musicians.[201] The contextual link with Madonna and Marilyn Monroe, however, juxtaposes popular culture's overall concept of repetition and re-contextualization with the problematic dynamics of cultural appropriation.[202]

Whereas Tuyen thus criticizes white discourses of power, she also assimilates to North American culture and rejects the Vietnamese identity of her parents. In this, she at times seems to echo her parents' aversion to their immigrant selves:

> "Why can't we eat like normal people?" she used to ask when she was little; when she was sent to school with minty soups and bean curd. [...] She loved milk. Despite the fact that her stomach reacted violently to it. But she insisted on drinking it. Or now buying it at least. She thought of this violent response as something to be conquered, like learning a new and necessary language. If nothing else, her tiny fridge could be counted on for storing putrefied sour milk that she had not had the courage to consume. (Brand 2005: 129–130)

Her desire to 'not be Asian' is apparently so strong that she forces herself to digest the milk although she is – like many Asians – lactose intolerant. The quote powerfully describes how the pressure to assimilate is still palpable for second-generation immigrants, which is further underscored by the fact that the narrative voice paraphrases her thoughts on this behavior in indirect speech as being

---

[201] Interestingly, the topic of cultural appropriation is not brought up in the ensuing discussion between Tuyen and Oku about her negative evaluation of Eminem, which largely focuses on the rapper's misogynistic and homophobic texts. The comparison with Presley is, however, telling.
[202] Madonna forms a fitting link in this juxtaposition since she is famous for taking up a virtually infinite number of roles in her music videos and shows, but also includes racial stereotypes in those performances.

similar to "learning a new and necessary language", although this comparison is in fact not very fitting since her body will probably not learn to be lactose tolerant. The quote could, therefore, be interpreted as an example of the materialization of power structures.[203]

Moreover, since the parents' life seems to center around the trauma of the loss of Quy – whose name tellingly means 'precious' in Vietnamese – Tuyen feels herself relegated to a position of "second-ratedness" (Brand 2005: 125), which again clashes with what the narrative voice describes as the North American values that Binh and Tuyen adapted to when growing up in Toronto:

> Their culture was North American despite their parents' admittedly ambivalent efforts to enforce Vietnamese rules, and in North American culture they knew it was *de rigueur* to love children equally and for children to claim that kind of love as a right. Binh picked up on that lost right and made all efforts to collect it. Tuyen, on the other hand, was made merely curious by its absence. She preferred to explore other aspects of North American birthright, such as independence, free love, and artistic irrelevance. (Brand 2005: 125)

The remaining children are thus marked by the fact that Quy was implicitly 'sacrificed' for them to grow up in another country, which imposes on them a burden of debt and duty towards their parents and deprives them of being loved in their own right. This becomes especially discernible in Tuyen's reflections on the reasons for leaving her family:

> She had left the embrace of her family – truthfully, not embrace, her family did not embrace. They fed you, they clothed you, they fattened you, but they did not embrace. Yet they held you. With duty, with obligation, with honour, with an unspoken but viselike grip of emotional debt. Tuyen wanted no duty. And perhaps that is what she had arrived at. Yet she wanted an embrace so tight, and with such a gathering of scents and touches. She wanted sensuality, not duty. She wanted to be downtown in the heat of it. Everyone walking in the city was senseless. She loved that. Everyone escaping the un-touch of familiars and the scents of fatalism gathered in close houses. Familiarity was not what she wanted or what would make her feel as if she were in the world. It was the opposite. The alien touch of sidewalks, the hooded looks of crowds. She loved the unfriendliness, the coolness. It was warmer than the warmth of her family in Richmond Hill. (Brand 2005: 61–62)

By moving out of her parents' house, Tuyen rejects the "emotional debt" that she feels confronted with in her family and exchanges it for the "sensuality" and "heat" of the city. The quote juxtaposes Tuyen's fixed identity as a 'second-

---

203 Nevertheless, the quote suggests that more often than not Tuyen does not actually drink the milk, but rather lets it turn sour in her refrigerator. Yet, this is only due to the fact that she "had not had the courage to consume" it, which further emphasizes how painful drinking the milk must be for her.

rate' child in her family with the ambivalent negotiation of identity in the city. Although Toronto is described in terms of "coolness" and "unfriendliness" and although the "touch of the sidewalks" remains "alien" and "looks" only betray the maskedness of their bearers, this anonymity – quite paradoxically – instills in Tuyen a hope for "sensuality" and tight embraces. Though this hope might remain unfulfilled in the end – as the word play on 'senseless' and 'sensuality' implies – the paradoxical notion of the "coolness" of the city being warmer than the warmth of Tuyen's family emphasizes the deprivation of love that Tuyen experiences. Drawing on the previous section's observations regarding the affective contingency and chance that the city entails, one could argue that this is the reason why Tuyen is looking for sensuality and warmth in the city rather than in her own family.

At the same time, she cannot really get away from her family since she still depends on them financially. While most of her other friends like Carla and Jackie have a more or less regular income, this is not the case for Tuyen who is fully aware of the fact that belonging to the Vu family also means that "he [her father] would not abandon her" (Brand 2005: 56) and that she can still borrow money from her mother every time she visits. In this, Tuyen's situation resembles that of Benjamin's flâneur who aims at being resistant while simultaneously becoming incorporated into capitalism. It is thus also somewhat ironic that she complains about her family "returning again and again" in her art, whereas, according to her, it actually serves the purpose of "stav[ing] off her family". Tuyen's financial dependency is of course neither the only nor the main reason why she cannot quite seem to shake off her family; a deeper reason lies in the set of "uncontrollable feelings" (Brand 2005: 69) that tie her to her parents and her siblings which are complicated by the power structures encroaching onto the family due to its immigrant status.

Similarly, Carla, the daughter of an Italian mother and a Jamaican-Canadian father, suffers from the consequences of her parents crossing a cultural border. As biracial children, she and her brother Jamal experienced at first hand the devaluing of the relationship between their parents by their mother's family: after the suicide of their mother Angie "no one claimed them [...] no one except [their] father" Derek, who apparently did so only "reluctantly" (Brand 2005: 106). While Carla's Italian grandmother does attack Derek after the inquest regarding Angie's death and thus voices her grief, she expresses no interest in raising Angie's children. This confirms Carla's presumption that "Angie had been dead to her family since the day she started up with Carla's father" (Brand 2005: 106). As a consequence, Carla identifies as Black – although she could have passed as white due to her biracial heritage (Brand 2005: 106) – in order to honor her mother's choices and thus to resist the rejection of the white family who abandoned their daughter for choosing what they must have perceived as a social downfall when Angie got involved with a Black man. Like Tuyen, Carla thus does not seem to be directly affected by racism, but rather suffers the consequences of the racism impressed on her parents.

The ensuing trauma, however, does affect the children deeply. Carla feels constantly deprived of love throughout her childhood, which causes her to deaden any kind of emotion that she might feel. While her brother Jamal is too young to consciously experience the death of his mother, Carla is five years old when her mother commits suicide and is therefore grieving intensely after her death. Yet, from the time she and her brother are taken in by her father and his wife – whom Derek cheated on with Angie for several years – there is no one to comfort Carla in her mourning. When the narrative focalizes on Nadine, Derek's wife, the reader learns that neither she nor Derek were able to properly take care of the grieving child:

> But Carla was a brooding, watchful little girl who was grieving for her mother. She would sometimes ask Derek when Angie was coming for her and the baby. Derek would bark at her eventually, saying that Angie wasn't coming back and that she should be quiet. The child was unhappy, and in those early days Nadine could not bring herself to comfort her. Carla would sink into quietness and strangeness. All Nadine could summon up was a prissy reprimand of Derek: "That little girl has lost her mother, you're her father. You should explain it to her." Nadine really meant "You'll spend a lifetime explaining it to me." (Brand 2005: 276)

Carla therefore seems to internalize her grief and becomes a "quiet [...] and strange [...]" child. As several scenes focalized through her imply, she has never stopped mourning: Derek and Nadine's house turns into a place of mourning for Carla that is marked by the absence of her mother and that causes her to envision the place as being constantly drenched in rain when her father is present (Brand 2005: 250).[204] Her behavior as an adult could be described in terms of what Freud (1969: 427–446) calls 'melancholic identification'; that is, she internalizes the lost – and forbidden – object of love, her mother, and identifies with it by taking care of her younger brother, and towards the end of the novel physically attacking her father as she had once observed her mother doing (see Brand 2005: 108 and Brand 2005: 253–255).[205] Moreover, Carla seems to be stuck

---

[204] "Through the window she could see that it was still the sunny crisp autumn day she had left outside. But in the room rain was falling."
[205] This is further emphasized by the fact that every aspect of Carla's identity seems to be determined by her love for Angie: "She hated her father because she loved Angie, she loved Jamal because she loved Angie, she loved her friends because she loved Angie, she was a bicycle cou-

in the moment immediately preceding her mother's suicide when Angie handed her Jamal and told her to take care of him. In order to preserve the memory of her mother, she "needed a clear empty path to Angie as a living being" and therefore "kept from loving because she loved Angie" (Brand 2005: 111).

Like Antigone's, her subject position is the product of an impossible desire and therefore her life was 'unlivable' from the very beginning.[206] As her reflections on the death of her mother imply, she only becomes aware of the fact that her mother broke a taboo by having a relationship with Derek when no one from her mother's side of the family took her in after Angie's death. Since she apparently does not understand the implications of this fact as a child, the norm still affects her process of identity formation, until she is able to recognize the workings of power which caused the situation and consequently begins to consciously identify as Black, thus honoring the choices of her mother. In Carla, the melancholic identification with the lost object of her dead mother and the impact of norms that assign an impossible subject position to her often combine in a paradoxical performance of disappearance. She seldom eats (Brand 2005: 131) and is therefore very thin (Brand 2005: 279), and she habitually cruises through the city on her bike in order to "burn [...] off a white light on her body" (Brand 2005: 28), frequently risking her life when doing so:

> Before long she was out on Bloor Street again, speeding east toward the centre of the city, flinging herself through the lights at Keele and bending southward to the lake; the bellowing horn and pneumatic brake of an eighteen-wheeler flinched her sinuous back, but she didn't stop for the trucker yelling curses at her. She left the drama of the shocked driver and skewered traffic behind. If she could stop, she would have, but she was light and light moves. (Brand 2005: 29)

As the quote implies, Carla might be effecting a double disappearance during her bike rides: on the one hand, she is attempting to rid herself of the "white light on her body"; on the other hand, she herself turns into that light, which prevents her from stopping while hazardously racing through the city. This constant movement could well result in Carla's death whenever she ignores traffic regulations due to her inability to stop – as is the case when she "fling[s] herself

---

rier because she loved Angie, she hated policemen and ambulances and bank tellers because she loved Angie. Loving Angie was a gate, and at every moment she made decisions based on that love, if the gate swung open or closed" (Brand 2005: 111).

206 I'm referring to Butler's analysis of the myth of Antigone, in which they point out that Antigone's life was unlivable from its very beginning, since, as offspring of the incestuous liaison between Jocasta and Oedipus, she is the product of a relationship that is forbidden by the matrix of power (see also section 4.2).

through the lights". While Carla is thus not directly affected by hegemonic power structures at the time that the novel takes place, her current state of trauma and depression is caused by the fact that the choices of her mother are denied by the matrix of power.

Oku, the son of Jamaican-Canadian parents who immigrated to Canada before he was born, not only has to deal with the traces that the painful process of immigration has left on his parents, but remains a constant victim to racism even in the present. The key passage in this context is strongly reminiscent of the concerns of today's Black Lives Matter movement since it describes Oku's first encounter with the police when he walks home alone one night.

> He stopped. Two cops came out of the car. He can't remember if they called him, if they told him to stop. His arms rose easily as if reaching for an embrace. One cop reached for him. He can't remember what they said or what they wanted. He only remembered that it was like an accustomed embrace. He yielded his body as if to a lover, and the cop slid into his arms. That was the fucked up thing about being dangerous. It was a surrender to violence, to some bruising, brutal lover. He remembered how instinctively his arms opened, how gently, as gently as they would have opened to embrace Jackie. But this was another kind of impeachment. A perverse fondling. [...] The cops didn't find anything on him, and he said nothing to them, just smiled and shook his head. They asked him his name, he smiled again. Their fondling became rougher. Oku let his body go limp. The cops folded him into their car with a few more shoves. He laughed. He was still high. They took him to fifty-two Division. They couldn't find anything to charge him with and let him go around 6 A.M.
>
> He had come to expect this passion play acted out on his body any time he encountered authority, and it was played out at its most ecstatic with the cops. Whenever he encountered them, he simply lifted his arms in a crucifix, gave up his will and surrendered to the stigmata. Some of his friends didn't. They resisted, they talked, they asserted their rights. That only caused more trouble. They ended up in the system fighting to get out. They ended up hating everyone around them. Homicidal. (Brand 2005: 164–165)

Apparently, the policemen had no specific reason for stopping Oku and took him to the police station without any evidence that he had committed a crime. While Oku could have asserted his rights the way his friends do, he refrains from doing so since he already knows that this will only exacerbate the situation. Instead, he becomes completely passive, drawing on performances of stereotypical femininity (Rosenthal 2011: 251) and the Christian imperative to 'turn the other cheek', as alluded to in the "passion play" reference, the crucifixion stance, and the mention of stigmata. Those stigmata, however, consist in the color of his skin which automatically assigns him the identity of "being dangerous". This identity – that of a "bad public hard-ass kind of black man everyone appreciated" (Brand 2005: 163–164) – is described in detail a few paragraphs before the passage quoted above as one of the main options for the construction of male Black identity.

While Oku does at times consider giving in to the allure of this performance option, he also tries to refrain from taking part in any criminal activities.[207] The policemen's projection of this identity onto Oku is emphasized in the ambivalence of the reference to his "surrender to violence, to some bruising, brutal lover". Whereas the actual performance of a 'dangerous' male Black identity would entail 'surrendering to violence' by actually performing acts of violence, the opposite choice is just as problematic since in this case Oku has to surrender to the violence of others who project this identity onto him. Either way, Oku cannot escape the stereotype and has to suffer its consequences.[208]

Moreover, Oku's other performance options are just as limited. Following in his father's footsteps, for example, would serve no purpose. Fitz, Oku's father, is depicted as an unhappy man who has been embittered by the unremitting racism he has experienced (Brand 2005: 86) and who constantly represses this experience of precariousness by re-affirming his sovereignty. Consequently, any kind of open conversation becomes difficult with Fitz because "[h]e always had to be right and certain about everything" (Brand 2005: 88). Like the 'dangerous' identity offered by Oku's peers, this sovereign male Black identity does not seem to offer a way forward.

Those two sovereign identity options are then juxtaposed with the precarious subjectivities of the Rasta and the musician.

> The Rasta and the musician would be an embarrassment to men like Oku's father. They had gone mad, the worst kind of giving into the system that could be imagined among black people in the city. Violence could be understood, but not madness. Violence at least had a traceable etymology – it protected your life, your remaining will, all your sense of beauty. But madness, madness was weak. Oku's boys in the jungle felt the same: "You see that crazy motherfucker playing air piano? What the fuck is wrong with him? Shame." The Rasta got a little more respect, even though they still thought him mad. At least he answered to higher powers, they said. That a steady stream of them lay open-chested on sidewalks and in the parking lots of after-hours clubs was just how the world was. (Brand 2005: 174)

---

207 Nevertheless, Oku is not entirely successful in doing so since he occasionally participates in selling stolen goods although he does not want to be implicated in actually stealing anything (Brand 2005: 163).

208 In this, the pressure to conform to stereotypical constructions of male Black identity is not only executed by white hegemonial discourses, but also by the Black community itself. Thus, Kwesi, a local gang leader, phones Oku on a regular basis in order to convince him to join in minor criminal activities (see, for example, Brand 2005: 162–163).

The quote echoes Foucauldian conceptions of subjectivity according to which those who are excluded from discourse or 'othered' by society are termed mad. As the juxtaposition between the "weak" identities of the Rasta and the musician implies, these two characters form the precarious other to a sovereign Black male identity. Both have "giv[en] into the system" by accepting their state of heightened precariousness. The Rasta strolls the streets as a panhandler and thus actively performs his financial precarity while also succumbing to his gambling addiction when he visits the racecourses. The musician, by contrast, became a victim of discrimination, according to him and the Rasta, when one of his compositions was denied performance after the Toronto Symphony found out that he is Black. As a consequence, he rejects his Black identity and starts attacking Oku when the latter calls him 'brother' at their first encounter. Traumatized by the experience of racial discrimination, the musician continues composing music and plays air piano while sitting on the streets. According to the Rasta, he is an exemplary case of what happens when Black men "[f]ollow the white man ways" (Brand 2005: 173) and aim at upward mobility.

Despite their state of deterioration both characters fascinate Oku and become "a strange source of friendship for" him (Brand 2005: 174). Moreover, as the quotation above suggests, their fate at least does not entail lying "openchested on sidewalks and in the parking lots of after-hours clubs". However, none of those options offers a convincing role model for Oku who remains stuck in a state of paralysis from which he cannot quite emerge. After dropping out of university he is still living at his parents' house and is constantly short of money. While spending his days at the market reading and watching the street, he tries to come to terms with his situation, yet at the same time "[e]very now and then he had an attack of panic so strong that he felt weak, he had pains in his stomach" (Brand 2005: 87).

Oku's love interest Jackie, on the other hand, struggles to escape from the financial precarity and desolate conditions of her upbringing. Whereas her parents took to petty crime when faced with the meagre job opportunities in Toronto, Jackie has opened a second-hand clothes store called Ab und Zu. As the German name indicates, however, the shop's existence is dependent on the fact that her German-Canadian boyfriend Reiner lives on the premises. While Jackie does not seem to be unsuccessful selling clothes, the novel leaves open the question of whether Jackie could pay the rent for it without his help. Moreover, Reiner is repeatedly described as offering safety and stability to Jackie, who is very much afraid of again feeling "out of control" (Brand 2005: 101), as she did when she was a child and was subjected to her parents' precarious lifestyle. The situation is all the more problematic since she simultaneously has an affair with Oku to whom she feels increasingly attracted. Upward mobility is for Jackie thus linked to Reiner so that her options for choosing a partner remain limited. Whether or not she gives in to Oku's wooing in the end, is left open by the novel.

Those four protagonists are then juxtaposed with the singular voice of Quy, who embodies a subjectivity that represents the utmost extreme of human precariousness. Growing up as an orphan in a refugee camp on Pulau Bidong, Quy is exemplary of those lives that have been deemed 'ungrievable' by western hegemonic discourses of power (see also Bernabei 2008: 123 and Lai 2014: 203–204). As autodiegetic creator of his own discourse he is left out of the western matrix of intelligibility – impersonated by the heterodiegetic voice telling the rest of the story – that still contains the other four characters, albeit in positions of heightened precariousness. This lack of a subject position within discourses of power manifests itself on the abstract level of individual identity, yet also on the very material level of basic survival. Due to the loss of his parents, Quy loses his identity as well as his means of survival. On the boat that first carried him to Pulau Bidong he was already being "mistreated, beaten back when [he] reached for the good water or when [he] cried for food" (Brand 2005: 7) since there were no parents to provide those basic necessities for him. Since he belongs to no one, no one protects him or makes sure that he survives. For Quy, identity becomes precarious in a primary sense because others either grant him the right to live or threaten him with death. Consequently, the construction of his own identity follows the simple guideline of whether or not a particular identity will ensure his survival, which also explains why he often quickly changes loyalties as soon as he realizes that attaching himself to someone else might increase his chances of survival (see Brand 2005: 76–78, 137, 198, 220, 284).[209] This is further emphasized in Quy's reflections on his encounter with Binh, which open up the possibility that Quy has been an unreliable narrator from the very beginning:

> By some coincidence, if you believe that kind of thing, I come to the name of a guy, Vu Binh, in the monk's e-mails. Young guy, M.B.A., all the money he wants, all the pussy he needs. And by some stranger coincidence, this one perhaps love, he's looking for a man who was a boy named Quy. Well, see for yourself. I already put two and two together. I appear. The guy is either very cunning or a *lo dit*. I arrive; he's convinced. I'm convinced. He turns out to be my brother. Isn't my name Quy? Wasn't I lost so he could come to me in his expensive shoes, in his silk shirt, his mouth slow and vulgar on his mother tongue, with his silver Beamer? He knows everything, he's a swift man, he looks at me like Picasso devouring an African mask – how can he use it, how can he change it, which part of his belly can he put it in? So I say to myself, Fine, let it play. (Brand 2005: 310)

---

209 Thus, Quy also points out that "[t]he *Dong Khoi* [that is, the boat that carried him away from his parents and to Pulau Bidong] had freed [him] of allegiances" (Brand 2005: 284).

Throughout the novel it remains unclear whether Quy is actually the son of Tuan and Cam or whether he simply adopted this identity (see also Sarkowsky 2018: 171) in order to be taken in by them as part of their family, a doubt further emphasized by the question "Isn't my name Quy?" as well as the ambiguous statement "I appear" which might either imply 're-appearing' after having been lost for a long time or 'appearing' for the first time as Quy, the role to be played by the narrator posing as Quy.[210] As he points out, the city offers ideal conditions for entirely changing one's identity and is thus marked by ethical relativism:

> There are times when I've said to myself, Who the hell are you? That's a dangerous question. And this is a dangerous city. You could be anybody here. That is what first took me when I walked among people on the streets. Then one morning I sat on the subway train and I heard a laughter and it reminded me of when I was little, and right away I knew it would be easy to disappear here. Who would know? The man living across the street from you could have fought in the Angolan war, he could've killed many people, and there he is sitting in a deck chair with his wife as if nothing happened, and one day he will mention the simple fact to you with a look of triumph as he remembers it only as a youthful adventure. (Brand 2005: 309)

Hence, similar to the heterodiegetic voice that tells the rest of the story, Quy perceives Toronto as a place that is defined by the fluidity of identity (see Rosenthal 2011: 222). In its most extreme form, this fluidity might result in disappearance and the construction of an entirely new identity that frees the subject from any prior responsibilities. Quy's take on ethical relativism, however, betrays the subjectivity of this perspective onto the city since "mention[ing] the simple fact" of having "killed many people" would probably not be met with indifference by the average inhabitant of Toronto, though it emphasizes the gateway to ethical relativism that this fluidity might constitute – thus recalling the relationship between the fluidity of identity and ethical relativism in *Open City*.

Moreover, the fact that Quy's narration changes from subsequent to simultaneous narration suggests that the purpose of his retrospective account of his growing up on Pulau Bidong lies in his present situation. This situation is rendered in the simple present tense and therefore constitutes a case of simulta-

---

[210] This is also suggested by an earlier passage where Quy describes the contents of the laptop of his former boss: "He'd been taking money from that one woman for more than ten years to find a boy named Quy. [...] This was the monk's most intense relationship, I could tell, until the factory girl came along. I came to believe that he was Quy himself; otherwise, why would he keep up so many letters with this one mother when with all the rest he robbed them and moved on? But then again the subject of all this could just as well have been me, for one of the names I go by is Quy and I was lost one night in a bay, or so I've told myself" (Brand 2005: 287–288).

neous narration which is juxtaposed with the subsequent narration relaying his past. His time of narration seems to change in the course of the novel from sitting in the subway train at the beginning of the narrated time, which is alluded to when he points out that he is experiencing a feeling of nonexistence "now riding this train" (Brand 2005: 74)[211] to sitting in Binh's car at the end of the novel – as well as the narrated time – when he remarks "[s]o I'm waiting, I'm going to rest my head here and wait" (Brand 2005: 312). His narration thus originates only when he arrives in Toronto and might just form part of his re-invention of himself. While the identity of the other characters is confirmed by the heterodiegetic voice who authorizes their identity, Quy's narrative might be unreliable and his identity is consequently only confirmed by himself.

Nevertheless, as mentioned above, Quy's fluid identity also turns him into a representative of a 'subaltern' multitude of immigrants whose lives are deemed 'ungrievable' by western discourses of power. Precisely because they do not form part of a western matrix of intelligibility except for their identity as 'undocumented immigrants' in a refugee camp far away from the 'western' world, their lives are especially precarious since hegemonic white discourses of power already construct them as a collective instead of individual, vulnerable lives. As Larissa Lai argues drawing on Said, western subjectivity defines itself by means of 'othering' that which is non-western as an unreadable multitude (2014: 204). The identity of this multitude is only generated by media coverage and thus limited to the options of the medium that transmits the message:

> When you look at photographs of people at Pulau Bidong you see a blankness. Or perhaps our faces are, like they say in places, unreadable. I know how you come by such a face. I was paralysed when we unfolded what was left of ourselves onto the shore of Bidong. I felt like you do with sunstroke. I felt dried out, though, of course, a child doesn't have these words, but don't give me any sympathy for being a child. I grew up. I lived. I've seen the pictures. We look as one face – no particular personal aspect, no individual ambition. All one. We might be relatives of the same family. Was it us or was it the photographer who couldn't make distinctions among people he didn't know? Unable to make us human. Unable to help his audience see us, in other words, in individual little houses on suburban streets like those where he came from. Had he done it, would it have shortened my time at Bidong?
>
> In one photograph you can see me stooped at the dress tail of a woman who could be my mother. She had two sons, and in the photograph I look like a third. Staring together into the camera's lens, perhaps by then we knew we were transformed into beggars for all time. I for sure had none of what you would call a character. Pulau Bidong was a refugee camp. A place where identity was watery, up for grabs. Political refugees, economic refu-

---

[211] The view that Quy is the man sitting in the subway train at the beginning of the novel is also supported by Langwald (2015: 362) and Siemerling (2008: 113).

gees – what difference? I was too young then for beliefs and convictions, thank heavens. Only at first I looked for love, for goodness, for favour. But after, I lived by one rule: Eat. Eat as much as you can. (Brand 2005: 8–9)

Quy's assessment of the seeming non-identity of the refugees at Pulau Bidong intricately alludes to the production of ungrievable lives in western discourses of knowledge. According to him, the "blankness" on the faces might result either from their fight for survival itself or from the way that the photographer saw them, namely as reduced to their bare existence and as representing the primary precariousness of human life itself. This is repeated in the second paragraph when Quy states that "perhaps by then [h]e knew [they] were transformed into beggars for all time" since this is the identity that is going to be assigned to them as soon as the image circulates in the press. The statement plays with the idea that photography freezes moments in time and links it to the construction of a fixed identity that is mirrored by the inescapability of their material condition of precariousness in this situation. Moreover, Quy suggests that this state of being reduced to the vulnerability of human existence and the subsequent deprivation of individual identity is caused by a lack of identification on the part of the photographer which in turn results in a lack of identification on the part of his audience due to his inability to make "his audience see [them] [...] in individual little houses on suburban streets like those where he came from". Hence, it is implied that the precariousness that determines the identity of the refugees cannot be empathized with through western eyes since western subjectivity is based on the norm of sovereignty that excludes the option of recognizing precariousness as a shared human condition. This is highlighted through the image of the "individual little houses on suburban streets" which, already at the beginning of the novel, are associated with sovereignty. Whether empathizing on the basis of similarity might actually have helped is, however, placed in question in the very next sentence.

Furthermore, the quote emphasizes how Quy's construction of identity is entirely subjected to this condition of primary precariousness since he explicitly names the one rule and thus the *hegemonikon* according to which he structures his life from this moment onwards: "Eat. Eat as much as you can." Thus, Quy represents humankind's general subjection to vulnerability on the level of matter as well as representation, which forms a mirror image to the precariousness that is manifest in the lives of the other four characters: albeit on a less primary level, precariousness infiltrates the level of material vulnerability for them as well. Moreover, it highlights the way in which supposedly sovereign western identities are built on the sacrifices made by those who are relegated to the sphere of the other (Rosenthal 2011: 252).

8.1.3 Metropolitan Aesthetics of Existence: Encounters with the Precarious City

Three of the five protagonists use the city as a means for their individual techniques of the self, albeit in different ways. Tuyen, the artist, roams the city with her camera or connects with its citizens by inquiring about their longings. Carla rides through Toronto on her bike in order to convince herself that she is in control and to shake off any disturbing emotions, whereas Oku walks the streets of Alexandra Park because he assumes that this will bring him closer to Jackie. Quy, by contrast, reflects (on) the city's potential for transformation in general and explicitly points out that the city itself is central to his process of acquiring a new identity.

The different means that Tuyen, Carla and Oku choose activate various processes in their techniques of the self and lead to different outcomes that reflect on issues of responsibility, sovereignty and empathy. In this, flânerie remains a precarious practice that revels in the fluid materiality, contact and representation that the city offers. However, while flânerie was transformed into text by the flâneurs themselves in *The Blindfold* and *Open City* and could thus be incorporated into techniques of the self as a means of reflection for the strolling subject itself, this is not the case here. In Brand's novel, flânerie is instead transformed into other art forms such as installations or photography, or serves an entirely non-artistic purpose. Hence, the text cannot offer reflexivity to the characters situated within the heterodiegetic discourse of the novel and thus cannot be read as an indicator for the truthfulness of processes of formation. This kind of reflexivity is, by contrast, entirely relegated to encounters between individuals – encounters that further enhance the circulation of affects in the city and that disrupt constructions of identity.

First of all, Tuyen's flânerie occurs on two levels. On the one hand, especially throughout the first half of the novel, she strolls through the city and asks its inhabitants about their longings, writes them down and creates an installation based on her findings. On the other hand, she roams the city during the 2002 World Cup with her camera in hand and tries to capture its multicultural spirit during various celebrations. Both practices are interlocked in their fascination with the multicultural plurality of Toronto. During the World Cup, she tries to capture the scenes of street parties held by different nationalities because "[s]he loved being in the middle of whirling people, people spinning with emotion" (Brand 2005: 204). Consequently, she actively participates in the various festivities standing, for example, "outside of the German pub and [being] shy to take pictures" or dancing "the samba in between shots" "at the Brazilian *cevejaria* [sic] on College Street" (Brand 2005: 204). Here, Tuyen's fascination with the city ties in with the narrator's description of it as an affective and diverse space. According to Tuyen, "that was the beauty of this city, it's polyphonic, murmuring. This is what always filled Tuyen with hope, this is what she thought her art was about – the representation of that gathering of voices and longings that summed themselves up into a kind of language, yet indescribable" (Brand 2005: 149). The city is thus a mixture of voices and affective drives for Tuyen which results in a language that cannot be described and thus can only partially be understood. The link between voices and longings already implies a focus on a fluid materiality that is reminiscent of the relationship between weather, affect and representation analyzed at the beginning of the chapter. This quality seems to be especially discernible to Tuyen who

> would turn around and find frames filled in with the life of the city. She would find discarded looks, which she tried to trace to their origins, or alternately their flights. On any given day, on any particular corner, on any crossroads, you can find the city's heterogeneity, like some physical light. And Tuyen found herself always in the middle of observing it. (Brand 2005: 142)

The reference to the "discarded looks" which Tuyen discovers like concrete objects in the city further emphasizes the reciprocal transgression of the immaterial and the material in the city. Therefore, "the city's heterogeneity" is also described in terms of the rather paradoxical phrase "physical light", which ascribes material characteristics to something immaterial. Tuyen's flânerie is thus explicitly located in a realm of transgression where the material turns into the immaterial and vice versa and where representation and concrete matter permeate each other, which is further exemplified in her focus on the 'longings' of the citizens of Toronto.

Nevertheless, the semantic field of vision looms large in Tuyen's apprehension of the city. While she seems to aim at a multifaceted sensual experience of the city, this experience often centers on visual perception. Thus, she finds "looks" in the city, which is itself compared to "light" – that is, a phenomenon that can be experienced only visually – and the quote above ends on the statement that "Tuyen found herself always in the middle of observing it" instead of actually finding herself in the middle of it. Tuyen's longing for contact, which manifests itself in her flânerie, is therefore juxtaposed with a distance that becomes especially palpable in her work with her camera. When attending a demonstration against globalization with Oku, she decides on documenting the whole event with her camera and using the photographs for an installation later on. Her interaction with the camera, however, seems to be closely linked with her family's trauma regarding the loss of Quy:

> Her eyes took in every human experience as an installation, her lids affecting the shuttering mechanism of a camera. It must have been a milky evening: the water was grey milk, the sky was stone grey, the boat was disappearing in a noisy rush, and Tuyen's mother and father must have seen Quy like this – slowly, slowly moving away. Floating, floated away, in the China Sea without a trace. Her mother's insomnia was caused by this sight. When she closed her eyes at night, she herself saw Quy floating away. So Tuyen kept clicking. She kept looking at what wasn't being seen, as her brother must have been unseen, and her mother noticing too late, harried with irrational fear. Tuyen saw, heard first Oku's voice unlike his voice, then saw, turning with her camera to click and click the declensions of Oku's body being dragged to the van. The arm of the cop entwined with Oku's flailing arms. She photographed this aggressive embrace, Oku falling to his knees, then pushed, pulled away by two friends, then the cops beating the friends back and shoving Oku into a white cube van with lines down the side. She called this "Tree Falling Against Van". (Brand 2005: 206)

The act of photography, during which Tuyen and her camera become one, also constitutes a way of trying to cope with her family's trauma since Tuyen tries to look "at what wasn't being seen" by documenting everything through her camera. This echoes her mother's obsession with documents and forms of identification and indicates how Tuyen still remains implicated in the familial trauma although she tries to get away from it. At the same time, the camera, her primary means of observation, establishes distance between Tuyen and her surroundings. While she actively partakes in city life, including the demonstration depicted here, she remains passive when it comes to active interference. Although Oku "yelled to her for help" (Brand 2005: 206), she just keeps photographing him. Like a typical flâneur, she is in the middle of the crowd, yet remains internally distanced from it. This stands in stark contrast to her longing for experiencing the sensuality of the city and implies that she is still held back from actively engaging with the city by this familial trauma. In fact, the relationship between her flânerie and the power structures she tries to escape is even more complex since the purpose of her art was originally "to stave off her family – to turn what was misfortune into something else. She had devoted all the time to it, and here they were – her family – returning again and again" (Brand 2005: 149). The desire to distance herself from her familial relations thus infiltrates her art and paradoxically keeps her from getting too entangled with the city. Hence, Tuyen's artistic practice as a photographer mirrors what the trauma had produced in her family, that is, the absence of proximity and love, and unveils how Tuyen's act of distancing herself from her family – and thus translating this distance into her flânerie – is a direct repetition of her experience of emotional distance within her family.[212]

---

[212] This is emphasized in Carla's reaction to the series of photographs that Tuyen produces

Nevertheless, her art does also open up a pathway towards a possible healing of this trauma, or at least further transformation. While drifting aimlessly through the city with her camera, Tuyen encounters her brother Binh with a young man whom she shortly after recognizes as her lost brother Quy. This moment is, however, also mediated through her camera:

> Tuyen was ecstatic. She spun around, her camera clicking off shots. She didn't yet know how she would use them. Through the lens she saw a familiar face and stroked the button to open the aperture; she clicked twice, trying to remember who it was. Binh! She hadn't expected to see him here, so the face of her own brother was familiar and unfamiliar to her. [...]
>
> Binh was grim-faced, talking to another man whose back was to Tuyen. It dawned on Tuyen that she was standing diagonally opposite Binh's store, XS. [...] Oddly, the man's body itself was rigid, a hand reaching out to touch Binh, to hold his pointing finger. Tuyen's lens caught this hand and the other reaching onto Binh's right shoulder. The embrace was both sinister and affectionate. Binh broke into a smile, then spun the man around, his left arm taking the man's right shoulder. Tuyen snapped this series of shots, her own shock translated into mechanical clicking of the shutter. Her camera almost slipped from her hand when she saw the man's face.
>
> It was the face of a boy, a baby, innocent and expectant. There was something wrong about it. It didn't go with the rest of his body – something she suspected when photographing his back. Binh clapped. Then they turned to watch the celebration in the street and Tuyen kept clicking her camera at them until the roll ended.
>
> [...] A pool of light set itself on that little familiar-unfamiliar knot of her brother and a stranger, a friend, an associate, a partner. (Brand 2005: 207–208)

On a metaphorical level, Tuyen's camera draws Quy back into their lives when she suddenly realizes that the man she has photographed is her brother Binh and afterwards observes him standing in front of his store with a man she later identifies as Quy. This sudden encounter is precipitated by a combination of Tuyen's desire for sensuality and the unpredictability of the city and the continuous action of photographing her surroundings. While she seeks to fulfil her desire for transformation by means of her aimless flânerie, her photography

---

from the demonstration: "The photographs made Carla queasy. She told Tuyen and Oku that they were sick. [...] The photographs, something about the motion in them, their sequence, reminded her faintly of the dream of her mother climbing onto a chair" (Brand 2005: 206). Hence, the sequence of the photographs as proof of Tuyen's persistent inactivity in the face of Oku's mistreatment by policemen is painful for Carla because it reminds her of the moment her mother climbed onto a chair in order to jump off the balcony and kill herself – the moment, that is, of giving up the responsibility for her children and abandoning them to whatever was to follow after her suicide. Tuyen's photographs then indicate her refraining from taking any kind of responsibility for her friends and therefore cause feelings of distress in Carla.

aims at 'seeing what is not being seen' and is marked by her familial trauma. Moreover, seeing the city through the lens of her camera changes Tuyen's perspective on her surroundings. While it gives her the opportunity to document everything that she sees in an instant, it also restricts her perspective onto the city and further contributes to her active attempt at disorientation. Flânerie as a technique of the self here links conscious wishes with more or less unconscious desires and results in an unexpected outcome precisely because Tuyen gives herself up to the unforeseeable city and becomes "ecstatic" in the original sense of the term.

The "familiar-unfamiliar" apparition that Tuyen then encounters on the street bears traces of an uncanny return of the repressed. While she tries to "stave off" her family by pursuing her art, those repressed relations return to her disguised as the 'unfamiliar' she is looking for. This process is in fact doubled in the passage mentioned above since Tuyen twice experiences seeing a brother as a stranger and then realizing that this stranger is actually her brother, once with Binh and once with Quy. Quy, however, remains uncanny to her because she is wary of his intentions and his identity. What causes him to give Tuyen "the creeps" (Brand 2005: 300) is the fact that, although he claims to be familiar and on the basis of this claim tries to enter Tuyen's family, a huge part of his identity is hidden. Yet, it is this identity that determines the extent of the family's repressed guilt towards Quy. Hence, Tuyen speculates about the anger that he must have stored up inside him through the years: "The lost boy would have to have been sad, lonely, angry, hurt, angry. Was that the scraping sound she had heard in his voice? Would he have had a life with love? A girlfriend, a wife, children perhaps? [...] Would he have let the past go as chance – unfair, but chance – and made the best of what he got?" (Brand 2005: 300). This ambivalence between apprehending familiarity and hidden resentment is also discernible in Tuyen's impression that Quy's behavior towards Binh is "both sinister and affectionate".

Ultimately, it can be argued that this technique of the self has transformed Tuyen since it brings her closer to her family and makes her develop a new position of responsibility with respect to her parents:

> She put her arm on Binh's to slow him. He turned to her at first brusquely, then, seeing the understanding of their mission in her face, slowed himself, as if to savour their mutual intuition. This is what they'd done all their lives, she thought. She felt comforted by their commonality, the same commonality that had made her so uneasy most of her life; it had made her long to be unexceptional. Yet, here was their specialness now carried between them to the door of the house, the recognitive gaze of an exception cherished through all this time. (Brand 2005: 307)

Encountering her brothers on the street outside XS has altered her position. It is only because she knows what Binh plans to do that she gets the opportunity to be involved in Quy's meeting with their parents. On that occasion, she assumes a position that is already familiar to her, yet towards which she develops a new attitude. The quotation suggests that she leaves off repeating her parents' aversion to their immigrant identity and instead affirms the attachment to her parents and her brother as forming part of a position of hybridity, a "specialness" to be "cherished".

As a consequence, Tuyen's plan for her installation changes and expands:

> She would need a larger space for the installation, three rooms really, very high ceilings. In the middle of each room a diaphanous cylindrical curtain, hung from the ceiling, that the audience could enter. At the centre of one cylinder would be the *lubaio* with all the old longings of another generation. She would do something with the floor here too, perhaps rubble, perhaps sand, water. In another cylinder there would be twelve video projections, constantly changing, of images and texts of contemporary longing. This one would be celebratory, even with the horrible. Again here the floor, the path, what material? The last cylinder would be empty, the room silent. What for? She still wasn't quite certain, what she was making; she knew she would find out only once the installation was done. Then some grain, some element she had been circling, but had been unable to pin down, would emerge. (Brand 2005: 308)

The installation reflects Tuyen's process of identity formation. While she is torn between her parents – represented by the *lubaio* and the "old longings of another generation" – and the multicultural city of Toronto – represented by the "constantly changing" video projections of "contemporary longing" – throughout the novel up until this point, the empty last cylinder points towards an uncertain future that opens up at the moment that Tuyen envisions this new concept for her installation. This last cylinder, however, is proof of the processuality of this identity since it will only "emerge" during the process of working on the installation. Tuyen's technique of the self thus includes her artistic production, which is intertwined with her flânerie.

Yet, the processuality of the aesthetics of existence produced by those techniques of the self always entails precarious results. When Tuyen and Binh leave Quy in Binh's car in order to prepare their parents for meeting their long-lost son, he is attacked by two petty criminals – Carla's younger brother Jamal and a friend – who want to steal Binh's silver Beamer. In one of the very last scenes of the novel the badly hurt Quy sees his parents running towards him before he loses consciousness. Whether he later dies or survives the attack remains unclear. In either case, Tuyen's feelings of guilt will intensify since it was she who suggested that Quy wait outside until they had spoken to Tuan and Cam, although she could not have foreseen what would happen to him. The precarious unpredictability and fluidity of different longings, including the "horrible" to which Tuyen also refers in her installation, brings Jamal and his friend to Richmond Hill and makes them attack the defenseless Quy. What served as a means of transformation in Tuyen's techniques of the self, that is, the precarious city itself, now changes her fate once again. Hence, the ending of the novel challenges Tuyen's celebratory stance towards the unpredictability of the city's longings and emphasizes the truly precarious character of flânerie as a technique of the self.[213]

Tuyen's flânerie is the only one among the novel's various techniques of the self that includes or results in artistic production. Oku's and Carla's interactions with the city, by contrast, serve other purposes. While Oku spends a lot of time in the city, he usually does not indulge in flânerie, but rather sits in a café and reads. Only towards the end of the novel does he stroll through Alexandra Park, a desolate area of the city where Jackie grew up, in order to find out how he might get closer to her. Oku's practice of flânerie becomes a material attempt at and metaphor for empathy which serves as a means of transformation for Oku.

Oku's flânerie deliberately aims at "know[ing] something about Jackie" and is described in terms of "research" (Brand 2005: 256). Knowledge thus becomes a material experience that derives from "walk[ing] where she had walked, and figur[ing] out the things that had given shape to her" (Brand 2005: 258). During his stroll, Oku reflects on the desolate state of Alexandra Park, briefly interacts with her father and muses on memories from their shared childhood. In this, space becomes a catalyst for various insights. Scrutinizing the neighborhood makes Oku aware that, although he didn't realize this when they were teenagers, Jackie actually comes from a poorer background than the other three characters: "They all lived in houses with their parents, but Jackie's parents' tiny apartment did not strike them at the time as so different. His walk now told him something else. His parents weren't rich or even well off by any means, but they obviously lived better than people in Vanauley Way. And this is where Jackie had always lived" (Brand 2005: 256). The encounter with Jackie's father, moreover, emphasizes the dangers of living in Alexandra Park, where "the poor waged wars for control of their small alleyways and walkways, their streets and the trade in unofficial goods" (Brand 2005: 257), while his memories mark the difference be-

---

[213] Fittingly, Jamal and his friends drive around rather aimlessly through Richmond Hill. Although they plan on stealing a car there, their encounter with Quy is entirely arbitrary and deviates from their original plan of breaking into one of the garages there.

tween a "teenage crush" and the feeling of love he now experiences towards Jackie.

The knowledge that he acquires, however, is by no means entirely correct, although some of his findings do coincide with ideas and beliefs that internal focalization on Jackie had already disclosed. First of all, despite never having seen the man before, Oku correctly identifies Jackie's father just by realizing that the way he holds his head is similar to hers. His observation that Jackie's father's limp is a matter of style instead of being brought about by an injury is mistaken, however, since the reader had learned earlier that Jackie's father gained this limp when he was attacked by another man in one of the nightclubs that he and Jackie's mother frequently went to. Moreover, Jackie might not be at all happy with Oku talking to her father in the first place, since she particularly dislikes her friends meeting her family. Oku's attempt at empathy therefore remains equivocal, neither entirely successful nor entirely fruitless.

This is underscored by the narrative voice's 'sliding' between different focalizers. The chapter in which Oku strolls through Alexandra Park starts with an internal focalization on Oku, yet in the next section – which ought to shift the focalization, as occurs in the rest of the novel – focalization briefly seems to remain with Oku when the narrative voice says "[w]hat must have scared Jackie was Vanauley Way" (Brand 2005: 260) before turning into either internal focalization on Jackie or zero focalization in the reference to "[t]he dry hot walkway in the summer, the dry cold walkway in the winter" (Brand 2005: 260). While the first sentence can be attributed neither to Jackie – since she would know what had scared her – nor to a possible zero focalization – since an omniscient narrator would also know what had scared her – it can only be attributed to Oku; the next line, by contrast, cannot be seen from his perspective since Oku, who strolls through Alexandra Park for the first time, cannot know about the quality of the walkways in different seasons.[214] Whereas the first sentence could simply be interpreted as a case of what Gérard Genette called *paralipsis*, that is, a rather unlikely restriction of perspective in cases of zero or internal focalization, it also ties in with a pattern that occurs on various other occasions in the novel: *What We All Long For* frequently employs slides between different levels of meaning that challenge the overall coherence of the story. Already in the first chapter on Quy, Quy's identity is put into question by an ambiguous reference to his fa-

---

[214] Moreover, the focalization seems to entirely change to Jackie for the rest of the section, recapitulating scenes from her childhood and further commenting on the state of Vanauley Way through the years.

milial relations. Here, Quy introduces himself by implicitly referring to two different fathers:

> How do I start to tell you who I am? Talking is always a miscalculation, my father, Loc Tuc, used to say.
>   I was a boy at that time. It was night. Because it is at night that these things happen. I was with my parents and my sisters. We had left the place where we lived and travelled along a road. (Brand 2005: 6)

Although the reader does not know it yet, the father who lost Quy when boarding the boat full of refugees is probably not called Loc Tuc, since Loc Tuc is the name of the criminal monk for whom Quy works later on. Moreover, if Quy actually is Tuyen and Binh's lost brother, the name of his father would be Tuan. Nevertheless, the quotation stages the rift in Quy's identity that causes Loc Tuc to become Quy's metaphorical and 'spiritual' father while his biological father disappears in the night that Quy starts to describe after referring to Loc Tuc. Similar metaphorical slides that deconstruct the difference or incompatibility between two signifiers or chains of signifiers occur for example in the description of Tuyen's preference for milk – where the narrative voice at first points out that Tuyen "loved milk" and forced herself to drink it despite being lactose intolerant, and then concedes that in fact she usually bought the milk and then left it in her refrigerator. Here it remains unclear whether Tuyen does sometimes drink the milk or always buys it simply to convince herself of being properly 'North American'. This ties in with the focus on constant instances of transformation in descriptions of the city. Thus, the city "smells of eagerness and embarrassment and, most of all, longing" at the beginning of spring. Not only does this wording refer to processes of transformation on the level of content, but it also establishes the catachrestic relation between the sensual experience of smelling and more abstract feelings of eagerness, embarrassment, and longing. The slides between different kinds of focalization taking place in the chapter mentioned above thus form part of a general structural feature within the novel, namely rather illogical combinations that disrupt coherence on levels of content and form while at the same time forming new connections.

What is more, this slide seems to imply that Oku might actually manage to empathize with Jackie on his walk through Alexandra Park since focalization on him seems to merge with hers. Nevertheless, this interpretation is counteracted by the pattern of meaning that has been established throughout the novel so far, namely that the beginning of a new section usually involves a change in focalization; hence, the difficulty of categorizing this first introductory line seems to indicate that empathy remains doubtful here. Moreover, it is also possible to read the whole section introduced by the line "[w]hat must have scared Jackie was

Vanauley Way" as part of Oku's attempt at empathizing with Jackie via his imagination. If this were the case, Oku would also imagine the rest of the content of this section and project ideas onto Jackie that he cannot know about – his supposed empathy would then remain his projection. While some of the conclusions he draws based on his stroll through Alexandra Park are confirmed by other scenes in the novel, his plan to get a job and work during the rest of the summer before going back to university is as ambiguous as his empathy, particularly in relation to his options for identity construction: whereas he strongly rejects identifying with his father up until this point, his project of getting a job and working for the rest of the year brings him close to the pattern established by his father. Whether Oku will actually return to the university remains doubtful, although the text does not deny the possibility. Flânerie as a technique of the self, then, might trigger a transformation, yet also remains precarious.

Carla's flânerie, by contrast, has frequently been interpreted in terms of a resistant spatial practice *sensu* De Certeau – that is, as an individual performance of the city text that produces "de-hierarchize[d] [...] spaces, calling into question the taken for granted social structure of the city" (Sarkowsky 2018: 168; see also Johansen 2008: 50). However, as has been mentioned above, what functions as a means of escape from her own emotional reactions towards others, especially her brother Jamal, also results in immediate danger to her life and threatens her with dissolution, while at the same time affirming Carla's place and existence in the city. When she rides through the city after having left her brother, she exchanges emotional precariousness for the physical precariousness of cruising through the city without paying attention to traffic rules. Her emotional distress and unrest are represented in her wish to "burn [...] off a white light on her body" (Brand 2005: 28), while the practice of riding through the city on her bike gives her "a feeling of weight and balance" (Brand 2005: 32). By overcoming the obstacles in her way, she assures herself of the physical existence of her body in the face of her deliberately precarious practice of flânerie. Unlike her brother Jamal, "she saw the city as a set of obstacles to be crossed and circled, avoided and let pass" (Brand 2005: 32) and thus adds a resistant power to her hazardous cruising. During her flânerie, Carla creates a tension between vulnerability and a rebellious affirmation of her own existence when becoming visible to others precisely because she ignores traffic rules, as explained above.

This paradoxical experience of feeling the most safe or powerful in the midst of chaos recurs in her preference for strolling through Toronto during a blizzard. For her, "[s]nowstorms stopped the pretence of order and civilization" (Brand 2005: 105) while at the same time "calm[ing] a city and mak[ing] things safe and quiet" (Brand 2005: 105). In this context, Carla again exchanges her experience of social precariousness – that is, the fact that within systems of "order and civilization" a place within the matrix of intelligibility is denied to her – for the physical precariousness of the blizzard. Here she oscillates between experiences of vulnerability and sovereignty: "[i]dentifying the direction of the wind, she would turn and turn in the blizzard and be lost, walk with it, walk against it, driving her feet through the thick gathering wall of it" (Brand 2005: 105).

Thus, Carla's practice of precarious flânerie transforms her and cleanses her of the emotional turmoil that her familial situation causes in her, although the positive effects it might have on her are limited. After her ride through the city, the "burning light" has left, yet now she feels that "her own weight and the thought of her brother at Mimico Correctional crushed her again" (Brand 2005: 32). Nevertheless, the novel also suggests that this particular technique prefigures Carla's ultimately giving up of her responsibility for Jamal when the narrative voice states that "[a]s she rode, she pictured him still standing there, waiting for her to turn around and come back, and all she could do was run, and all she could find was this well of heat and cold depth" (Brand 2005: 31). As the transformation into light and the reference to the "well of heat and cold depth" imply, Carla's bike rides contribute to a gradual burning out with regard to her feelings of "protectiveness" (Brand 2005: 313) towards her brother and her cruises can therefore be likened to running away from him. This process, however, does not make her 'more' aware of her condition of precariousness, as was the case with other examples of flânerie discussed in this study – which in any case would be difficult to achieve since she is already very much aware of it – but rather aims at a gradual restitution of independence.

The different outcomes of Carla's and Tuyen's flânerie then serve the overall problematization of responsibility in the novel. Although towards the end of the novel Tuyen seems to accept the precariousness that she associates with the feelings of dependency in her family, she simultaneously develops a sovereign attitude of control with regard to Quy. While she is not sure how to judge him throughout her various encounters with him, her actions imply that she still perceives him as a threat when, in the end, she decides that he has to wait outside in order to lessen the shock to her parents. Hence, for Tuyen, taking responsibility for her family also entails a sovereign judgement and behavior with regard to Quy. Together with Carla's giving up of her own responsibility for Jamal, Tuyen's actions partly cause the attack on Quy and are therefore marked as potentially violent. Yet, in the case of each character, the opposite action could likewise have been problematic since the novel also implies that Carla is actually no longer able to bear the responsibility for her brother and since Tuyen's mistrust of Quy seems to be at least somewhat justified.

In all three cases, strolling or cruising through the city serves as a precarious technique of the self by means of which the characters transform themselves in various ways and alter their emotional predispositions. In this, the materiality of the city engages with the emotional landscape of the characters. Thus, Tuyen is led to her brother by giving herself up to the city while at the same time trying to overcome her familial trauma. The encounter with her brother then induces Tuyen's participation and ensuing transformation. Oku tries to empathize with Jackie by means of strolling through Alexandra Park and thus lets himself be guided by the city in his attempt at empathy, whereas Carla uses the city in her hazardous encounters with Toronto traffic in order to cleanse herself of emotional turmoil. The outcome of those practices as well as the practices themselves, however, remain precarious so that there is no guarantee that those techniques of the self will result in the expected outcome or any outcome that might have positive effects on the characters. What distinguishes them from the protagonists of Hustvedt's and Cole's novels is the fact that their techniques of the self do not rely primarily on representation and signification, but rather on engaging with the material city that is – due to the flow of people, yet also other circumstances – subject as much to fluidity and chance as to the workings of *écriture*. This fluidity, however, is caused by other people. Tuyen, for example, is drawn to Binh's store – where she encounters him and Quy – by people celebrating Korea's victory during World Cup 2002. The traffic with which Carla engages is, of course, manmade and Oku's transformation is brought about by his longing for Jackie. Longing itself, as the title of the novel already suggests, is a central motor in the city and constitutes a central trigger for processes of transformation and identification.

Reflexivity, by contrast, is mostly relegated to the other. On the one hand, characters in the novel are repeatedly questioned and challenged in their attitudes by other characters. Carla's friends, for example, on various occasions try to convince her to give up her responsibility for Jamal (see, for example, Brand 2005: 26) and Tuyen re-evaluates her opinions concerning her brother Binh several times after interacting with him (see e.g. Brand 2005: 147). On the other hand, the other is also the uncanny other to be found in instances of doubling in the novel. As has already been mentioned, when Tuyen sees Quy for the first time, he is constructed as not only Binh's doppelgänger, but also Tuyen's. What they share is their condition of precariousness in western hegemonic discourses of power, although Quy experienced this vulnerability in a more existential way than Tuyen. His technique of the self, however, is also a mirror image of the other characters' techniques. While their practices of flânerie engage with the fluidity of the city, Quy's technique is narration itself and thus based on the fluidity of signs. Quy's autodiegetic narrative produces an identity that oscillates between being Tuan and Cam's lost son and being any other refugee who experienced a similar fate. The processual act of narration enables Quy to enter the novel's matrix of intelligibility and, therefore, create his own precarious identity. While this identity seems to be located outside the heterodiegetic discourse that produces the other characters, he explicitly enters their world on the level of plot in the last third of the novel so that his existence is confirmed by the heterodiegetic voice as well. The potential untruthfulness of his narration, however, highlights the problem of accountability for one's actions that was already discussed in the chapter on *Open City*. Quy's narrative highlights the dangers of completely fluid identities and thus constitutes an uncanny double to Oku's, Carla's and Tuyen's techniques of the self, while his precariousness brings to the surface what is repressed in western constructions of sovereign subjectivity.

It is then also Quy who becomes the victim of the potential violence of chance and contingency in the city when he is beaten by Jamal and his friend. Here, the violent potential of stereotypes – focalization on Jamal reveals that they drive to Richmond Hill because there are "rich motherfuckers" (Brand 2005: 316) – combines with the violent potential of contingency and emphasizes once more the precariousness of human existence under those conditions. Hence, the novel emphasizes the dangers as well as opportunities for constructions of subjectivity in the precarious city, of which the characters are also aware: "They believed in it, this living. Its raw openness. They saw the street outside, its chaos as their only hope. They felt the city's violence and its ardour in one emotion" (Brand 2005: 212).

8.1.4 City of Longing and Belonging: Affect and Identity in *What We All Long For*

In Brand's ever-moving Toronto, identity, materiality, representation and affects can constantly be changed so that the city becomes a vital part in the characters' techniques of the self. Those techniques of the self involve the fluidity of matter, representation and affect, yet affects seem to constitute the focal point in each character's individual aesthetics of existence. Indeed, the circulation and movement which are so central to the role of the city in their techniques of the self are frequently represented by affect itself, in particular in its manifestation as the emotion of longing. Thus, Tuyen's representation of the city in her installation centers on the longings of the inhabitants of the city and by doing so foregrounds the emotion of longing as common ground between all citizens. This is confirmed by the discourse of the narrative voice which repeatedly refers to the transformational effect of emotions and longing in the city from the very first pages of the novel. Hence, Toronto becomes what Sara Ahmed calls an "intense" (2004: 10) space through which objects and subjects of emotion circulate and turn the city into a "site of personal and social tension" (Ahmed 2004: 11), yet also become sites of tension themselves. They trigger movement as much as they manifest themselves in movement. When Carla cycles through the city, she is thus driven by her emotions, yet she even seems to turn into emotion itself. And while she tries to get rid of the "burning light" that she feels has taken over her body after having left the Mimico Correctional Institute, she turns into this light itself. The light marks the inscription of histories of hate on Carla's body. Carla is condemned to an 'unlivable life' due to her multiracial heritage, for the hatred that Angie's family exhibits towards Jamaican-Canadians is inscribed in Carla by means of Angie's suicide. Since "the work of emotions involves the 'sticking' of signs to bodies" (Ahmed 2004: 13), the emotion of hate sticks the sign 'unlivable life' onto Carla's body when it is repeated on various occasions such as the violent fight between Angie and Carla's father, Angie's suicide and Carla's life at her father's house. The notion of 'unlivable lives' constitutes an intensification of the overall precariousness of the subject so that Carla is reminded of her status as an 'unlivable life' every time she experiences a loss of control and sovereignty, as when her brother asks her for help when in prison. The "burning light" that she then tries to shake off while cycling through the city marks her as a site of social tension.[215]

Experiencing the hatred towards her heritage as an object of this emotion turns Carla at the same time into a subject regarding the feeling of vulnerability. According to Ahmed, subjects can become subjects as well as objects of emotion, or one could say that subjects are subjected to emotion in a Foucauldian sense of the term. This is emphasized not only through Carla's auto-aggressive reenactment of racist hatred, but even more so through the novel's focus on desire and longing. While *What We All Long For* showcases in Carla's case how emotions 'stick' to bodies and thus construct certain bodies as hateful surfaces, it also highlights how objects of emotion and words for feeling 'move' and 'slide'. Both Oku and Tuyen 'long for' one of the other characters and their long-

---

[215] See also Roupakia (2015: 36) who likewise uses Ahmed as an interpretative lens in her reading of Brand's novel: "In *What We All Long For* Brand explores the invidious ways in which the cultural memories of loss acquire almost material texture, impress upon the malleable surface of affiliated diasporic psyches and bodies [...]" and Chariandy (2006: 106) who points out that "Tuyen and her companions encounter their ancestor's [sic] legacies of displacement and disenfranchisement not through official histories or family tales, but through a doubly unwilled circulation of feeling. In contemporary theoretical parlance, we might suggest that, here at least, the second generation awakens to its diasporic legacy not through conscious communication, but through an unconscious transmission of affect."

ing turns the others into objects of feeling. Moreover, it orients Oku and Tuyen towards the other and influences their behavior. This is most notably the case with Oku when he strolls through Alexandra Park and decides on taking a new direction in his life at the end of his walk. Longing for Jackie transports him out of himself and reconstructs his identity so that longing turns into belonging as a marker of identity.

This connection between being oriented towards another person and this person's influence on one's identity resurfaces on various occasions in the novel when characters claim another person as "mine" (for example, Brand 2005: 26).[216] Carla, for example, voices her orientation towards as well as her attachment to her brother by referring to him as 'mine' and by doing so transfers the idea of this kind of relationality to Tuyen who from then on tries to transform her relationship with her brother Binh to whom she did not feel attached in a similar way. By emphasizing the link between affective attachments and identity, the novel thus foregrounds the relationality and hence the precariousness of identity itself. It is only due to this relationality that the four protagonists can be transformed by other characters. All the slides mentioned in the previous section mark ruptures in the identity of one of the characters. While the slides in Quy's and Tuyen's stories mark the trauma of loss – in Quy's case – and displacement – in Tuyen's case – the slide in the chapter on Oku's walk through Alexandra Park indicates the possibility of empathy and adds a positive connotation to those slides. Hence, the 'sticking' and 'sliding' of emotions are interdependent, and transformation due to one's longing for another person can coalesce into identity, while identity can conversely be disrupted due to the orientation towards another person and the ensuing transformation.

In the case of all four characters, their friendship with the other three establishes a new community of belonging far from the politics of racial and cultural identity to which their parents subscribed. Thus, Carla happily imagines her future with her friends after having let go of the responsibility for her brother Jamal:

> She'll go back to her apartment and live her life. She'll have parties with Tuyen, she'll go to the Roxy Blue, she'll go to jazz concerts, she'll wait in line to hear U2, she'll go with Tuyen to Pope Joan, to Afrodeasia. They'll dance together. She'll check out the open-mike spoken word at Caliban with Oku. She'll cut her hair, she'll go to Jackie's Ab und Zu and get a new wardrobe. She'll be seduced by someone. She can't hold the baby any longer. (Brand 2005: 315)

---

216 See also Brand (2005: 297): "Of course it was her brother Quy. Of course it wasn't. What difference would it make? This man had arrived in their orbit, and he was therefore theirs."

To Carla, this is a moment of transformation precipitated by the continuous advice from her friends to give up her responsibility for Jamal (Brand 2005: 26). As the quote indicates, she now constructs an identity based on the multicultural community with her friends.

Yet, *What We All Long For*'s take on multicultural western society is more sinister. Before sitting down in the café where her mother worked, Carla muses "that she couldn't hold the baby any more either. She knew all this when Jamal came by in the black Audi. She knew Derek hadn't lent it to him. Derek would never lend anyone his car" (Brand 2005: 315). Carla is thus fully aware of the fact that Jamal has committed his next crime right away, yet refrains from calling her father or acting upon this awareness in any way. In the cruel montage following her ride to the café, the reader learns that while Carla is celebrating her new freedom, Jamal and his friend drive to Richmond Hill, encounter Quy sitting and resting in Binh's car, and beat him (nearly) to death.[217] While the pressure resting on Carla has become palpable in the course of the novel up until this point, her flight from this situation alongside with her father's disinterest in his son cause the brutal ending of the novel. Giving up the responsibility that has put Carla under an almost unendurable pressure due to its connection with the traumatic loss of her mother, causes more violence. Similar dark undercurrents to an idealization of a multiculturalism beyond cultural attachments occur in scenes of doubling between Toronto and Pulau Bidong. While the Canadian metropolis is continuously depicted as a place for the reinvention of identity, Quy also emphasizes – as mentioned before – that "Pulau Bidong was a [...] place where identity was watery, up for grabs". Although his previously quoted assumption that his criminal activities might become an anecdote to laugh about as soon as he has been firmly established in Toronto is unlikely to be confirmed, the doubling implies that a fluid identity might equally include a very fluid stance with regard to ethical issues. This is further underscored by Quy's doubling with Binh, who makes most of his money by means of various criminal activities:

> Binh was that strange mix of utter overconfidence and insecurity, utter ruthlessness and squeamishness. So while he invested fifteen thousand dollars in a shipload of migrants from Fushen to British Columbia, he did not want to know the details or, of course, be named if they were discovered. Though if they were not discovered, and even if they were, he stood to make a profit of three or four hundred percent on his investment. His

---

[217] Research on *What We All Long For* has interpreted this scene differently. Whereas Roupakia (2015: 43) argues for Quy's survival, Birkle (2019: 70) remarks that Quy is "killed before his parents can even meet him".

was not the lion's share in this enterprise. He was a small investor. But he stood to make even more if some of those migrants found their way to Toronto, from which he and several colleagues would arrange their transportation to New York City with proper documents. He also had a small investment in a home-based Ecstasy manufacturing plant, which distributed to high schools and raves. Binh, like all businessmen who run multinational operations, could swiftly pull his money out of one concern or another and invest elsewhere. (Brand 2005: 122–123)

Especially Binh's involvement with human trafficking illustrates the problematic link between the Global North and the Global South. As the child of former immigrants who had to experience exploitation and hardship during their flight to Canada, Binh is now transporting migrants from Vietnam to the North American continent who are subjected to similar conditions. By contrast to his brother, however, he does not need to rely on crime in order to survive, but his criminal activities rather derive from a capitalistic greed for more and more money.[218] While Quy's fate emphasizes that the divide between the Global North and the Global South can only be overcome by means of breaking the rules, Binh represents an unnecessary breach of rules by the westernized sovereign subject. Similarly, Carla giving up her responsibility for Jamal can only lead to catastrophe because there is no one else who could take over this responsibility from her so that her precarious suffering is juxtaposed with the sovereign irresponsibility of her father. The novel thus implies that a post-sovereign ethical subject needs to be developed by those who already are in a position of power since they are not those who are in a position of heightened precariousness. Oku's, Tuyen's and Carla's practices of flânerie constitute examples of techniques of the self that might contribute to the formation of a post-sovereign subjectivity that affirms its precarious relationality with others. Thus, Oku takes a first step towards developing an identity that acknowledges his primary state of dependency as well as that of Jackie when he asks himself "[h]ow could he tell her that he wasn't wreckage? How could he, when he was depending on her to tell him that?" (Brand 2005: 265). Tuyen finally accepts the precarious attachment to her family due to recognizing the heightened vulnerability of her parents in the face of Quy's arrival, and Carla accepts the precariousness inherent in letting go of the responsibility for Jamal.

---

[218] This is also suggested by the narrative voice's description of Binh's development: "Binh had been sent to the University of Toronto to do business and had left with all the credentials of an M.B.A., namely a distaste for the straightforward and honest, a mistrust of social welfare, and a religious fervour for what was called the bottom line. His education had enhanced his penchant for ungenerousness and solidified his resolve that only he mattered [...]" (Brand 2005: 122).

Nevertheless, the success of those techniques is necessarily also precarious and still implicated in power structures that call into question the transformational potential of the techniques themselves. Whereas Carla's transformation becomes linked to the violent encounter in Richmond Hill, it is especially Tuyen whose technique of the self is depicted as problematic. Tuyen's artistic activity and thus her flânerie as well depend on an economic freedom that can only be achieved because she relies on money she receives from her parents as well as from Binh. Especially the fact that she actually takes money from her brother, of whose criminal activities she is aware, links her to the chain of exploitation detailed above. In terms of the continuum of flânerie derived from the work of Walter Benjamin, Tuyen occupies a position that seems resistant to discourses of power while she in fact depends on them financially just like her brother. This is not to say that her art cannot be understood in terms of resistance, but the novel clearly problematizes her entanglement with the very same power structures that she criticizes, for example, in her photographic series *Riot* (see Brand 2005: 206).[219]

Based on my argument so far, I suggest reading *What We All Long For* as a sinister meditation on the possibility of emancipation and resistance in times of globalization and late capitalism.[220] Nevertheless, especially Tuyen, Carla and Oku manage to partly resist the power structures that have assigned them an inferior position, and this is partially due to their reliance on flânerie as a precarious technique of the self. Moreover, the novel emphasizes how discourses of power rely on emotion, yet also how emotion can just as much become a motor for transformation and resistance. *What We All Long For*'s strong emphasis on emotion and the possibility of empathy is highlighted by the variable internal focalization that juxtaposes different kinds of perspectives and thus enables insight into the emotional landscape of each of the characters.[221] The discrepancy between the heterodiegetic voice of the four protagonists' world and Quy's autodiegetic narration, however, contrasts the order and relative safety of the so-called 'First World' with the precarious chaos from which Quy emanates. Yet,

---

[219] A rather harmless analogy to Tuyen's subjection to discourses of power due to her flânerie might be found in Oku's decision to get a job and let go of his bohemian lifestyle since the flânerie that led him to this decision seems to have precipitated this incorporation into the market.
[220] See also Roupakia (2015: 33), who argues that *What We All Long For* "marks a shift [in Brand's writing] from a clear-cut politics of resistance to a more difficult ethics of recognizing co-option, complicity, interdependency and complexity."
[221] Roupakia (2015: 45) even claims that "Brand's employment of a range of narrative points of view in *What We All Long For* invites readers to enter her literary text in various relations of critical intimacy."

chaos also recurs in a different form in the multicultural city and might become a motor of freedom and transformation there, while the city itself is built on rigid power structures that cannot be overcome as easily.

Those power structures also loom large in the last text to be analyzed, Robin Robertson's *The Long Take, Or a Way to Lose More Slowly*, which also focusses on lending visibility to those marginalized in the city. Robertson's text, however, also adds another dimension to the negotiation of post-sovereign subjectivity by foregrounding different modes of perception through various kinds of intermediality which then ultimately lead back to the juxtaposition of the ethical subject with *flâneurisme* as 'ultimate play'.

8.2 Turning Film into Scripture: Intermedial Encounters in Robin Robertson's *The Long Take*

Robin Robertson's narrative poem *The Long Take, Or a Way to Lose More Slowly* (2018) is the most recent among the works discussed in this book and is the only one that crosses the boundaries of the genre of the novel. It has been awarded several prizes, such as the Goldsmiths and the Roehampton Poetry Prize, and was shortlisted for the Man Booker Prize. While Robertson has already published five collections of poetry, *The Long Take* is his first attempt at longer poetic forms. Nevertheless, it continues to develop several aesthetic tendencies that were already discernible in his earlier work, like a propensity for highly aestheticized depictions of violence or an inclination towards Greek mythology[222] that recurs in *The Long Take* on the level of form, which is highly reminiscent of the ancient Greek epic poem.

Like many other city novels such as James Joyce's *Ulysses* (1922), Saul Bellow's *Herzog* (1964) or Ian McEwan's *Saturday* (2005), Robertson's experiment in form features a modern-day Ulysses whose life in the city is described in terms of the heroic quest. In *The Long Take*, this hero is a Canadian D-Day veteran called Walker who struggles with bouts of post-traumatic stress disorder, loss of identity and feelings of guilt deriving from his experiences in the war. In the course of the book, he moves from New York to Los Angeles to San Francisco and then back to Los Angeles to escape his feelings of unrest and loss, yet cannot shake them off in the disturbing environment of the cities. In all three metropolises he is confronted with the experience of violence, extreme poverty

---

[222] Robertson has also published translations of Euripides's *Medea* and *The Bacchae*, which both also feature drastic depictions of violence.

and racism, giving him a grim perspective on the post-war USA. The text ends when Walker, having lost his friend Billy Idaho to gang violence, confesses how he tortured a German SS soldier in order to take revenge for his comrades who had been executed by the SS. When his interlocutor Frank, called 'glassface' due to a facial deformation that is the result of being himself tortured by SS soldiers, tells him "You're no better than them" (Robertson 2018: 222), Walker gives up his habit of strolling, settles in among the unhoused people in LA's skid row district and gives in to alcoholism.[223]

What is particularly striking about this text is its constant transgression of not only generic, but also medial boundaries, which has led to varying categorizations of it by reviewers. John Banville, for example, refers to the "epical feel" (2018: n. pag.) of Robertson's poem, Colin Burrow describes it in terms of a "historical verse novel" (2018: n. pag.) and Sibbie O'Sullivan opts for its classification as a "narrative poem" (2018: n. pag.). The blurb on the dustjacket of Picador's paperback edition, however, categorizes the text as a "noir narrative" and thus already indicates the text's intermedial crossing to the genre of film noir. This highly idiosyncratic style nevertheless ties in with the transgressive nature of the flânerie text, whose analogy with it will be delineated below.

8.2.1 The Ultimate Flânerie Text: Formal Peculiarities and the Aesthetics of Transgression in *The Long Take*

As explained in chapter 2.6, I suggest that such texts feature an emphasis on the particular – as opposed to an attempt at totality – as well as a transgression of boundaries. Whereas *The Blindfold* and *Open City* transgress the boundary between author and protagonist and *What We All Long For* crosses the border between heterodiegetic and homodiegetic narration alongside its frequent employment of catachrestic slides on the levels of form and content, *The Long Take* takes this structural property to the extreme by transgressing boundaries of narrative voice (if it could even be called thus in this case), genre and various media.

The entire text is made up of short snippets that are sometimes written in verse form and sometimes in prose. On the whole, four different types of snippets can be distinguished in Robertson's book. The lion's share is taken by strings of text, written in free verse, that comprise the plot of the text and

---

[223] This is symbolized by Walker opening a bottle of Thunderbird wine, a brand of flavored fortified wine common among unhoused people in the US due to its low price, which is mentioned several times in the context of alcoholism in the book.

refer to Walker, the protagonist, in the third person. These parts delineate Walker's present situation in contrast to the second-most frequent kind of snippets which contain his memories of the past and are either located on the Nova Scotian island near Broad Cove where Walker lived until he went to war, or in France, covering his experiences in the war. Here, the text is in italics and features an autodiegetic narrator who recounts his memories in prose form. Apart from these two main types, the text is interspersed with snippets in bold print that seem to represent Walker's private notes and reflections on what he sees in the city – possibly preparations for his work as a journalist at the *Press* – as well as a few postcards he has sent to his ex-girlfriend Annie in Nova Scotia. These parts are always accompanied by a mention of the date and thus provide further temporal orientation within the individual chapters whose titles give the year in which they start.[224] Only at the end of the novel does another type of text occur, used just once in the book. This text is written in a different font than the other parts, yet does not feature italics or bold print. Like Walker's memories, it is justified and written in prose form, but employs no personal pronouns beyond addressing the reader right at its beginning by means of the pronoun 'you'. The content is somewhat reminiscent of Christian mythology's Revelation of John, with an apocalyptic description of an earthquake of epic proportions engulfing all of Los Angeles until "[t]he ground opens, swallowing pieces of itself, cracking apart, rising in places to a twenty-foot cliff, and lifts now into two huge moving plates, under which something seems to be breathing" (Robertson 2018: 224). This prophetic vision is introduced by the appearance of the coyote who – echoing Native American mythology – ambiguously "steal[s] fire and bring[s] it to mankind" (Robertson 2018: 108) according to Walker's friend Billy, and by a boy quoting loosely from the Book of Hosea: "But I will send a fire upon your cities, / and it shall devour your palaces. / The days of visitation are come. / You shall reap the whirlwind" (Robertson 2018: 223). While the text's equation of Los Angeles with the Biblical sinful city here employs a motif common in city literature, it also explicitly links LA's 'sinfulness' to capitalist ideology since Walker's apocalyptic vision of LA is set against the frame of the so-called Bunker Hill Renewal Plan that included the eviction of up to 9,000 people and a rebuilding of the entire area that was mostly populated by LA's poor, a process that is aptly summarized by Billy with the words "They call this *progress*, when it's really only greed" (Robertson 2018: 79; original emphasis). The Promethean

---

[224] The headings themselves provide only partial temporal orientation since they are separated from each other according to the cities in which they are set and do not comprise only the year mentioned in their title.

fire brought by the coyote is thus the neo-liberal promise of the possibility of upward mobility on which the American Dream's entanglement with capitalism is based. This last type of text seems to describe Walker's emotional landscape in the face of the Bunker Hill area being torn down and in the face of Frank's reaction to Walker's confession since it is followed by another sequence in free verse returning to the text's primary mode of narration: "If he could drain his eyes of this. The split world, the world / burning" (Robertson 2018: 224). Two pages before the end of the text this new type of snippet therefore sums up Walker's hopeless situation.

Similarly, the other three types can be differentiated by means of their overall function in the text. The first type could best be described in terms of narrative free indirect discourse's characteristic dual voice which makes the voice of the focalizer be heard next to the narrator's voice. While those sequences often give an insight into Walker's very subjective perspective onto the city, they also show him from the outside and press this perspective into the outward form of free verse. His memories, by contrast, are usually triggered by his experiences in the city, yet might just as well influence the way he perceives the city so that there are numerous sequences written in free verse that depict the city by relying on the semantic fields of battle and war, as is the case in the following example: "He remembered every bar as a battlefield / sodden with carnage, / and the blurred ghosts of drinkers, / their glasses emptying, filling, emptying" (Robertson 2018: 21). Moreover, the prose parts are particularly interesting in the context of the history of flânerie texts and the genre of the prose poem that originally gained popularity due to Baudelaire's posthumously published *Petits Poèmes en prose* (1869; *Paris Spleen*), and which, according to Baudelaire, can be considered particularly apt for descriptions of the experience of metropolitan life.[225] Baudelaire's poems, however, only constitute the modernist actualization of the general form of the *poème en prose*, which simply refers to longer prose texts that claim to have the aesthetic value of poetry or translations of epic poetry (see Bunzel 2009: 587). Significantly, Baudelaire's poems are called **Petits Poèmes en prose** and thus adapt the older form of highly stylized longer prose texts to the conditions of capitalist modernity. In *The Long Take*, both forms of 'prosaic poetry' occur in the interplay between the short prose poems that give a brief insight into Walker's memories and the longer stretches of epic poetry that serve the direct description of the city. This prose poetry thus mirrors the impression that the city makes on Walker's consciousness, on the one hand by means of the link to Baudelaire's short prose poetry that is specifically designed

---

[225] See chapter 2.1.

to reflect the environment of the city and on the other hand by means of the epic poem's use of the third person which further underscores his subjection to the various discourses that make up and sustain the city. The parts written in bold print then add Walker's deliberate reflections on the city to this dynamic and could be interpreted as a result of the interaction between city and memory:

> They stopped off there, one day, among the bulldozers
> and backhoes, cement trucks and cranes,
> to get some shots of the progress,
> but the pile drivers ... the hammer-drills ... the blasting
> from the building site ...
> the noise ...
>
> *The noise of it, the noise of the guns, the heavy machine-gun fire, and nowhere to hide and they were getting closer all the time and the flares were burning and the noise was so loud, and all the shouting and the guns were going and now their 88s had found us, they'd found us out and were pounding our positions, pinning us down, pinning us, so many of us down.*
>
> He had his hands over his ears for twenty minutes,
> even in the car, and they took it easy, driving round,
> before stopping at a bar on 2nd and Spring,
> near the *Press*, for a drink.
> [...]
>
> **People come to Los Angeles for refuge, sanctuary, but what they get is this massed, mechanized population moving in a confined space almost without collision or accident. The sounds, the movement of war: a ballet of battle without the guns.**
> (Robertson 2018: 58–59)

Here, Walker's perception of the city seems to trigger his memories of war and ultimately results in his reflection on the experience, written down in the form of one of his notes. Although the dynamics between the environment of the city, Walker's memories and his notes is not always as explicit as in this case, the relationship between the three is often similar. Like a typical flâneur, Walker thus indulges in a combination of observation and reflection tinged with his subjective experiences.

Already at this level, the text transgresses generic boundaries as well as the boundary between different types of narrative perspective, yet it also features cases of overt as well as covert intermediality:[226] each section dedicated to one of the three metropolises is framed by two black-and-white photographs – one at the beginning of the section and one at the end of it – of locations to

---

[226] For a definition of the distinction between overt and covert intermediality see chapter 2.4.

which the respective section explicitly refers.[227] This visualization of the text's settings is supported by a detailed map of downtown Los Angeles at the beginning of the book.

Even more striking is the covert intermediality which the text employs. As the title already indicates, the text contains numerous references to the medium of film on the level of content as well as on the level of form. Thus, the whole book is interspersed with a plethora of references to movies belonging to the genre of film noir since Walker often visits the cinema (see e.g. Robertson 2018: 12, 43 or 90) and frequently encounters the sets of those movies when walking through Los Angeles (see e.g. Robertson 2018: 69, 70 or 95–97). Whereas many allusions in the text remain unexplained – like *Open City*, *The Long Take* features a lot of historical detail, yet is much more reluctant to explain its references – the book also contains a rather extensive appendix that mostly consists of detailed information about the movies alluded to in the text (see Robertson 2018: 230–236). What is more, *The Long Take* explicitly mirrors the medium of film on the structural level by means of its formal peculiarities. The text is – as mentioned above – made up of individual snippets that are separated from each other not only by means of different types of font as well as generic form, but also by means of small asterisks that neatly cordon each snippet off from the others, and this emulates the material structure of a movie that is likewise made up of individual scenes linked as well as separated from each other by means of cuts. *The Long Take* thus becomes a movie turned into text:

> The treetops are swaying, but there's no wind.
> *
> Pike was always in a movie, the cameras always rolling;
> he sweeps his hair from his eyes:
> long shot, close-up, man of the moment –
> roving reporter; editor in waiting.
> *
> Birds broke from the trees, in every direction.
> *
> '*Yeah-yeah-yeah*,' was his machine-gun way of saying:

---

227 Moreover, the photographs often emphasize central motifs or topics discussed in the individual chapters. The photographs enclosing the section on New York, for example, center on the play between light and shadow (see Robertson 2018: 1 and 33) which is also alluded to several times in the text. The image introducing the first section on Los Angeles mimics an upward glance at Bunker Hill (see Robertson 2018: 35) where Walker is going to find a home in the chapter to follow, and the second section on Los Angeles starts with a photograph gazing downward onto the dead-end of Olive Street (see Robertson 2018: 143), thus alluding to Walker's gradual descent depicted in this section.

> *Look, I know all this. I'm a busy man.*
>
> *
>
> Outside on the line, a white shirt on a wire hanger begins to dance.
> (Robertson 2018: 205; original emphasis)

As the quote self-reflexively implies – "Pike was always in a movie" – *The Long Take* is a textualized movie consisting of small scenes that add up to a longer filmic narrative. Here, the focus on Walker's colleague Pike is interrupted by scenes indicating the advent of the earthquake that will take place in the last pages of the book. The scenes are focalized through Walker whose perspective switches from focusing on the trees to focusing on Pike. Whether they represent something that Walker actually sees or are instead a product of his mental landscape, however, does not become clear since the earthquake is also linked to his apocalyptic vision at the end of the text and thus could just as well be interpreted as an illustration of his inner turmoil. While such a representation of emotional landscapes might also be possible in film, the written text seems to lend itself to it more readily, since the reception process itself relies on imagination and interpretation, which is not necessarily the case when watching a movie.

Returning to the tradition of the flâneur, *The Long Take* can be seen to merge several of its strands. First of all, activities traditionally associated with the flâneur, such as observation and reflection, occur on the level of content. Second, those activities are relayed in a form that is strongly reminiscent of the medium of film and accompanied by several photographs, media that are both also deeply rooted in flânerie's overall emphasis on visual perception and whose theorizations frequently employ the flâneur as a central metaphor. While the text thus emphasizes the 'activity of the eye' in the city, it also defamiliarizes it by transferring it to the medium of scripture. Paradoxically, the subdivision into small texts that mimics the medium of film is what instils a heightened necessity for interpretation and reflection on the part of the reader since any kind of narrative coherence is disrupted. This focus on the particular, however, is typical of flânerie texts like Benjamin's *One-Way Street* (1928) or Baudelaire's *Paris Spleen* (1869) and usually serves the function of representing the disorientation and transience of perception in the modern metropolis. *The Long Take* thus fuses forms that have been used to illustrate the experience of modern city life with intermedial references to the medium of film, and by means of the double-coding of its central structural principle suggests filmic perception as forming the 'mental life' of the metropolitan citizen in the twentieth and twenty-first centuries. Transferring the filmic structure to the text then represents the flâneur's particular form of resistance as 'a way to lose more slowly' and to partly escape this filmic structure of perception.

What is more, Walker's story can be interpreted as a kind of "promiscuous obedience" that enacts a deferral of the twenty-first century's norms of perception by transferring them to another medium and therefore emphasizes their arbitrariness and constructedness. While viewers usually do not tend to actively recognize the cuts that link one perspective to another, *The Long Take* emphasizes the patched-up nature of the medium of film and foregrounds techniques of cutting and editing that can be used in order to manipulate seemingly realistic images. Fittingly, long-take techniques – that is, continuous shots that are longer than the normal pace established by a particular movie – usually give up precisely this privilege, just as transferring Walker's filmic perception to the medium of the literary text dismantles the filmic medium's potential for manipulation. Alfred Hitchcock himself points out that movies consisting of a small number of shots and thus endorsing long-take techniques tend towards the aesthetics of the theatrical play (see Bordwell 2008: 39). The title of Robertson's text might thus suggest an emphasis on authenticity and a deliberate refraining from opportunities of manipulation. However, the fact that *The Long Take* is actually not a 'long take', but instead consists of individual snippets that suggest techniques of cutting, adds an ambivalence common to flânerie texts since the title now suggests authenticity as well as deception. The proximity to the medium of theatre then might emphasize the ambivalent notion of performance on the level of plot. This performance might be one that adapts itself to the wishes of its audience – as the example of the character Pike suggests – or it might be resistant, as in the way Walker defies those expectations and the text itself takes up a societal norm and decontextualizes it.

The Long Take thus already creates a multi-layered, individual performance of resistance on the level of form by drawing on central characteristics of the flânerie text. By combining different kinds of snippets of text within a long transgeneric narrative poem it emphasizes particularity and coherence alike and thus creates a complex form of post-sovereign subjectivity. By transgressing boundaries between different perspectives, genres and media it highlights the restrictions each individual category imposes on recipients and producers alike and thus manages to partly escape discourses of power by self-reflexively questioning those very same boundaries. In the following, I will elucidate the link between those formal features and flânerie as a technique of the self on the level of content.

8.2.2 "A Way to Lose More Slowly": Flânerie as a Technique of the Self in *The Long Take*

The text's structural peculiarities are closely linked to the book's central topics of trauma, capitalism and violence and present flânerie mostly as a technique that is diametrically opposed to the continuous acceleration taking place in metropolises since the nineteenth century. At the same time, the text suggests that Walker needs the anonymity of the city to stave off feelings of guilt and a loss of moral integrity that result from war crimes that he has committed during World War II. While flânerie thus might form a means of resistance against the proliferation of the ideal of progress and continuous acceleration, *The Long Take* once again also links it to the dissolution of boundaries between good and evil, only this time the deconstruction of this particular binary opposition is paradoxically tied to Walker's discourse of resistance itself, which further underscores the critique of the system the product of which Walker has become.

First of all, flânerie seems to become Walker's *modus vivendi* after the war and is – as his name already indicates – the focal point of his identity. Thus, the text introduces him with the words "He walks. That is his name and nature" (Robertson 2018: 4), without specifying whether this has always been his name or whether he only developed this habit after his experiences in the war. This habit is caused by a feeling that is repeatedly metaphorized as a "*coal-seam fire*" (Robertson 2018: 4; original emphasis) burning inside him; that is, a fire that is smoldering and that might break out after a certain amount of time. The text then directly likens this fire to "*The road*" (Robertson 2018: 4; original emphasis), and in the course of the book Walker often reacts to the occurrence of the feeling of the coal-seam fire by going for a walk or even leaving a city (see Robertson 2018: 30 or 80). Walking seems to constitute a technique that keeps this fire from actually breaking out; it represses what is "crackling underground" (Robertson 2018: 80) and therefore ensures that Walker's descent into dissolution, which finally occurs on the last pages of the book, is further postponed. Like Carla's bike rides in *What We All Long For*, walking serves Walker as a way to deal with emotional turmoil.

Moreover, walking is directly linked to practices of writing and reflecting. As the example quoted in the previous section shows, Walker reflects on what he perceives during his walks in short notes that he seems to produce after or during the walks themselves. The combination of the practice of writing with his interest in cities in general is the reason why Walker is offered a job at the *Press* and therefore further contributes to his reinvention of himself in Los Angeles:

> 'Have you worked on a newspaper before?'
> 'Well, sir, I was in the war...'
> 'Mr. Walker, that's not really the kind of experience I meant.'
> 'I'm well-read. Well-traveled. And I can write.
> I keep abreast of things.' And here he pulled out
> *City Development: Studies in Disintegration & Renewal*
> by Lewis Mumford, which Billy had given him as he left.
> (Robertson 2018: 54)[228]

Although Walker's job mostly consists in working at the city desk, covering often shocking cases of criminal activity that have taken place in the city, he also draws a new sense of purpose from his project of writing about impoverished and unhoused people in the skid row districts of Los Angeles and San Francisco. This particular project is once again linked to his practice of flânerie since he encounters those people during his walks on the streets of both cities. The combination of strolling, reflecting and writing actively produces a new sense of self in Walker and establishes his new identity. Flânerie, therefore, becomes a method of searching that leads to several kinds of transformation in Walker.

Moreover, the articles Walker produces based on his research constitute examples of active political resistance when published in the *Press* and derive directly from what De Certeau defined as the tactics of the ordinary citizen.[229] Thus, Walker's flânerie produces spaces later on translated into his reports which unveil a perspective onto the city that is different from the authorities' view of it as a playground for "*corporate* development" (Robertson 2018: 149; original emphasis). Importantly, the strength of his argument relies to a certain extent on Walker's particular perspective as a veteran since he often connects with the people on skid row through their shared experience of war and thus emphasizes the fact that those who risked their lives during the war and "fought for freedom" (Robertson 2018: 47) are now left alone by the very same country that sent them to war.

Nevertheless, flânerie is also ambivalent since Walker actively seeks out the anonymity of the city and the opportunity to constantly dissolve his identity and therefore temporarily free himself from his feelings of guilt. Already at the beginning of the text, the speaker indicates that Walker, like everyone else in the city, was drawn to it for its anonymity: "People; just like him. / Having given up the country for the city, / boredom for fear, the faces / gather here in these streets /

---

228 Mumford's study *City Development*, published in 1945, ties in with a general critique of capitalist and technocratic discourses of power that is often articulated by Walker's friend Billy Idaho and that constitutes one of the central political discourses in *The Long Take*.
229 See chapter 2.3.

like spectators in a dream. / They wanted to be anonymous / not swallowed whole, not to disappear" (Robertson 2018: 7).[230] The anonymity in the city, here, is explicitly constructed as being different from the idea of total disappearance and therefore seems to constitute a state in between the fixed identity that 'the country' might offer and the complete dissolution that the city in fact inflicts on its inhabitants according to Walker's first impression of it. Similarly, 'Walker', the flâneur, develops a new identity that is in between the dissolution implied at the end of the book and the fixed identity on the island that is described at the beginning, when he moves to the city:

> Back there in Broad Cove, on the island, it was just working the mines or the boats. Taking on the habit of the old ones – the long stare out to sea – becoming like a thorn tree, twisted hard to the shape of the wind, its grain following the grain of the weather; cloth caps and tweed, ruddy, raw-boned faces, wet eyes, silences that lasted weeks; the women wringing red hands or dishcloths or the necks of chickens just to make more silence. (Robertson 2018: 4)

As the quote indicates, options for identity construction on the island in Nova Scotia, where Walker was born, are limited – *"it was just working the mines or the boats"* – and follow a small set of rules already established by older generations. The zeugma in the last sentence seems to emphasize the elimination of difference which ultimately creates *"more silence"*.

His (new) identity as 'Walker', by contrast, is defined by his constant walking and thus allows for change without giving up the fixed characteristic of walking. The text itself represents this identity which finally disintegrates as soon as Walker's identity as a torturer is revealed and he refrains from or is no longer capable of using the practice of strolling as a flight from his feelings of guilt.

Before this, however, he creates an in-between space for himself that becomes possible because the city itself is marked by the dissolution of clear ethical boundaries between light and shadow – that is, good and evil – which is typical of the genre of film noir. On several occasions, the city is described as a labyrinth where light and shadow blend into each other so that orientation becomes difficult:

> Night.
>
> The city's gone.
> In its place, this gray stone maze, this
> locked geometry of shadows, blind and black,

---

[230] This is again emphasized in the first note he produces from his wanderings: **"Manhattan's the place for re-invention, mobility, anonymity, where everything is possible. It's what I came for"** (Robertson 2018: 17).

> and angles hurt into the sky, symmetries breaking
> and snapping back into line.
> The green Zs of fire-escapes; wires criss-
> crossing what's left of the light
> to a tight mesh.
> The buildings close
> around a dead-end, then
> spring open to the new future: repetition,
> back-tracking, error, loss.
> (Robertson 2018: 5–6)

At night – and much of Walker's strolling takes place at night – the city turns into a "gray stone maze" and thus dissolves the categories of black and white or light and shadow into a unified gray. The description of the city then features various verbs that all imply violence – such as "hurt", "breaking" or "snapping" – and discloses how the "geometry of shadows" impinges on "what's left of the light". The depiction of the buildings further suggests disorientation when dead-ends suddenly "spring open to the new future", even though this future only seems to lead to the association of "repetition, / back-tracking, error, loss" for Walker.

While the images of light and shadow are already traditionally coded as symbols of good and evil, this connection is underscored by *The Long Take*'s continuous reference to the genre of so-called film noir. As the term itself already implies, noir movies often depict a world that is marked by a blurring of the border between good and evil which is then again emphasized by the movies' play with light and shadow within the aesthetics of black-and-white film (see Spicer 2002: 4–5). *The Long Take* frequently indulges in images that allude to this dynamic (see, e.g., Robertson 2018: 9, 15 or 21 *et passim*) and further highlights the connection through the addition of black-and-white photographs, which in the case of the photographs enclosing the chapter on New York play quite explicitly with the dynamics of light and shadow (see Robertson 2018: 1 and 33).

Against this backdrop, Walker manages to escape a fixed classification of his identity according to the categories of what is morally good or evil:

> He walked for hours –
> Following the glow
> in the sky uptown he'd been told
> was the lights of Times Square –
> his shadow moving with him
> below the streetlamps: dense, tight,
> very black and sharp, foreshortened, but already
> starting to lengthen as he goes, attenuating
> to a weak stain. Then back in

> under another streetlight, shadow
> darkening again, clean and hard.
> Who he really is, or was,
> lies somewhere in between.
> (Robertson 2018: 11–12)

Walker's shadow – that is, his feelings of guilt that follow him throughout the entire text – sharpens as soon as it is confronted with light, whereas it seems to turn into nothing more than "a weak stain" as soon as he moves through the dark spaces between the street lights. The last two lines then link the image to Walker's identity which "lies somewhere in between" light and shadow or in between an amount of guilt that is symbolized by a very dark shadow and one that is represented by hardly visible contours.[231] In this sense, the practice of walking constantly transforms this shadow and finally culminates in a variable, hybrid identity with regard to moral integrity.[232]

Hence, Walker's flânerie serves as a technique of the self that enables the production of a counter-discourse on the level of plot that becomes manifest in the articles he publishes in the *Press*. Strolling through the city and communicating with its citizens creates a new identity for Walker that temporarily staves off feelings of guilt and loss. However, as the title suggests, Walker's flânerie enables the production of his resistant discourse, but cannot finally absolve him from his guilt, so that it only functions as "a way to lose more slowly", postponing his final descent into alcoholism. Yet, flânerie is once again also marked as an ambivalent practice that repeats central dynamics of the twentieth-century metropolis and is complicit with the loss of moral integrity described above. Walking itself therefore becomes a metaphor for a technique of the self that occupies a space between a negatively coded mode of acceleration and a resistant mode of deceleration which forms an explicit counterpoint to the rapid changes taking place in each of the metropolises depicted in the text.

---

231 Importantly, it is the shade that weakens the intensity of Walker's shadow, which conveys the impression that compared to the crime that takes place around Walker, his crimes are diminished.

232 To a certain extent, this dynamic is reminiscent of Edgar Allan Poe's short story "The Man of the Crowd" that showcases the unreadability of those who continue walking the city and thus, by lacking a place also lack an identity and cannot be discovered to be criminal.

8.2.3 History Repeating Itself? Precariousness and Circular Performances of Sovereignty in *The Long Take*

It is not only Walker's work as a journalist that is potentially resistant; *The Long Take* itself repeats the counter-discourse that Walker produces in his article. Especially through the voice of Billy Idaho, the text articulates its critique of capitalist ideology and demagogic hate speech, while at the same time foregrounding precariousness as a shared human condition. By implying the constant repetition of the logic of "war and struggle" (Foucault 2003b: 18) in the course of time, Robertson's book ultimately bridges the gap between Walker's period in history and the time of *The Long Take*'s publication – that is, the years covered by the Trump administration in the US.

Most of the text's overall criticism is uttered quite explicitly by the character Billy Idaho, a Black WWII veteran whom Walker meets on first moving to Los Angeles. Whenever the two of them meet Billy delivers short speeches, in which he dismantles the power structures defining the city in trenchant statements:

> When the war was over, the jobs were over,
> and the blacks moved south and the Japs were moved on.
> Just like all the ethnics – all zoned out.
> The Mexicans got pushed east and the Chinese north.
> That's what they do here – demolish houses and build freeways.
> It's the only city-planning there is – segregation.
> And greed, of course.
> (Robertson 2018: 47–48)

Like most of Walker's conversations with Billy, this first monologue focusses on the topic of the city's constant renewal and the ensuing marginalization of minorities in the wake of its continuous adaptation to the needs of hypercapitalism. Most importantly, Billy's criticism also dismantles the hate speech employed to create support for such transformations in the population:

> 'So, you see how it's changing?'
> 'I saw that freeway stack coming in on the plane. They finally did it.'
> 'No one to stop them. That's almost the end of public transport;
> now they're killing public housing. You hear about that?'
> 'Police Chief Parker?'
> 'Yeah. Anything Senator McCarthy can do …
> So Parker fingers the Housing Authority as a bunch of Commies,
> public housing as "creeping socialism" and now – wait for it –
> community development is shelved for *corporate* development.
> *Much* more important.

> And, courtesy of Mr Chandler's *Los Angeles Times*,
> he's got a Republican mayor on his side, Norris Poulson,
> and they're going after Chavez Ravine'.
> 'How do you mean? That's allocated for housing, eh?'
> 'At the moment. But they've cleared it – most of it –
> all those Mexican farmers, growing their own food on that land
> the last hundred years. Once it's cleared, that's it.
> The CRA can do anything.
> *We're only doing our jobs*, they keep saying.
> Seems like lying's just part of that job.'
> (Robertson 2018: 148–149; original emphasis)

Billy's explanation clearly points out how the language of McCarthyist politicians produces metaphorical slides in public discourse that attach the concept of public housing to what they call "creeping socialism" and thus to everything that might be linked to McCarthyist anxieties about Communism infiltrating the US. At the same time, the connection between economic interests and the construction of discourses of fear is explicitly pointed out alongside a reference to the minority who will suffer from the consequences of such political actions. This emphasis on dismantling the metaphorical connections in discourses of hate speech is a trademark of Billy's parrēsiastic monologues and serves the additional function of disclosing the precariousness of those groups who are affected by McCarthy's politics of fear:

> 'See, it's all about *functionality* now,
> which is speed, efficiency and profit.
> They call it a *clean sweep*
> to eradicate *crime* – which means blacks – to fumigate
> and disinfect the city against *disease*
> – Which means the black and the poor –
> to demolish *slums* and *blighted areas* – which means
> the homes and communities of the black and poor and old.'
> Billy took another mouthful of coffee, looked up at Walker:
> 'They call this *progress*, when it's really only greed.'
> (Robertson 2018: 79; original emphasis)

Here, Billy's translation has a twofold function: on the literal level he explains who McCarthyist politicians are actually referring to when they talk about 'crime', 'disease' and 'blighted areas' and thus points out how they associate negative attributes such as crime and sickness with precarious groups in postwar US society. Apart from that, Billy also hints at the real-life consequences of those strategies. Thus, the Republican politics aiming at an eradication of crime will be launched against Black communities because they are associated with crime according to the Republican mindset; the fumigation of the city against disease will be directed at those who are assumed to be counterproductive – and therefore unhealthy – for the capitalist ideal of functionality, like the Black population (who has already been identified with crime) and the poor (who cannot contribute to practices of consumption); and the demolition of slums will ultimately result in the destruction of the homes of those who cannot afford more expensive housing. The last remark here is especially interesting because it alludes to the reflection of power structures in the material reality of the city. Whereas the first two strategies imply that actions will be directed towards individual representatives of each group, the reference to the demolition of the impoverished parts of the city proves that actions are taken against entire targeted groups of the population. Moreover, Billy's counterdiscursive disentangling of the 'sticking' of emotions and concepts to certain groups of people highlights how the Republican hate speech uses terms belonging to the semantic field of destruction and eradication in order to refer to groups of human beings and thus to perpetuate the logic of war.

Importantly, Billy not only dismantles the rhetorical strategies employed in hate speech discourse, but also invokes the construction of a community based on the shared condition of the precariousness of human life. By adding ever larger parts of the population to the groups he refers to, he also points out how the ideal of functionality threatens those who are or might become vulnerable. The polysyndetic accretion of "the black and poor and old" crosses the borders of discursive othering and emphasizes how everyone could fall into a state of heightened precariousness. While members of the white population might feel safe from falling victim to the hate speech that is aimed at the Black population, this might not be the case with the other two groups that are named: even those who might not identify as poor could become poor one day – especially in the hypercapitalist social system of the US – and even those who are not old *will* inevitably become old one day. By joining several precarious groups into one community, Billy's discourse invites identification with those who are in a state of heightened precariousness and therefore forms an explicit counterpoint to a politics of functionality tied to an ideal of sovereignty that excludes precisely those states of vulnerability.

Whereas Billy Idaho's perspective on the politics of city renewal is just one among the many perspectives that Walker encounters during his strolls through the city, it is not only the one which takes up the most space, but also one that is supported by Walker's own observations. The racist structures that Billy explicitly names surface on various other occasions in the book, such as the racial slurs the bartender uses in order to refer to some of his customers during Walker's visit to a bar (see Robertson 2018: 29) or the very explicit remark of Walker's colleague Pike after having witnessed how Billy has been burnt alive (see Robertson 2018: 218). The city's measures against the poor and the old then become discernible in the gradual 'cleaning' of skid row and the district of Bunker Hill (see Robertson 2018: 208–226) which leads to the eviction of thousands of people who become unhoused due to those strategies of urban renewal. Walker's perspective therefore confronts the abstract discourses of hate speech with the immediate materiality of their effects. What is more, Walker's experiences in the impoverished districts of Los Angeles emphasize the possibility of a construction of community out of a shared sense of vulnerability when he attends the Bethel Gospel Mission's Christmas lunch titled *"For those of you alone at Christmas"* (Robertson 2018: 171; original emphasis) and makes new friends talking to veterans he encounters there.

But because Walker's particular point of view is framed by his sense of guilt, it deviates from Billy's perspective as regards the juxtaposition between the experience of war and the experience of the city. Although Billy acknowledges that he "know[s] what the war does to men" (Robertson 2018: 80), he also emphasizes the clear distinction between good and evil in the war: "You know something... / The war made sense at the time: / all in black and white, good and evil, they said" (Robertson 2018: 46). This situation is according to Billy very much opposed to what he experiences now after his return to the US: "At least in the war there was some common purpose – / in the same boat, all in it together, y'know? / Now here we are, in our own country, / scrambling over each other, just / trying to stay afloat" (Robertson 2018: 79).

Walker, by contrast, repeatedly associates the city and its dynamics with war when he thinks, for example, that "[c]ities are a kind of war" (Robertson 2018: 206) or remembers "every bar as a battlefield" (Robertson 2018: 21), therefore implying that the ethical relativism that Billy associates only with the city was, for him, already present during the war. As mentioned above, this analogy is supported by Walker's flashbacks and the numerous times in which what he sees or perceives in the city triggers memories of war in him. The common denominator between both experiences is the dehumanization of the other that takes place in contexts of war and the ensuing construction of 'ungrievable lives'. The focal point of Walker's experience of a deconstruction of the binary opposition between good and evil consists in the very plastic act of dehumanization that Walker committed when torturing an officer belonging to the SS by cutting off his ears, nose and lips during the war.

Drawing on Butler's reinterpretation of the Levinasian notion of the 'face' "as the extreme precariousness of the other" (Levinas 1996: 167), Walker's action can be interpreted in terms of a very literal act of "defac[ing]" (Butler 2004b: 143) the other. In *Precarious Life*, Butler explains how the representation of faces in the media and their association with absolute evil serves as a practice of dehumanization in order to advocate the necessity for war. *The Long Take* now shifts this dynamic to the level of experience: the face of the other is not created by the media, but primarily by Walker's very experience of war, and this complicates Butler's thesis by transferring it to the messy reality of war. The mutilation of the SS officer is thus Walker's direct affective reaction to having seen how the SS executed his comrades. At the same time, it showcases the precariousness that even this human being shares with others in the simple display of physical vulnerability. This is further emphasized through the judgement of Walker's acquaintance Frank who has been disfigured by SS soldiers during the war and to whom Walker confesses his story.

Interestingly, the "extreme precariousness" which the face represents does not take the form of an articulation of suffering in the actual scene that Walker remembers. Instead, the whole scene is weirdly muted and focuses almost exclusively on olfactory, visual and tactile impressions:

> He'd checked for the SS blood-tattoos, he remembered that: the hot stink there, inside of their left arms. But not the officer, the one with the Iron Cross at his neck. He kept looking into the distance, up into the burning sky. He smelled of French cologne. The edge was blunt by then, or maybe his face was really tough. The skin kept being dragged by the knife, not sliced, so he had to hold it flat, cursing, and work at it with a sawing motion. Where was he? Oh yes. Here. By the end there was so much blood his hands were getting slippery. He hated that: not being in control. Hated it. He cut off the ears. The nose. The lips. He left the eyes, so the German could see what had happened to him. So he would see. (Robertson 2018: 222)

While Walker's action is described in shocking detail, the officer's reaction seems to consist in "looking into the distance", which seems highly improbable. Suffering is implied by means of Frank's judgement, but it is not represented in Walker's memory since Walker does not perceive it according to the logic of war that requires erasing the shared condition of precariousness in the other. Walker's act of violence is then also a reflection of the attack on his own condition of precarious interdependence, which has been violated by the execution of his comrades. Taking revenge is a representation of his own experience of precariousness, thus reinstating feelings of sovereignty by locating vulnerability in the other.

Walker's confession, by contrast, becomes a technique of the self that he launches as an act of resistance against the ethically relativist world around him. Contrary to *Open City*'s Julius, Walker thus affirms the opposition between good and evil by constructing his subjectivity according to norms that distinguish between good and evil and that do not give in to the allure of ethical relativism. Walker's hope that Frank "would get it" (Robertson 2018: 220) is therefore ambiguous and might simply be fulfilled when Frank tells him "You're no better than them" (Robertson 2018: 222), thus affirming the norm of a clear distinction between good and evil by assigning an identity to Walker that assimilates him to the Nazis he has fought in the war. Although this entails Walker being confronted with his feelings of remorse and precipitates the end of his flânerie, it is also the sacrifice that enables him to performatively affirm a clear difference between good and evil.

At the same time, it has become increasingly clear by now that *The Long Take*, in accordance with Butler's claims in *Giving an Account of Oneself*,[233] suggests that Walker cannot be held fully accountable for his actions due to the traumatization he has undergone during the war. Frank's judgement, however, assumes precisely this and reduces Walker to an identity that he abhors, which contributes to his implied descent in the last pages of the novel. Hence, the novel problematizes the issue of accountability as discussed by Butler: whereas Walker's confession counteracts the violent potential of ethical relativism he might otherwise affirm, Frank's judgement likewise carries a certain amount of violence. A relativization of this judgement, however, would be equally problematic if it were extended to Frank's torturers. The central issue of the novel, the ethical evaluation of Walker's deeds, therefore, establishes two values at the same time: on the one hand, the text argues for a clear distinction between good and evil; on the other hand, it demands a differentiated and nuanced examination of each individual case.

Nevertheless, *The Long Take* also aims at a sedimentation of Butler's postulate of non-violence since it implicitly condemns violating the precariousness of the other by criticizing circular performances of sovereignty. Thus, Walker's action explicitly aims at regaining control and is therefore a performance of sovereignty that is supposed to cover and annihilate the losses (of control) he has experienced. In order to perform this sovereignty, Walker has to install precariousness in the other, which he does by torturing the SS officer. Importantly, this act of 'defacement' that occurs in contexts of war according to Butler, repeatedly resurfaces in the novel not just in Walker's memories of war, but – on the level of representation – also in the politics of fear championed by McCarthyist discourse. When Billy describes how the terms 'crime', 'disease' and 'blighted areas' are used in order to refer to actual human beings, he points out how McCarthyist politics actively deface those whom they attempt to eradicate. This analogy is further highlighted by the merging of the paradigm of war with the

---

[233] See chapter 4.3.

8.2 Intermedial Encounters in Robin Robertson's *The Long Take* — 261

depiction of the city as seen from Walker's perspective. And indeed, the link to fascism is explicitly drawn by one of Walker's interlocutors in San Francisco: "McCarthyism is fascism. Exactly the same. Propaganda and lies, / opening divisions, fueling fear, paranoia. Just like the thirties: / a state of emergency, followed by fascism, followed by war. / You've just defeated Hitler. / Can't anyone see you've made another, all of your own?" (Robertson 2018: 130). The authority of this statement is underscored by the fact that the speaker is a "Social Democrat and Jew, who'd lived through Weimar, / got out of Berlin in '33, knew his history of displacement, tyranny" (Robertson 2018: 129).[234]

Hence, the text suggests a circular movement of history which repeats the same performances of sovereignty based on a dehumanization of the other over and over again, and this raises the question as to what a text published in 2018 might refer to by depicting this kind of dynamic in the 1940s and '50s in the US. An answer might already be gleaned from the above quotation's allusion to "Propaganda and lies, / opening divisions, fueling fear, paranoia", but the link is made explicit in the appendix to Robertson's text: there, an explanation is added to a reference to the Army-McCarthy hearings which points out that "McCarthy's legal adviser was Roy Cohn, who had been instrumental in the 1951 trial of the Rosenbergs for espionage and their subsequent conviction and execution based on manipulated evidence. In the 1970s, Cohn was the friend, mentor and legal adviser to Donald Trump" (Robertson 2018: 235). The mention of Donald Trump, who at the time of *The Long Take*'s publication had been president of the US for two years, is telling in this context because it builds a trail to a couple of legal cases regarding discrimination quite similar to what is depicted in *The Long Take*, yet this time the culprit is Trump himself. Roy Cohn, for example, represented Trump in a lawsuit that accused the Trump Management Corporation of refusing to rent their apartments to African Americans (see Kaplan 1973: 1; Dunlap 2015: n. pag.). According to this logic, African Americans are again associated with 'crime', 'disease' and 'blighted areas' and therefore are denied housing. Based on this analogy, additional parallels can be drawn between the McCarthyist politics of fear and Trumpist propaganda. Moreover, the allusion to Trump further underscores the economic motivation behind strategies of discrimination. What is more, the text gains an even prophetic quality when seen from the perspective of the events of 6 January 2021, when demagogic hate speech was in fact turned into physical attack, thus affirming the analogy between Trumpist politics and fascism that *The Long Take* implicitly suggests. How-

---

234 However, the aforementioned problematization of judgement also implies that those parallels still have to be placed under scrutiny and are still marked by deferral.

ever, a differentiated and nuanced examination is once again called for by the text owing to the difference that any repetition entails and that is emphasized through the temporal distance between the events on the level of plot and the political reality of its recipients.

The Long Take's 'deep focus' on the dynamics of war and struggle and strategies of dehumanization in political discourse then draws a trajectory of various repetitions of those performances of sovereignty that project precariousness onto the other instead of acknowledging it as a shared condition throughout history. In this, Walker's flânerie forms the basis for the text's overall negotiation of subjectivity, sovereignty and precariousness which reflects on the possibilities of post-sovereign subjectivity.

8.2.4 The Aestheticization of City Life: Film Noir and the Tradition of Flânerie in *The Long Take*

The Long Take adds one more level of reflection to its overall performance of resistance. As delineated in section 8.2.1, the book also relies on an intermedial connection to film in general and to the genre of film noir in particular. Especially this last relationship can be linked to flânerie as an ambivalent mode of resistance with regard to its problematic entanglement with capitalism. Similarly, the text alludes to film noir's ambivalent dealings with the historical circumstances of the McCarthy era and, more broadly, to film's connection, as a medium, to general phenomena of capitalist acceleration.

First of all, film noir is *the* governing paradigm that determines the structure and content of the whole text. Not only does the text contain several references to film noir movies, but Walker also talks to director Fred Zinnemann in Los Angeles and encounters several film sets during his strolls through the city. Moreover, the book features several stock characters of film noir among which the "alienated, often psychologically disturbed, male anti-hero" (Spicer 2002: 5) is especially prominent. While "the hard, deceitful *femme fatale* he encounters" (Spicer 2002: 5) might be absent from the cast of characters, her place is taken up by the cities themselves which are traditionally metaphorically charged with femininity (see Weigel 1990). Fittingly, Walker is taken in by the allure of New York's glamour when approaching the city for the first time:

> And there it was: the swell
> and glitter of it like a standing wave –
> the fabled, smoking ruins, the new towers rising
> through the blue,

> the ranked array of ivory and gold, the glint,
> the glamour of buried light
> as the world turned round it
> very slowly
> this autumn morning, all amazed.
> (Robertson 2018: 3)

This first impression of New York links the beauty of the city to its display of wealth and thus combines its feminine beauty with capitalist achievements that cause the world to "turn[] round it" "all amazed". As soon as Walker and the truck driver get closer to it, however, the city disappears and what remains is "a black wetness / of streets trashed and empty" (Robertson 2018: 3). This motif of deception is even more palpable with respect to Los Angeles, which is described by Billy in the following way: "But none of it's real, and nothing's *from* here. I'm not, / you're not, *nobody* is – not even the *palm trees* are from here – / the buildings are all just sets and stage-flats / because no one can keep up with the city" (Robertson 2018: 52; original emphasis).

Second, the convoluted dynamics of light and vision in the cities mirror the disorienting aesthetics of film noir's visual style where "deep, enveloping shadows are fractured by shafts of light from a single source" and along with "odd angles and wide-angle lenses" create "unstable, decentred combinations" (Spicer 2002: 4). Most often, those aesthetics occur in descriptions of the "dark, night-time city", "claustrophobic alleyways and deserted docklands alternat[ing] with gaudy nightclubs and swank apartments" (Spicer 2002: 4) – that is, basically all the locations where *The Long Take*'s plot takes place.

Third, even the narrative structure is reminiscent of film noir aesthetics with its frequently occurring flashbacks and ellipses and the heterodiegetic narrative voice that describes Walker's experiences in the city and that could be interpreted as representative of film noir's common technique of the voice-over.

In brief, *The Long Take* is a film noir turned into text that puts up a mirror to American society. In the same way that film noir critically reflects the anxieties and paranoia of the post-war era (see Spicer 2002: 19–22), *The Long Take* draws on this genre's central characteristics in order to dismantle the dehumanizing strategies of Trumpist America's politics of fear.

Nevertheless, the text also alludes to the way in which art might become complicit with oppressive forces when referring to Edward Dmytryk's movie *Sniper:*

> A few days after, they've sealed off Filbert Street at Grant,
> and cops with megaphones are keeping back crowds
> at the auto repair shop on the corner.

> He knows the director from a mugshot in the papers:
> Dmytryk, one of the Hollywood Ten,
> back in business after naming names.
> (Robertson 2018: 127)

What the quote refers to is Dmytryk's return to the United States film industry after having denounced several members of the American Communist Party. Dmytryk had been banned from working in the US due to being listed among the so-called Hollywood Ten, a group of American film-industry individuals who were accused of being affiliated with Communist activities (see Barson 2013: n. pag.). After his return, his movies became apolitical due to the pressure and restrictions of the McCarthyist government, to which he had yielded.

While *The Long Take* indulges extensively in film noir aesthetics, it nevertheless also reflects on the more problematic entanglements of its production. Moreover, the text not only deviates from the genre's overall cynical tone when emphasizing the possibility of friendship between Walker and other veterans, but it also critically reflects on the medium of film itself. Most importantly, although *The Long Take* seems to emulate the genre of film noir, it, in fact, is not a film. Likewise, the text's subtitle, *A Way to Lose More Slowly*, does not refer only to Walker preferring a stroll to a drive through the city, but just as much to the fact that *reading The Long Take* as a text takes up much more time than *watching* it as a movie would take. As the ending of the book implies, the medium of writing has, temporarily, actually suspended Walker's downfall, yet the text is finally taken over by the end of the roll of film, which terminates with one last sequence:

> He saw old people dancing in slow motion, in the scratchy
> black-and-white of a ciné-film, moving in their long strathspey,
> slow and stately to some silent fiddle and accordion, passing
> through each other, through each other's hands and bodies,
> the women turning
> under the turning hands, disappearing. Ghosts of one another.
> The film sticks, the projector judders to a halt, jams.
> The celluloid burning yellow, bubbles, tearing to white.
>
> *click*
>
> He reached the corner of 5th and Pedro,
> posting the knife with a *plip* through the ribs of a storm-drain,
> laid down copies of the *Press* on the blackened sidewalk,
> the one with the last of his bulletins,
> then set his duffle bag on top.
> Someone offered a cigarette, some pieces of bread,

another passed him a bottle, which he twisted open.
Thunderbird Red. It was the best thing he'd ever tasted.

click

He thought he could hear the weather: the last reel
played on the pipes, the wind in the trees, the sound of deer
running in the high fields.
He looked around at his comrades-in-arms, 'Remember me,'
then closed his eyes.
'I can stop now,' he said,
putting his mouth to the mouth of the bottle,
'I'll make my city here.'
(Robertson 2018: 225–226; original emphasis)

The first of the three images already foreshadows the fast-approaching ending of the book by metareflexively referring to a projector "judder[ing] to a halt" and linking this to the gradual disappearance of the people in the movie. The "*click*" that separates the three images from each other then refers to the sound of the movie projector slowly coming to a halt until Walker affirms that he "can stop now" and gives in to alcoholism. Hence, the passage suggests that turning this "noir narrative" into written text has indeed been a tactic of deceleration while being at the same time unable to escape writing's and film's shared characteristic of linearity that inevitably propels the protagonist forward.

The replacement of the usual asterisks that represent the cuts between individual scenes with the clicking of the movie projector acquires an additional twist through its connection with the character Pike who has been called "a progenitor of selfie culture" by reviewer Sibbie O'Sullivan (2018: n. pag.). As O'Sullivan notes, Pike represents the future, but above all else he represents a future performed via moving images. Thus, Pike "was always in a movie" (Robertson 2018: 205), "pushing into the frame" and "waiting for the moment to smile" (Robertson 2018: 153). He is associated with constant performance, being "**[l]oud, full of brag**" (Robertson 2018: 68) and "look[ing] around, / [to give] the room one of his fascinating smiles" (Robertson 2018: 105). Moreover, Pike is diametrically opposed to Walker in terms of velocity: if Walker represents deceleration in an increasingly accelerated world, then Pike has entirely submitted to this acceleration so that he "just wouldn't stop moving" (Robertson 2018: 105), "restless, learning the short cuts / eating anything" (Robertson 2018: 153) and "snapping the lid of his Zippo, clicking it / up and down, up and down / as if to illustrate his restless intelligence" (Robertson 2018: 85). The leitmotif of restlessness is further emphasized by the continuous clicking sound that turns into a polyvalent symbol in the course of the book, becoming associated with the aforementioned lighter, with the "clicking of his ballpoint pen down the corridors" (Robertson 2018: 153) or with Pike "clicking his fingers impatiently" (Robertson 2018: 154) before stealing an apple, until it transforms into the sound of the movie projector at the end of the book when, before the very last section, the narrative voice states that "Pike was following him, at a distance. / *Click. Click. Click.*" (Robertson 2018: 225; original emphasis)

The ending highlights once more Walker's – as well as the flâneur's – paradoxical relationship to acceleration. While the act of sitting down on the sidewalk and the simultaneous slowing down and halting of the movie projector obviously cause Walker's ending as well as that of the book, he is also driven towards this fate by several factors that all include acceleration or movement. Thus, on the level of plot, Walker partly gives in to Los Angeles's dynamics of renewal and reinvention which engender the destruction of the district in which he has lived so far and in which he started to find a home after having felt "fucking lost" (Robertson 2018: 69) for most of the book. Second, the fact that Pike's clicking sound at first approaches and then increasingly infiltrates Walker's story further implies that acceleration plays a vital part in Walker's ending. Finally, the book itself relies on the linearity of forward movement which is again emphasized in its uncanny doubling with the moving images of film. Similarly, Walker needs the city to re-invent himself anew after his experiences in WWII, but he is just as much threatened by the city's submission to capitalist forces.

Consequently, just as text and film become doppelgangers, complementing as well as fighting each other in *The Long Take*, Walker and Pike can also be considered as forming a pair of doppelgangers, with Pike representing the uncanny aspects of Walker's flirtation with the opportunities of the city. Both characters are young men working at the *Press* and both have a conflictual relationship with morality. Yet, while Walker struggles with his feelings of remorse, Pike, like *The Blindfold*'s Paris, is the embodiment of ethical relativism. Thus, Walker describes him as being "**[a]ssertive, but with no real personality, no balance or integrity**" (Robertson 2018: 68) and the narrative voice refers to him as having "the moral integrity of George Raft" (Robertson 2018: 85).[235] Pike then represents the journalism of the tabloid press, striving for attention from all sides, irrespective of moral reservations, and therefore hints at one strand of the 'future' of American journalism that will later become manifest in media such as Fox News or Rush Limbaugh's take on the genre of 'talk radio'. Consequently, Pike is also a racist and antisemite, as his comments about Billy's death (Robertson

---

235 George Raft was a Hollywood actor known for his involvement with the LA underworld (see Aaker 2013: 1).

2018: 218) and about the Jewish director Joseph H. Lewis show (Robertson 2018: 166).

Pike ultimately returns us to what Bauman has called the 'postmodern flâneur', the representation of late-capitalist constructions of identity already referred to in the Introduction. This "*flâneur* mode of life" (Bauman 2015: 152), marked by the notion of "ultimate play" (Bauman 2015: 142), prefers fiction over reality and ultimately dissolves reality by means of fiction. One consequence of this is that identity based on fiction can always be created anew so that "the game never ends" (Bauman 2015: 152). Bauman's 'postmodern flâneur' is closely linked to Baudrillard's concept of the 'hyperreal' which recurs in Bauman in the form of Baudrillard's famous example of Disneyland. It is no surprise therefore that the 'postmodern flâneur' should encounter his true medium in the videotape, which finally absolves him from moving around because now, the images move for him:

> You can buy or rent the tape that does the dreaming and playing for you. If you are lucky and privileged, you may buy or rent a camcorder so that you can script and direct the lives of yourself and your nearest and dearest after the pattern of bought or rented dreams and plays, and make it feel *real*, after the standards of reality they set, by recording it as a play. To be sure, there is not much choice, as by now you probably know of no other way of living your life. (Bauman 2015: 155)

The moving images offer a selection of dreams, scripting how one can play one's own life. The flâneur, who is observer and performer at once, re-creates his identity on screen "by recording it as a play". The comparison seems even more fitting in light of the new opportunities that the internet and social media like Twitter, Instagram, Snapchat or TikTok offer to their users who can reconstruct their identity in the virtual realm according to prescribed templates. *The Long Take*'s Pike, who is "always in a movie", fits this description exceptionally well. He constantly rebuilds his identity according to the demands of the market and thus consumes the roles that are on offer for him. But Walker is also performing his identity in the city according to the template of film noir since he does not know of any "other way of living [his] life". The fact that this filmic performance is transferred to the realm of text, however, constitutes an instance of resistance, although it is not quite discernible due to the heterodiegetic voice that dominates most of the text, whether this transferral is Walker's own decision to talk about himself in the third person – which would turn the text into his own resistant performance – or whether discourse has assigned him only a marginalized position and therefore relocated him to the medium of scripture. *The Long Take*'s transgressive form therefore emphasizes the blurred border between intentional acts of resistance and the unintentional kind of resistance implicit in any deviation from the norm.

Cities, and especially Los Angeles, with its connection to the movie industry and its generalized unreality – as noted above – then become Walker and Pike's Disneyland, which is even further emphasized by each of the cities' as well as the entirety of California's link to carnival. Thus, while dwelling in San Francisco Walker reflects on his experience of California as **"a playground, solely designed for our entertainment – colorful, exotic, transporting, like a carnival – and it *is* just that: a carnival. A crude travesty of childhood happiness: a pageant of loss"** (Robertson 2018: 134). This idea of carnival as "a travesty of childhood happiness" occurs several times in Walker's descriptions of different manifestations of carnival. Coney Island, for example, is exposed as an illusion where "[b]y day, you can see she's made of pasteboard, held together / by nuts and bolts, metal frames – that the huge clown's head / is chipped, the painted façades all faded, peeling" (Robertson 2018: 18) and the funfair he strolls through in San Francisco is revealed to be governed by the principle of "fear" and "the high-wheel of fortune and despair: that / thin glimpse of joy and freedom, before / rattling back to earth, loose-legged and spinning" (Robertson 2018: 132). Thus, the space of the city is linked to the dynamics of hyperreality as well as the concomitant ethical relativism – both embodied in the character Pike – yet the city is also the space of those who live in precarious conditions, as emphasized by the text's focus on materiality. By means of the carnivalesque funfair's metonymical relationship to the city – the narrative voice points out with regard to Coney Island that "Manhattan's the same, just better made" (Robertson 2018: 18) – the bleak materiality of the precarious city breaks through the glamourous surface of the possibility of endless play.

This dynamic places Walker in the conflictual situation of the Benjaminian flâneur and its variations: he is drawn to the city and its masses, but he is also in a relation of antagonism to its acceleration and its orientation towards capitalist profit. The text's intermedial relationship to film noir then reflects this overall condition since Walker is to a certain extent intrigued by the opportunities of the city as much as he is fascinated by the possibilities of the medium of film. Consequently, his flânerie is only a temporary phenomenon and will at some point run the risk of being entirely absorbed into the city's game of hyperreality. As Baudrillard writes in *The Spirit of Terrorism*, there is only one way to escape the logic of exchange that allows capitalism to devour whatever comes in its way, and this option is death itself since it cannot be exchanged for anything else (Baudrillard 2012: 7). Walker's decision to "stop now" at the end of *The Long Take* and thus give up his identity as 'Walker, the flâneur' is also a last attempt at resistance to the constant fluidity of the hyperreal metropolis. His death as a flâneur here coalesces with the end of the story and his implied descent into alcoholism, but it also problematizes the issue of effective resistance by finally excluding him from any further participation in the discourses that shape this society. Fittingly, the copies of the *Press* he brings with him contain "the last of his bulletins" and therefore mark the end of his work as a journalist.

The depiction of the precariousness of Walker's situation and that of the other unhoused people is what *The Long Take* sets against capitalism's endless game of reinvention. While – as the reference to "Thunderbird Red" implies – their situation can still be exploited by the market, this is not the case with death itself. Everything that happens before runs the risk of becoming incorporated into the market along with the highly aestheticized description of the precarious cities themselves. In the same way that the Parisian flâneur's aestheticization of the city which is being transformed according to the plans of Baron Haussmann collaborates with the capitalist discourses of power (see Brand 1991: 7–8), *The Long Take*, too, is an homage to the city as well as to the medium of film and thus contributes to the celebration of movement and acceleration which it at the same time criticizes. The reference to film noir thus also points towards the text's own ambiguous status with regard to the capitalist forces it criticizes. After all, *The Long Take*, like most works of art in our days, is a commodity that needs to be sold to its audience. The noir aestheticization – as horrific as it might be at times – of the city as *femme fatale* ruled over by the mechanisms of technocratic capitalism then might lure the reader into the dynamics of endless play while also warning them of the dangers of their alignment with discourses of power.

The numerous medial, formal and generic transgressions that *The Long Take* undertakes open up ever new perspectives onto the arbitrariness of the norms produced by discourses of power and therefore emphasize the necessity to defer norms in ever new performances of 'promiscuous obedience'. As the ambivalent coding of the trope of the flâneur suggests, however, this principle needs to be checked by an affirmation of ethical norms, the application of which needs to be subjected to continuous reflection.

9 Conclusion

As the works discussed in this book show, contemporary Anglophone flânerie texts negotiate post-sovereign performances of subjectivity in a variety of ways. Drawing on the paradoxical basic constellation of the trope of the flâneur and its link to conditions of subjection and performances of resistance as envisioned by Walter Benjamin, the texts analyzed in my study showcase individual examples of the Foucauldian aesthetics of existence and explicitly affirm the precarious as a *conditio humana*, thus deferring the conceptual norm of subjectivity towards the post-sovereign. In this, the ambivalence of flânerie highlights the complexity of resistance and critique in the twentieth and twenty-first centuries, yet also serves as a paradigm that allows for the conceptualization of ethical subjecthood after the 'death of man'.

The trope of the flâneur as well as the paradigm of flânerie are notoriously hard to define due to the plethora of functionalizations and redefinitions that the flâneur has undergone over time. Although there is already a certain contradiction implied in the fact that the flâneur stands for acceleration and deceleration at the same time, numerous paradoxical constellations have been added to the trope such as a combination of proximity and distance, performance and observation or simply life and death, due to the flâneur's continuous revitalization in discourses which simultaneously announce the end of flânerie. Those contradictions then famously recur in Walter Benjamin's functionalization of the flâneur in his historical-materialist analysis of the nineteenth century which interprets the figure as directly representative of the incorporation of the writer into the market and thus locates the flâneur in a complex web of resistance and subjection. Particularly Benjamin's additional configuration of flânerie as a *techne* that centers on giving up one's sovereignty offers an interesting link to the concepts of Foucault and Butler. This connection surfaces, for example, in conceptions of walking as performance which mostly occur in poststructuralist theories of space that envision space as being dynamically produced by means of movement. The concept of flânerie as performance then ties in with those approaches while also foregrounding flânerie as a kind of walking whose resistant potential is particularly emphasized. Apart from this new focus on the material side of flânerie, I have also suggested a reconsideration of the significance of intermediality in the tradition of flânerie and the ways in which it represents and problematizes the flâneur's primary modes of perception.

Like the connection between flânerie and intermediality, the tradition of flânerie in British, American and New English literatures is still a somewhat neglected field of study, although a great variety of Anglophone flânerie literature does exist. Interestingly, a variant of the flâneur *avant la lettre* occurs almost a century earlier in Great Britain than in France and it is especially this flâneur as well as his nineteenth-century successors who fit Benjamin's analogy between flâneur and commodity exceptionally well. This, however, is not to say that the British as well as the Anglophone tradition of flânerie do not contain just as many examples of sociocritical flânerie as the French, for example, in the work of Charles Dickens.

Ultimately, although flânerie is a phenomenon that is particularly hard to define, a couple of characteristics emerge from the various perspectives onto flânerie presented here which can be collected into a heuristic model of what could be called the flânerie text. Thus, flânerie texts usually feature a somewhat episodic form that might, for example, result in a reduction of plot in narrative texts. Moreover, they are always set in the space of the city and are particularly prone to different kinds of hybridity and the concomitant notion of transgression. Especially the last characteristic makes the flânerie text particularly well suited to the negotiation of forms of partly resistant subjectivity.

Models of those forms of subjectivity are offered by the late writings of Michel Foucault and the work of Judith Butler. The Foucauldian ethics of the self center around the idea of a partly autonomous subject which is still subjected to discourses of power, yet at the same time manages to not be governed 'that much' by them. This subject can be described in terms of the 'aesthetics of existence', an active self-stylization and self-formation of the subject that relies on various practices of the care of the self; these take the form of techniques of the self as methods of searching in which the subject seeks to transform itself employing various techniques derived from ancient Greek dietetics. Among those practices the dimensions of writing, truth-speaking and experience are particularly noteworthy in their production of difference in the subject.

The Foucauldian 'aesthetics of existence', however, do not yet envision a conception of ethics that focuses on the self as being primarily relational, although the other at times plays a significant role in the techniques of the self. It is then only in Butler's concept of post-sovereign subjectivity that the aspect of relationality is put into focus. In their work, Butler expands on a Foucauldian conception of subjectivity based on the assumption that subjects are not only subjected to discourses of power, but produced by them. According to Butler, subjects form themselves by means of potentially resistant performances which are based on the norms offered by a matrix of intelligibility consisting of different options of performance. Those norms, however, are only transmitted by means of the performance of individual subjects and thus always already deferred. Moreover, each encounter with an other bears the potential of further transformation so that the individual subjects' longing for recognition becomes a gateway to resistance. This longing for recognition derives, according to Butler, from the subject's primary condition of vulnerability and precariousness, which produces an "ecstatic" subject that is located outside of itself. In order to protect this primary condition of vulnerability, a post-sovereign subjectivity has to be developed that acknowledges its own precarious condition and orientates its actions towards this shared condition of precariousness. In this, resistance to normalization in the form of a "promiscuous obedience" that aims at maximizing the individual's performance options is just as important as the sedimentation of certain norms which protect the subject from succumbing to ethical relativism.

Both Foucault's and Butler's approaches then contribute to the imaginary of a new post-sovereign subjectivity, yet in order to sediment into a new, persistent narrative of the subject, they have to be continually translated into the socio-political reality of the twentieth and twenty-first centuries, as exemplified by the five flânerie texts I have analyzed in my study.

Ian McEwan's *Saturday* constitutes a case that marks the border between technologies of the self and technologies of domination and serves as a counterpoint to the other examples of post-sovereign subjectivity discussed in the book. McEwan's Henry Perowne, a Benjaminian 'man of the crowd' who is not a flâneur himself but does evoke the tradition of flânerie, remains a sovereign subject in his actions towards Baxter despite his confrontation with his own condition of primary vulnerability. What is more, the novel highlights how the demand to perform sovereignty leads to repetitive cycles of violence and thus subjects the individual to the necessity of engaging in potentially hazardous behavior. However, whereas transformation seems to be mostly denied to Perowne, the novel's intense intertextual play opens up a literary memory space to the reader that de-centers the writing as well as reading subject. By means of this intertextual flânerie, the text paves the way for the potential development of a non-sovereign reading subject. Nevertheless, the novel does not offer any explicit model of post-sovereign subjectivity, which is then only offered by the novels to follow.

In Siri Hustvedt's *The Blindfold*, flânerie is shown to be a precarious performance of resistance that constitutes a technique of the self in the protagonist's aesthetics of existence which become manifest in the text itself. During her wanderings, Iris Vegan gives herself up to a possible transformation through the eyes of others who perceive her as masculine due to the practice of cross-dressing that she adopts when strolling through the nighttime metropolis of New York. In this context, the way in which Iris's suit "effectively blurs [her] gender" is of particular importance because it questions the norm of a clear-cut division between masculinity and femininity and thus forms a model for her practice of deconstructing the binary opposition between a human predetermination to violence and the possibility that humans are not predetermined to violence. The subjectivity which she projects in her account of her time in New York is decidedly precarious, but at the same time admits the possibility of escaping the circular violence that continuous performances of sovereignty and the ensuing "logic of war" might produce. Consequently, her narrative openly emphasizes the restriction of her perspective and self-reflexively marks the non-sovereignty of her account, thus affirming the ontological 'fiction' of precariousness.

Teju Cole's *Open City* dovetails nicely with Hustvedt's novel, with which it shares several characteristics. Like Hustvedt's protagonist Iris Vegan, *Open City*'s autodiegetic narrator Julius is construed as an alter ego of his author so that both novels deliberately play with the boundary between fact and fiction while remaining explicitly rooted in the realm of fiction. However, *Open City* engages centrally with societal norms of truth-production and truth-speaking by means of Julius's parrēsiastic aesthetics of existence. In the novel, flânerie becomes a technique of the self for Julius that actively aims at juxtaposing his strictly regulated environment at work with the disorientation and chaos that the city offers. Here, knowledge and perception become fragile since Julius's assumptions are constantly challenged by his experiences in the city, with direct communication as well as reflection often revealing the limited validity of visual perception, although neither of these can produce anything like a sovereign subject of knowledge. The impossibility of sovereign knowledge in the form of an absolute notion of truth is further underscored by the formal peculiarity of Julius's 'underreporting', a rather rare case of unreliable narration. This is particularly interesting since Julius's account – albeit fictional – usually mimics factual speech so that the truthfulness of his narration is marked by norms which pertain to the construction of truth in the twenty-first century. Nevertheless, the parrēsiastic speech of his friend Moji uncovers the sinister entanglement of power and truth in Julius's story without rendering the entire narration untruthful. In this, her act of *parrēsia* emphasizes the limitation and potential violence of Julius's perspective in a similar way that his parrēsiastic collection of marginalized voices in the city counteracts white hegemonic discourses of power. The inclusion of her account constitutes an important paradox with respect to the form of subjectivity represented in Julius's narrative. Here, Julius instrumentalizes the precariousness and opacity of perspective in order to turn himself into a sovereign subject as regards his moral evaluation. Yet, although he claims that his audience will not be troubled upon hearing of his "being the villain in someone else's story", this assessment appears doubtful given Moji's accusations. Moreover, the question remains as to why exactly Julius has included her narration in his story in the first place if he actually thinks that it will not influence the reader's judgement. Contrary to his claims that "we are not the villains of our own story", the inclusion of her account in fact affirms the relationality of identity construction because he also deems it necessary to indirectly comment on it. Ultimately, Julius's narration could be interpreted as an instance of parrēsiastic critique which, by means of a fictional performance, uncovers not only a central paradox in our production of truth – namely that an extreme objectivization of discourse might become just as potentially violent as an extreme subjectivization of discourse – but also the problematic proximity of the Foucauldian 'aesthetics of existence' to a dandyesque amoralism. The text itself then emphasizes precariousness as a shared *conditio humana*, while at the same time negotiating the potential entanglement of the techniques of the self with new performances of sovereignty, which is based on a transformation towards ethical relativism. As in *The Blindfold*, flânerie is shown to be a precarious practice that oscillates between instilling sovereignty and non-sovereignty in the subject.

Hustvedt's and Cole's novels then showcase two variants of the Foucauldian aesthetics of existence that, given the homodiegetic narration employed in the texts, rely on writing as well as strolling as techniques of the self. The contrast in form between the texts, however, is striking: while Iris Vegan's asymmetrical account of her time in New York explicitly develops towards coherence and thus suggests a process of development and transformation, Julius's narration is decidedly symmetrical and therefore emphasizes formation over a possible transformation, or rather makes constant transformation its norm, thus showcasing an entirely fluid identity. In both cases, the texts themselves exemplify self-reflexive performances of resistance situated in – in Hustvedt's case – feminist as well as – in Cole's case – postcolonial counter-discourses.

Dionne Brand's novel *What We All Long For* shares *Open City*'s postcolonial agenda, but places a stronger emphasis on the significance of the other as well as an affective relationality in the development of post-sovereign subjectivity. Brand presents a variety of different aesthetics of existence against the backdrop of a continuously fluid, affectively charged metropolis that offers the ideal precondition for any kind of transformation. Flânerie occurs here in different forms and with different aims as a technique of the self that potentially transforms each of the characters, although the results of those transformations are also problematized and contribute to the novel's overall negotiation of responsibility. Thus, Tuyen, the daughter of Vietnamese immigrants, incorporates flânerie in her general strategy for staving off her family by means of her artistic projects, only to be led back to it through her encounter with her brother Quy on one of her strolls, albeit with a changed attitude that accepts the 'more precarious' part of her identity. Her "ecstatic" flânerie here truly carries her out of herself by paradoxically bringing her back to her family and involving her in her brother's project of redemption. Tuyen's practice of strolling is noteworthy because it relies to a large extent on the modification of her perspective by means of her camera and therefore suggests how techniques of the self can incorporate specific media in order to defamiliarize the surroundings and thus to 'experiment in foreign knowledge'. The further results of her transformation, however, are problematic since Tuyen's newfound identification with her family also entails taking control of their process of reconciliation which ultimately causes the near-death of her brother Quy.

Tuyen's assumption of responsibility is juxtaposed with Carla's relinquishment of responsibility for her brother Jamal, a transformation that is likewise precipitated by her specific kind of flânerie as a technique of the self. Carla's bike rides can be located at the border between rigid power structures that assign her what Butler calls an 'unlivable life' due to her parents' infringement of societal norms of racial separation, and specific means of resistance that affirm her existence through physical movement and a deliberate confrontation with her material environment. Although her hazardous engagement with the city has an auto-aggressive side to it that repeats the inscription of the 'unlivable life' on her body, Carla's ability to cruise the city on her bike actively invokes her physical presence despite its supposed 'impossibility'. Nevertheless, this practice also leads to Carla cutting the remaining ties to her family and leaving her brother to his criminal activities, which ultimately results in the tragic ending of the novel. By juxtaposing Carla's activities with those of Tuyen, *What We All Long For* problematizes various approaches to responsibility, emphasizing its entanglement with power and control in the case of Tuyen and highlighting the potentially brutal consequences of letting go of responsibility in the case of Carla, even though the novel also points out that it would be equally problematic for Carla to continue shouldering responsibility for her brother. By problematizing those different modalities of responsibility, the novel effectively engages in a critique of ethical violence.

The character Oku, by contrast, performs a more 'traditional' kind of flânerie when strolling through the desolate area of Alexandra Park in order to learn more about his love interest Jackie, who grew up in this area. His attempts at empathy, however, are problematized by catachrestic slides on the level of form that highlight the proximity between empathy and projection. Despite the partly contested validity of his assumptions, Oku's flânerie most definitely causes a transformation in him since he decides at the end of his stroll to let go of his rather hedonistic lifestyle and try to provide what he assumes to be a safe environment for Jackie, due to his recognition of their mutual interdependence. This example, in particular, illustrates the novel's emphasis on the transformative power of the sliding of affects; it thus ties in with Butler's notion of emotions as a gateway to transformation and the recognition of relationality – and consequently a post-sovereign subjectivity.

Nevertheless, *What We All Long For* also foregrounds how emotions contribute to the sedimentation of power structures by 'sticking' certain concepts to certain bodies, as exemplified by Carla, who repeatedly experiences her existence as an 'unlivable life' owing to the continuous emotion of hate that has been attached to her. Affects are therefore shown to perform an ambivalent function in processes of subject formation and can either counteract or support discourses of power. The foregrounding of emotion ties in with the affirmation of an overall human condition of precariousness in *What We All Long For*, yet the novel also emphasizes that there are lives that biopower subjects to a state of heightened vulnerability and that the responsibility for an active development of post-sovereign subjectivity lies with those who can afford to do so. In this context, the novel especially foregrounds the protagonists' entanglements with the dynamics of capitalism which often indirectly turn them into supporters of their actual or former condition of oppression.

This dynamic also looms large in Robin Robertson's narrative poem *The Long Take*, which productively engages with the overall hybridity of the flânerie text, here cast in terms of intermediality, generic hybridity and hybridity on the level of voice, in order to problematize notions of justification and ethical violence. The protagonist engages in flânerie as a technique of the self in an effort to come to terms with his feelings of guilt as well as traumatic experiences and thus produces a non-sovereign, relational subjectivity that voices a counter-discourse against the accelerated dynamics of hypercapitalism. The book's criticism then aims not only at the post-war paranoia of the 1950s in the US, but also at the rhetoric and performance of Trumpist America and its emphasis on sovereign conceptions of individual as well as national subjectivity. Moreover, *The Long Take*'s overt as well as covert intermediality displaces the basic structure of film to the text and in so doing explicitly targets the kind of accelerated perception that forms the basis both of a fluid identity that refrains from ethical considerations and also of the constant processes of urban renewal that endanger the lives of the city's most precarious population. In contrast to this, the text presents an ethical subject trying to come to terms with the upheavals of its past. Walker's final confession and Frank's reaction to it then problematize the notion of ethical violence: while the confession locates Walker within an ethical framework that distinguishes between good and evil – and thus builds a contrast with the ethical relativism performed by other characters – Frank's reaction is built on the assumption that Walker can be held fully accountable for his actions. Although this might be placed in question by other aspects of *The Long Take*, the idea that subjects cannot be held fully accountable for their actions becomes highly problematic if extended to Frank's own torturers. Hence, even on a meta-level the text affirms the flâneur's ethical ambivalence: while on the one hand potentially supporting the notion of ethical relativism, on the other hand it demands the affirmation of normative ethical frameworks that protect the primary vulnerability of human subjects.

The texts discussed in my study thus showcase different examples of post-sovereign subjectivity and negotiate the possibilities of performances of resistance in the twentieth and twenty-first centuries by drawing on the trope of the flâneur and the paradigm of flânerie. In doing so, they tie in with Butler's call to imagine a new story of the subject that envisions it as primarily relational. For this to be possible, the flâneur had to be freed from isolation and solipsism as well as from disinterestedness and projection, thus deviating from some of its most traditional characteristics while retaining the paradoxical structure that has been particularly emphasized by Walter Benjamin. The strolling subject thus performs another *conversio ad se*, again overcoming the conditions of its own death by putting itself into a relation with itself – that is, escaping from the 'ultimate play' of the *flâneurisme* of the man of the crowd by relocating itself in a field of "ethical enmeshment with others". In so doing, the subject gives up the potential sovereignty of ethical relativism for the sake of a continuous practice of critique.

Works Cited

Aaker, Everett. 2013. *George Raft: The Films*. Jefferson, NC: McFarland.
Adams, Ann Marie. 2012. "Mr. McEwan and Mrs. Woolf: How a Saturday in February Follows 'This Moment of June'". *Contemporary Literature* 53.3: 548–572.
Addison, Joseph and Richard Steele. 1967. *The Spectator*. Ed. Gregory Smith. 4 vols. Introd. Peter Smithers. London: Dent.
Ahmed, Sara. 2004. *The Cultural Politics of Emotion*. Edinburgh: Edinburgh University Press.
Alexander, Michael. 2013. *A History of English Literature*. 3rd ed. Basingstoke: Palgrave Macmillan.
Aragay, Mireia, Cristina Delgado-García and Martin Middeke. 2021. "Introduction". In: Aragay, Delgado-García and Middeke (eds.). *Affects in 21st-Century British Theatre*. Cham: Palgrave Macmillan.
Aragon, Louis. 1987. *Paris Peasant*. Trans. Simon Watson Taylor. London: Picador.
Artt, Sarah. 2018. "*Femme Publique:* The Brothel Sex Worker as Anti-Flâneuse in the Television Series *Maison Close*". In: Monika Prietrzak-Franger, Nora Pleßke and Eckart Voigts (eds.). *Transforming Cities: Discourses of Urban Change*. Heidelberg: Winter. 91–106.
Bachmann-Medick, Doris. 2009. "Fort-Schritte, Gedanken-Gänge, Ab-Stürze: Bewegungshorizonte und Subjektverortung in literarischen Beispielen". In: Wolfgang Hallet and Birgit Neumann (eds.). *Raum und Bewegung in der Literatur: Die Literaturwissenschaften und der Spatial Turn*. Bielefeld: transcript. 257–279.
Balzac, Honoré de. 2010. *Treatise on Elegant Living*. Trans. Napoleon Jeffries. E-book ed. Cambridge, MA: Wakefield Press.
Banville, John. 2018. "The Long Take by Robin Robertson Review – A Melancholy Love Song to America". *The Guardian* March 24. <https://www.theguardian.com/books/2018/mar/24/long-take-robin-robertson-poetry-review> [accessed 08 December 2020].
Bar-Yosef, Eitan. 2020. "Dr. Perowne and Mr. Baxter: Gothic Resonances in Ian McEwan's *Saturday*". *ANQ: A Quarterly Journal of Short Articles, Notes and Reviews* <Dr. Perowne and Mr. Baxter: Gothic Resonances in Ian McEwan's Saturday: ANQ: A Quarterly Journal of Short Articles, Notes and Reviews: Vol 0, No 0 (tandfonline.com)> [accessed 25 December 2020].
Barret-Ducrocq, Françoise. 1991. *Love in the Time of Victoria*. Trans. John Howe. London: Verso.
Barson, Michael. 2013. "Edward Dmytryk – American Film Director". *Britannica.com*. Encyclopædia Britannica, n. d. <https://www.britannica.com/biography/Edward-Dmytryk> [accessed 08 December 2020].
Baudelaire, Charles. 1970. *Paris Spleen*. Trans. L. Varèse. New York: New Directions Books.
Baudelaire, Charles. 1972. *Selected Writings on Art and Artists*. Trans. and ed. P. E. Charvet. Harmondsworth: Penguin.
Baudrillard, Jean. 1994. *Simulacra and Simulation*. Trans. Sheila Faria Glaser. Ann Arbor, MI: University of Michigan Press.
Baudrillard, Jean. 2012. *The Spirit of Terrorism*. Trans. Chris Turner. London: Verso.
Bauman, Zygmunt. 2015. "Desert Spectacular". In: Keith Tester (ed.). *The Flâneur*. London: Routledge. 138–157.

Bein, Britta. 2016. "Mysterious Illness and the Acceptance of Ambiguity". In: Johanna Hartmann, Christine Marks and Hubert Zapf (eds.). *Zones of Focused Ambiguity in Siri Hustvedt's Works*. Berlin: De Gruyter. 225–236.
Belenky, Masha. 2019. *Engine of Modernity: The Omnibus and Urban Culture in Nineteenth-Century Paris*. Manchester: Manchester University Press.
Benesch, Klaus and François Specq (eds.). 2016. *Walking and the Aesthetics of Modernity: Pedestrian Mobility in Literature and the Arts*. New York: Palgrave Macmillan.
Ben Gouider Trabelsi, Hajer. 2010. "Rethinking Community in Dionne Brand's *What We All Long For*, Ahdaf Soueif's *The Map of Love*, Michael Ondaatje's *Anil's Ghost* and Joseph Boyden's *Three Day Road* and *Through Black Spruce*". Unpubl. PhD dissertation, University of Montreal at Montreal. <https://papyrus.bib.umontreal.ca/xmlui/bitstream/handle/1866/7074/Ben_Gouider_Trabelsi_Hajer_2011_these.pdf?sequence=10&isAllowed=y> [accessed 11 November 2020].
Benjamin, Walter. 1974. "Benjamin an Horkheimer: Paris, 24.6.1939". In: Benjamin. *Gesammelte Schriften*. Volume 1.3: *Abhandlungen*. Eds. Rolf Tiedemann and Hermann Schweppenhäuser. Frankfurt/Main: Suhrkamp. 1121–1122.
Benjamin, Walter. 1985. "Berliner Chronik". In: Benjamin. *Gesammelte Schriften*. Volume 6: *Fragmente vermischten Inhalts, Autobiographische Schriften*. Eds. Rolf Tiedemann and Hermann Schweppenhäuser. Frankfurt/Main: Suhrkamp. 465–519.
Benjamin, Walter. 2002. *The Arcades Project*. Trans. Howard Eiland and Kevin McLaughlin. Cambridge, MA: Belknap.
Benjamin, Walter. 2000. "Brief an Theodor W. Adorno". In: Benjamin. *Gesammelte Briefe*. Volume 6: *1938–1940*. Ed. Christoph Gödde. Frankfurt/Main: Suhrkamp. 181–190.
Benjamin, Walter. 2006. *The Writer of Modern Life: Essays on Charles Baudelaire*. Ed. Michael W. Jennings. Trans. Howard Eiland, Edmund Jephcott, Rodney Livingston and Harry Zohn. Cambridge, MA: Belknap.
Benjamin, Walter. 2013. *Charles Baudelaire: Ein Lyriker im Zeitalter des Hochkapitalismus*. Ed. Rolf Tiedemann. Frankfurt/Main: Suhrkamp.
Benjamin, Walter. 2017. "The Flaneur's Return". Trans. Adrian Nathan West. In: Franz Hessel. *Walking in Berlin: A Flaneur in the Capital*. Trans. Amanda DeMarco. Cambridge, MA: MIT Press. xiii–xix.
Berensmeyer, Ingo and Catharina Löffler. 2018. "Challenging Urban Realities in Recent London Writing: Iain Sinclair's *Ghost Milk* and John Lanchester's *Capital*". In: Christoph Ehland and Pascal Fischer (eds.). *Resistance and the City: Challenging Urban Space*. Leiden: Rodopi. 164–180.
Berg, Klaus van den. 2009. "Staging a Vanished Community: Daniel Libeskind's Scenography in the Berlin Jewish Museum". In: D. J. Hopkins, Shelley Orr and Kim Solga (eds.). *Performance and the City*. London: Palgrave. 222–239.
Bernabei, Franca. 2008. "'What We All Long For': Dionne Brand's Transatlantic Metamorphoses". In: Annalisa Oboe and Anna Scacchi (eds.). *Recharting the Black Atlantic: Modern Cultures, Local Communities, Global Connections*. New York: Routledge. 109–127.
Best, Stephen and Douglas Kellner. 1991. *Postmodern Theory: Critical Interrogations*. New York: Guilford Press.
Biendarra, Anke. 2002. "Der Erzähler als 'popmoderner Flaneur' in Christian Krachts Roman *Faserland*". *German Life and Letters* 55.2: 164–179.

Birkle, Carmen. 2019. "Geographies, Ethnicities, and the Cultures of Belonging: Dionne Brand, *What We All Long For* (2005)". In: Maria Löschnigg and Martin Löschnigg (eds.). *The Anglo-Canadian Novel in the Twenty-First Century*. Heidelberg: Winter. 61–74.
Blair, Gregory. 2019. *Errant Bodies, Mobility and Political Resistance*. Cham: Springer.
Blake, William. 1996. "London". In: Margaret Ferguson, Mary Jo Salter and Jon Stallworthy (eds.). *The Norton Anthology of Poetry*. New York: Norton. 681–682.
Bock, Oliver and Isabel Vila-Cabanes (eds.). 2020. *Urban Walking: The Flâneur as an Icon of Metropolitan Culture in Literature and Film*. Wilmington, DE: Vernon Press.
Böhme, Hartmut. 2005. "Einleitung: Raum – Bewegung – Topographie". In: Böhme (ed.). *Topographien der Literatur: Deutsche Literatur im transnationalen Kontext*. Stuttgart: Metzler. ix–xxiii.
Bolle, Willi. 1994. *Physiognomik der modernen Metropole: Geschichtsdarstellung bei Walter Benjamin*. Köln: Böhlau.
Borden, Iain. 2000. "A Performative Critique of the City: The Urban Practice of Skateboarding, 1958–98". In: Malcolm Miles, Tim Hall and Borden (eds.). *The City Cultures Reader*. New York: Routledge. 291–297.
Bordwell, David. 2008. *Poetics of Cinema*. New York: Routledge.
Borges, Jorge Luis. 1989. *Obras Completas*. Volume 2: *1952–1972*. Barcelona: Emecé.
Bossinade, Johanna. 2000. *Poststrukturalistische Literaturtheorie*. Stuttgart: Metzler.
Boutin, Aimée. 2012. "Rethinking the Flâneur: Flânerie and the Senses". *Dix-Neuf* 16.2: 124–132.
Brand, Dana. 1991. *The Spectator and the City in Nineteenth-Century American Literature*. Cambridge: Cambridge University Press.
Brand, Dionne. 2001. *A Map to the Door of No Return: Notes to Belonging*. Toronto: Doubleday Canada.
Brand, Dionne. 2005. *What We All Long For*. New York: Thomas Dunne Books.
Briggs, Jo. 2014. "Flâneurs, Commodities, and the Working Body in Louis Huart's *Physiologie du flâneur* and Albert Smith's *Natural History of the Idler upon Town*". In: Richard Wrigley (ed.). *The Flâneur Abroad: Historical and International Perspectives*. Newcastle upon Tyne: Cambridge Scholars Publishing. 117–141.
Brynhildsvoll, Knut. 2020. "The Bohemian and the Flâneur – Two Complementary Terms of a Life-Style Design: Reflections on the Role of (Sub)Cultural Outsiders in Scandinavian Art and Literature in the Late Nineteenth and the Beginning of the Twentieth Century". In: Oliver Bock and Isabel Vila-Cabanes (eds.). *Urban Walking: The Flâneur as an Icon of Metropolitan Culture in Literature and Film*. Wilmington, DE: Vernon Press. 49–58.
Bublitz, Hannelore. 2010. *Judith Butler zur Einführung*. 3rd ed. Hamburg: Junius.
Bublitz, Hannelore. 2014. "Subjekt". In: Clemens Kammler, Rolf Parr and Ulrich Johannes Schneider (eds.). *Foucault Handbuch: Leben – Werk – Wirkung*. Spec. ed. Stuttgart: Metzler. 293–297.
Buck-Morss, Susan. 1986. "The Flaneur, the Sandwichman and the Whore: The Politics of Loitering". *New German Critique* 39 (Autumn): 99–140.
Buck-Morss, Susan. 1989. *The Dialectic of Seeing: Walter Benjamin and the Arcades Project*. Cambridge, MA: MIT Press.
Bunzel, Wolfgang. 2009. "Prosagedicht". In: Dieter Lamping, Sandra Poppe, Sascha Seiler and Frank Zipfel (eds.). *Handbuch der literarischen Gattungen*. Stuttgart: Kröner. 587–592.

Burrow, Colin. 2018. "Slice of Life". Rev. of *The Long* Take, by Robin Robertson. *London Review of Books* 40.16: n. pag. <https://www.lrb.co.uk/the-paper/v40/n16/colin-burrow/slice-of-life> [accessed 08 December 2020].
Butler, Heidi. 2011. "The Master's Narrative: Resisting the Essentializing Gaze in Ian McEwan's *Saturday*". *Critique* 52: 101–113.
Butler, Judith. 1993. *Bodies That Matter: On the Discursive Limits of "Sex"*. New York: Routledge.
Butler, Judith. 1997a. "Performative Acts and Gender Constitution: An Essay in Phenomenology and Feminist Theory". In: Katie Conboy, Nadia Medina and Sarah Stanburg (eds.). *Writing on the Body: Female Embodiment and Feminist Theory*. New York: Columbia University Press. 401–415.
Butler, Judith. 1997b. *The Psychic Life of Power: Theories in Subjection*. Stanford, CA: Stanford University Press.
Butler, Judith. 1999. *Gender Trouble: Feminism and the Subversion of Identity*. 2nd ed. New York: Routledge.
Butler, Judith. 2000. *Antigone's Claim: Kinship Between Life & Death*. New York: Columbia University Press.
Butler, Judith. 2002. "What is Critique? An Essay on Foucault's Virtue". In: David Ingram (ed.). *The Political*. Malden, MA: Blackwell. 212–228.
Butler, Judith. 2004a. *Undoing Gender*. New York: Routledge.
Butler, Judith. 2004b. *Precarious Life: The Powers of Mourning and Violence*. London: Verso.
Butler, Judith. 2005. *Giving an Account of Oneself*. New York: Fordham University Press.
Butler, Judith. 2009. *Frames of War: When is Life Grievable?* London: Verso.
Butler, Judith. 2020. *The Force of Nonviolence: An Ethico-Political Bind*. London: Verso.
Butzer, Günter. 2009. "Selbst-Bildung: Michel Foucaults 'Ästhetik der Existenz'". In: Butzer and Hubert Zapf (eds.). *Theorien der Literatur: Grundlagen und Perspektiven*. Volume 4. Tübingen: Francke. 217–240.
Byerly, Allison. 1999. "Effortless Art: The Sketch in Nineteenth-Century Painting and Literature". *Criticism* 41.3: 349–364.
Carluccio, Cristina. 2020. "Urban Abstraction in Literary Modernism: Virginia Woolf's Street-Haunting Adventures". In: Oliver Bock and Isabel Vila-Cabanes (eds.). *Urban Walking: The Flâneur as an Icon of Metropolitan Culture in Literature and Film*. Wilmington, DE: Vernon Press. 97–118.
Carrera Suárez, Isabel. 2008. "Toronto in the Global City: Flows and Places in Dionne Brand's *What We All Long For*". In: Charlotte Sturgess and Martin Kuester (eds.). *Reading(s) from a Distance: European Perspectives on Canadian Women's Writing*. Augsburg: Wißner. 187–199.
Chariandy, David. 2006. "What We All Long For: Dionne Brand". *New Dawn: Journal of Black Canadian Studies* 1: 103–107.
Clark, Rebecca. 2018. "'Visible only in speech': Peripatetic Parasitism, or, Becoming Bedbugs in *Open City*". *Narrative* 26.2: 181–200.
Clifford, James. 1992. "Travelling Cultures". In: Lawrence Grossberg, Cary Nelson and Paula A. Treichler (eds.). *Cultural Studies*. London: Routledge. 96–112.
Cole, Teju. 2011. *Open City*. London: Faber & Faber.

Cole, Teju. 2015. "A True Picture of Black Skin". *The New York Times Magazine* February 18. <https://nytimes.com/2015/02/22/magazine/a-true-picture-of-black-skin.html> [accessed 15 September 2021].

Conlin, Jonathan. 2014. "'This Publick Sort of Obscurity': The Origins of the Flâneur in London and Paris, 1660–1780". In: Richard Wrigley (ed.). *The Flâneur Abroad: Historical and International Perspectives*. Newcastle upon Tyne: Cambridge Scholars Publishing. 14–39.

Coverley, Merlin. 2010. *Psychogeography*. Harpenden: Pocket Essentials.

Cresswell, Tim. 1997. "Imagining the Nomad: Mobility and the Postmodern Primitive". In: Georges Benko and Ulf Strohmayer (eds.). *Space and Social Theory: Interpreting Modernity and Postmodernity*. Oxford: Blackwell. 360–382.

Currie, Mark. 2007. *About Time: Narrative, Fiction and the Philosophy of Time*. Edinburgh: Edinburgh University Press.

Dallmann, Antje. 2009. *ConspiraCity New York: Großstadtbetrachtung zwischen Paranoia und Selbstermächtigung*. Heidelberg: Winter.

De Certeau, Michel. 1988. *The Practice of Everyday Life*. Trans. Steven Rendall. Berkeley, CA: University of California Press.

De Lacroix, Auguste. 1840. "Le Flâneur". *Les Français peints par eux-mêmes* 3: 65–72.

Debord, Guy. 1995. "Theorie des Umherschweifens". In: *Der Beginn einer Epoche: Texte der Situationisten*. Trans. Pierre Gallissaires, Hanna Mittelstädt and Roberto Ohrt. Hamburg: Edition Nautilus. 64–67.

Debord, Guy. 2006. "Introduction to a Critique of Urban Geography". *Situationist International Anthology*. Ed. and trans. Ken Knabb. Rev. and expand. ed. Berkeley, CA: Bureau of Public Secrets. 8–12.

Deleuze, Gilles and Felix Guattari. 1986. *Nomadology: The War Machine*. New York: Semiotext(e).

Dell'Amico, Carol. 2005. *Colonialism and the Modernist Moment in the Early Novels of Jean Rhys*. New York: Routledge.

DeMaria, Robert. 2005. "The Eighteenth-Century Periodical Essay". In: John Richetti (ed.). *The Cambridge History of English Literature, 1660–1780*. Cambridge: Cambridge University Press. 527–540.

DeRitter, Margaret. 2011. "Teju Cole, a K-College Grad, Writes What He Observes Through Narrator in 'Open City'". *Kalamazoo Gazette* May 27. <https://web.archive.org/web/20150225175753/http://www.mlive.com/entertainment/kalamazoo/index.ssf/2011/05/teju_cole_a_k-college_grad_wri.html> [accessed 16 August 2020].

Detmers, Ines. 2008. "Saturday (2005)". In: Susanne Peters, Klaus Stierstorfer and Laurenz Volkmann (eds.). *Novels. Part II*. Trier: WVT. 363–378.

Dickens, Charles. 1994. *The Dent Uniform Edition of Dickens' Journalism*. Volume 1: *Sketches by Boz and Other Early Papers, 1833–39*. Ed. Michael Slater. London: Phoenix.

Dickens, Charles. 2000. *The Dent Uniform Edition of Dickens' Journalism*. Volume 4: *The Uncommercial Traveller and Other Papers, 1859–70*. Ed. Michael Slater and John Drew. London: Phoenix.

Dinter, Sandra. 2019. "Re-Walking the Paths of *Pride and Prejudice*: Intersectional Perspectives on Pedestrian Mobility in Jo Baker's *Longbourn*". *Anglia: Journal of English Philology* 137.1: 105–125.

Doane, Mary Ann. 2000. "Film and the Masquerade: Theorizing the Female Spectator". In: Joanne Hollows (ed.). *The Film Studies Reader*. London: Arnold. 248–256.
Duden. 2020. Berlin: Bibliographisches Institut. <www.duden.de> [accessed 25 March 2020].
Dunlap, David W. 2015. "1973: Meet Donald Trump". *The New York Times* July 30. <https://www.nytimes.com/times-insider/2015/07/30/1973-meet-donald-trump/> [accessed 08 December 2020].
Eaglestone, Robert. 2004. "Postmodernism and Ethics against the Metaphysics of Comprehension". In: Steven Connor (ed.). *The Cambridge Companion to Postmodernism*. Cambridge: Cambridge University Press. 182–195.
Eco, Umberto. 1995. *How To Travel with a Salmon and Other Essays*. Trans. William Weaver. San Diego: Harcourt.
Ehland, Christoph and Pascal Fischer (eds.). 2018a. *Resistance and the City: Challenging Urban Space*. Leiden: Rodopi.
Ehland, Christoph and Pascal Fischer (eds.). 2018b. *Resistance and the City: Negotiating Urban Identities: Race, Class and Gender*. Leiden: Rodopi.
Ellin, Nan. 1996. *Postmodern Urbanism*. New York: Princeton Architectural Press.
Elze, Jens. 2017. "Cosmopolitan Place, Postcolonial Time, and the Politics of Modernism in Teju Cole's *Open City*". *Zeitschrift für Anglistik und Amerikanistik: A Quarterly of Language, Literature and Culture* 65.1: 85–104.
Epstein Nord, Deborah. 1995. *Walking the Victorian Streets: Women, Representation and the City*. Ithaca, NY: Cornell University Press.
Faisst, Julia. 2018. "Strolling the Biophilic City: Flâneurism, Urban Nature and Eco-Fiction". In: Monika Prietrzak-Franger, Nora Pleßke and Eckart Voigts (eds.). *Transforming Cities: Discourses of Urban Change*. Heidelberg: Winter. 43–58.
Featherstone, Mike. 1998. "The *Flâneur*, the City and Virtual Public Life". *Urban Studies* 35.5–6: 909–925.
Ferguson, Priscilla Parkhurst. 2015. "The *Flâneur* on and off the Streets of Paris". In: Keith Tester (ed.). *The Flâneur*. New York: Routledge. 22–42.
Finocchiario, Briana. 2019. "Solipsism and Solitude: The Alignment of Impressionism and Flânerie in Teju Cole's *Open City*". *Scaffold: A Showcase of Vanderbilt's First-Year Writing* 1: 1–7.
Fischer, Ralph. 2011. *Walking Artists: Über die Entdeckung des Gehens in den performativen Künsten*. Bielefeld: transcript.
The Flâneur in the Salon, or M. Bonhomme; Joyful Review of Paintings, Mixed with Vaudevilles. Trans. Isabel Vila-Cabanes. 2016. In: Isabel Vila-Cabanes. *Re-Imagining the Streets of Paris: The French Flaneur in Nineteenth-Century Literature*. Trier: WVT. 103–109.
Flieger, Jerry Aline. 1997. "Postmodern Perspective: The Paranoid Eye". *New Literary History* 28.1: 87–109.
Flynn, Thomas. 1987. "Foucault as Parrhesiast: His Last Course at the Collége de France (1984)". *Philosophy & Social Criticism* 12.2–3: 213–229.
Foden, Giles. 2011. "Open City by Teju Cole – Review". *The Guardian* August 17. <https://www.theguardian.com/books/2011/aug/17/open-city-teju-cole-review> [accessed 07 September 2020].
Fongang, Delphine. 2017. "Cosmopolitan Dilemma: Diasporic Subjectivity and Postcolonial Liminality in Teju Cole's *Open City*". *Research in African Literatures* 48.4: 138–154.

Forna, Aminatta. 2018. "Power Walking: Aminatta Forna on the Streets of London, Freetown and NYC". *Literary Hub* September 19. <https://lithub.com/power-walking/> [accessed 08 April 2020].

Foucault, Michel. 1976. "Von den Martern zu den Zellen". In: Foucault. *Mikrophysik der Macht: Über Strafjustiz, Psychiatrie und Medizin*. Berlin: Merve. 48–53.

Foucault, Michel. 1984. "Politics and Ethics: An Interview". In: Foucault. *The Foucault Reader*. Ed. Paul Rabinow. New York: Pantheon. 375–380.

Foucault, Michel. 1985. "Hermeneutik des Subjekts: Vorlesung am Collége de France (1982): Nachschrift und Übersetzung von Helmut Becker in Zusammenarbeit mit Lothar Wolfstetter". In: Helmut Becker and Lothar Wolfstetter (eds.). *Freiheit und Selbstsorge: Interview 1984 und Vorlesung 1982*. Frankfurt/Main: Materialis.

Foucault, Michel. 1988. "The Ethic of Care for the Self as a Practice of Freedom". In: James Bernauer and David Rasmussen (eds.). *The Final Foucault*. Cambridge, MA: MIT Press. 1–20.

Foucault, Michel. 1990. "The Return of Morality". Interview by Gilles Barbadette and André Scala. In: Foucault. *Politics, Philosophy, Culture: Interviews and Other Writings, 1977–1984*. Ed. Lawrence D. Kritzman. New York: Routledge. 242–254.

Foucault, Michel. 1991. *Remarks on Marx: Conversations with Duccio Trombadori*. Trans. R. James Goldstein and James Cascaito. New York: Semiotext(e).

Foucault, Michel. 1992. *The History of Sexuality*. Volume 2: *The Use of Pleasure*. Trans. Robert Hurley. London: Penguin.

Foucault, Michel. 2000a. "Technologies of the Self". In: Foucault. *Essential Works of Michel Foucault 1954–1984*. Volume. 1: *Ethics: Subjectivity and Truth*. Ed. Paul Rabinow. Trans. Robert Hurley et al. London: Penguin. 223–252.

Foucault, Michel. 2000b. "The Masked Philosopher". In: Foucault. *Essential Works of Michel Foucault 1954–1984*. Volume 1: *Ethics: Subjectivity and Truth*. Ed. Paul Rabinow. Trans. Robert Hurley et al. London: Penguin. 321–328.

Foucault, Michel. 2000c. "What is Enlightenment?" In: Foucault. *Essential Works of Michel Foucault 1954–1984*. Volume 1: *Ethics: Subjectivity and Truth*. Ed. Paul Rabinow. Trans. Robert Hurley et al. London: Penguin. 303–320.

Foucault, Michel. 2000d. "Self Writing". In: Foucault. *Essential Works of Michel Foucault 1954–1984*. Volume 1: *Ethics: Subjectivity and Truth*. Ed. Paul Rabinow. Trans. Robert Hurley et al. London: Penguin. 207–222.

Foucault, Michel. 2000e. "The Hermeneutics of the Subject". In: Foucault. *Essential Works of Michel Foucault 1954–1984*. Volume 1: *Ethics: Subjectivity and Truth*. Ed. Paul Rabinow. Trans. Robert Hurley et al. London: Penguin. 93–108.

Foucault, Michel. 2000f "On the Genealogy of Ethics: An Overview of Work in Progress". In: Foucault. *Essential Works of Michel Foucault 1954–1984*. Volume 1: *Ethics: Subjectivity and Truth*. Ed. Paul Rabinow. Trans. Robert Hurley et al. London: Penguin. 253–280.

Foucault, Michel. 2003a. "What is Critique?" In: Foucault. *The Essential Foucault: Selections from Essential Works of Foucault, 1954–1984*. Ed. Paul Rabinow and Nikolas Rose. New York: New Press. 263–278.

Foucault, Michel. 2003b. *"Society Must Be Defended": Lectures at the Collège de France, 1975–76*. Ed. Mauro Bertani and Alessandro Fontana. Trans. David Macey. New York: Picador.

Foucault, Michel. 2004. *Geschichte der Gouvernementalität*. Volume 1: *Sicherheit, Territorium, Bevölkerung: Vorlesung am Collège de France (1977–1978)*. Ed. Michel Sennelart. Trans. Claudia Brede-Konersmann and Jürgen Schröder. Frankfurt/Main: Suhrkamp.
Foucault, Michel. 2005. "Diskussion vom 20. Mai 1978". In: Foucault. *Schriften in vier Bänden: Dits et Ecrits*. Volume 4: *1980–1988*. Eds. Daniel Defert and François Ewald. Trans. Michael Bischoff et al. Frankfurt/Main: Suhrkamp. 25–43.
Foucault, Michel. 2007. "Die Hermeneutik des Subjekts". In: Foucault. *Ästhetik der Existenz: Schriften zur Lebenskunst*. Ed. Daniel Defert and François Ewald. Frankfurt/Main: Suhrkamp. 123–136.
Foucault, Michel. 2018. "The Return of Pierre Riviére". In: Foucault, Patrice Maniglier and Dork Zabunyan. *Foucault at the Movies*. Ed. and trans. Clare O'Farrell. New York: Columbia University Press. 159–170.
Foucault, Michel. 2019. *Discourse & Truth and* Parrēsia. Eds. Henri-Paul Fruchaud and Daniele Lorenzini. Trans. Nancy Luxon. Chicago, IL: University of Chicago Press.
Foucault, Michel and Richard Sennett. 1982. "Sexuality and Solitude". In: David Rieff (ed.). *Humanities in Review*. Volume 1. Cambridge: Cambridge University Press. 3–21.
Fournel, Victor. 1867. *L'Odyssee d'un flâneur ou Ce qu'on voit dans les rues de Paris*. Nouvelle edition revue, corrigée et augmentee. Paris: Dentu.
Freud, Sigmund. 1966. "Das Unheimliche". In: Freud. *Gesammelte Werke: chronologisch geordnet*. Volume 12: *Werke aus den Jahren 1917–1920*. 3rd ed. Ed. Anna Freud et al. Frankfurt/Main: Fischer. 227–268.
Freud, Sigmund. 1969. "Trauer und Melancholie". In: Freud. *Gesammelte Werke: chronologisch geordnet*. Volume 10: *Werke aus den Jahren 1913–1917*. 5th ed. Ed. Anna Freud et al. Frankfurt/Main: Fischer. 427–446.
Friedberg, Anne. 1993. *Window Shopping: Cinema and the Postmodern*. Berkeley, CA: University of California Press.
Frisby, David. 2015. "The Flâneur in Social Theory". In: Keith Tester (ed.). *The Flâneur*. London: Routledge. 81–110.
Fuest, Leonhard. 2008. *Poetik des Nicht(s)tuns: Verweigerungsstrategien in der Literatur seit 1800*. München: Fink.
Gamso, Nicholas. 2019. "Exposure and Black Migrancy in Teju Cole". *New Global Studies* 13.1: 60–79.
Ganteau, Jean-Michel. 2014. "Ghosts, Texts, Phantom Texts: McEwan's *Saturday* and Joyce's 'The Dead'". In: Brigitte Johanna Glaser and Barbara Puschmann-Nalenz (eds.). *Narrating Loss: Representations of Mourning, Nostalgia and Melancholia in Contemporary Anglophone Fictions*. Trier: WVT. 223–238.
Garvey, Johanna X. K. 2011. "Spaces of Violence, Desire and Queer (Un-)Belonging: Dionne Brand's Urban Diasporas". *Contemporary Women's Writing and Queer Diasporas*. Spec. issue of *Textual Practice* 25.4: 757–777.
Gauthier, Tim. 2013. "'Selective in Your Mercies': Privilege, Vulnerability, and the Limits of Empathy in McEwan's *Saturday*". *College Literature* 40.2: 7–31.
Gehrmann, Susanne. 2015. "Cosmopolitanism with African Roots: Afropolitanism's African Mobilities". *Journal of African Cultural Studies* 28.1: 61–72.
Genette, Gérard. 1980. *Narrative Discourse: An Essay in Method*. Trans. Jane E. Lewin. Foreword by Jonathan Culler. Ithaca, NY: Cornell University Press.

Gikandi, Simon. 2010. "Between Roots and Routes: Cosmopolitanism and the Claims of Locality". In: Janet Wilson (ed.). *Rerouting the Postcolonial*. London: Routledge. 22–35.

Gilloch, Graeme. 1999. "The Return of the *Flâneur*: The Afterlife of an Allegory". *New Formations* 38: 101–109.

Gleber, Anke. 1999. *The Art of Taking a Walk: Flanerie, Literature and Film in Weimar Culture*. Princeton, NJ: Princeton University Press.

Goebel, Rolf J. 1998. "Benjamin's Flaneur in Japan: Urban Modernity and Conceptual Relocation". *The German Quarterly* 71.4: 377–391.

Goebel, Rolf J. 2001. *Benjamin Heute: Großstadtdiskurs, Postkolonialität und Flanerie zwischen den Kulturen*. München: Iudicium.

Goldmann, Marlene. 2004. "Mapping the Door of No Return: Deterritorialization and the Work of Dionne Brand". *Canadian Literature* 182: 13–28.

Gomolla, Stephanie. 2009. *Distanz und Nähe: Der Flaneur in der französischen Literatur zwischen Moderne und Postmoderne*. Würzburg: Königshausen & Neumann.

Gregori, Flavio. 2005. "The 'Audacious' Art of Walking: The Metropolis and the Proto-Flâneur in John Gay's 'Trivia'". *South Atlantic Review* 70.1: 71–96.

Groes, Sebastian. 2009. "Ian McEwan and the Modernist Consciousness of the City in *Saturday*". In: Groes (ed.). *Ian McEwan: Contemporary Critical Perspectives*. London: Continuum. 99–114.

Groh, Dieter. 1987. "Kompensationsmodell – Historismusbegriff – Flaneurtypus". In: Helmut Pfeiffer, Hans Robert Jauß and Françoise Gaillard (eds.). *Art social und art industriel: Funktionen der Kunst im Zeitalter des Industrialismus*. München: Fink. 48–52.

Gros, Frédéric. 2019. Introduction. *Discourse & Truth and* Parrēsia. By Michel Foucault. Eds. Henri-Paul Fruchaud and Daniele Lorenzini. Trans. Nancy Luxon. Chicago, IL: University of Chicago Press. xiii–xx.

Haarmann, Anke. 1995. *Disziplin und Differenz: Erfahrung bei Michel Foucault*. Berlin: Freie Universität Berlin.

Hallemeier, Katherine. 2014. "Literary Cosmopolitanisms in Teju Cole's *Every Day is for the Thief* and *Open City*". *Ariel: A Review of International English Literature* 44.2–3: 239–250.

Hartmann, Johanna. 2016. *Literary Visuality in Siri Hustvedt's Works: Phenomenological Perspectives*. Würzburg: Königshausen & Neumann.

Hartwiger, Alexander Greer. 2016. "The Postcolonial Flâneur: *Open City* and the Urban Palimpsest". *Postcolonial Text* 11.1: 1–17.

Harvey, David. 2003. *Paris: Capital of the Modernity*. New York: Routledge.

Head, Dominic. 2007. *Ian McEwan*. Manchester: Manchester University Press.

Herbert, Robert L. 1988. *Impressionism: Art, Leisure and Society*. New Haven, CT: Yale University Press.

Hessel, Franz. 1999. "Vorschule des Journalismus: Ein Pariser Tagebuch". In: Hessel. *Sämtliche Werke*. Volume 2: *Prosasammlungen*. Ed. Karin Grund-Ferroud. Oldenburg: Igel. 292–330.

Hessel, Franz. 2017. *Walking in Berlin: A Flaneur in the Capital*. With an Essay by Walter Benjamin. Trans. Amanda DeMarco. Cambridge, MA: MIT Press.

Hicklin, Aaron. 2019. "Interview: Siri Hustvedt: 'I'm writing for my life'". *The Guardian* March 3. <https://www.theguardian.com/books/2019/mar/03/siri-hustvedt-i-am-writing-for-my-life-memories-of-the-future-interview> [accessed 20 May 2020].

Hohmann, Angela. 2000. "Der Flaneur: Gedächtnis und Spiegel der Moderne". *Die Horen* 4: 123–145.
Hollington, Michael. 1981. "Dickens the Flaneur". *The Dickensian* 77: 77–81.
Huart, Louis. 2007. "Physiologie du Flâneur: Vignettes de Alophe, Daumier et Maurisset". In: Margaret Rose (ed.). *Flaneurs & Idlers*. Bielefeld: Aisthesis. 75–200.
Hustvedt, Siri. 1993. *The Blindfold*. London: Sceptre.
Hustvedt, Siri. 1998. "Yonder". In: Hustvedt. *Yonder: Essays*. New York: Holt. 3–45.
Hustvedt, Siri. 2006. "Being a Man". In: Hustvedt. *A Plea for Eros*. London: Sceptre.
Hustvedt, Siri. 2011. *The Summer Without Men*. London: Sceptre.
Hustvedt, Siri. 2014. *The Blazing World*. London: Sceptre.
Hustvedt, Siri. 2016a. *A Woman Looking at Men Looking at Women: Essays on Art, Sex and the Mind*. London: Sceptre.
Hustvedt, Siri. 2016b. "Foreword". In: Teju Cole. *Blind Spot*. London: Faber & Faber. ix–xvi.
Jameson, Alice. 2010. "Pleasure and Peril: Dynamic Forces of Power and Desire in Siri Hustvedt's *The Blindfold*". *Studies in the Novel* 42.4: 421–442.
Jauß, Hans Robert. 1989. "Spur und Aura: Bemerkungen zu Walter Benjamins 'Passagen-Werk'". In: Jauß. *Studien zum Epochenwandel der ästherischen Moderne*. Frankfurt/Main: Suhrkamp. 189–215.
Johansen, Emily. 2008. "'Streets are the Dwelling Place of the Collective': Public Space and Cosmopolitan Citizenship in Dionne Brand's *What We All Long For*". *Canadian Literature* 196 (Spring): 48–62.
Joyce, James. 1986. *Ulysses*. Ed. Hans Walter Gabler. New York: Random House.
Kafka, Franz. 1995. *Erzählungen*. Ed. Michael Müller. Stuttgart: Reclam.
Kaiser, Tina Hedwig. 2007. *Flaneure im Film: La Notte und L'Eclisse von Michelangelo Antonioni*. Marburg: Tectum.
Kaiser, Tina Hedwig. 2008. *Aufnahmen der Durchquerung: Das Transitorische im Film*. Bielefeld: transcript.
Kaplan, Morris. 1973. "Major Landlord Accused of Antiblack Bias in City". *The New York Times* October 16. <https://www.documentcloud.org/documents/2186612-major-landlord-accuse-of-antiblack-bias-in-city.html> [accessed 08 December 2020].
Keidel, Matthias. 2006. *Die Wiederkehr der Flaneure: Literarische Flanerie und flanierendes Denken zwischen Wahrnehmung und Reflexion*. Würzburg: Königshausen & Neumann.
Knirsch, Christian. 2010. "In a Time-Warp: The Issue of Chronology in Siri Hustvedt's *The Blindfold*". *Current Objectives of Postgraduate American Studies* 11: n. pag. <https://copas.uni-regensburg.de/article/view/122/146> [accessed 2 August 2020].
Kock, Bernhard. 1994. *Michelangelo Antonionis Bilderwelt*. München: Schaudig & Leidig.
Köhn, Eckhardt. 1989. *Straßenrausch: Flanerie und kleine Form. Versuch zur Literaturgeschichte des Flaneurs von 1830–1933*. Berlin: Das Arsenal.
Kracauer, Siegfried. 1980. "Straße ohne Erinnerung". In: Kracauer. *Schriften*. Volume 5.3: *Aufsätze 1932–1965*. Ed. Inka Mülder-Bach. Frankfurt/Main: Suhrkamp. 170–174.
Kracauer, Siegfried. 1994. *Jacques Offenbach und das Paris seiner Zeit*. Frankfurt/Main: Suhrkamp.
Lachmann, Renate. 1990. *Gedächtnis und Literatur: Intertextualität in der russischen Moderne*. Frankfurt/Main: Suhrkamp.
Lai, Larissa. 2014. *Slanting I, Imagining We: Asian Canadian Literary Production in the 1980s and 1990s*. Waterloo, OH: Wilfried Laurier University Press.

Laing, Olivia. 2016. *The Lonely City: Adventures in the Art of Being Alone*. Edinburgh: Canongate.
Lamarque, Peter. 2014. *The Opacity of Narrative*. Lanham: Rowman & Littlefield.
Langwald, Sylvia. 2011. "The Self and the City: Narrating 'Glocal' Spaces and Identities in Dionne Brand's *What We All Long For*". *Zeitschrift für Anglistik und Amerikanistik* 59.2: 123–134.
Langwald, Sylvia. 2015. *Diasporic Generationality: Identity, Generation Relationships and Diaspora in Selected Novels from Britain and Canada*. Augsburg: Wißner.
Lauster, Martina. 2007. *Sketches of the Nineteenth Century: European Journalism and its Physiologies, 1830–50*. Basingstoke: Palgrave Macmillan.
Lejeune, Philipp. 1994. *Der autobiographische Pakt*. Trans. Wolfram Bayer and Dieter Horning. Frankfurt/Main: Suhrkamp.
Lettenewitsch, Natalia. 2019. "Prekäre Flanerie: Filmische Streif- und Beutezüge in Berlin". In: Jörn Glasenapp, Georgiana Banita and Judith Ellenbürger (eds.). *Die Lust zu gehen: Weibliche Flanerie in Literatur und Film*. München: Fink. 167–193.
Levinas, Emmanuel. 1996. "Peace and Proximity". In: Levinas. *Basic Philosophical Writings*. Ed. Adriaan T. Peperzak, Simon Critchley and Robert Bernasconi. Bloomington, IN: Indiana University Press. 161–170.
Li, Stephanie. 2018. *Pan-African American Literature: Signifyin(g) Immigrants in the Twenty-First Century*. New Brunswick, NJ: Rutgers University Press.
Lipp, Carola. 1986. "Frauen auf der Straße: Strukturen weiblicher Öffentlichkeit im Unterschichtsmilieu". In: Carola Lipp (ed.). *Schimpfende Weiber und patriotische Jungfrauen: Frauen im Vormärz und in der Revolution 1848/49*. Baden-Baden: Moos. 16–24.
Löffler, Catharina. 2017. *Walking in the City: Urban Experience and Literary Psychogeography in Eighteenth-Century London*. Stuttgart: Metzler.
Lyotard, Jean-François. 1984. *The Postmodern Condition*. Minneapolis, MN: University of Minnesota Press.
Makropulous, Michael. 2007. "Benjamins Theorie der Massenkultur". In: Bernd Wirkus (ed.). *Die kulturelle Moderne zwischen Demokratie und Diktatur: Die Weimarer Republik und danach*. Konstanz: UVK. 263–286.
Marks, Christine. 2014. *"I am because you are": Relationality in the Works of Siri Hustvedt*. Heidelberg: Winter.
Mazlish, Bruce. 2015. "The *Flâneur*: From Spectator to Representation". In: Keith Tester (ed.). *The Flâneur*. New York: Routledge. 43–60.
McEwan, Ian. 2006. *Saturday*. London: Vintage.
McKibbin, Molly Littlewood. 2008. "The Possibilities of Home: Negotiating City Spaces in Dionne Brand's *What We All Long For*". *Journal of Black Studies* 38.3: 502–518.
McLaren, Peter. 1997. "The Ethnographer as Postmodern *Flâneur*: Critical Reflexivity and Posthybridity as Narrative Engagement". In: William G. Tierney and Yvonna S. Lincoln (eds.). *Representation and the Text: Re-Framing the Narrative Voice*. Albany, NY: State University of New York Press. 143–178.
Meeks, Spencer. 2019. "Affective Images: The Transformative Power of Photography in Siri Hustvedt's *The Blindfold*". *Comparative Studies in Modernism* 14: 199–208.
Michael, Magali Cornier. 2014. *Narrative Innovation in 9/11 Fiction*. Amsterdam: Rodopi.

Middeke, Martin. 2012. "The Victorian Age". In: Middeke, Timo Müller, Christina Wald and Hubert Zapf (eds.). *English and American Studies: Theory and Practice.* Stuttgart: Metzler. 56–77.
Miller, Stephen. 2015. *Walking New York: Reflections of American Writers from Walt Whitman to Teju Cole.* New York: Fordham University Press.
Minnaard, Liesbeth. 2013. "The Postcolonial Flaneur: Ramsey Nasrs Antwerpse Stadsgedichten". *Dutch Crossing* 37.1: 79–92.
Missinne, Lut. 2019. "Autobiographical Novel". In: Martina Wagner-Egelhaaf (ed.). *Handbook of Autobiography/Autofiction.* Volume 1: *Theory and Concepts.* Berlin: De Gruyter. 464–472.
Mock, Roberta (ed.). 2009. *Walking, Writing and Performance: Autobiographical Texts by Deirdre Heddon, Carl Lavery and Phil Smith.* Bristol: Intellect.
Moers, Ellen. 1960. *The Dandy: Brummell to Beerbohm.* London: Secker & Warburg.
Morozov, Evgeny. 2012. "The Death of the Cyberflâneur". *The New York Times* February 4. <https://www.nytimes.com/2012/02/05/opinion/sunday/the-death-of-the-cyberflaneur.html> [accessed 24 February 2021].
Morrell, Carol (ed.). 1994. *Grammar of Dissent: Poetry and Prose by Claire Harris, M. Nourbese Philip, Dionne Brand.* Fredericton, NJ: Goose Lane.
Müller, Wolfgang G. 2013. "Der Flaneur: Begriff und kultureller Kontext". In: Volker Knapp, Kurt Müller, Klaus Ridder, Ruprecht Wimmer and Jutta Zimmermann (eds.). *Literaturwissenschaftliches Jahrbuch.* Neue Folge 54. Berlin: Duncker & Humblot. 205–225.
Müller, Wolfgang G. and Isabel Vila-Cabanes. 2012. "Dickens's 'Uncommercial Traveller' as a Flaneur". In: Francesca Ortesano and Norbert Lennartz (eds.). *Dickens's Signs, Readers' Designs: New Bearings in Dickens Criticism.* Rome: Aracne. 227–252.
Munt, Sally. 1995. "The Lesbian Flâneur". In: David Bell and Gill Valentine (eds.). *Mapping Desire: Geographies of Sexualities.* London: Routledge. 114–125.
Murail, Estelle. 2016. "'Du croisement de leurs innombrables rapports': Baudelaire and De Quincey's *flâneurs*". In: Klaus Benesch and François Specq (eds.). *Walking and the Aesthetics of Modernity: Pedestrian Mobility in Literature and the Arts.* New York: Palgrave Macmillan.
n. A. 1976. "Die Theorie der Momente und die Konstruktion von Situationen". In: *Situationistische Internationale: Gesammelte Ausgaben des Organs der Situationistischen Internationale.* Hamburg: Ed. Nautilus. 125–127.
Nava, Mica. 1996. "Modernity's Disavowal: Women, the City, and the Department Store". In: Nava and Alan O'Shea (eds.). *Modern Times: Reflections on a Century of English Modernity.* New York: Routledge. 38–76.
Neumann, Birgit and Gabriele Rippl. 2017. "Celebrating Afropolitan Identities? Contemporary African World Literatures in English". *Anglophone World Literatures.* Ed. Neumann and Rippl. Spec. issue of *Anglia: Journal of English Philology* 135.1: 159–185.
Neumann, Birgit and Gabriele Rippl. 2020. *Verbal-Visual Configurations in Postcolonial Literature: Intermedial Aesthetics.* New York: Routledge.
Neumeyer, Harald. 1999. *Der Flaneur: Konzeptionen der Moderne.* Würzburg: Königshausen & Neumann.
Nies, Fritz. 1964. *Poesie in prosaischer Welt: Untersuchungen zum Prosagedicht bei Aloysius Bertrand und Baudelaire.* Heidelberg: Winter.

Nietzsche, Friedrich. 2001. *The Gay Science*. Ed. Bernard Williams. Cambridge: Cambridge University Press.

Nigg, Marie-Louise. 2017. *Gehen: Raumpraktiken in Literatur und Kunst*. Berlin: Kadmos.

Nolan, Petra Desireé. 2004. *The Cinematic Flâneur: Manifestations of Modernity in the Male Protagonist of 1940s Film Noir*. PhD dissertation, University of Melbourne at Melbourne. <https://minerva-access.unimelb.edu.au/bitstream/handle/11343/38754/65805_Nolan.pdf?sequence=1&isAllowed=y> [accessed 14 January 2021].

Nünning, Ansgar. 1998. "Unreliable Narration zur Einführung: Grundzüge einer kognitiv-narratologischen Theorie und Analyse unglaubwürdigen Erzählens". In: Nünning (ed.). *Unreliable Narration: Studien zu Theorie und Praxis unglaubwürdigen Erzählens in der englischsprachigen Erzählliteratur*. Trier: WVT. 3–39.

Nunius, Sabine. 2009. *Coping with Difference: New Approaches in the Contemporary British Novel (2000–2006)*. Berlin: LIT.

OED = *Oxford English Dictionary*. 2000–. 3rd ed. online. Oxford: Oxford University Press. <http://www.oed.com/> [accessed 25 March 2020].

Oniwe, Bernard Ayo. 2016. "Cosmopolitan Conversation and Challenge in Teju Cole's *Open City*". *Ufahamu: A Journal of African Studies* 39.1: 43–65.

Ortheil, Hanns-Josef. 1986. "Der lange Abschied vom Flaneur". *Merkur* 40.443: 33–42.

O'Sullivan, Sibbie. 2018. "Poetry Need Not Be a Call to Action, But 'The Long Take' Is". *The Washington Post* November 19. <https://www.washingtonpost.com/entertainment/books/poetry-need-not-be-a-call-to-action-but-the-long-take-is/2018/11/16/eb327d54-e833-11e8-b8dc-66cca409c180_story.html> [accessed 08 December 2020].

Papadimitriou, Nick. 2013. *Scarp: In Search of London's Outer Limits*. London: Sceptre.

Parker, Simon. 2015. *Urban Theory and the Urban Experience: Encountering the City*. London: Routledge.

Parsons, Deborah. 2000. *Streetwalking the Metropolis: Women, the City, and Modernity*. Oxford: Oxford University Press.

Phelan, James. 2005. *Living to Tell About It: A Rhetoric and Ethics of Character Narration*. Ithaca: Cornell University Press.

Pietrzak-Franger, Monika, Nora Pleßke and Eckart Voigts. 2018. "Transforming Cities: Discourses of Urban Change from Victorian London to Global Megacities – An Introduction". In: Pietrzak-Franger, Pleßke and Voigts (eds.). *Transforming Cities: Discourses of Urban Change*. Heidelberg: Winter. 7–27.

Piggott, Gillian. 2012. *Dickens and Benjamin: Moments of Revelation, Fragments of Modernity*. Farnham: Ashgate.

Pleßke, Nora. 2014. *The Intelligible Metropolis: Urban Mentality in Contemporary London Novels*. Bielefeld: transcript.

Poe, Edgar Allan. 1965. "The Man of the Crowd". In: Poe. *The Complete Works of Edgar Allan Poe*. Ed. James A. Harrison. New York: AMS. 134–145.

Pogossian, Tatiana. 2016. "The Art of Walking in Space and Time: The Quest for London". In: Klaus Benesch and François Specq (eds.). *Walking and the Aesthetics of Modernity: Pedestrian Mobility in Literature and the Arts*. New York: Palgrave Macmillan. 129–140.

Pollock, Griselda. 1988. *Vision and Difference: Femininity, Feminism and the Histories of Art*. London: Routledge.

Porombka, Stephan. 1999. "Schwarze Flaneure: Versuch über den Zusammenhang zwischen Flanerie und Amoklauf". In: Stephan Porombka and Susanne Scharnowski (eds.). *Phänomene der Derealisierung*. Wien: Passagen. 283–312.
Rachmann, Stephen. 1975. "Es lässt sich nicht schreiben: Plagiarism and 'The Man of the Crowd'". In: Shawn Rosenheim and Rachmann (eds.). *The American Face of Edgar Allan Poe*. Baltimore, MD: Johns Hopkins University Press. 49–90.
Rajewsky, Irina O. 2005. "Intermediality, Intertextuality and Remediation: A Literary Perspective on Intermediality". *Intermédialités* 6: 43–64.
Redecker, Eva von. 2011. *Zur Aktualität von Judith Butler: Einleitung in ihr Werk*. Wiesbaden: VS Verlag.
Reipen, Corinna. 2014. *Visuality in the Works of Siri Hustvedt*. Frankfurt/Main: Lang.
Rhein, Jan. 2015. *Flaneure in der Gegenwartsliteratur: Réda, Wackwitz, Pamuk, Nooteboom*. Marburg: Tectum.
Richardson, Tina. (ed.). 2015a. *Walking Inside Out: Contemporary British Psychogeography*. Bielefeld: transcript.
Richardson, Tina. 2015b. "Introduction: A Wander through the Scene of British Urban Walking". In: Richardson (ed.). *Walking Inside Out: Contemporary British Psychogeography*. Bielefeld: transcript. 1–30.
Riedelsheimer, Martin. 2020. *Fictions of Infinity: Levinasian Ethics in 21st-Century Novels*. Anglia Book Series 71. Berlin: De Gruyter.
Riedelsheimer, Martin and Eva Ries. 2021. "This Narrator Nothing Affirms, Therefore He Lies? Truth-speaking and Discursive Power in Teju Cole's *Open City*". In: Monika Fludernik and Stephan Packard (eds.). *Being Untruthful: Lies, Fictionality and Related Nonfactualities*. Baden-Baden: Ergon. 305–322.
Riedl, Eva. 2017. *Raumbegehren: Zum Flaneur bei W.G. Sebald und Walter Benjamin*. Frankfurt/Main: Lang.
Ries, Eva Katharina. 2020. "Precarious Flânerie – Towards the Formation of an Ethical Subject". In: Oliver Bock and Isabel Vila-Cabanes (eds.). *Urban Walking: The Flâneur as an Icon in Metropolitan Culture in Literature and Film*. Wilmington, DE: Vernon Press. 1–28.
Rignall, John. 1992. *Realist Fiction and the Strolling Spectator*. New York: Routledge.
Rimmon-Kenan, Shlomith. 2002. *Narrative Fiction: Contemporary Poetics*. 2nd ed. New York: Routledge.
Rippl, Gabriele. 2012. "Film and Media Studies". In: Martin Middeke, Timo Müller, Christina Wald and Hubert Zapf (eds.). *English and American Studies: Theory and Practice*. Stuttgart: Metzler. 314–332.
Rippl, Gabriele. 2018. "The Cultural Work of Ekphrasis in Contemporary Anglophone Transcultural Novels". *Poetics Today* 39.2: 265–285.
Riquelme, John Paul. 2007. "[Dedalus and Joyce Writing the Book of Themselves]". In: James Joyce. *A Portrait of the Artist as a Young Man: Authoritative Text, Backgrounds and Contexts, Criticism*. Ed. Riquelme and Hans Walter Gabler. New York: Norton. 366–381.
Robertson, Robin. 2018. *The Long Take, Or a Way to Lose More Slowly*. London: Picador.
Rohr, Susanne. 2003. "On 'The Perils of Going Astray': Female Figures in the City". In: Günter H. Lenz and Utz Riese (eds.). *Postmodern New York City: Transfiguring Spaces – Raum-Transformationen*. Heidelberg: Winter. 89–97.

Roob, Alexander. 2018. "Exkursion, Trivia und Montage: Zur englischen Früh-Flanerie/ Excursion, Trivia and Montage: On Proto-Flânerie in England". In: Volker Adolphs and Stephan Berg (eds.). *Der Flaneur: Vom Impressionismus bis zur Gegenwart/From Impressionism to the Present.* Bonn: Kunstmuseum Bonn/Köln: Wienand. 229–254.

Rose, Margaret A. 2007. *Flâneurs and Idlers.* Bielefeld: Aisthesis.

Rosenthal, Caroline. 2009. "Transgressing the 'Poetics of the Anglicized City': The Figure of the Flâneuse in Dionne Brand's *What We All Long For*". In: Doris G. Eibl and Caroline Rosenthal (eds.). *Space and Gender: Spaces of Difference in Canadian Women's Writing/ Espaces de difference dans l'écriture Canadienne au féminin.* Innsbruck: Innsbruck University Press. 231–247.

Rosenthal, Caroline. 2011. *New York and Toronto Novels after Postmodernism: Explorations of the Urban.* New York: Camden House.

Rosenthal, Caroline. 2016. "'A carnival in hell': Representations of New York City in Siri Hustvedt's Novels". In: Johanna Hartmann, Christine Marks and Hubert Zapf (eds.). *Zones of Focused Ambiguity in Siri Hustvedt's Works.* Berlin: De Gruyter. 51–65.

Rosenthal, Caroline. 2017. "Die Kunst des Gehens: Weibliches Flanieren in Siri Hustvedts *The Blindfold* und Tessa McWatts *Out of My Skin*". In: Georgiana Banita, Judith Ellenbürger and Jörn Glasenapp (eds.). *Die Lust zu gehen: Weibliche Flanerie in Literatur und Film.* Paderborn: Fink. 77–101.

Rossbach, Susanne. 2002. *Des Dandys Wort als Waffe: Dandyismus, narrative Vertextungsstrategien und Geschlechterdifferenz im Werk Jules Barbey d'Aurevillys.* Tübingen: Niemeyer.

Roupakia, Lydia Efthymia. 2015. "'Art-iculating' Affective Citizenship: Dionne Brand's *What We All Long For*". *ATLANTIS: Journal of the Spanish Association of Anglo-American Studies* 37.1: 31–50.

Rummel, Andrea. 2012. "People in the Crowd: British Modernism, the Metropolis and the Flâneur". In: Regina Rudaitytė (ed.). *Literature in Society.* Newcastle upon Tyne: Cambridge Scholars. 57–76.

Ruoff, Michael. 2018. *Foucault-Lexikon: Entwicklung, Kernbegriffe, Zusammenhänge.* 4th ed. Paderborn: Fink.

Said, Edward. 1994. *Culture and Imperialism.* London: Vintage.

Sandten, Cecile. 2012. "'Metroglorification and Diffuse Urbanism': Literarische Repräsentationen des Postkolonialen im Palimpsestraum der 'neuen' Metropolen". *Anglia: Journal of English Philology* 130.3: 344–363.

Sandten, Cecile. 2020. "Challenging and Reconfiguring Flânerie in Fictions of Contemporary Indian Metropolises". In: Oliver Bock and Isabel Vila-Cabanes (eds.). *Urban Walking: The Flâneur as an Icon of Metropolitan Culture in Literature and Film.* Wilmington, DE: Vernon Press. 195–214.

Sarasin, Philipp. 2012. *Michel Foucault zur Einführung.* 5th ed. Hamburg: Junius.

Sarkowsky, Katja. 2018. *Narrating Citizenship and Belonging in Anglophone Canadian Literature.* Cham: Palgrave Macmillan.

Schmid, Christian. 2005. *Stadt, Raum und Gesellschaft: Henri Lefebvre und die Theorie der Produktion des Raums.* München: Steiner.

Schmid, Wilhelm. 2000. *Auf der Suche nach einer neuen Lebenskunst: Die Frage nach dem Grund und die Neubegründng der Ethik bei Foucault.* Frankfurt/Main: Suhrkamp.

Schmider, Christine and Michael Werner. 2011. "Das Baudelaire-Buch". In: Burkhardt Lindner (ed.). *Benjamin Handbuch: Leben – Werk – Wirkung*. Stuttgart: Metzler. 567–584.
Schmidt, Alfred. 1994. "Walter Benjamin und die Frankfurter Schule". In: René Buchholz and Joseph A. Kruse (eds.). *"Magnetisches Hingezogensein oder Schaudernde Abwehr": Walter Benjamin 1892–1940*. Stuttgart: J.B. Metzler. 122–134.
Schneider, Christiane. 1996. "Von der Schildkröte zur Datenautobahn: Verlaufsformen und Funktionen des Flaneurs". In: Jörg Döring, Christian Jäger and Thomas Wegmann (eds.). *Verkehrsformen und Schreibverhältnisse: Medialer Wandel als Gegenstand und Bedingung von Literatur im 20. Jahrhundert*. Opladen: Westdeutscher Verlag.
Schwalm, Helga. 2012. "The Eighteenth Century". In: Martin Middeke, Timo Müller, Christina Wald and Hubert Zapf (eds.). *English and American Studies: Theory and Practice*. Stuttgart: Metzler. 37–45.
Severin, Rüdiger. 1988. *Spuren des Flaneurs in deutschsprachiger Prosa*. Frankfurt/Main: Lang.
Shaya, Gregory. 2004. "The Flâneur, the Badaud, and the Making of a Mass Public in France, circa 1860–1910". *The American Historical Review* 109.1: 41–77.
Shields, Rob. 2015. "Fancy Footwork: Walter Benjamin's Notes on *Flânerie*". In: Keith Tester (ed.). *The Flâneur*. New York: Routledge. 61–81.
Shohat, Ella and Robert Stam. 1994. *Unthinking Eurocentrism: Multiculturalism and the Media*. New York: Routledge.
Sicher, Efraim. 2007. "The 'Attraction of Repulsion': Dickens, Modernity, and Representation". In: Lawrence Philips (ed.). *A Mighty Mass of Brick and Smoke: Victorian and Edwardian Representations of London*. Amsterdam: Rodopi. 35–60.
Siemerling, Winfried. 2008. "Writing the Black Canadian City at the Turn of the Twenty-First Century: Dionne Brand's Toronto and Mairuth Sarsfield's Montreal". *Canadian Studies/ Études Canadiennes* 64: 109–122.
Sidney, Philip. 2012. *The Defense of Poesy. The Norton Anthology of English Literature*. Ed. Stephen Greenblatt et al. 9th ed. Volume B. New York: Norton. 1044–1083.
Simmel, Georg. 1971. "The Metropolis and Mental Life". In: Simmel. *On Individuality and Social Forms: Selected Writings*. Ed. and with an Introduction by Donald N. Levine. Chicago, IL: Chicago University Press. 324–340.
Sinclair, Iain. 2003. *London Orbital*. London: Penguin.
Solnit, Rebecca. 2001. *Wanderlust: A History of Walking*. London: Penguin.
Solnit, Rebecca. 2014. *Men Explain Things To Me And Other Essays*. London: Granta.
Sontag, Susan. 1990. *On Photography*. New York: Doubleday.
Spicer, Andrew. 2002. *Film Noir*. Harlow: Pearson Education.
Steckenbiller, Christiane. 2018. "Diasporic Ways of Knowing: Teju Cole's *Open City*". In: Sarah Ilott, Ana Christina Mendes and Lucinda Newns (eds.). *New Directions in Diaspora Studies: Cultural and Literary Approaches*. London: Rowman & Littlefield. 71–85.
Stein, Howard F. 1987. *Developmental Time, Cultural Space: Studies in Psychogeography*. Norman, OH: University of Oklahoma Press.
Stein, Howard F., and William G. Niederland (eds.). 1989. *Maps from the Mind: Readings in Psychogeography*. Norman, OH: University of Oklahoma Press.
Stevenson, Robert Louis. 2003. *Strange Case of Dr. Jekyll and Mr. Hyde*. Ed. Katherine Linehan. New York: Norton.
Tambling, Jeremy. 2009. *Going Astray: Dickens and London*. Harlow: Pearson Longman.

Tappen-Scheuermann, Diana. 2012. *Literarischer Narzissmus: Spiegelverhältnisse zwischen Autor, Text und Leser*. Marburg: Tectum.
Tappen-Scheuermann, Diana. 2016. "Reality Bites: Fractured Narrative and Author-Reader Interaction in Siri Hustvedt's Work". In: Johanna Hartmann, Christine Marks and Hubert Zapf (eds.). *Zones of Focused Ambiguity in Siri Hustvedt's Works*. Berlin: De Gruyter. 39–50.
Tester, Keith. 2015. "Introduction". In: Tester (ed.). *The Flaneur*. New York: Routledge. 1–21.
Thiemann, Jule. 2019. *(Post-)Migrantische Flanerie: Transareale Kartierung in Berlin-Romanen der Jahrtausendwende*. Würzburg: Königshausen & Neumann.
Thorne, Robert. 1980. "Places of Refreshment in the Nineteenth-Century City". In: Anthony King (ed.). *Buildings and Society: Essays on the Social Development of the Built Environment*. London: Routledge & Kegan Paul. 228–254.
TLFi = *Le Trésor de la langue française informatisé*. 2020. Nancy: Université de Lorraine. <http://atilf.atilf.fr/> [accessed 25 March 2020].
Tseng, Ching-fang. 2006. "The Flaneur, the Flaneuse, and the Hostess: Virginia Woolf's (Un)Domesticating Flanerie in *Mrs Dalloway*". *Concentric: Literary and Cultural Studies* 32.1: 219–258.
Vermeulen, Pieter. 2013. "Flights of Memory: Teju Cole's *Open City* and the Limits of Aesthetic Cosmopolitanism". *Journal of Modern Literature* 37.1: 40–57.
Vermeulen, Pieter. 2015. *Contemporary Literature and the End of the Novel. Creature, Affect, Form*. New York: Palgrave Macmillan.
Versluys, Kristian. 2003. "New York as a Maze: Siri Hustvedt's *The Blindfold* (1992)". In: Günter Lenz and Utz Riese (eds.). *Postmodern New York City: Transfiguring Spaces – Raum-Transformationen*. Heidelberg: Winter. 99–108.
Vila-Cabanes, Isabel. 2014. "The *Flâneur* and the Grotesque Figures of the Metropolis in the Works of Charles Dickens and Charles Baudelaire". In: Isabelle Hervouet-Farrar and Max Vega-Ritter (eds.). *The Grotesque in the Fiction of Charles Dickens and Other 19th-century European Novelists*. Newcastle upon Tyne: Cambridge Scholars. 108–120.
Vila-Cabanes, Isabel. 2016. *Re-Imagining the Streets of Paris: The French Flaneur in Nineteenth-Century Literature*. Trier: WVT.
Vila-Cabanes, Isabel. 2018. *The Flâneur in Nineteenth-Century British Literary Culture: "The Worlds of London Unknown"*. Newcastle upon Tyne: Cambridge Scholars.
Vila-Cabanes, Isabel. 2020. "Remapping Late Nineteenth-Century London: Arthur Machen's Dyson Mysteries and the 'Art of London'". In: Oliver Bock and Vila-Cabanes (eds.). *Urban Walking: The Flâneur as an Icon of Metropolitan Culture in Literature and Film*. Wilmington, DE: Vernon Press. 59–96.
Voss, Dietmar. 2001. *Dialektik der Grenze: Aufsätze zu Literatur und Ästhetik einer unverantwortlichen Moderne*. Würzburg: Königshausen & Neumann.
Waldow, Stephanie. 2013. *Schreiben als Begegnung mit dem Anderen: Zum Verhältnis von Ethik und Narration in philosophischen und literarischen Texten der Gegenwart*. München: Fink.
Walkowitz, Rebecca. 2006. *Cosmopolitan Style: Modernism Beyond the Nation*. New York: Columbia University Press.
Walter, Roland. 2003. "Between Canada and the Caribbean: Transcultural Contact Zones in the Works of Dionne Brand". *International Journal of Canadian Studies* 27: 23–41.

Weidle, Roland. 2009. "The Ethics of Metanarration: Empathy in Ian McEwan's *The Comfort of Strangers*, *The Child in Time*, *Atonement* and *Saturday*". In: Pascal Nicklas (ed.). *Ian McEwan. Art and Politics*. Heidelberg: Winter. 57–72.
Weigel, Sigrid. 1990. *Topographien der Geschlechter: Kulturgeschichtliche Studien zur Literatur*. Reinbek: Rowohlt.
Wellmann, Angelika. 1991. *Der Spaziergang: Stationen eines poetischen Codes*. Würzburg: Königshausen & Neumann.
Werner, James V. 2004. *American Flaneur: The Cosmic Physiognomy of Edgar Allan Poe*. New York: Routledge.
Weymann-Teschke, Stefanie. 2018. *The City as Performance: The Contemporary American Novel and the Power of the Senses*. Heidelberg: Winter.
Williams, Adebayo. 1997. "The Postcolonial Flâneur and Other Fellow Travelers: Conceits for a Narrative of Redemption". *Third World Quarterly* 18.5: 821–841.
Wilson, Elizabeth. 1992. "The Invisible Flâneur". *New Left Review* 191.1: 90–110. <https://newleftreview.org/issues/I191/articles/elizabeth-wilson-the-invisible-flaneur.pdf> [accessed 26 May 2020].
Winterhalter, Teresa. 2010. "'Plastic Fork in Hand': Reading as a Tool of Ethical Repair in Ian McEwan's *Saturday*". *The Journal of Narrative Theory* 40.3: 338–363.
Wolf, Werner. 2001. "Intermedialität". In: Ansgar Nünning (ed.). *Metzler-Lexikon Literatur- und Kulturtheorie: Ansätze – Personen – Grundbegriffe*. 2nd rev. and exp. ed. Stuttgart: Metzler. 284–285.
Wolf, Werner. 2005. "Intermediality". In: David Herman, Manfred Jahn and Marie-Laure Ryan (eds.). *Routledge Encyclopedia of Narrative Theory*. Routledge. 252–256.
Wolff, Janet. 1989. "The Invisible *Flâneuse*: Women and the Literature of Modernity". In: Andrew Benjamin (ed.). *The Problems of Modernity: Adorno and Benjamin*. London: Routledge. 141–156.
Woolf, Virginia. 2000. *Mrs Dalloway*. London: Penguin.
Wrigley, Richard (ed.). 2014. *The Flâneur Abroad: Historical and International Perspectives*. Newcastle upon Tyne: Cambridge Scholars.
Wuthenow, Ralph-Rainer. 1978. "Der Dandy als Verkleidungsform des Künstlers". In: Wuthenow (ed.). *Muse, Maske, Meduse: Europäischer Ästhetizismus*. Frankfurt/Main: Suhrkamp. 185–199.
Zackodnik, Teresa. 1995. "'I am blackening in my way': Identity and Place in Dionne Brand's *No Language is Neutral*". *Essays on Canadian Writing* 57: 194–211.
Zauner-Schneider, Christiane. 1995. *Die Kunst zu balancieren: Berlin-Paris: Victor Auburtins und Franz Hessels deutsch-französische Wahrnehmungen*. Heidelberg: Winter.

Index

acceleration 2f., 5, 19, 21, 28, 37, 48, 105, 250, 254, 262, 265f., 268–270
Addison, Joseph 54f., 58–61, 65, 68, 106
Addison, Joseph
– The Spectator 54f., 58–61, 64, 67f., 106
affect 12, 46, 59, 198, 203, 205–209, 214, 224f., 236–238, 259, 274–276
Ahmed, Sara 203, 236f.
alienation 2, 52, 93, 150, 168
Althusser, Louis 91
Aragon, Louis 29, 66
Arnold, Matthew 126–129, 151
– "Dover Beach" 126–129
Auster, Paul 57, 150
Austin, John L. 88f.
Austin, John L.
– How to Do Things with Words 88

badaud 22, 25f., 28
Balzac, Honoré de 23f.
Baron Haussmann, Georges Eugéne 4, 269
– Haussmannization 4f., 7
Baudelaire, Charles 1–3, 15f., 21, 24f., 27–30, 32–37, 39, 41, 52, 61, 67f., 72, 135–137, 163, 179, 245, 248
Baudelaire, Charles
– Paris Spleen 15, 30, 245, 248
– Parisian Scenes 27, 29, 52, 67f., 179
– The Painter of Modern Life 24, 52, 72, 135
Baudrillard, Jean 173, 175, 267f.
Baudrillard, Jean
– Simulacra and Simulation 175
– The Spirit of Terrorism 268
Bauman, Zygmunt 4, 114, 116, 168f., 267
Benjamin, Walter 2–5, 8f., 11–13, 18f., 21, 27, 29–44, 46, 48, 53, 56, 59–61, 64, 66–68, 101, 105f., 109, 113f., 116, 121, 134–136, 138, 163, 170–172, 177, 179f., 182, 214, 241, 248, 270f., 277
– arcades 36, 39, 44
– shock 39, 131, 227, 234
– "The Flaneur's Return" 41

Benjamin, Walter
– A Berlin Chronicle 41
– Arcades Project 41, 135
– Erlebnis 60
– One-Way Street 21, 30, 67, 248
– The Paris of the Second Empire in Baudelaire 30, 32–35, 37, 39
Blake, William 49, 58, 65
– "London" 49, 58
bourgeoisie 16, 23–25, 49, 55
Brand, Dionne 10, 12, 54–60, 62, 203–241, 274
Brand, Dionne
– What We All Long For 10, 53, 203, 205, 209f., 231, 237, 239, 241, 243, 250, 274–276
Butler, Judith 7–9, 12, 35, 68, 87–105, 107–111, 120, 124, 129, 137, 144, 147, 156, 160, 166, 190, 205, 209, 216, 258–260, 270–272, 275, 277
Butler, Judith
– Antigone's Claim 93
– Frames of War 98
– Gender Trouble 88
– Giving an Account of Oneself 96, 260
– Precarious Life 97, 258
– The Force of Nonviolence 101
– The Psychic Life of Power 90, 96
– Undoing Gender 95, 101

capitalism 1, 3f., 6f., 32, 39, 58, 60f., 65, 106, 113–115, 121, 130, 214, 241, 245, 250, 262, 268f., 276
Certeau, Michel de 6, 8, 12, 45–47, 50, 105, 233, 251
– *carte* 45–47, 50
– *parcours* 45–48, 50
– "Walking in the City" 8, 45
Cole, Teju 10, 12, 131, 166f., 172–183, 185, 187, 189, 191–194, 196–202, 235, 273f.
Cole, Teju
– Blind Spot 166

– Open City   53, 131, 166, 172f., 175–177, 180, 183f., 188, 192, 195f., 200–203, 209, 221, 224, 236, 243, 247, 259, 273f.
consumption   4f., 60f., 67, 114f., 257

dandy   22–24, 26, 49, 72, 136
Debord, Guy   6, 47f., 108
– *dérive*   6, 48
– situationist   6, 47–50, 108
deceleration   19, 21, 37, 105, 254, 265, 270
detective   38
Dickens, Charles   56, 58, 61–65, 106, 204, 271
– "The Uncommercial Traveller"   65, 67
Dickens, Charles
– Sketches by Boz   61–65

écriture   78, 85, 129, 131, 235
Engels, Friedrich   113
Enlightenment   66, 73, 106
ethical relativism   80, 146f., 161f., 164, 186, 197, 202, 221, 258, 260, 266, 268, 272, 274, 276f.
ethical turn   7, 9, 105, 150, 209

film noir   52, 243, 247, 252f., 262–264, 267–269
flâneuse   56, 126, 134–139, 145
Foucault, Michel   7–9, 12, 35, 45, 68–91, 94, 102–111, 130, 151, 166, 184, 186, 188, 194f., 255, 270–272
– aesthetics of existence   12, 23, 71–75, 77–79, 82, 85f., 97, 102, 104, 107, 110, 131, 166, 172, 195, 202, 229, 236, 270–274
– care of the self   74, 81, 107, 194, 271
– *hypomnêmata*   75, 77, 85
Foucault, Michel
– The History of Sexuality   69, 74, 83, 85f.
Fournel, Victor   25–28, 52
fragmentation   29
Freud, Sigmund   92f., 100, 215

Hessel, Franz   9, 15, 26–28, 41f., 53, 179
Hessel, Franz
– Walking in Berlin   15, 26, 41f., 179

Huart, Louis   15, 23, 52, 56
Huart, Louis
– Physiologie du Flâneur   56
Hustvedt, Siri   10, 12, 131–133, 139–166, 197, 200, 202, 235, 272–274
Hustvedt, Siri
– A Woman Looking at Men Looking at Women   139
– The Blazing World   139
– The Blindfold   53, 131–133, 137, 139, 143, 147f., 150, 154, 163–166, 177, 197, 200, 202, 209, 224, 243, 266, 272, 274
– The Summer Without Men   139
hybridity   30, 168–172, 205, 210, 229, 271, 276

industrialization   2–4, 28, 35, 39, 55, 58, 61, 65
– industrialized   18f., 28f., 35, 39
intermediality   12, 51–53, 68, 105, 242, 246f., 270, 276
intertextuality   126, 129

Joyce, James   67, 111f., 123, 126, 128f., 133, 242
– "The Dead"   126
Joyce, James
– Ulysses   67, 111–114, 123, 128, 242

Kracauer, Siegfried   24, 27, 52f.

Lachmann, Renate   126f.
Laing, Olivia   1–3, 7
Laing, Olivia
– The Lonely City   1
Levinas, Emmanuel   97, 258

male gaze   135f., 139–142, 147, 149, 151f., 171
materialization   88f., 213
McEwan, Ian   10, 12, 19, 57, 110f., 113–115, 117–126, 128f., 242, 272
McEwan, Ian
– Saturday   12, 19, 110–113, 116f., 120f., 123, 126–130, 209, 242, 272
melancholia   88, 92–96, 98, 107, 215f.
memory space   126, 129f., 272

Mercier, Louis-Sébastien   15, 29f., 52, 58, 61, 65
Mercier, Louis-Sébastien
– Tableau de Paris   15, 29, 52, 58, 61, 65, 67
modernity   5, 24, 26, 29–31, 34, 39, 57, 67, 72, 132, 134f., 171, 245
– modern life   6, 72, 115

nomad   168–170

opacity   94, 156, 184, 186, 191–193, 273

palimpsest   174
parrēsia   79–82, 85, 158, 166, 183f., 194f., 199, 273
– parrēsiastic   79f., 107, 158f., 166, 176, 183, 194f., 199f., 202, 256, 273f.
performative turn   44
physiologies   14, 22, 27, 37f., 40, 52, 56
Poe, Edgar Allan   3f., 25, 33, 35, 38f., 41, 56f., 64, 254
– "The Man of the Crowd"   3, 5, 25, 35, 38, 254
post-sovereign subjectivity   3, 7, 9, 12, 88, 94f., 97, 105, 108–111, 125f., 130f., 150, 165f., 172, 203, 240, 242, 249, 262, 270–272, 274, 276f.
prose poem   30, 203, 245
psychogeography   6, 47, 49f., 108

relationality   2, 12, 86, 108, 196, 206, 209, 238, 271, 274, 276
responsibility   97, 202, 206, 224, 227f., 234f., 238–240, 274–276
responsiveness   97, 144

Robertson, Robin   10, 12, 203, 242–261, 263–268, 276
Robertson, Robin
– The Long Take, Or a Way to Lose More Slowly   53, 203, 242f., 245, 247–251, 253, 255, 259–264, 266–269, 276

Said, Edward   168, 171, 222
Simmel, Georg   21, 28, 131, 135, 179f.
– "The Metropolis and Mental Life"   135
Sinclair, Iain   6, 47, 50, 56
spatial turn   44, 108
– spatiality   45
speech act   6, 47, 88f., 105, 155
Steele, Richard   54f., 58–61, 65, 68, 106
Steele, Richard
– The Spectator   54f., 58–61, 64, 67f., 106
Stevenson, Robert Louis   122
Stevenson, Robert Louis
– Strange Case of Dr Jekyll and Mr Hyde   122, 126, 128

uncanny   3, 38, 45, 58, 100, 132, 150, 154f., 157, 228, 235, 266
unreliable narration   163f., 195, 220
– 'underreporting'   184, 190, 192, 199, 202, 273

vulnerability   2, 7, 12, 95, 99f., 102, 104, 107f., 112, 121, 125, 129f., 134, 145, 147, 150, 161f., 175, 191, 205, 223, 233–235, 237, 257–259, 272, 276f.

Woolf, Virginia   56f., 111f., 115, 126, 128
Woolf, Virginia
– Mrs Dalloway   111–114, 116, 126–130

www.ingramcontent.com/pod-product-compliance
Lightning Source LLC
Chambersburg PA
CBHW020222170426
43201CB00007B/286